Mastering Digital Color

A Photographer's and Artist's Guide to Controlling Color

David Saffir

THOMSON
COURSE TECHNOLOGY
Professional ■ Technical ■ Reference

ISBN-10: 1-59200-543-8

ISBN-13: 978-1-59200-543-7

Library of Congress Catalog Card Number: 2004108526

Printed in the United States of America

07 08 09 10 11 BU 10 9 8 7 6 5 4 3 2 1

Publisher and General Manager, Thomson Course Technology PTR:
Stacy L. Hiquet

Associate Director of Marketing:
Sarah O'Donnell

Manager of Editorial Services:
Heather Talbot

Marketing Manager:
Heather Hurley

Executive Editor:
Kevin Harreld

Marketing Coordinator:
Adena Flitt

Project Editor:
Kezia Endsley

Series Editor:
Harald Johnson

Technical Reviewer:
Andrew Behla

PTR Editorial Services Coordinator:
Erin Johnson

Copy Editor:
Kezia Endsley

Interior Layout:
Shawn Morningstar

Cover Designer:
Mike Tanamachi

Indexer:
Larry Sweazy

Proofreader:
Gene Redding

THOMSON
COURSE TECHNOLOGY
Professional ■ Technical ■ Reference

Thomson Course Technology PTR, a division of Thomson Learning Inc.
25 Thomson Place ■ Boston, MA 02210 ■ http://www.courseptr.com

To my Uncle Howard Levin,
who made so many things possible.

May his memory be a blessing.

Acknowledgments

My thanks to my teachers and mentors, who have helped me to see the possibilities, and to make some of them become reality. A partial list includes Harald Johnson, Jack Duganne, Lee Thomas, Ted Dayton, Ramona MacFadyen, David Bacon, Mike Lehman, Tommy Durian, Eileen Fritsch, Teri Ritter, and Cynthia Saffir.

About the Author

David Saffir is a nationally-recognized portrait, commercial, and fine art photographer and printmaker, living in the Santa Clarita Valley, California. Formerly a resident of Santa Barbara, California and New England, David has had a lifelong interest in photography, and particularly the world of nature. He also writes on a number of subjects, and has authored articles on color management, digital capture, and large-format digital printmaking. David has enjoyed an extensive career leading marketing, planning, operations, graphic design, and creative teams as a general manager and vice president for high-tech medical companies. He has led design, art, and communications groups in the U.S., Europe, and Japan. Leaving corporate life behind, he chose to focus his time on work, and pursue his love of crafting images through photography.

Now, David works extensively in portrait and commercial photography. He works primarily with the Hasselblad H1, using Phase One digital camera backs. He also uses Nikon and Canon DSLRs. David is also an accomplished digital printmaker. He finishes all of his work, and makes limited edition prints for other artists and photographers. He uses HP and Epson professional inkjet products. David teaches workshops in digital printing, including the Clear Focus Studios seminar sessions scheduled in a number of cities this year. He has also written numerous nationally-published articles on digital image capture, color management, printing software, and digital printing. Most recently, he taught web seminars for the Professional Digital Imaging Association on digital capture, color control, and printing. He was a conference-level speaker at WPPI and other venues during 2006.

His images have won awards in a variety of print competitions, and they have appeared in a number of publications. His e-mail is dsaffir@mac.com. His website is www.davidsaffir.com.

About the Series Editor

Harald Johnson has been immersed in the world of commercial and fine-art imaging and printing for more than 25 years. A former professional photographer, designer, and creative director, Harald is an imaging consultant, the creator of the website DP&I.com (www.dpandi.com), and the author of the groundbreaking books, *Mastering Digital Printing: The Photographer's and Artist's Guide to High-Quality Digital Output* (2003), *Mastering Digital Printing, Second Edition* (2005), and *Digital Printing Start-Up Guide* (2005). Harald is also the founder of YahooGroup's digital-fineart, the world's largest online discussion group on the subject of digital fine art and digital printing.

Contents

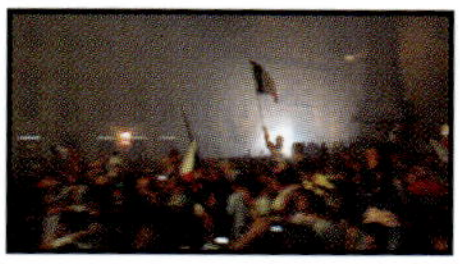

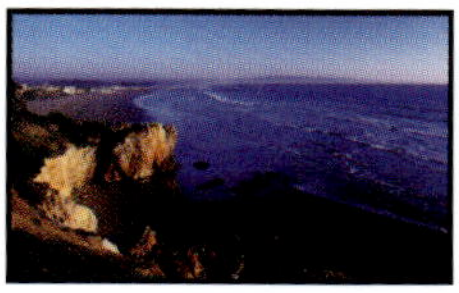

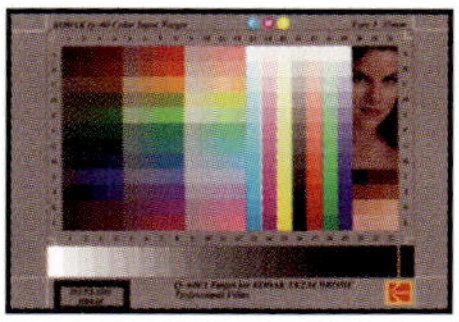

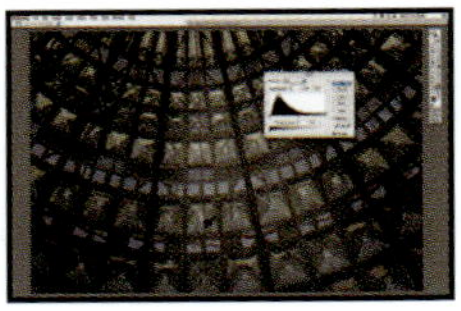

4 Production Guide for Photographers 61

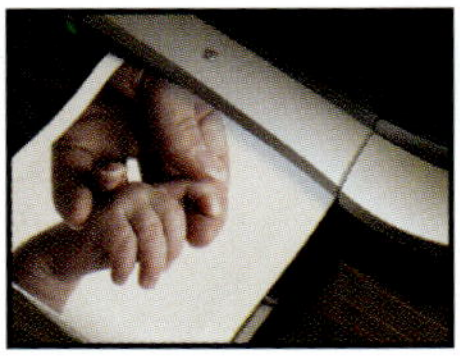

5 Color Management Policies for Photographers 103

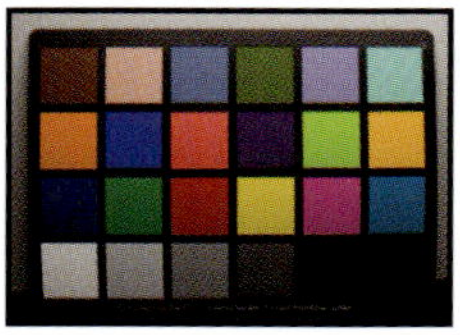

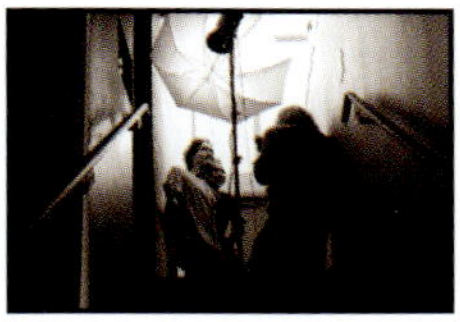

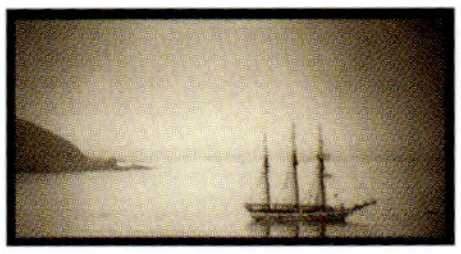

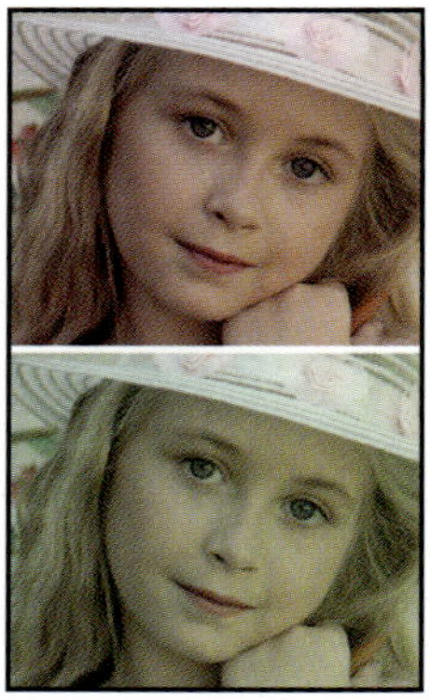

9 Preserving Color: Archiving and Storage .207

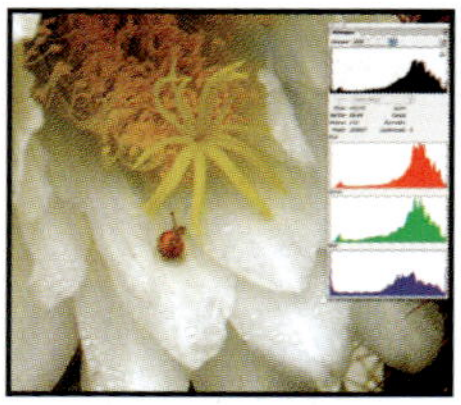

A Helpful Tips and Tricks .221

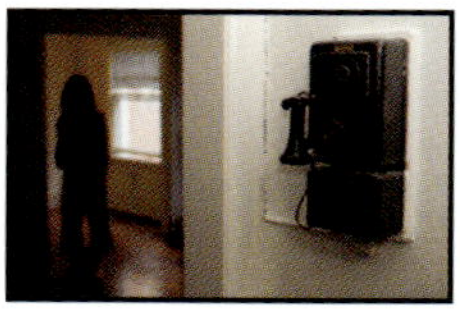

B Art Gallery .237

Index .249

1

Introduction: Imagine the Possibilities

This book is intended to help photographers and artists master the skills needed to realize their vision, using color management tools available in the digital world.

I'll focus on the practical aspects of color management, the connections between end and beginning, and the links between cause and effect in making our art come to life on our chosen media.

In some ways, articles and other publications on this subject have become how-to manuals for Photoshop. That is not intended here; in fact, I assume that the reader understands the basics of Photoshop or their chosen image editor.

I've tried to include just the aspects of color management for photographers and artists that will help you to achieve your editing and production goals in the shortest amount of time—and deliver high quality, too.

It has become in many ways easier than ever for an artist change what a piece of art will look like when complete—whether it originates on a computer, starts with transparency scanned to digital, is a pure digital capture, or is any of a number of hybrids.

Many artists believe that visualization, both of concept and result, is key. Ansel Adams said, "In my mind's eye, I visualize how a particular... sight and feeling will appear on a print."

Although he is "only" a photographer, this phrase speaks volumes to artists of all kinds. He refers first to pre-visualization, developing in his mind's-eye the concept, composition, color, and other aspects of his art.

But second, he speaks to the issue of anticipating what the final version will look like when completed. He implies that he knows how the media he might use will behave, how art may appear to him at each stage—this includes film, the developing process, and printing paper he selects.

He was capable of performing this visualization and producing great art because he worked so hard to understand the behavior and the strengths and weaknesses of the tools he chose to use.

A watercolorist and good friend of mine, Greg Wilsey, often tells me of how he will visit a location again and again, looking at it in different light. He makes sketches and preliminary paintings to help him bring his ideas into focus.

I've heard stories of Marc Chagall, who while planning the stained glass windows of a new structure, sat on the planned building site for many hours and in different seasons, watching the interaction of the sun and landscape and the changing colors. I've been told he personally selected every piece of glass for its unique properties.

All of these artists understood the importance of using their tools to accomplish their goals, of working in stages—and all of them, on some level, used their tools and did not let the tools run them.

In this book, you will methodically work through the modern digital color management toolbox. You'll start with how people perceive light and color and continue through to electronic and media-based production. In most aspects, the book stays away from theory and focuses on practicality and results.

2

Getting a Grip on Your Color: Definitions and a Road Map

One of the biggest problems involved in discussing the subject of color management tools used by photographers and artists is the issue of finding the balance—between generalities and detail, between everyday practicality and theory, and between one technical option and another.

There are plenty of available definitions of color management. Here are a few examples:

- In computerized processes, attempting to hold colors the same no matter in what medium they are displayed or printed (Zelanski)
- Software that translates the colors of an original image into the truest representation obtainable on the output device (Computer Dictionary/Farlex)
- A technology to calibrate the color of input devices (such as scanners or digital cameras), display devices, and output devices (such as printers or offset presses). Parts of this technology are implemented in the operating system (OS), or directly in the application (Dictionary/Labor Law Index)

Many of the reviews, articles, and the like that I've seen, although written by brilliant individuals, leave me a bit underwhelmed or even confused when it comes to translating these ideas into everyday successes. Sometimes we're offered too many options.

As you'll notice more than once while reading this book, I'm focused less on a detailed discussion of every possible alternative and more interested in getting high-quality results at reasonable cost in time and money.

I'm going to leave out the pictures of eyeballs in cross-section and the optical physics charts. What I hope to do is to help you understand how you can create the best possible images in the most efficient manner.

I'm also going to do my best to stick to using everyday language in this book and ask that you learn new terms only as necessary and as they support your understanding of the subject.

Much of this discussion of getting a grip on your color and how we define color management centers on managing your tools from the earliest stages of your work to completion:

- From the eye to the camera
- From the camera to the computer
- Film scanner image processing and RAW image processing
- Editing and saving the digital file

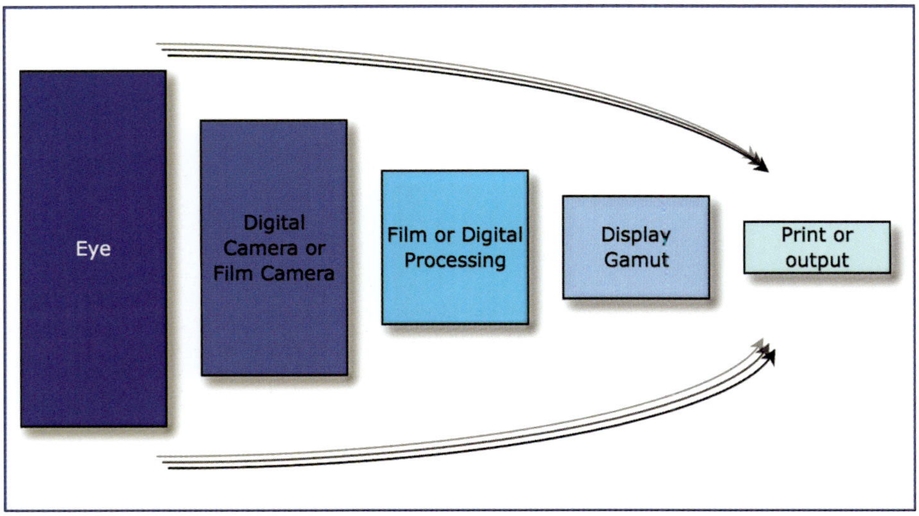

Figure 2.1

Good color management involves keeping as much of the color and detail as possible in the image, from capture, through production, to final output.

This kind of "road map" might not be exactly what you had in mind when you picked up this book. But it is critical that you understand this idea and that mastering it will help preserve the color inherent in your work from the beginning and will enhance its appearance and marketability when it is completed.

This road map describes efficient, effective management of the tools available to you as a photographer and artist. This chapter will, hopefully, show you:

- Important aspects of how each tool handles color
- What may be available for you to control the effect or influence of each tool on color and image detail
- How you can choose to use these tools to get the high-quality result you want at reasonable cost

From the Eye to the Camera

Our eyes, developed and refined over millions of years, work in close harmony with our brains to aid us in perceiving what we call "color." The complex range of light intensities and colors that we can see is the result of this incredible combination.

I'm sure we've all noticed from time to time that not everything we can see can be recorded on camera film or on a digital camera sensor. A classic example is an image of a "perfect" sunset, as shown in Figure 2.2, which once developed, just doesn't quite live up to the vibrancy seen at the time the image was taken.

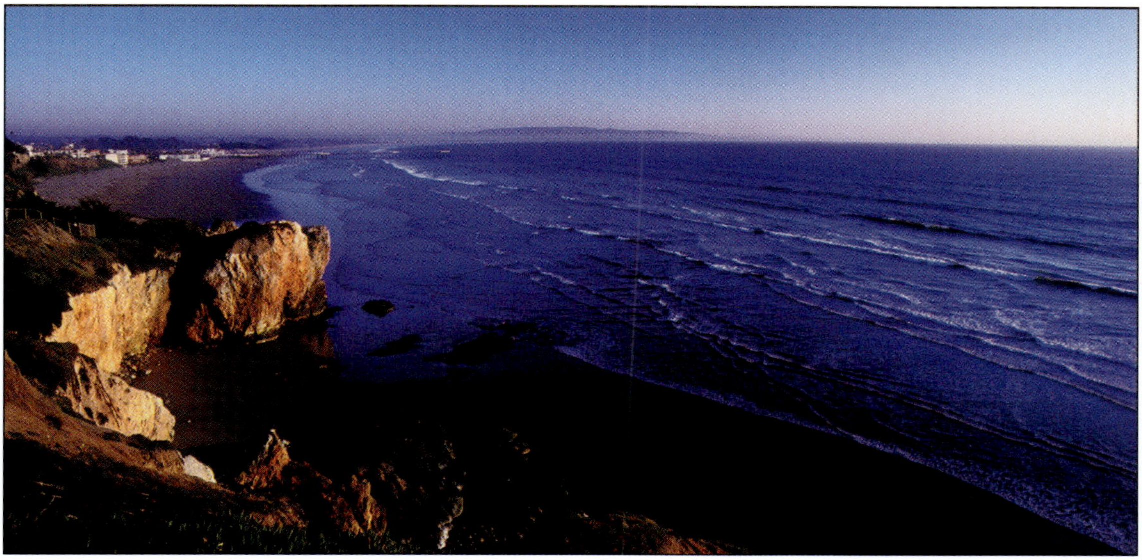

Figure 2.2

This image captures a very wide range of tones but still can't match what I saw when the photograph was taken. (Fuji Velvia 50, scanned)

The fact is that our eyes and brain can see far more than any digital sensor or film can record. In both range of color and range of tones from light to dark, our eyes and brain in concert can see far more than film.

Using a common term, such as *a stop* in photography, is quite useful here. As you know, stops in photography represent a progression in the intensity of light reaching a sensor or film. Examples include 1, 1.4, 2, 2.8, 4, 5.6, 8, 11, 16, and 22.

Each step from left to right in this progression represents a reduction of 50% in light intensity; so, for example, the numeral 2 represents half as much light as the numeral 1.4, and so on.

Our eyes and brain, looking at an entire scene (the whole thing, not just a portion of it), can perceive about 15 stops of difference from the brightest part of a scene and the darkest. Film can perceive around 7–10 stops, transparencies can perceive only 4–5 stops, and photographic darkroom prints can perceive approximately 3–4 stops.

Another way to look at this is that our eyes and brain can perceive a range, from deep shadows to brightest highlights, of about 10,000:1. Most printed photography media, on average, can render 200:1.

This has several implications, as follows:

- Given the tools available now, we can't really expect that the full range of color and details that we can see in person can be fully represented in a final print.
- What we record on film or via a digital sensor involves a "translation" of the color we see into the color the film or sensor can actually record. One way to refer to the color that the film or sensor can record is its *color space.*
- Any additional step in processing that we take, from film developing techniques, to scanning, to editing via computer, to printing, involves additional "translations" of the image and color from one media or device to the next.

These translations from one color palette or color space to another are an important part of color management. A good translation, as with any language, means that the message will be understood. A poor translation, obviously, means the opposite—it can introduce distortions in the image. Color management tools allow you to manage these translations to your benefit.

So, what happens to all of the color that we can perceive but that is probably not kept on film or digital sensor, for example? Some of this color is recorded accurately by the film or sensor, some of it is lost, and some color is placed into the color space of the film or digital sensor.

Color Space

Color space is a term that drives many people up the wall, and sometimes that includes me. I think that this is the case, at least in part, because this phrase is used by so many people who are using different tools and are trying to achieve different goals.

As a photographer and artist, I tend to think of color space as I might imagine a painter's color palette. In a sense, a color space describes what is contained in that palette: how many individual colors there are, how many variations exist of each color, how dark or light they are, where they are located in the palette, and so on. Some palettes are bigger and more varied than others, and some palettes have different colors—and the same is true of different color spaces.

Just as with an artist's palette, most color space models that have been created represent only a portion of what we can actually see. For example, the human eye and brain can see millions of colors and tones. The color space that most closely represents this is called LAB color space.

Among other things, different color spaces can be collected into libraries. Each color space has its strengths and weaknesses and so is used in turn for a specific purpose. The most commonly used color space on the Internet, and in many displays, is sRGB, which can only provide 256 tones in each channel of red, green, and blue. It works just fine on the computer displays most people see every day.

The sRGB color space is limited; it can't handle many of the colors that can be printed using an ordinary four-color printing press or by many digital inkjet printers. These four-color printing machines commonly use what is called CMYK (Cyan, Magenta, Yellow, Black) inks, which are combined into a range of colors; digital inkjet printers intended for printing photographs typically have at least six colors of ink, which can be combined in printing an even broader range of colors than CMYK.

Another important color space is Adobe RGB (1998), which is designed among other things to incorporate most of the colors that can be printed via CMYK (see Figure 2.3). In the past, most digital cameras used sRGB; now an increasing number of models provide sRGB and Adobe RGB (1998). This makes Adobe RGB (1998) one of the better choices for photographers.

Film Capture

In the case of film, layers of light-sensitive materials each respond in their unique way to exposure to varying colors and intensities of light. Some films record only black and white tones, others color. Some films render color as closely to human vision as possible, and others emphasize certain colors to make the final image more pleasing or unusual. Figure 2.4 shows a schematic cross-section of modern camera film.

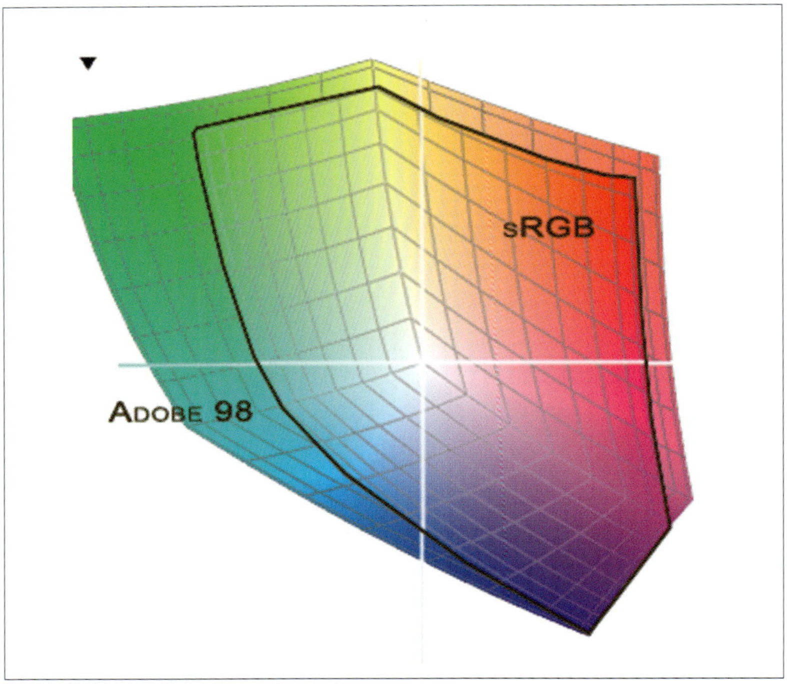

Figure 2.3

This figure compares the coverage of sRGB to Adobe RGB (1998). Notice how the sRGB color space (defined by the dark line) is more limited than Adobe RGB (1998).

One of the important differences between film products is the way they interpret, sometimes called *render*, the light they are exposed to. Many films have a distinctive rendering or interpretation of color combinations in a scene, and this is one reason a photographer might choose one type of film over another.

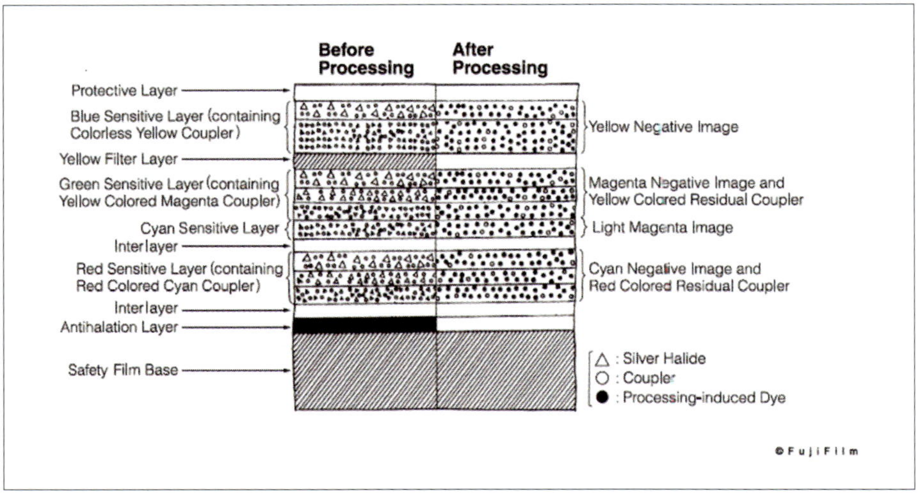

Figure 2.4

Modern film is made up of a number of light-sensitive layers, sandwiched together to make up the film. Each layer is designed to record a specific portion of the color and light intensity of the exposure. (Courtesy Fujifilm)

Interestingly, images captured on film may again be altered when the latent image is developed, for example, when the film is placed in a chemical solution that causes the image to become visible to us. And it may be altered again when the image is projected onto light sensitive paper and run through another set of chemicals.

Digital Capture

A digital camera chip is made up of an array of thousands and thousands of small electronic light sensors (called *pixels*). Each pixel records varying intensities of light, as illustrated in Figure 2.5. Some of these pixels (sometimes referred to as *photosites*) are allocated to "see" green, another portion is dedicated to seeing red, and others see blue.

Actually, each one "sees" in varying tones of gray—allocated portions of the photosites have red, green, and blue filters over them. They are assigned by the manufacturer to represent either red, green, or blue. A color image is created by the camera using a complex set of calculations, using the preset camera hardware (sometimes called *firmware*) and on-board software to combine the signals from all the photosites.

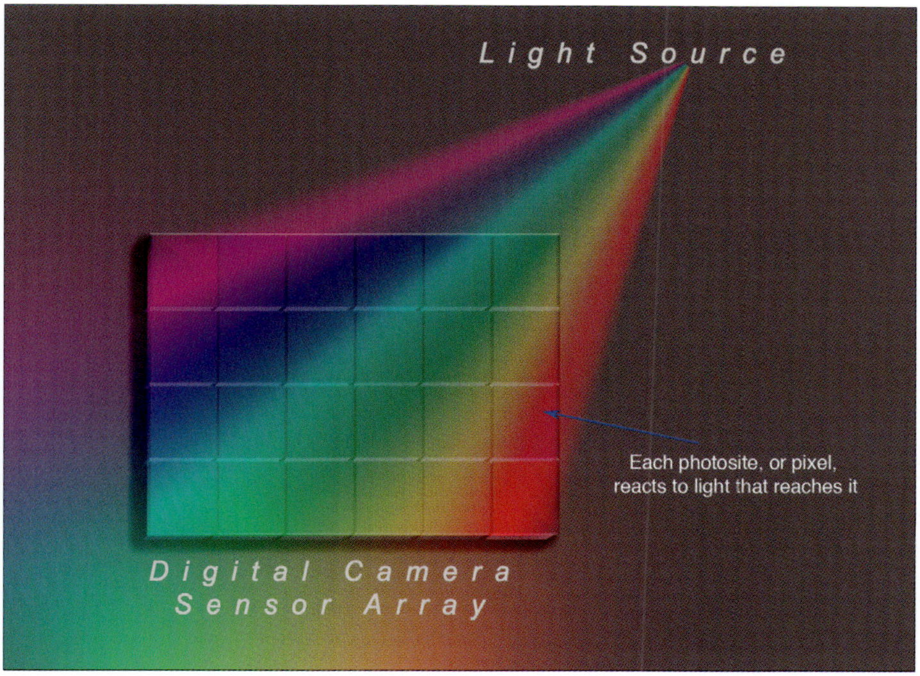

Figure 2.5

A digital sensor's photosites respond to varying intensities of different colors.

Controlling In-Camera Image Processing

It's important to capture images with your digital camera using the highest quality possible. Most mid-level and professional-level digital cameras offer photographers a range of choices in this area.

Some of the choices available to you in controlling your digital camera include:

- Color saturation
- Contrast (sometimes referred to as *tone compensation*)
- Hue
- Color space
- White balance (also referred to as color *temperature*)
- ISO (digital sensor sensitivity, very similar to film speed)
- Sharpening
- File quality

It is a matter of basic principle to me to keep my options open when creating an image. What I mean by this is that I would rather choose camera options that give me the greatest flexibility down the road in regard to image editing and creativity. In a way, this is one of the areas where digital capture potentially gives photographers flexibility beyond what film can offer.

On the other hand, most digital cameras come out of the box programmed to process images fairly aggressively. This means that the program in the camera applies liberal amounts of color saturation, contrast, and other modifications to the image file.

As an example, a pro-level digital camera that I purchased earlier this year came out of the box programmed like this:

- Mid-range contrast
- Mid-range saturation and hue adjustment
- sRGB color space
- Auto-ISO
- Mid-range sharpening
- Auto white balance
- Saved images in JPEG file format

Now here's the problem: The camera was set up to take good, but not necessarily great, images most of the time. It plays it safe in many ways, combining auto-exposure and processing to make the images pleasing at first glance. It uses a relatively limited color space, automatic white balance, and saves the image in a JPEG format.

So the first thing I do when I take a new camera out of the box is to put the battery in, mount a lens on it, take a few test shots, and examine the images. (Being a typical photographer, I only read the manual if I'm desperate.) If the camera works, I change some of the more important camera settings:

- Adobe RGB (1998) color space
- Manual ISO (refers to film speed or digital sensor sensitivity)
- White balance preset, or manual
- Low in-camera sharpening
- RAW file format

To JPEG or not to JPEG?

JPEG (which means Joint Photographic Expert's Group) refers to a file format that can be used to save digital images. JPEG files usually compress, or squeeze, a file into a smaller size for convenience in storage and in e-mail transmission. One of the biggest drawbacks to using JPEG files is file compression—each time the file is saved, some information is modified or discarded. This does not apply when a file is copied, unchanged, from one place to another. Also, if you are going to save a file only once or twice, chances are you'll see only minor differences.

But when the camera saves your photograph as a JPEG file, it locks in all of the in-camera processing—in other words, every option on the list provided earlier in this chapter. You can modify the appearance of the image after the image is captured—but your options are limited.

For example, once an image is saved as a JPEG in sRGB, there is nothing you can do to expand the color space to meet your needs. This is somewhat like over-exposing or under-exposing an image—if you don't capture the image information on the first pass, you can't put it back.

If you can be satisfied with an image that is limited in a number of ways, or you have a need for really quick production turnaround, shoot JPEG. When shooting JPEG, be meticulous in exposure and white balance, because the image file can be edited only conservatively before distortion shows in the photograph. Otherwise, use RAW file capture, discussed later in this chapter.

Tip: AUTO WHITE BALANCE VS. CUSTOM WHITE BALANCE

Automatic white balance is a great feature. It can save time in image editing, as it color-corrects in real-time, while you're capturing the shot. It's also true that if you use automatic white balance, and you capture a series of images, they might not match one another in their color appearance. If your lighting situation changes, it is likely that the camera's on-board processor will modify the color appearance of the image. At best, this means that you may be forced to spend time after the shoot trying to match the color appearance of the images using Photoshop or another image editor—or accept that they look different.

It's frequently better to use a custom white balance preset, such as Tungsten or Daylight. This will auto-correct, but if there are variations in the images you capture, they will usually be closer in appearance and easier to correct. Even better in some situations, use the on-camera White Balance feature to photograph a white card in the light you'll be shooting in and set the white balance exactly on target. If the light changes, reset this White Balance feature. See your camera's instruction manual for details on this important feature.

This depth of image information gives me much more control over the camera during the shoot and keeps my options open during image editing and post-production. Using a larger color space and using a file-saving option that does not discard image information through file compression are big advantages all by themselves.

Using a larger color space usually means that I can edit an image and still minimize distortions in color accuracy and image details. This is frequently not the case when using sRGB. Using RAW file format means that I can easily edit exposure, contrast, saturation, hue, color temperature/white balance, and other image attributes. And because RAW files are typically saved in high-bit format, image distortions such as banding or posterization are minimized.

From the Camera to the Computer (Scanning)

In many cases, once the image is captured on film and developed in the lab, it is transferred to the computer via a scanning device. Digital images may be processed via specialized software. In either case, the photographer can, and should, be in control of range of color and quality of detail rendered during this process.

In the case of the scanner, film is handled by a device that projects light through it and a lens onto a digital sensor. As with the digital camera, the operator can choose among exposure options, color spaces, and more. In a way, the scanner "exposes" the image on the film onto a chip. A scanner captures an electronic "exposure" of your film using an electronic sensor that is similar to the designs used in digital cameras. A digital file is saved to your computer for additional processing and editing.

It is important to note that some film scanners cannot capture the full range of tones and color offered by most films, negative, or transparency. There's a lot of engineering, physics, and math involved in explaining this—and the marketing spin the manufacturers try to put on their products isn't all that helpful in understanding the issues, either.

What is important to know is that you should select a higher-quality film scanner for your use, and you should squeeze every drop of information possible out of every film scan. This means, usually, following these guidelines:

- Create the highest-quality film image possible in the camera
- Use the highest-quality film scanner available, one that has a claimed density range rating of 4.2 or better
- Scan in a reasonably large color space, such as Adobe RGB 98
- Scan at the highest resolution available, 4000 to 6000 dpi
- Ensure that the scan exposure is correct and that you are not under- or overexposing the scan
- Save the scan in TIFF or Photoshop file format

Let's review some of these bulleted points. First, it is as important as ever to get your image right in the camera. If you are capturing your image on film, that means using a good quality lens, the correct exposure, shutter speed, and aperture settings, shooting from a stable platform, protecting the lens from unwanted incoming light or reflections, shooting in the light that's appropriate for the image, and so on.

Second, there are quite a few scanner models available on the market today. Some scan only film, and others can be used for scanning film, prints, and other reflective materials. These are usually called *flatbed scanners* and look quite a bit like a photocopying machine.

As a general rule, the best film scans are produced using a dedicated film scanner. They kind of look like a shoebox on steroids. These are available from a number of companies, including but not limited to Nikon, Microtek, and Imacon. They can scan sizes from APS all the way up to 8×10, depending on the manufacturer and model. I'm going to leave drum scanners out of this discussion, at least for now, simply because acquisition cost significantly restricts their use.

You Want That RAW??

Digital photography has more acronyms than a dog has fleas. Most of them really don't make much sense, taken at face value. Look at the term *RAW files*, for example: RAW indicates that the image file is not finished or completely processed in the camera. It really should be referred to as "raw," or "uncooked," or undeveloped in much the same way a latent image is stored on film. It contains information recorded from the digital sensor, something like the way that an image is recorded on film that has not been developed.

A number of settings and similar things are noted in the file, but most of these settings are not permanent. They are just notes, or indicators, of what happened during image capture. A RAW file, unlike other file formats, can be changed during editing.

White balance, exposure, tint, sharpening, contrast, saturation, brightness, and development curve can all be adjusted. In fact, they can be adjusted many times, as the adjustment process does not permanently change your image file!

One of the most important characteristics of RAW files is that they are recorded in high-bit format. Why be concerned about capturing an image in a high-bit file? It is all in the numbers—an ordinary JPEG image file, used by most consumer level cameras, uses an 8-bit file. What this translates into is that each of the color channels, R, G, and B, has 256 steps, or tones available to render the image. A RAW file, however, has over 65,000 tones available per color channel.

This gives you incredible power in editing your images. A few years ago, when personal computers were not quite powerful enough to handle all this information, it often made sense to shoot in JPEG; it just took too long to process RAW files. Now, a very large RAW file from a 22-megapixel camera can be processed and exported as a 16-bit TIFF in about 30 seconds. Not bad. (TIFFs are kind of the jack of all trades in digital image files—TIFF stands for Tagged Image File Format. TIFFs can be saved in varying bit depths, unlike JPEGs.)

Using high-bit image files provides additional benefits in post-production and image editing. The more information available per color channel, the less you'll see the *posterization* (as shown in the figure), banding, and pixilation gremlins in your finished images.

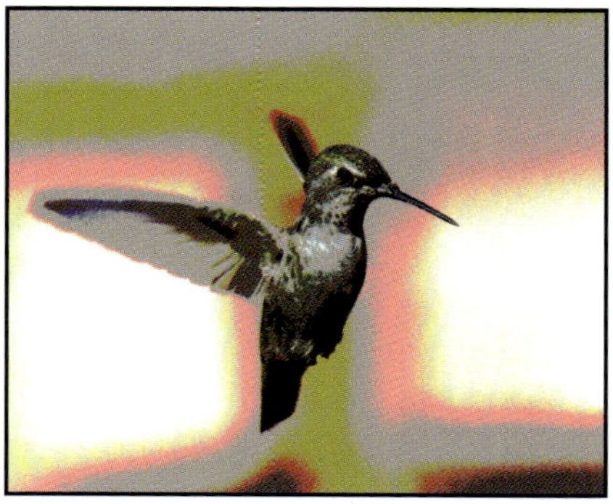

For 35mm, I recommend a dedicated film scanner that incorporates a lens of high optical quality and provides scan resolution of at least 3200 dpi (preferably 4000 dpi), the ability to scan to high-bit resolution in at least Adobe RGB (1998) color space, and a claimed density range rating of at least 4.2. For medium format film, a dedicated film scanner that provides 3200 dpi is preferred. There are desktop scanners available that can scan at resolutions up to 8000 dpi.

When scanning, be sure that you set the scanning software to match the type of film you are scanning, such as color negative, transparency, or black and white. Some experts advocate that you set the scanner for color negative when scanning black and white; this is usually a good idea, because it provides more digital information in the scan than a pure grayscale approach.

One of the reasons it is preferable to use a scanner that provides good density range and a high-bit scan is that you will see noticeable improvements in the details and reduced color distortion in the shadow areas than if you are using a lesser machine. In fact, the combination of these two is more important than either alone. In other words, use a high-quality scanner that gives you the option of scanning at least 14 bits per color channel and has a claimed density range rating of at least 4.2. A scanner that provides high-quality, true 16-bit scans is even better.

Last, the scanning software usually has an exposure control. This controls the intensity of light being transmitted from the light source inside the scanner, through the film, and onto the digital sensor. This is a slider control, much like those used in other image editing software like Photoshop, Aperture, Lightroom, and others. When you adjust exposure, make small moves, and watch your scan on the screen—over-adjustment of the exposure slider can result in color distortions and loss of highlight or shadow detail. See Figure 2.6 for a screen shot of scanner software controls.

Examples of scanners that might suit your needs include:

- Nikon 5000: 35mm, extra-low distortion lens, 16-bit, claimed 4.8 density range
- Minolta Multi-Scan Pro: 35mm, 120/220, 16-bit, claimed 4.8 density range
- Imacon 848 (all sizes up to large format) 16-bit, claimed 4.8 density range

Each of these has its strengths and weaknesses. If you plan to make a decision about purchasing one, be sure that you get a detailed demo of the software that drives the scanner and that you feel comfortable with it.

As you gain experience in working with scans of your film, you will see how well (or badly) your film image turns out in the digital world. *Scanning* is a way of interpreting, or translating, a film image into another medium. Stretching an analogy a bit, there are parallels here to decisions made in the darkroom when making a print. ("The negative is the score, the print is the performance".) Building up your experience in scanning and making your own personal judgments about image appearance, color rendition, contrast, and other criteria with different types of film are just as important as knowing the technical specifications of the machine you are using.

In any case, your scanned image is now stored on your computer and is ready for editing and printing.

Density Range and Scanners

Density range refers to the theoretical range of tones, from utter black all the way to whitest white, that can be recorded by photographic media and digital sensors. In theory, the higher the claimed density range a scanner has, the more it can see into the shadows in your film image, drawing out the details.

However, there is much more to choosing a scanner than finding a machine that claims be the king of the hill in density range. The fact is that most scanners' claimed density range is far beyond what they actually deliver and also beyond anything film or transparencies can render. And, by the way, a badly shot photograph can't be magically transformed in the scanner into something better. Get it right in the camera first!

In scanners, a number of factors contribute to scanned image quality: the quality and type of the scanner sensor, the quality of the electronic hardware that processes the image information, the ability to reduce digital noise generated during the scan, scanner control software, the light source used to expose the image in the scanner, and more.

Scanning in 16-bit, for example, does not guarantee that your scanner will deliver its maximum performance in terms of image quality. The combination of a 16-bit scan, combined with excellent on-board electronics to process the signal, will definitely get you closer to this goal. Adding a high-end sensor chip, which delivers lower noise, is a big asset in producing high-quality scans. You *do* get what you pay for.

A final tip: Many high-end scanners and their software permit you to make more than one pass when scanning an image. Sometimes this is called *multi-sampling*; the big advantage to multi-sampling is that it reduces noise in the digital scan. I strongly suggest that you give this a try; start with 4x re-sampling, and work your way up. I personally multi-sample critical images at 4x or 8x and get good results from my Nikon and Minolta film scanners. Multi-sampling does increase scan time significantly. (Note: Multi-sampling is not a replacement for software-based dust and scratch removal, such as GANE or Digital ICE.)

Film Scanner Image to Computer and RAW Image Processing

Scanner controls are in many ways similar to the software controls provided in most RAW image conversion software. They allow you to choose your color space, exposure, image size/resolution, hue/saturation, contrast/brightness, and more.

Mastering these controls, shown in Figures 2.6 and 2.7, is important in several respects: Finding the right combination of settings will help you protect color, highlight, and shadow detail in your image.

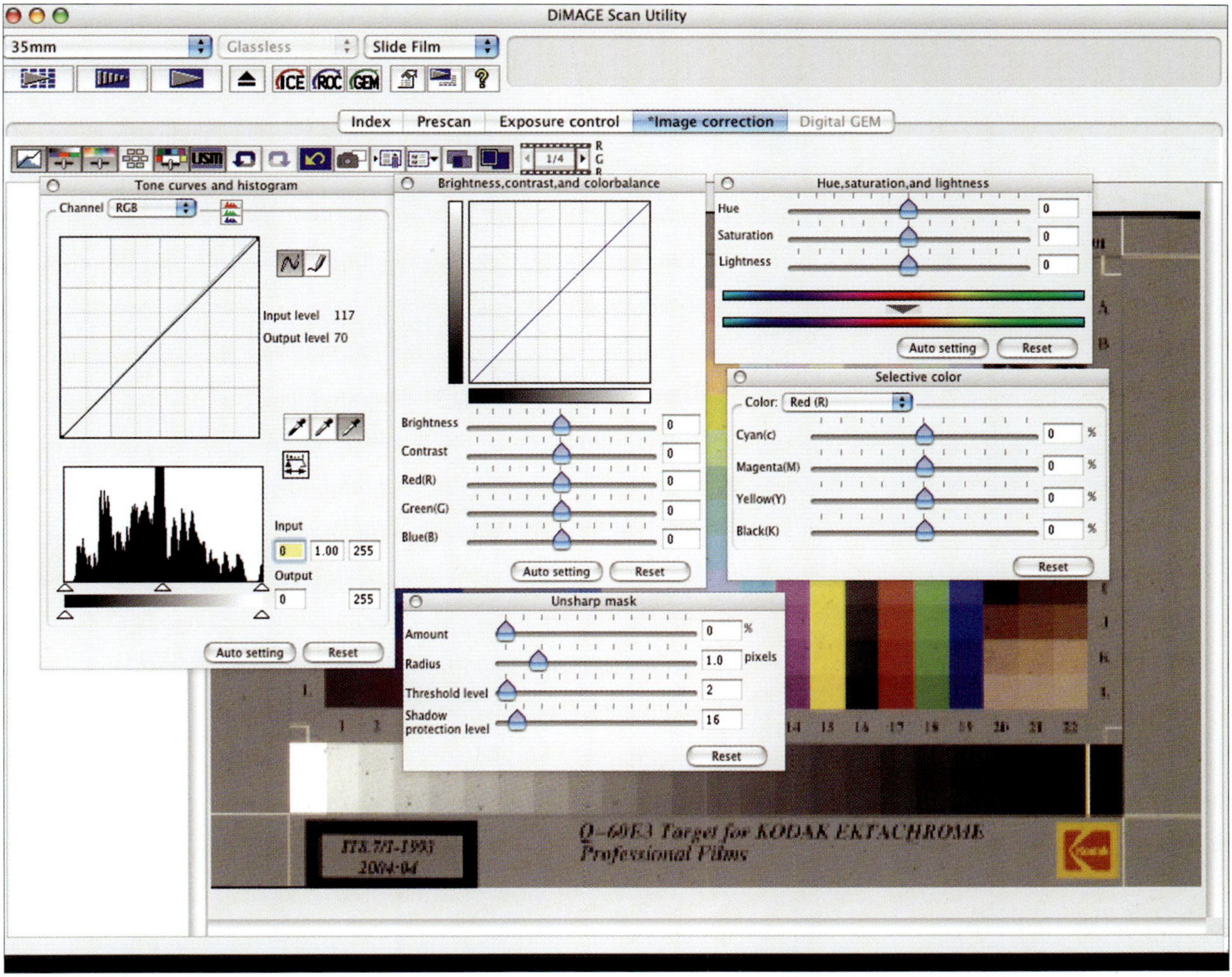

Figure 2.6

Scanner controls put you in the driver's seat for exposure, color, resolution, and more.

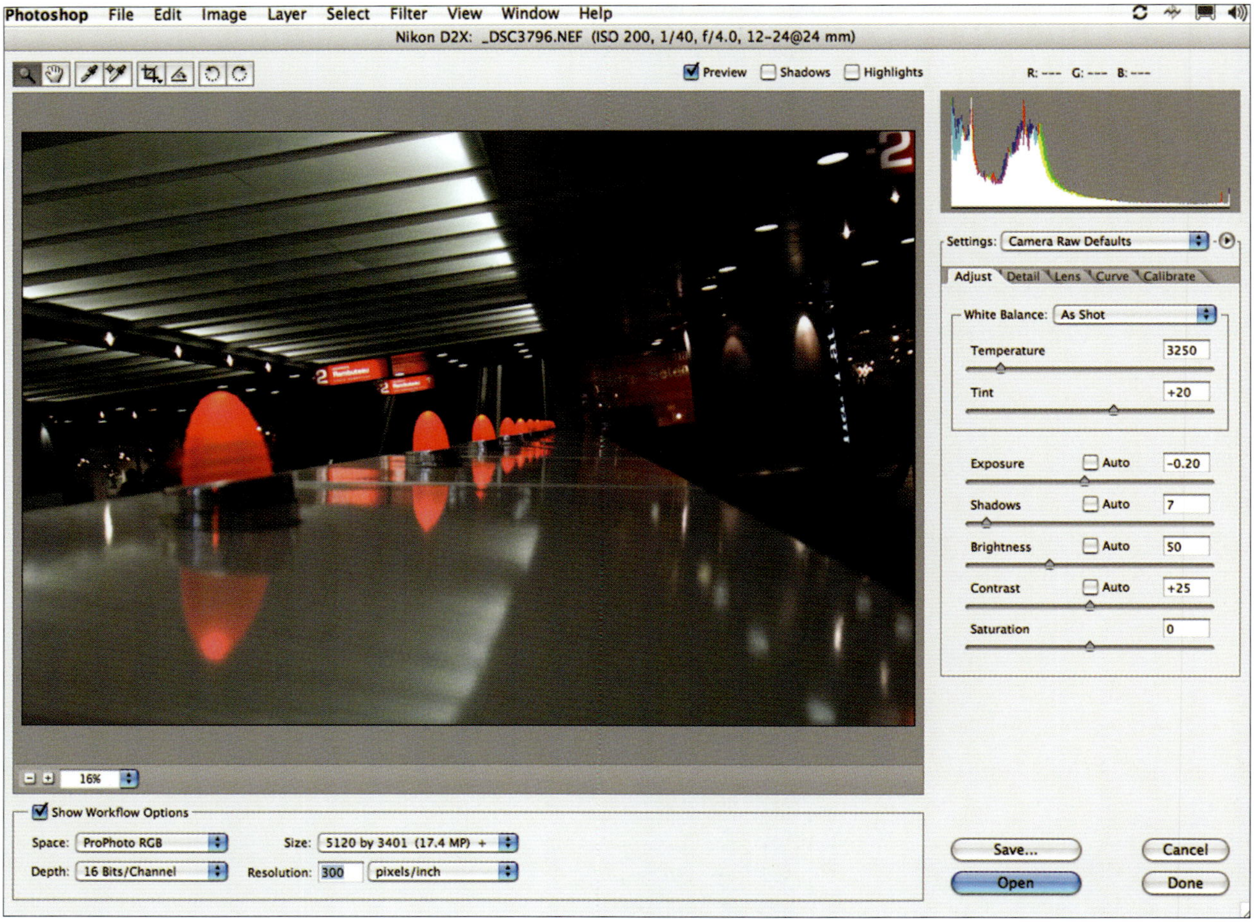

Figure 2.7

RAW software is available through Adobe, Phase One, Apple, and a variety of camera manufacturers.

Typically, camera images are recorded on a removable memory card, such as an SD or Compact Flash card. This card is taken from the camera and inserted into a card reader, and the image files are transferred to the computer. At this point, the conversion software comes into play.

This image conversion software gives you a wide range of control over the processing of the image before you transfer it into an image editing software package, such as Adobe Photoshop.

About the only thing you can't adjust effectively in conversion software is the original ISO, or rated light sensitivity of the sensor when the image was taken. This can produce the equivalent of film grain, usually called *noise*. Sometimes this noise can cause color distortion, hence the term "color noise."

RAW software controls permit you to adjust a wide range of image attributes. Figures 2.8 through 2.11 point to some of the key controls. One big advantage of making major adjustments in a RAW converter is that color distortions and other image defects that result from image editing are kept to a minimum—in many cases, much less than you would see when editing a JPEG in an ordinary image editor.

The reason for this is that, at this stage, the image file has the maximum amount of information it will ever have—for example, in terms of color—giving you as much latitude as possible to edit without undue penalties.

There are other controls available in most RAW converters, but I suggest that you reserve additional editing for Photoshop or a similar application.

Tip

Another key point to keep in mind is that RAW file adjustments are *not* permanent. The RAW software saves your instructions, along with your original image file, but these instructions do not alter your image information. You can go back again and again, make further adjustments, and fine-tune your image over time.

RAW files permit adjustments for increased total exposure and decreased total exposure. Take a look now at Figure 2.8. Note that there is a histogram at the top right of the RAW processing dialog box; observe that when you move the exposure slider, the histogram responds in real-time and will show you the effect of increased or decreased exposure. Note that this particular histogram has a strong peak on the left, and that this peak is nearly touching the left side of the histogram. If the peak begins to overlap on the right or left of the histogram, this means you might have adjusted the image too much, and you are potentially discarding color information and image detail.

Figure 2.9 shows the preset white balance drop-down menu and the color temperature slider. These tools are very useful in setting the overall color balance of your image. For example, if you have taken a photograph indoors in tungsten lighting, you can click on the white balance drop-down menu and select Tungsten. Usually, this will color balance your image nicely. The second red arrow points to the color temperature slider control. This control allows you to fine-tune your color temperature decision; moving the slider to the left will "cool down" your image (emphasizing blue tones), and moving it to the right will "warm up" your image (emphasizing red and yellow tones).

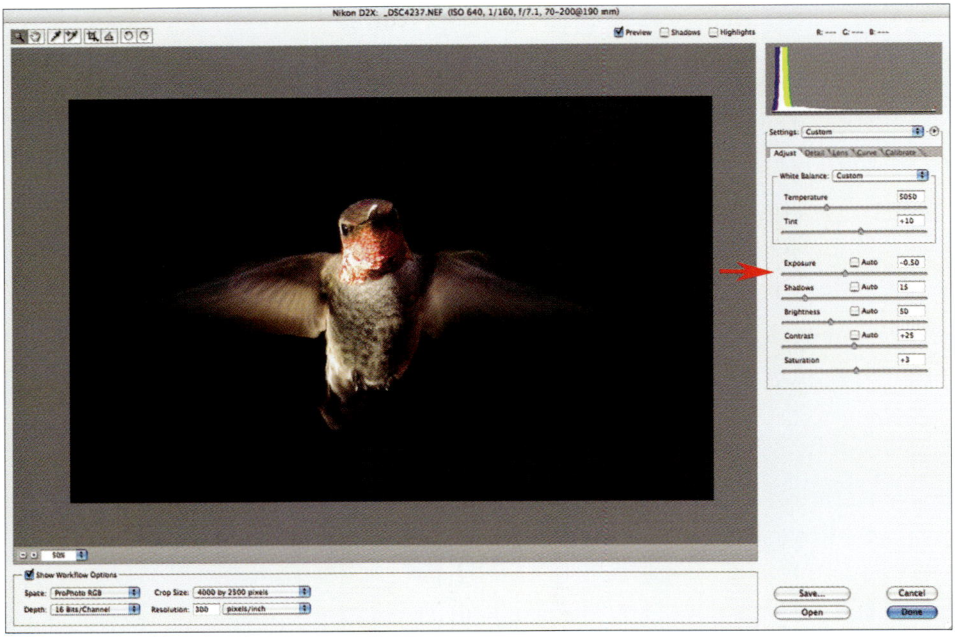

Figure 2.8

The red arrow points to the Exposure control slider.

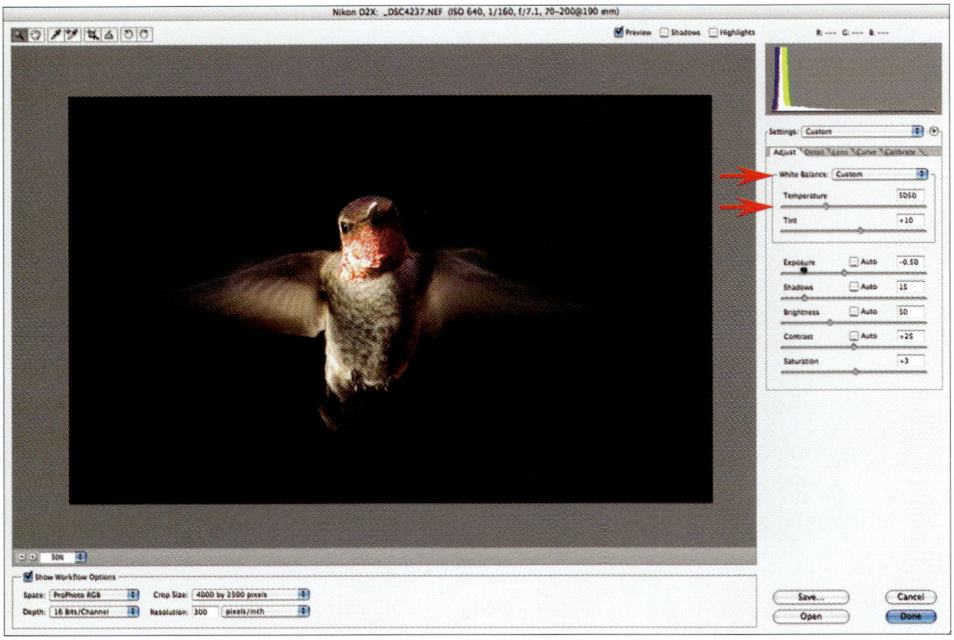

Figure 2.9

The red arrows point to the preset white balance drop-down menu and to the color temperature slider.

In Figure 2.10, the red arrow points to the white point eyedropper. This eyedropper can be very useful in making quick white balance adjustments. Left-click on the eyedropper, and then mouse over with the eyedropper to a bright white area that has a neutral tone. The best white point to select for scanning/digital imaging is the flat white area, like a shirt collar, or a fence or a wall, where it's not a catchlight/specular highlight and not a detailed highlight such as lace or a golf ball.

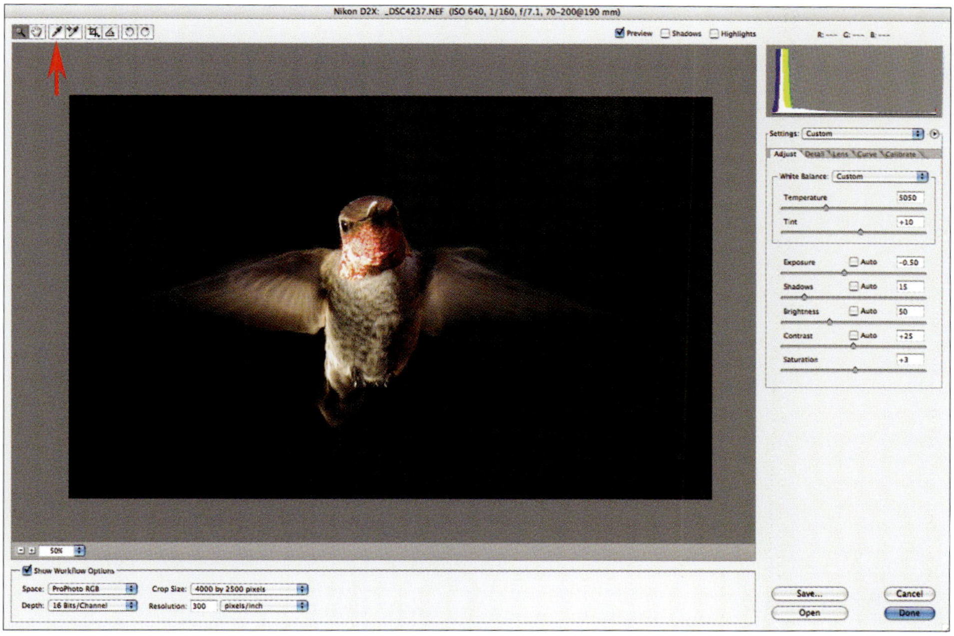

Figure 2.10

The white point eyedropper allows you to make quick white balance adjustments.

In Figure 2.11, the red arrow points to the drop-down menu presets for the color space that your RAW file will be processed in when it is converted to a TIFF or JPEG. (I strongly recommend TIFF file format and Adobe RGB 1998 or ProPhoto RGB.) Note also the Depth drop-down menu. It helps you specify 8-bit or 16-bit color depth. Now that Photoshop and many other image editors allow editing in 16 bits, there's really no reason to pass this option up. Output your file in 16-bit color depth, and see for yourself as posterization and banding are reduced, if not eliminated, from blue skies, water, and brightly colored fabrics portrayed in your images.

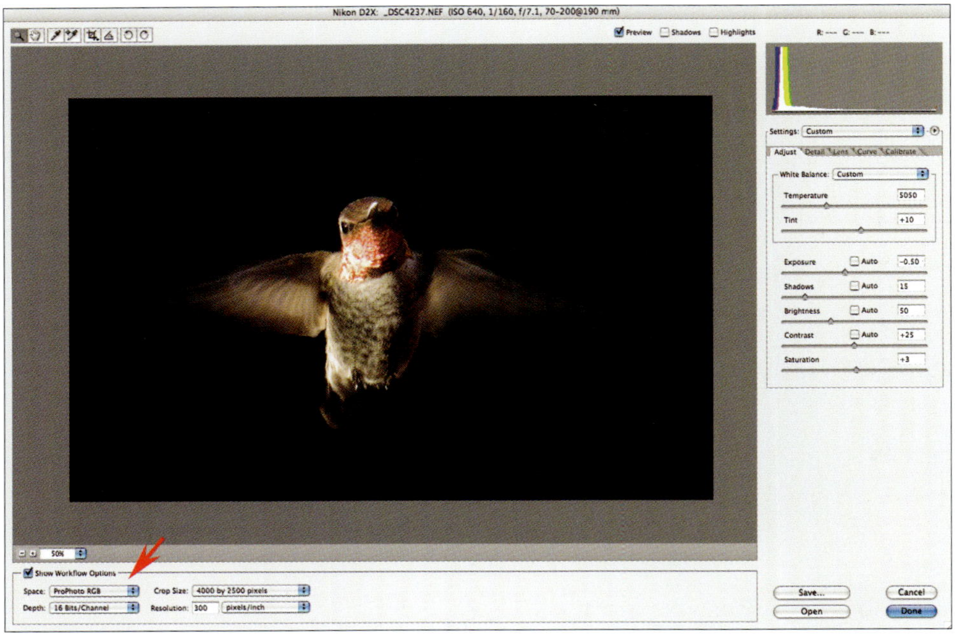

Figure 2.11

Here, you choose the color space that your RAW file will be processed in when it is converted to a TIFF or JPEG.

Last, you can choose to click Open, which will open your image in Photoshop; you can choose Done, which will save your edits and close the RAW dialog box (leaving your original image undamaged); you can click Save, which brings up a dialog box that allows you to save your file in several formats and gives you the option of keeping your RAW file intact.

RAW file processors also provide utilities for saving your adjustments to a file and then applying those adjustments to another file, or even an entire folder of images. This is sometimes called *batch processing*, and it can be an incredible productivity tool.

Editing and Finishing the Digital File

Adobe Photoshop is one of the most commonly used image editors today. It offers an incredibly wide range of image adjustment and editing tools. One of the important things to control in Photoshop is how the software application manages color. An interesting alternative to Photoshop CS2 is Photoshop Elements 4.0, which is much less expensive and incorporates many CS2 features. Figure 2.12 shows the Color Settings dialog box in Photoshop CS2. (From the menu bar in CS2, go Edit>Color Settings. In Photoshop CS, go to Photoshop>Color Settings.)

Note the features of the Color Settings dialog box:

- On the upper right of the box, note the Fewer Options button. Click on this so you can see all choices available.
- Working Spaces RGB: The default is sRGB. Change it to Adobe RGB (1998) for photographers. Set the other options in this section as shown in the figure.
- In the Color Management Policies section, set the first three drop-down options to Preserve Embedded Profiles, as shown in the figure.
- For Profile Mismatches, enable the Ask when Opening and Ask when Pasting checkboxes.
- For Missing Profiles, enable the Ask when Opening checkbox.
- Under Conversion Options, choose Adobe ACE, and for photographers, choose Perceptual.

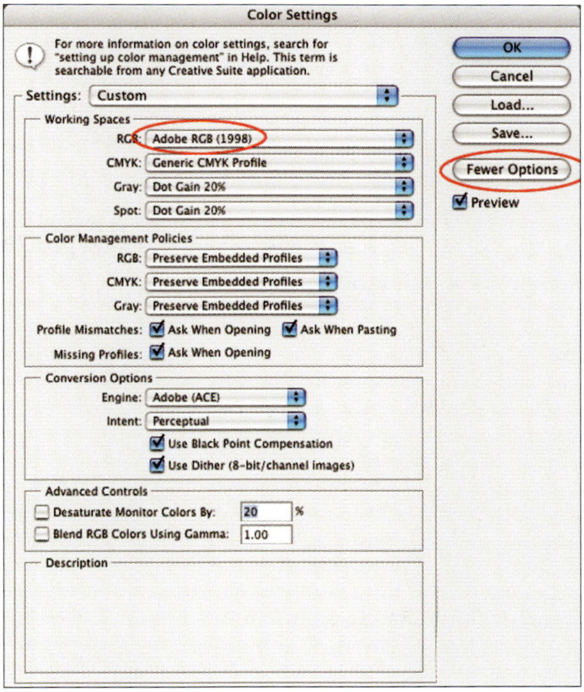

Figure 2.12

This dialog box, and its color settings, is the "gatekeeper" for managing color of all the images you bring into Photoshop.

Note that the default working space is set to Adobe RGB (1998). This ensures that your carefully scanned or captured Adobe RGB (1998) image is preserved and is protected from conversion to sRGB or another inappropriate color space.

In combination with the other settings shown here and later in this book, you'll achieve consistent control over color of images coming into your system and over images that you export from your system. For example, if you open an image that was captured in the sRGB color space, Photoshop will notify you that this image uses this color space and ask you if you want to change it. This is much better than flying blind, not knowing what you are working with.

Editing and finishing your image includes making adjustments in contrast, color, and clarity. Perhaps just as important as these is the issue of ensuring that the image will look the way you want it to when it goes to print or on a computer display.

Tip

If an image is captured in sRGB, it is better to keep it in that color space while editing. Attempting to change it to a broader color space such as Adobe RGB (1998) is at best ineffective and, at worst, damaging to your image. As a general rule, I recommend image capture in Adobe RGB (1998), and that you use this color space consistently through image editing, printing, and archiving.

I try to use a standardized approach to editing color in my image files. Once the image is opened in Photoshop or another image editor, I make the changes provided in the following list. Each change is made on its own layer or its own adjustment layer.

- Overall levels adjustment
- Overall color cast correction
- Selected area correction or change to color
- Selected area change in brightness or tonality
- Retouching (removing or smoothing out unwanted elements)
- Save as a master file, with all layers intact

Let's review these steps further in the following sections.

Making Levels Adjustments

To make an overall levels adjustment from the Photoshop menu bar, choose Image>Adjustment>Levels. You'll see the dialog box provided in Figure 2.13. The histogram in this dialog box (it kind of looks like a mountain, doesn't it?) shows the amount of information in your image, from the darkest tones on the left to the brightest tones on the right.

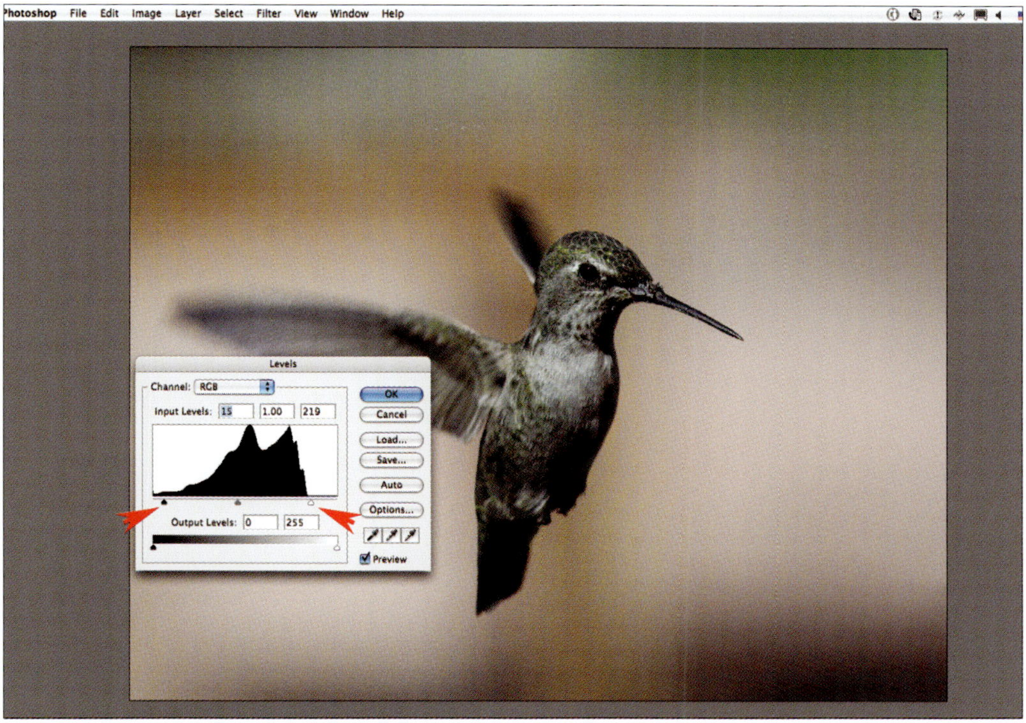

Figure 2.13

Levels adjustment improves the overall contrast and dimensionality of your image.

Note the red arrows in the figure; the arrow on the left points to an adjustable slider that's been moved to the right, improving contrast in the dark tones of the image. The right arrow shows how the right-hand slider, which controls brighter tones, has been adjusted. Generally, you'll want to move these two sliders in toward the right and left edges of the histogram. Make small moves, and watch the appearance of the image as you do this.

Note that a significant levels adjustment will introduce a warm color cast (reds and yellows) into your image. The most basic way to eliminate this is to choose Edit>Fade Levels, and then select Luminosity in the drop-down menu.

Making Color Cast Corrections

To make an overall color cast correction, you must consider what your image needs. The image shown in Figure 2.14 has a fairly warm color case, with yellow predominating. One quick and easy way to balance this is through the Curves dialog box. Choose Image>Adjustment>Curves, and you'll see the Curves dialog box. Click on the Channel drop-down menu at the top of the box to select individual color channels of red, green, or blue.

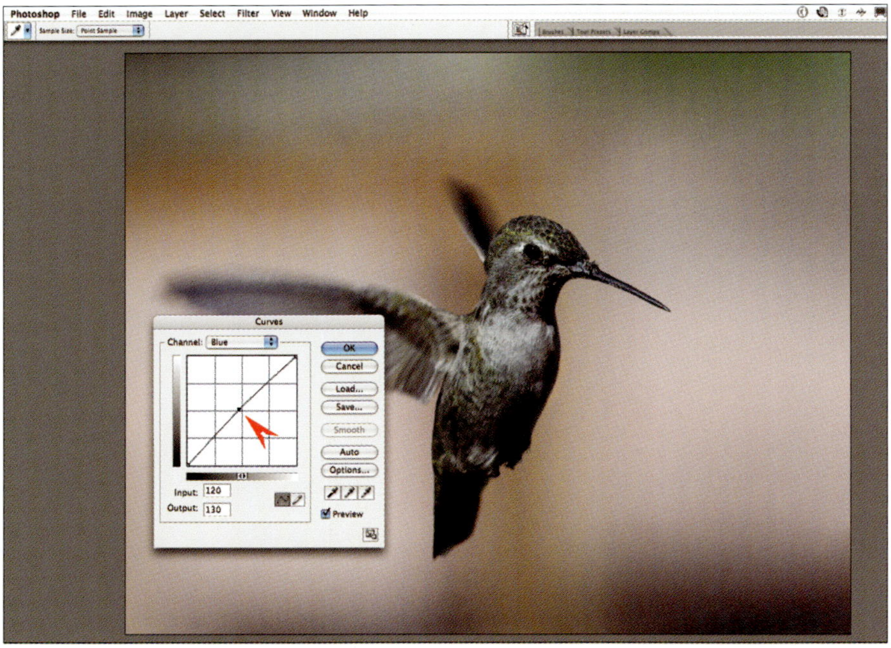

Figure 2.14

You can use Curves adjustments to produce quick and easy overall color corrections.

Because you want to correct a yellow color cast in this example, you select the blue channel. As you can see in the Figure 2.14, the red arrow points to the center of the Curves adjustment line. If you left-click on the center of this line, it will create an adjustment point, which you can left-click/drag upward or downward. Dragging this adjustment point upward increases the blue tones in the image, balancing the yellow color cast and color-neutralizing the image.

Another way to achieve overall color correction is to use the white or gray eyedropper in the Curves dialog box. In the following example, shown in Figure 2.15, the gray (middle) eyedropper is selected, and we are going to click with this tool in a relatively neutral gray area of the image. This will cause the color cast in the image to be corrected.

Next, it's time to add a layer for retouching. Believe it or not, retouching has a place in landscape work, commercial photography, and portraits. Beer cans, dust spots, or skin imperfections can all be eliminated. And keeping this retouching layer separate from your color adjustment layers protects your color from inadvertent changes or distortions.

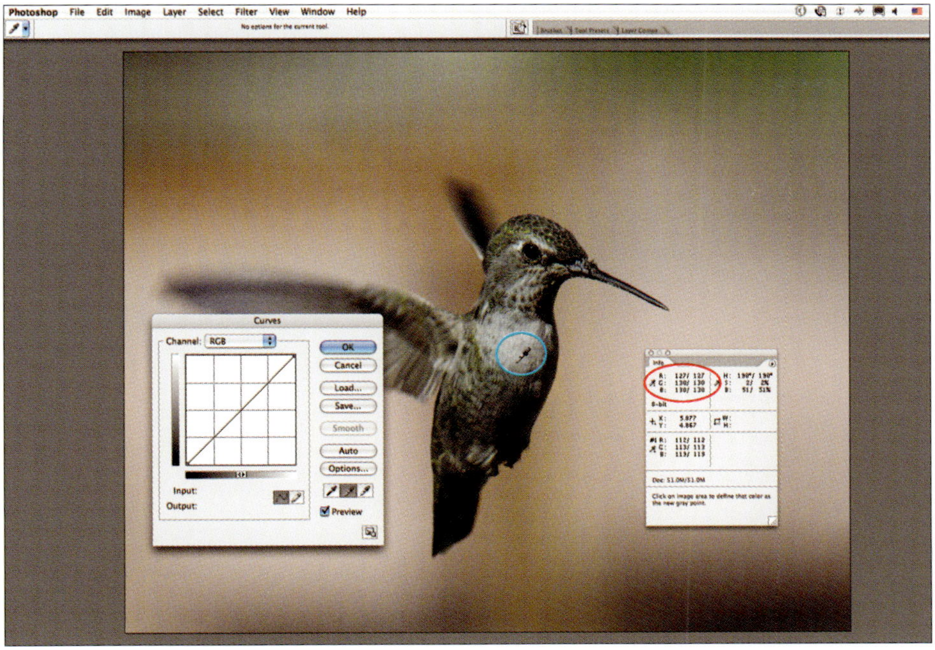

Figure 2.15

The gray eyedropper tool available in the Curves dialog box can be used to make quick, accurate color corrections.

Many of the tools I've been describing are available in new programs, such as Aperture and Lightroom. They also offer some interesting alternatives, including presets for specific color styles, such as cyanotype, old black and white, and others. These can be quite useful in developing alternatives to conventional color adjustments.

Tip

Image editors such as Photoshop provide quite a few methods for color correction and adjustment. There are extensive tutorials provided under the Help menu—and they are free!

Saving the Master File with All Layers Intact

Last, make it a matter of habit to save your files as master images with the layers intact. Do *not* flatten images before saving them. Once an image is flattened, your individual adjustments can be changed only with a great deal of work—or they can't be changed at all. Save your file as a TIFF or Photoshop file with the layers intact. And archive your file on one of the new metal-based CDs and store it in a physical location separate from your computer—such as a safety deposit box.

Summary

Most photographers use only a small fraction of what is available to them; there's a great deal of improvement to be gained in color management with a modest amount of thought and effort. Again, the best part of this is that the finished image will help you communicate your vision clearly with other photographers, artists, and customers.

Given imaging technology that's become available, you can capture and keep more color in your images than has ever been possible. Now you can capture images in dozens of ways and publish them via hundreds of different media.

It's absolutely vital to your success as an artist and photographer to have a clear understanding of these basic concepts and of the tools you can use to manage color in your work. You should understand how color is captured by your preferred film or digital sensor, what impact choosing a color space will have on your work, and how to use image editors to achieve the color and look you envision.

3

Controlling Your Color: Tools for Photographers

Recent developments in technology have made it much easier to create and color-manage your work. The acquisition cost of technology and the technical learning curve are both much more manageable.

What's the *real* benefit of effective color management? If you plan to use your image or artwork for just about any commercial purpose or even share it via the Internet—if you want reasonable consistency of appearance—or if you want to print your work—you'll find that good color management will enhance your work, save time, and help you make money.

Using color management in today's world enables you to:

- Think ahead and effectively harmonize the look of your art or image capture with your intended output device or media.
- Make adjustments, edits, or changes in real-time, see them on your computer display, and preview the effect of these changes before you make costly proofs or final prints.

- Re-purpose an original image for use on the Web, in video, TV/DVD playback, photographic printing, four-color press, and more. Given good color controls and systematic workflow, the number of iterations from an original is nearly unlimited.

On the side of your artwork, not only will you have a more accurate preview, but your artwork or reproduction will likely be truer to your original vision. Photographers use color management from the moment of capture, through final output.

One good analogy for color management is tuning an ensemble of musical instruments, as shown in Figure 3.1.

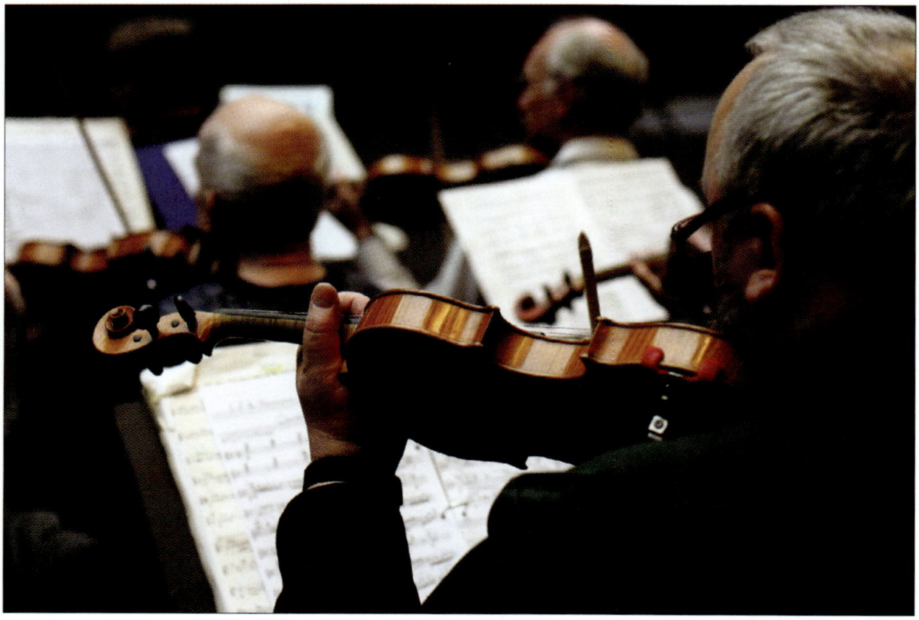

Figure 3.1

All of the instruments in an ensemble should be in tune. (Image licensed from istockphoto.)

Any instrument might be tuned by itself and played alone and sound fine—but for any combination of them to be played together, *they all must be tuned together.*

Color management not only provides tools for you to tune your capture, display, and output—it allows others to work with you in harmony—and to see your work as you intend it to be seen.

Manufacturers and software engineers have improved their products dramatically. And contrary to conventional wisdom, a significant portion of this technology remains usable for an extended time—there is much less pre-programmed obsolescence than most people believe.

For photographers or artists who want to print their work, color management can reduce time and production costs by 50%—and perhaps more.

Let's compare a color-managed production cycle with one that's *not* color managed:

Color Managed	Not Color Managed
Create Image	Create Image
Image Edit	Image Edit
Soft Proof*	Test Print
Final Print	Image Edit
	Test Print
	Image Edit
	Final Print

* Soft proofing involves accurate preview of print on computer display.

This is a simplified example, and there will be variations among the population of artists or photographers. But if you eliminate even one test print per production cycle, you cut your costs significantly.

Here's an example of the difference in media cost (if you assume that it costs one dollar to make an 8×10 print on your "SnappyPrint 6000," that you are making 30 prints a month (about one roll of film), and that you make only one test print in a non-color–managed work environment.

Color Managed	Non-Color Managed
30 Final Prints/Month = 360 Prints/Year =	30 Final Prints/Month +
$360 Total Costs	30 Proof Prints/Month =
	720 Prints/Year =
	$720 Total Costs

One hidden cost in this is your production time. If you figure out your desired hourly rate, multiplied by your current printing time, you can assume that you can cut that cost/hour in half with a well-calibrated display. This isn't imaginary, it's based on my personal experience and my work helping other photographers get a grip on their own studio equipment.

My own informal survey of people attending my Photoshop and printing workshops indicates that most people make two test prints for every final print they produce, and that the majority do not use the most basic color management tools.

This is a conservative scenario. As an alternative, imagine that you do not have a color-managed workflow, and that you are printing via an outside lab.

If the color is not acceptable, you will usually find yourself asking for a re-make. This involves your time to mail the unacceptable print back to the lab or travel there yourself, explain the problem, and then return again to pick it up.

Or, imagine that you want to make a change in color, saturation, density, or any other variables in an image that you want to print yourself. In a non-color–managed scenario, you would be forced to guess at the impact of a change—and perhaps make additional test prints. Using color management, you can see the image onscreen, understand what it will look like down the road, make the adjustment, and move on.

No matter how you look at it, large scale or small scale, using color management can save most of us time and money.

Costs in adding color management tools can be reasonable or, in some cases, expensive. If you already own a display of reasonable quality that was manufactured in the last couple of years, you can get improved results simply by using the display adjustment software that is provided with your operating system (Windows or Mac).

If you go beyond the basics, you might include the following (in approximate order of cost and inconvenience):

- Software calibration (Mac or Windows)
- Workroom management (inside lighting controls, room color, control of outside light)
- Basic display upgrade (display hardware)
- Basic display calibration (hardware and software)
- Basic output device calibration, such as printer profiling
- Advanced display upgrade (display and video card upgrade)

If you do a lot of image editing, it really pays to work in a room where the primary lighting source comes from the display and the influence of other lighting is as little as you can get by with. And even though it sounds like a cliché, wear a dark shirt to minimize screen reflections. This will keep fatigue and eyestrain lower, make you work more efficiently, and help you make more money.

You can add a display color calibration device, shown in Figure 3.2, at a cost of less than $200 and begin to color manage your work. I strongly recommend this to anyone who is using a computer for image editing or layout work and is serious about his or her work as a photographer or artist.

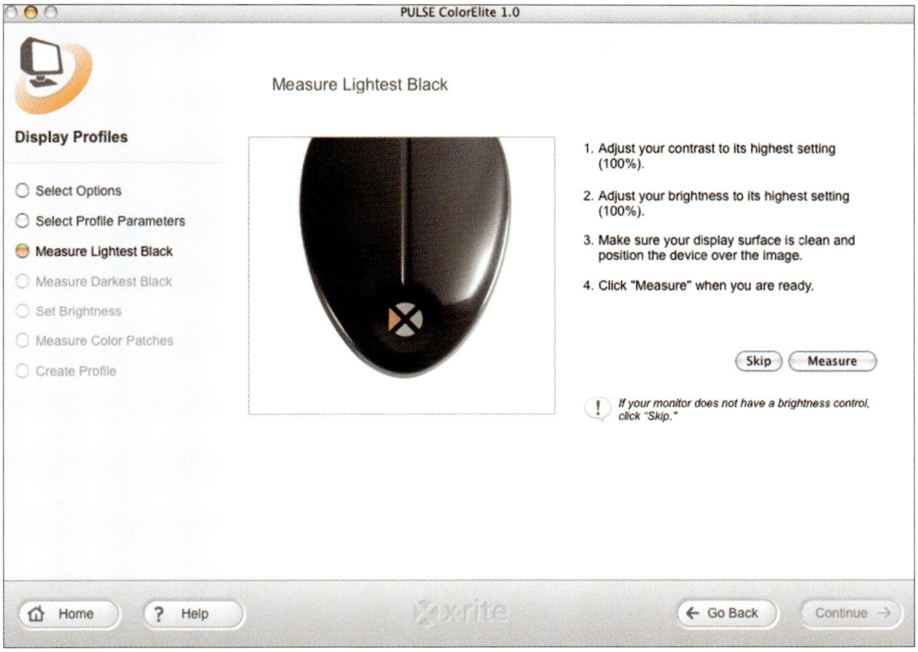

Figure 3.2

Display calibration devices are the most accurate way to tune up your display—you'll see improved color and highlight/shadow detail.

On the other hand, if you do need to replace an older display, you could add $500 to $1,200 to your budget for a unit that will give decent results. Manufacturers provide basic software along with the device. (See Chapter 5 for a discussion of recent developments in display technology and color management.)

The learning curve should not be a problem for those who are only moderately familiar with computers and software. Tutorials are available via the Internet. See Appendix A for details.

If you need to control camera input, display, and prints, you may opt for a higher-end system, which ranges from $1,500 to several thousand dollars. See Appendix A for more detailed examples of a business model and a brief analysis of how these devices and software can also pay for themselves.

Options for Scanning or Capturing Your Digital Image

This section reviews the following options in scanning or capturing a digital image:

- Film media (transparency or negative)
- Scanners—film, flat work, and art
- Camera—film
- Camera—digital

Film Media

In the last 20 years, we have all been spoiled by the incredible flexibility of film—transparency and negatives alike. In the case of negative film, one can create images with an amazing range of colors, even in situations where artificial and natural light are mixed.

Transparency film has also evolved. Although transparencies do not have the extraordinary latitude of negative film, they are now available in a variety of what I'll call "color interpretations." In some cases, they render color in a neutral fashion. In many others, they emphasize certain colors or color ranges.

Described another way: Given neutral, daylight balanced lighting (5,000 degrees Kelvin, or 5000K), some films will render color in a scene differently than others.

One way to measure these differences among films is by their "neutral rendering point," or NRP. Each film records light a bit differently, and the lab chemistry can also play a role in the color of film. Table 3.1 compares color temperatures of the light required to make different films render pleasing colors.

Table 3.1 Examples of the Neutral Rendering Point for Different Film Stocks

Film	Neutral Rendering Point
Fuji Astia 100	5150K
Fuji Velvia	5600K
Kodak E100S	5250K
Kodak E100 SW	5500K

*Table courtesy of Will Crockett.

Understanding these differences can help the photographer or artist to tailor the image capture to anticipated production requirements. In other words, the decisions you make up front will save time and money later on. Photographers can create avoidable post-production problems when they choose a film with an inappropriate NRP.

Assuming a light source of 5000K, the higher the NRP, the more you will see a shift to warmer colors, such as reds and oranges, in the final image.

Fuji Velvia will record a subject in a neutral lighting situation in fairly warm tones. In addition, Velvia is well known for its total palette of highly saturated, vibrant colors, particularly when used in landscape work.

If I were capturing an image of someone's artwork so that I could make reproductions for them, I might choose Fuji Astia, which has a lower NRP than Velvia and also provides more conservative (some might say more natural) color saturation.

In addition, some films and transparencies will scan more readily than others. Color transparencies are still preferred for scanning to digital in traditional photography in terms of rendering fine detail and ease of managing color in the digital world.

Scanners and Scanning

Digital cameras aside, the most commonly used bridge between the analog (film) world and digital is the scanner. Available in a variety of configurations, scanners can create very high-quality image files at reasonable cost.

Film scanners, whether they are consumer-level flatbeds (which look like a desktop photocopying machine) or highly sophisticated drum scanners, all use a light source and a digital sensor to capture the image.

The basic scanner setup for film or transparency works like so. The scanner light is transmitted through the film or transparency, and the digital sensor records the information to your computer's memory or a file.

Color rendered in the scan can be determined by combination of these variables:

- Film stock used
- Scanner and scanner sensor characteristics
- Exposure, contrast, and other adjustments made by the scanner operator
- Color space used during the scanning process
- Scanner characteristics

Scanners and digital cameras do have at least one thing in common: Image quality is largely determined by the imaging sensor hardware and the software that controls it.

As with digital cameras, scanners are made in a number of configurations. Nikon, shown in Figure 3.3, makes a number of models for scanning 35mm film, as does Minolta and Pacific Image. Figure 3.3 shows the Nikon Coolscan 5000, and Figure 3.4 shows the Imacon 828.

At the top of the film scanner food chain is the drum scanner. These devices still have the edge when it comes to top quality, detailed scanning. Most individuals, and even small studios, can't afford the expense and labor involved in using these machines. At a cost of $30,000 to $50,000, these scanners are used by publishing houses, service bureaus, and design companies.

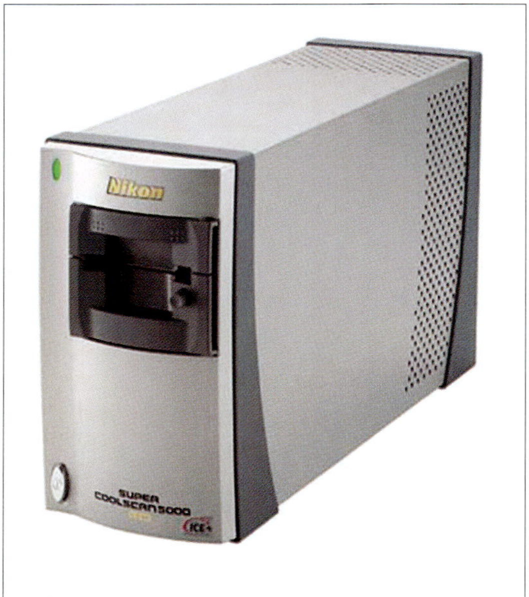

Figure 3.3

The Nikon Coolscan 5000 scans 35mm and APS-sized film and transparencies and provides 16-bit analog/digital conversion and 4000 dpi. (© Nikon)

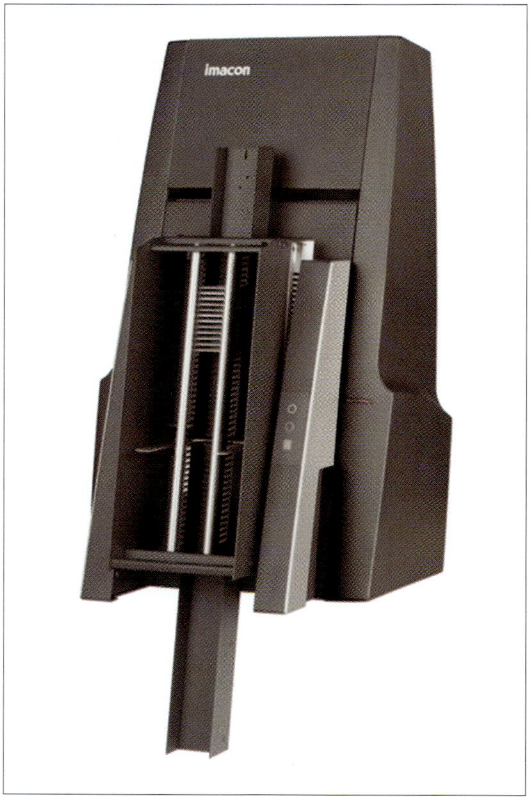

Figure 3.4

The Imacon 828 can handle film or transparencies up to 12×25cm. Its maximum resolution is 8,000 dpi. © Imacon.

You can send your film out to a service bureau that provides drum scanning services—and you can expect to pay at least $30 for a 35mm scan and close to $100 for a high-resolution scan of a 4×5 transparency (some scanning houses charge by the megabyte, so you might want to shop around).

If you do send your film out to be scanned, here are a few recommendations:

- Specify the maximum resolution, or dpi, that your budget can handle. You can always downsize an image file, but it's very difficult to upsize it.
- Ask for your scan in Adobe RGB (1998) color space or better. Some scanner operators advocate Ekta color space, others Wide Gamut RGB. If your original is black and white, you should still ask for an RGB scan; it maximizes the information in your file. As a general rule, I ask for Adobe RGB (1998) unless the scanner operator recommends a large space for technical reasons.

Tip

Wide Gamut RGB is an expanded version of Adobe RGB (1998), and it is one of the giants in the color space universe. In fact, it contains some colors that can't be displayed on a computer monitor and some colors that just can't be printed. Like ProPhoto RGB, it is often a specialists' tool, used for image editing that is intended to be output to film. If you do decide to use a larger color space, keep the image in 16-bit mode to avoid color distortion and posterization.

- In scans of film under 4×5 inches, ask for a 16-bit scan. According to some opinions, at 4×5 and up, there is so much information available in the scan that bit depth is less critical. If you plan to crop the scan or do significant color adjustment, go for the 16-bit scan.
- Specify a TIFF file format and avoid JPEG. TIFF files are uncompressed, so they suffer no loss of information. (Remember that TIFF files are the jack-of-all trades in the digital world. They do not compress the image data, they can be saved as high-bit files, and they can be read by most software applications. JPEG files, however, are limited to 8 bits and, depending on software choices, apply small or larger amounts of compression to reduce file size.)

Last, there are a number of good flatbed type scanners available. Epson, Canon, HP, and MicroTek are just a few of the manufacturers in the market. These look like a desktop photocopying machine, but they have much higher resolution.

Flatbed scanners can be used to scan both film and printed materials. The quality of these devices has improved greatly over the past few years; however, I still recommend a dedicated film scanner or a drum scanner for the serious amateur or professional.

Color Depth

Scanner resolution differs from company to company. More important from a color management standpoint, some scanners capture a broader range and depth of color.

Color depth is a measurement of the amount of color information captured in each pixel of a scan or digital capture. (A pixel, or "picture element," is a single element of an image. For the purposes here, it typically consists of red, green, and blue color elements combined in varying amounts to render a desired color.)

The color depth captured by your scanner can make a big difference in your final product. Sometimes described as *bit depth,* higher color depth provides better color representation and gives you more "elbow room" in editing and manipulating colors.

Here are some examples:

- Consumer-level camera: 8 bits
- Prosumer camera: 8 bits or 12 bits
- Professional digital SLR: 12 bits
- Professional medium-format digital camera back: 16 bits
- Desktop dedicated film scanner: 14 bits
- Virtual drum, or drum scanner: 16 bits

These measurements might seem closer together than they really are. There is a huge difference between an 8-bit image and a 16-bit image, because these numbers are exponential.

A pixel that has a bit depth of 1 can be black or white. A pixel that has a bit depth of 8 has 28 tones, which equals 256 tonal values.

A pixel with a bit depth of 16 is expressed as 216 and has 65,536 potential tonal values.

Going further down this road and making the calculation for RGB or CMYK color shows that we have billions and billions of possible tones (apologies to Carl Sagan).

It's also true that current technology can't display or print 100% of this range of colors. However, it is important that you understand that higher bit depth images give you the ability to manage or manipulate color more effectively and with significantly less distortion of final product.

Figure 3.5 shows an example of what can happen when an 8-bit image is edited, versus a 16-bit image.

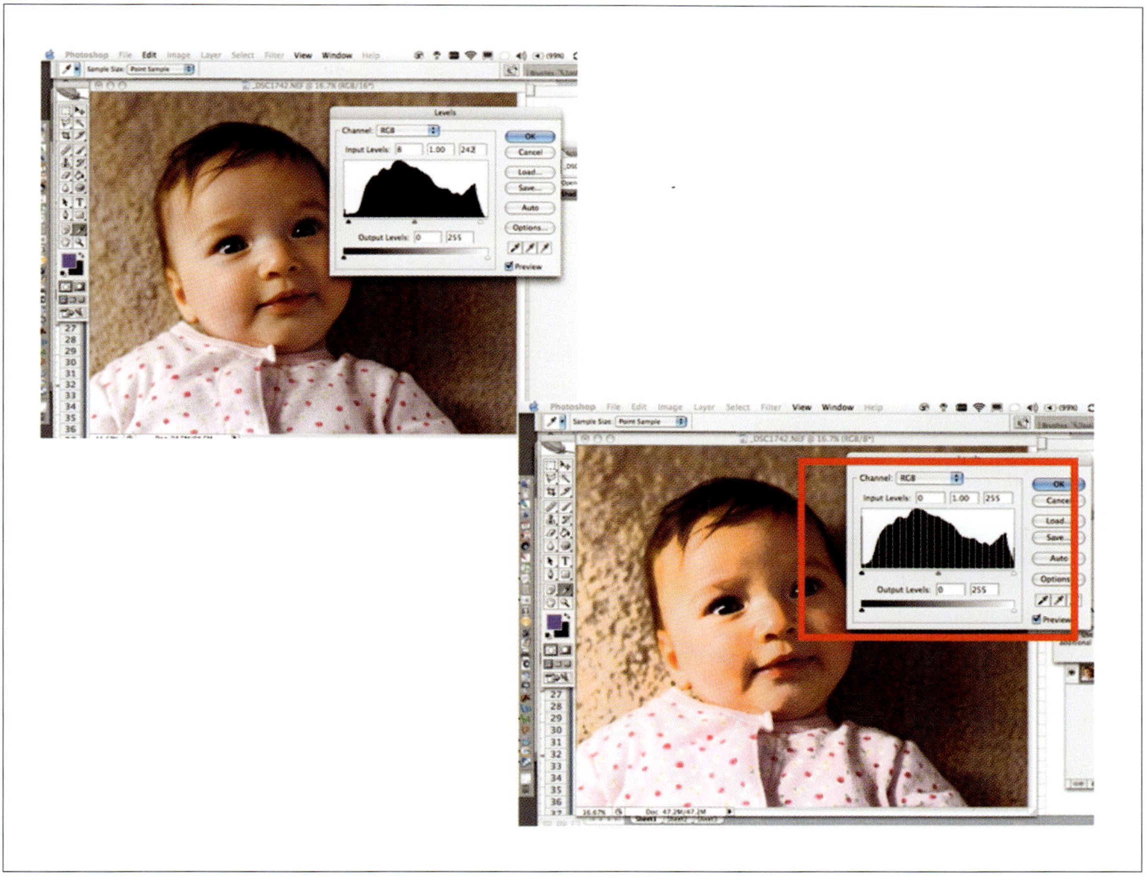

Figure 3.5

The image on the left is the 16-bit image; notice how the image on the right (the 8-bit image) is now suffering from posterization.

The gaps in the histogram on the left show where the 8-bit image information was "stretched"—in other words, the 8-bit image is likely to suffer from posterization, banding, or other nasty digital artifacts when you try to print it.

Choosing a Color Space

When scanning, you can choose one of a number of color spaces. As you saw in Chapter 2, some of the commonly used color spaces include sRGB, Adobe RGB, Wide Gamut RGB, and so on.

If you are scanning film, keep in mind that film has a much bigger potential to render color than any of these. Even now, most digital cameras and scanners do not even come close to fully translating "analog" film into the digital world.

So, what do you do? If you are scanning for the Web, computer display, video, and the like, you can do just fine scanning with sRGB in 8-bit mode. Remember that sRGB is quite limited compared to Adobe RGB 98, as illustrated in Figure 3.6.

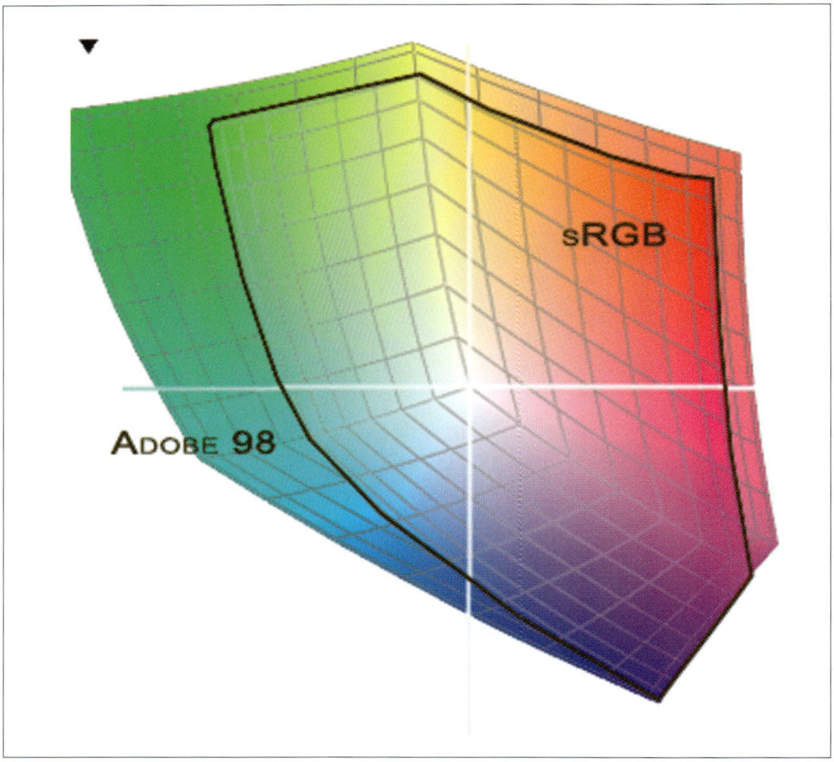

Figure 3.6

This is a two-dimensional map of the colors available in a color space. Each color space map will look different.

If you are scanning for printing, whether in a book, magazine, or other four-color device, I strongly recommend that you choose Adobe RGB (1998) at minimum.

Other options include Wide Gamut RGB, ProPhoto RGB, and Ekta color space. In Figure 3.6, the inner triangle represents Adobe RGB (1998), and the outer triangle represents ProPhoto RGB.

All four of these spaces provide a range of color that cannot be printed in full using current technology. However, the breadth and depth of these gives you plenty of elbow room for editing and modifying your images.

Scanner Controls and Adjustments

Figure 3.7 illustrates a typical set of scanner controls, with an image of a color target used for color calibration of the scanner. (Scanner is Minolta Dimage Multi Scan Pro. Target provided by X-Rite.)

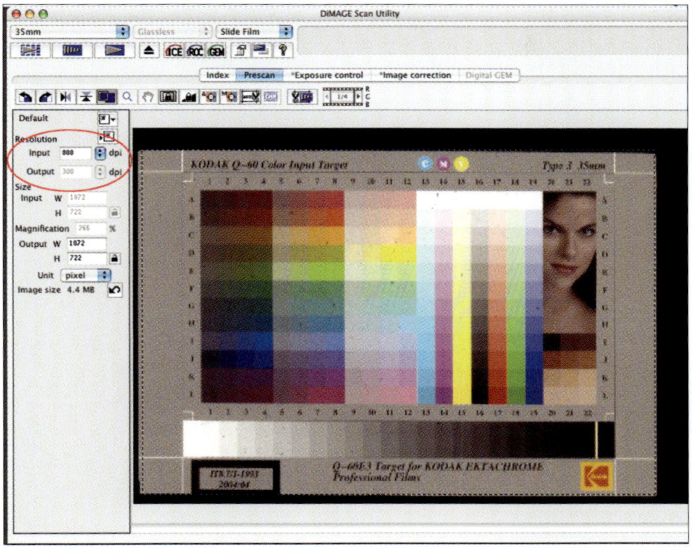

Figure 3.7

An example of scanner controls, with an image of a color target used to calibrate the scanner. (Scanner software by Minolta, color target from X-Rite.)

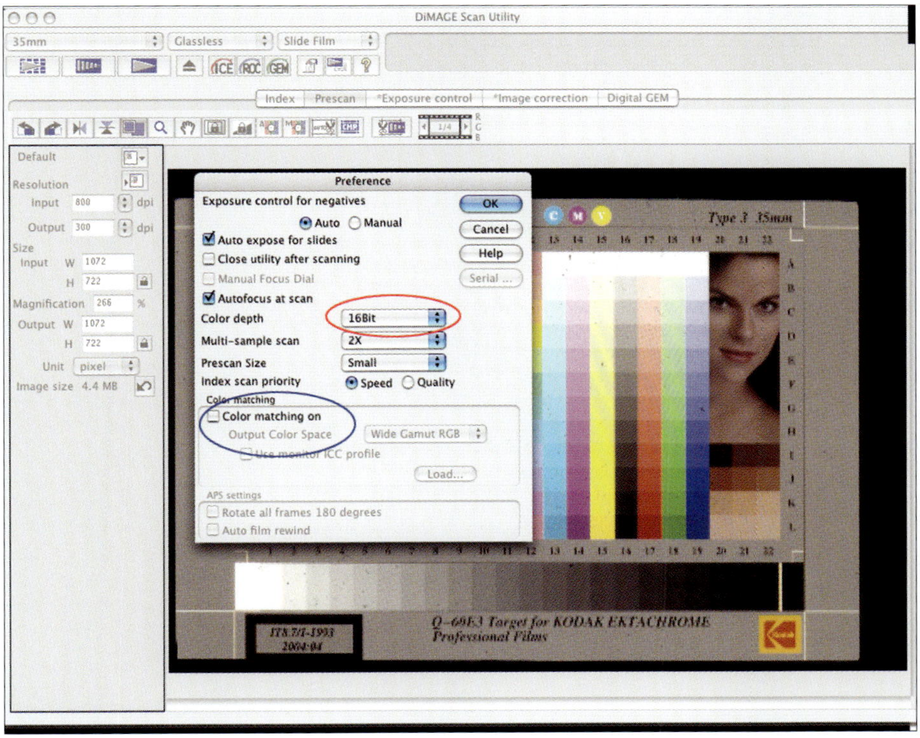

Note the red circle around Scanning Resolution. This is the recommended resolution for this target. If I scan a 35mm slide for printed output, I use 4,200 dpi.

Next, I have selected the Preferences dialog box, which specifies bit depth and color space, among other things.

Note the red circle around Color Depth, set to 16-bit, and the blue circle, which denotes color matching or color space. In this case, Color Matching is not enabled, denoted by the blue circle. This eliminates any software changes to color, preserving the color target's original color values.

If I were scanning a 35mm slide, I would likely specify Adobe RGB (1998), Wide Gamut RGB, or ProPhoto RGB as my color space. Again, the reason for this is that a broad, robust color space will give maximum room for image editing in the future, including perhaps re-purposing the image for a four-color press, inkjet printing, the Internet, projection, and so on.

Note

There is some controversy over use of a larger color space, because some people say that you can't see the entire range of color on your monitor anyway, or that some of the color is outside the range that inkjet printers can reproduce. Both of these observations are correct.

I have found in my personal work that use of ProPhoto RGB is most helpful in studio portrait work, particularly when the appearance of skin tones is important. So from the standpoint of real-world results, not theory, I'm satisfied that ProPhoto RGB can be a useful tool. An extra note: Once I've finished the full range of edits on the image, I then make a duplicate output copy that's been converted to Adobe 1998 (RGB). This output copy is compatible with all of my printer profiles.

There is also a variety of tools available through the scanner software. These include 1) tone curves and levels (histogram), 2) brightness, contrast, and color balance, 3) hue and saturation, 4) selective color adjustment, and 5) unsharp mask controls. These are all similar in function to tools that are available in Adobe Photoshop.

However, these are not color management tools; they are color adjustment and sharpening tools. Generally, I recommend that adjustments be made in a fully featured image editor, such as Photoshop.

A dedicated image editor is more flexible and powerful than the tools provided in most scanning software. Additionally, good image editors allow you to edit non-destructively in layers, in other words, without permanently altering the information in the image. Scanner software that I'm aware of does not permit this.

In most instances, I adjust only the resolution and the general exposure when scanning. All color controls and adjustments are set to neutral, or the software defaults.

The next section reviews the details of the software process involved in creating a profile for your scanner and discusses how you can use that profile to better manage color in your scans.

Creating a Scanner Profile

Creating a film scanner profile is relatively easy. In fact, getting to the finish line mostly depends on leaving things alone, rather than complex maneuvering.

To create an accurate scanner profile, you need:

- A color target that you can scan into a digital image file.
- Software that will use the scan to measure what your scanner has done.

A good scanning target can be a 35mm or 4×5 inch transparency or a printed version on photographic-quality paper. A typical target looks like Figure 3.8.

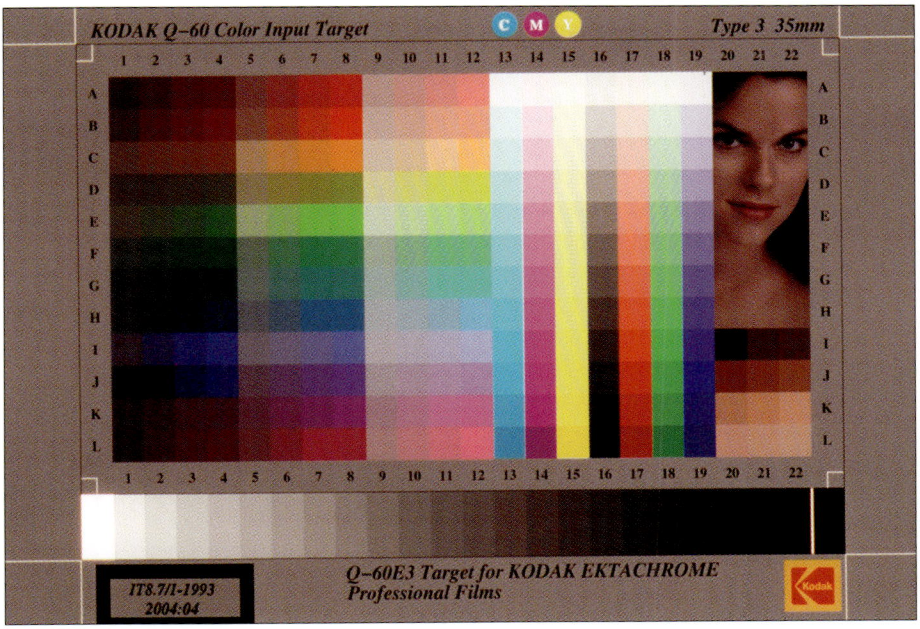

Figure 3.8

This is a color target used for scanner calibration.

The scan is usually made without using any color controls or adjustments. This allows the software, which is discussed next, to measure the color information the scanner produces without any interference.

The instructions from X-Rite are as follows:

- Position the target.
- Turn off all of your scanner's automatic correction options and any color management options.
- Set the scanner's resolution to 800 dpi.
- Prescan the target, and then crop the prescan to include only the IT8 target before scanning. Save a TIFF of the scan.
- As with other scanning jobs, it's best to turn image sharpening off.

Write down the scanner settings you use. You will need to use the same setting each time you scan an image to use with the profile. (Also, please note that other manufacturers' profiling software may require you to use different scanner settings.)

After this, you process the scanned image using the profiling software.

Next, you select Input Profile, which provides the dialog box shown in Figure 3.9.

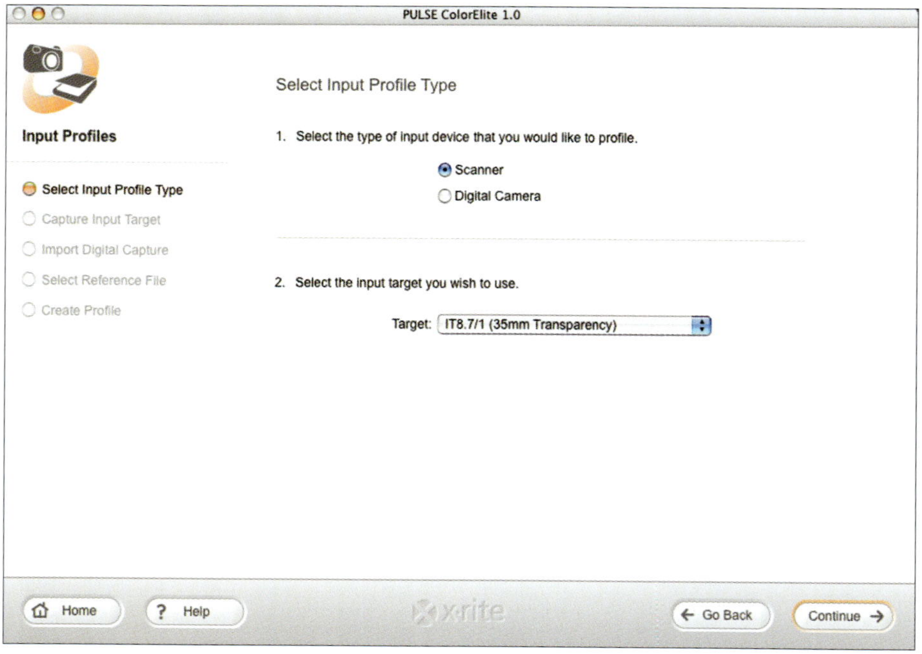

Figure 3.9

In this dialog box, you select your input profile type.

Next, you choose to load the image file created by the scanner. This is just like opening any file in any other software package. Figure 3.10 shows the dialog box.

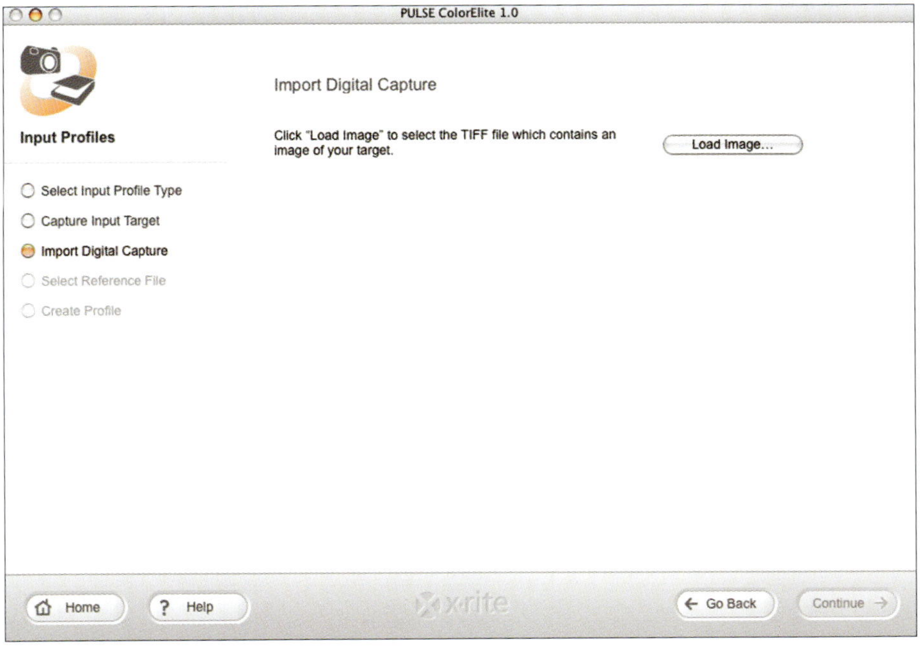

Figure 3.10

Next, you load the scanner image.

The next two dialog boxes, shown in Figure 3.11, are simple. They instruct you to identify the type of target you have and next to process it.

Once processing is complete, you will have a profile of your scanner's performance. This is a measurement of, and comparison between, the known color values in the target and the color values the scanner delivers. These files always have a suffix of .icc, or .icm—Mac or Windows, respectively.

If you are calibrating for scanning of flat work, such as a photographic print or art work, the process is much the same. You use a reflective target that is printed on paper, rather than a transparency.

Tip

Here's a little-known tip for enhancing your scanner profiles' accuracy—if you plan to scan a particular film type, such as Kodak or Fuji, purchase and use a color target that is produced on *that* film. Use that target to create a profile in your scanner. Remember the discussion of neutral rendering point, and how different films render color differently? I own and use color targets produced on film made by several companies—it works!

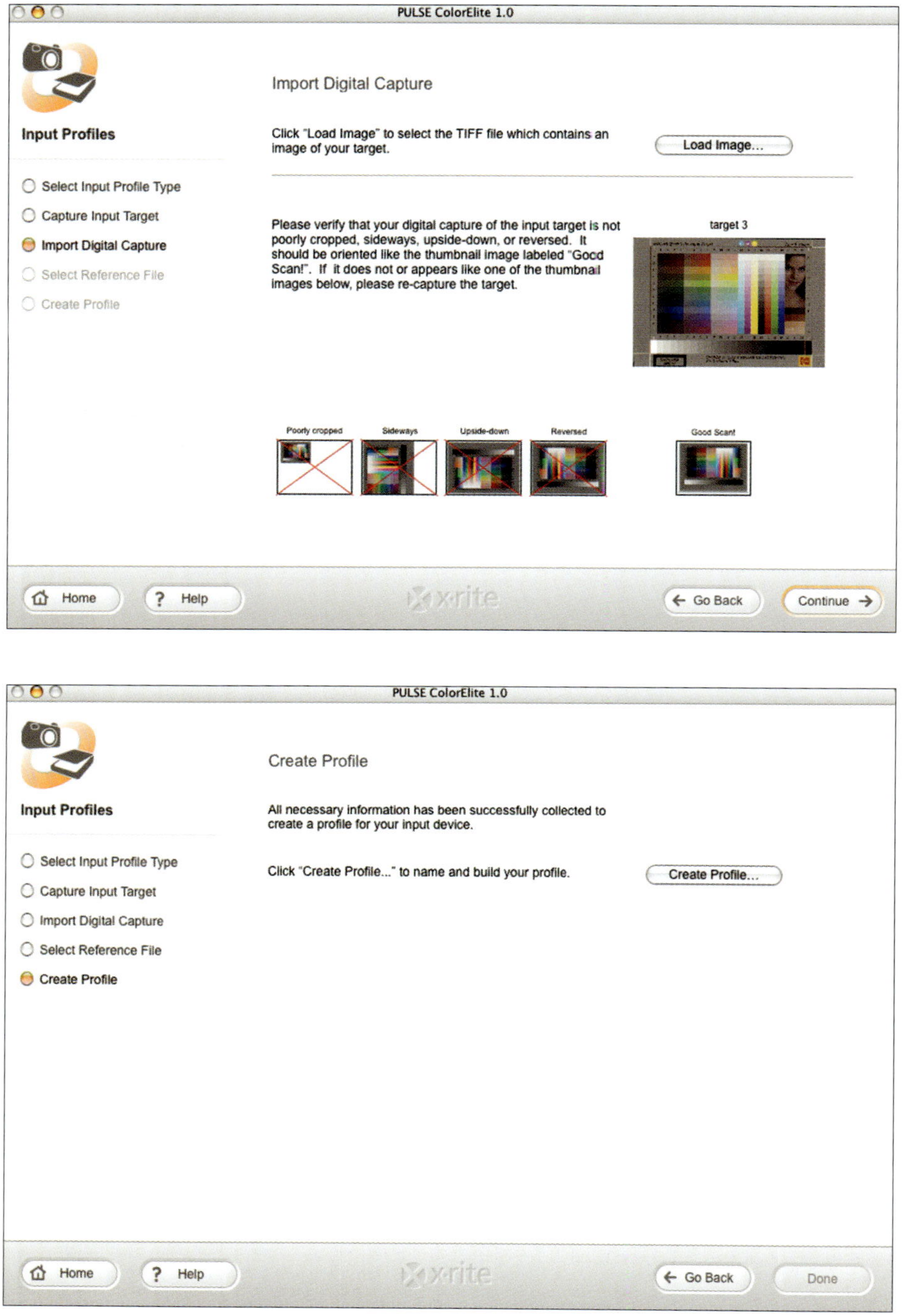

Figure 3.11

Creating your profile takes just a few clicks.

Using a Scanner Profile

A scanner profile is applied in your image editing software. For the purposes of this review, I assume that you are using Adobe Photoshop.

First, open the image in Photoshop. If you have set up Photoshop color preferences according to the recommendations in Chapter 2, you will see a dialog box that asks you if you want to assign a profile to the image. Choose not to assign any profile to the image ("Don't color manage this document").

Next, choose Edit>Assign Profile. You will see the dialog box shown in Figure 3.12.

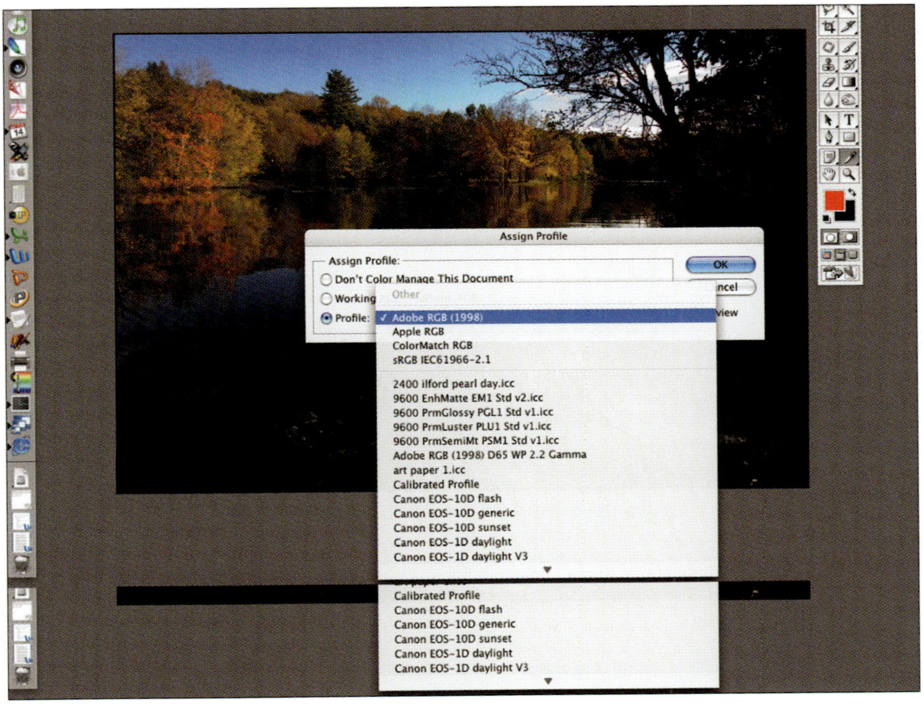

Figure 3.12

Use the drop-down menu to choose the scanner profile you created, and assign it to this image.

If you click on the drop-down menu, you should see a list of available profiles; choose the one that you created previously, and then click OK. This adjusts the image colors to compensate for any color shifts or related bias built into the scanner.

Next, you need to convert the image to the color space that you prefer to work in. My recommendation is to keep as much color information in the image as possible. To do this, you will convert the image to a color space that is relatively large, such as Adobe RGB (1998).

Here's how:

1. Select Edit>Convert to Profile. Then, from the drop-down menu, select your working color space and click OK. Keep in mind that Convert to Profile is not the same as soft proofing. See Chapter 7, "Color Quality Control," for more information on this important tool.
2. Now save your image file under a new name, and you're ready to begin final editing. If you've done a good job of shooting the original and your scanner profile is accurate, you will usually have just a little cleaning up to do.

Digital Cameras

Digital cameras come in hundreds, if not thousands, of models and configurations. However, they can be divided into several major categories.

First, these cameras come into two very broad categories: consumer and professional. Consumer-level cameras are characterized by emphasis on convenience over flexibility, automation over manual controls, and lower image quality.

Professional level cameras emphasize image quality and usually have interchangeable lens options, adjustable color and exposure settings, and more. As you will learn in the next part of this section, the choices available to you with professional-level cameras enhance image quality and shorten total time required for image editing.

There are a number of important options available to you in digital capture. Managing these choices in your hardware can determine the quality of your final image, as illustrated in Figure 3.13. They include:

- Color space
- Exposure
- Camera profile or color calibration
- File type
- Image resolution

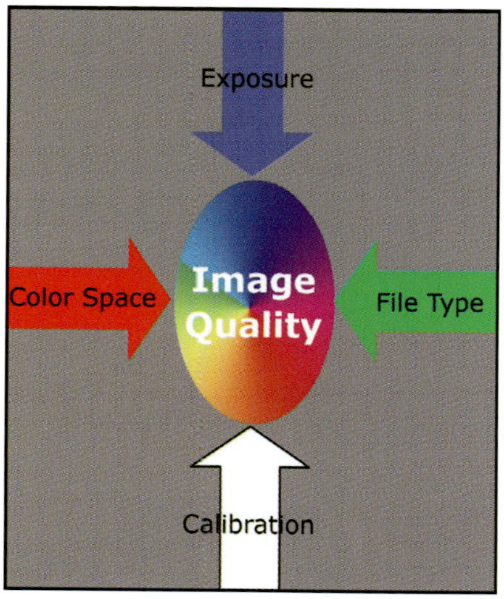

Figure 3.13

Getting all the important elements to come together is the key to creating great images.

Digital Camera Sensors

It's possible to write an entire book on the characteristics of currently available digital imaging sensors. Ranging from those used in inexpensive pocket cameras to multi-shot large format *digital backs* (attached to the camera, much like a traditional film holder), the image quality rendered ranges from barely acceptable to astonishingly detailed photographs with rich, accurate color. The difference in price can be tens of thousands of dollars.

A guide to matching sensor performance to intended use is provided in the following table:

Category	Quality		
Sensor size	< APS size = 1	Approx 35mm = 2	6x4.5+ = 3
Photosite size	< 6 microns = 1	6 microns = 2	9 microns = 3
ISO capability	200 ISO = 1	100 ISO = 2	50 ISO = 3
Sensor resolution	Low = 1	Med = 2	High = 3
Color capability	sRGB = 1	Adobe RGB (1998) = 2	Wide Gamut/ProPhoto RGB = 3

Tip

Photosite refers to the location of each of the light-sensitive pixels on a digital sensor. These rows of photosites are sometimes referred to as *arrays*. In many digital sensor designs, each photosite is constructed like a tiny dimple, or well, that protects the pixel from light bouncing around inside the camera, and other gremlins.

For everyday snapshots that you print at 4×6 inches or send via e-mail, a score of 5–8 will do. For 8×10 portraiture, event, and average wedding photography, a score of 10 or higher is needed. For commercial work, such as a high quality reproduction on packaging or in publications, a total score of 12–15 is highly desirable.

Note that photosite size is included because it frequently determines the amount of noise in the image, particularly at ISO 200 and higher.

Color Space

Most high-end digital cameras provide choices among color space. It's a good thing to be aware of this and choose your color space to fit the job you are working on.

The color space that you decide to use can be determined by a number of variables. It can be driven by your final output destination, such as an inkjet printer or press. Or it can be determined by how accurately it renders precise colors in a particular color range—a good example is photographing colors included in a company logo or other commercial design.

At the end of the day, however, you do have to look at a color space in terms of whether it can or can't capture the color you want. And if any post-production or editing will be performed, you need to know whether or not that color will survive its treatment in Photoshop or another image editor.

One of the things that still amazes me is that nearly all digital cameras, professional and consumer, default to sRGB, as does Photoshop (an exception to this is medium-format digital camera backs). The good news is that most pro-level digital cameras can capture sRGB and Adobe RGB (1998) RGB—and some can capture even more.

Compare sRGB to Adobe RGB (1998) RGB to ProPhoto RGB in Figure 3.14.

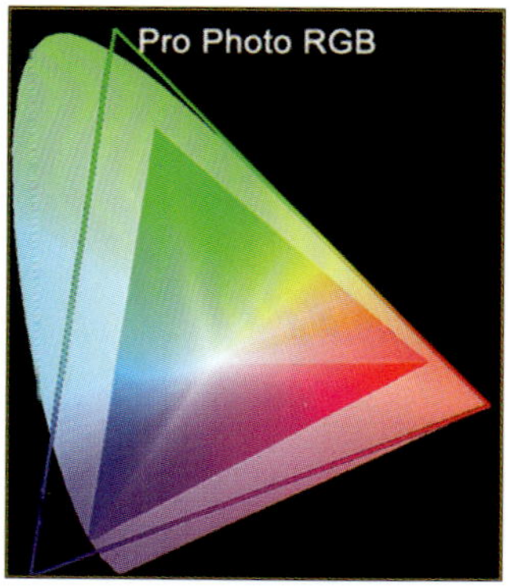

Figure 3.14

This is a color map comparing sRGB to Adobe RGB 1998, and ProPhoto RGB. sRGB is the smallest color space; ProPhoto is the largest.

Although a diagram like this doesn't show you everything there is to know about a color space, it does give you some idea of how they compare to one another and allows you to roughly estimate the impact of using a color space on your image capture.

Now sRGB works quite well in some circumstances. If your images are intended for a Web site or are going straight to output at a lab that uses sRGB, you'll probably be fine.

However, sRGB has significant limitations. It excludes, or "clips," quite a bit of color from its range as compared to other options. This means that it is smaller in capacity than, say, Adobe RGB (1998) or ProPhoto RGB.

In the digital world, size matters. Given two unedited images that are otherwise identical, one shot in sRGB, and the other in Adobe RGB (1998), at first they look identical on your computer display.

But nearly every time you edit an image in Photoshop, you lose some information from the image, as shown in Figure 3.15. In this case, the vertical white lines in the histogram represent information lost in the image during levels adjustment.

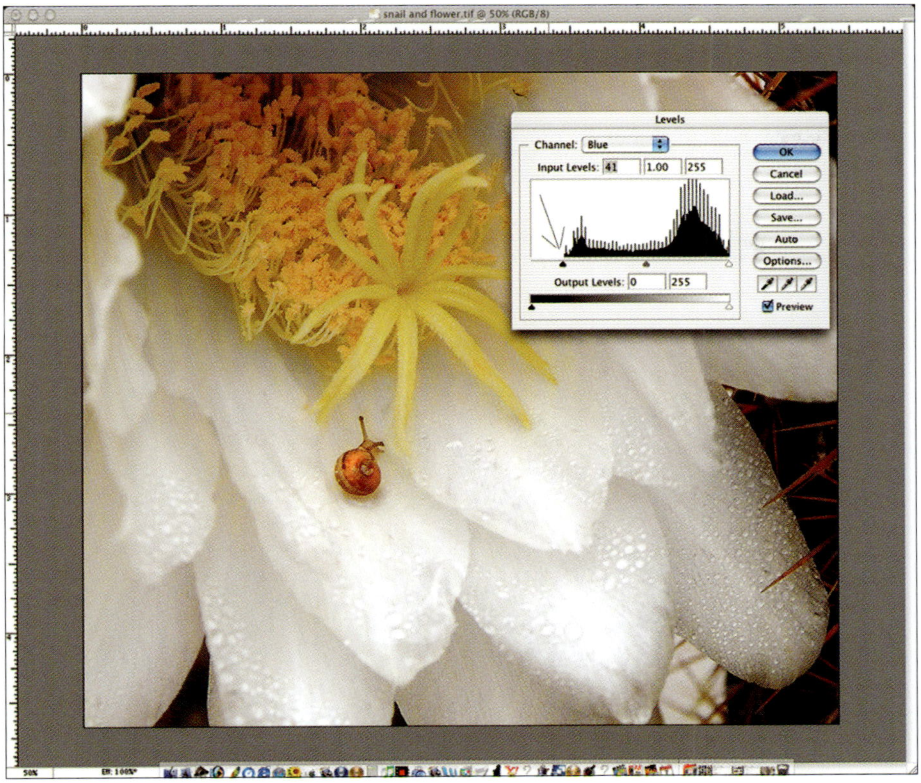

Figure 3.15

The white stripes, or gaps, in the histogram show where tonal information is missing from the image.

Whether in Curves, Levels, Hue/Saturation, or others—every time you make a significant adjustment you lose, bruise, or bend pixels in your image.

If you start with a large color space, you have some elbow room. Start with a smaller one, and you run out of elbow room more quickly.

Notice how the histogram in Figure 3.15 (which can be seen when you open the Levels dialog box) changes when color is adjusted in sRGB. These changes indicate lost or missing information—information that was lost during editing, and information that you can't put back into the image.

Think of it like this: We all know that we can probably get away with cleaning a negative or transparency one time using poor technique. But over time, repeated cleaning like this damages it, making it scratched and less usable. The damage is cumulative, and the same is true in digital.

The more you bruise the pixels, the worse the image gets. The more you can protect the pixels, the better the final work will be.

Correct Exposure

Digital capture is more demanding than shooting film or transparencies. In fact, a variance of 1/10 of a stop can make the difference between success and a painful, difficult post-production process.

Digital capture is very sensitive to under- or over-exposure, and either of these can affect color in unexpected ways. I use a hand-held exposure meter more than ever. (An exposure meter is a device that measures light intensity and calculates shutter and aperture settings appropriate for a selected film/sensor ISO, or light sensitivity.)

This is directly linked to the physical characteristics of digital camera sensors. Our eyes and brain see much differently than a digital sensor. Our eyes adjust to a scene with amazing flexibility, allowing us to see a range of brightness that is many times greater than any currently available recording device.

Digital sensors record images in terms of light levels. The brightest part of an image provides most of the information, and the darkest part the minority of information. This type of recording is linear in nature.

Some photographers think that now that they have digital, they can fix a poor exposure in Photoshop. But given the recording characteristics of digital sensors, any over-exposure will make your life difficult, if not downright miserable.

Like transparencies, information lost in the highlights is difficult, or impossible, to recover. And the highlights contain the majority of the information in your image! How do you tell when your exposure is correct? If you are in the studio, use a hand-held exposure meter. I recommend that you put your set-ups together the old-fashioned way—one light at a time, metering each light separately. This has of course been the subject of many books.

On location, you will often use the in-camera exposure meter to assist in setting your exposures. However, it is still best to back up your decision with information from a hand-held meter. If this is not practical, do try to use a range of exposures, from slightly under-exposed to slightly over-exposed (this is called *bracketing*). Many pro-level cameras offer this as an option and allow you to choose two- or three-frame bursts.

Next, many people use the LCD screen on the camera to preview the image—but this display is often limited in terms of correct brightness, contrast, and color.

The best way to evaluate your exposure once the image is taken is to use the histogram display on your camera. Although this option also has some limitations, it is a much better indicator than the LCD display on the camera, particularly when you are in bright ambient lighting. As you gain experience with a particular camera, you'll soon know how accurate your histogram is (see Figure 3.16).

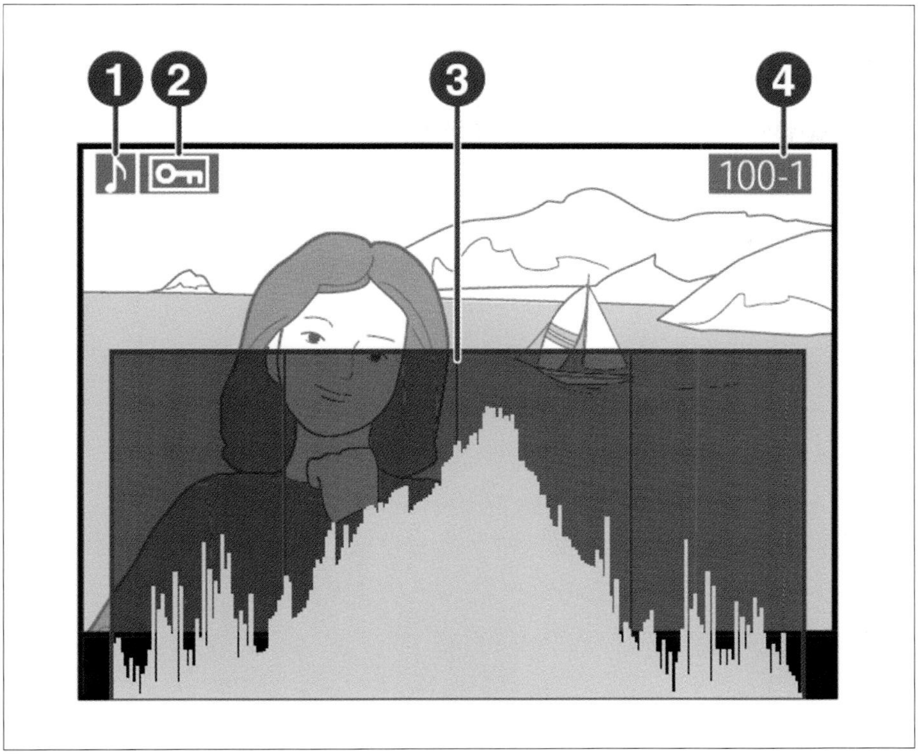

Figure 3.16

This is a histogram display on a Nikon camera. © Nikon

Camera Color Calibration

Usually thought of as something that is reserved for control-obsessed photographers, calibrating your camera can save you a great deal of time and money.

Color calibration can take several forms in digital capture. Unlike film, digital hardware settings can be changed. Interestingly, all but one of these involve hardware settings on the camera:

- Performed automatically in-camera
- Pre-set color balance in-camera, such as daylight or tungsten
- Shooting a gray or white card and using this to calibrate color in post-production

Automatic color balance has one thing going for it: convenience. If, for example, you are shooting an image in mixed lighting, auto color balance can save you time—in some cases.

This is based on an in-camera calculation, which averages the mix of colors and attempts to average them in a pleasing way. But, like in-camera metering, the camera's color sensors can sometimes be fooled.

In-camera presets offer a somewhat higher level of control. These selections allow you to choose the in-camera color balance in advance. In more predictable lighting, such as studio flash, daylight, or tungsten, they offer a pleasing color adjustment.

Both of these methods depend on use of pre-set calculations, color averaging, or in-camera calculations. Although convenient, it is not possible for the engineers to build every possibility, or range of calculations, into the camera.

On top of this, each camera's combination of hardware sensor and lenses renders color differently. Just from the outside, these cameras are very different from one another—never mind the internal engineering.

A method that offers a higher degree of control is shooting a white card and using the camera's custom white balance feature to control your color.

This option involves selecting a menu choice on the camera and then photographing a piece of neutral white material. This is the secret reason so many photographers wear white socks! Figure 3.17 shows an example of menu choices for custom white balance.

3 To measure white balance using a neutral gray or white object...
...frame the reference object so that it fills the viewfinder and press the shutter-release button all the way down. The camera will measure a value for white balance and store it in preset d-0. No photograph will be recorded; white balance can be measured accurately even when the camera is not in focus.

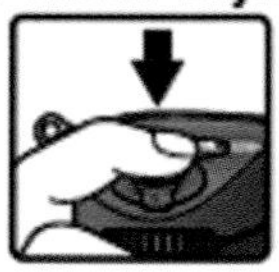

To measure the color of the light source...
...make sure that the ambient light sensor is lit by the light source and press the FUNC. button. The camera will calculate a value for white balance and store it in preset d-0.

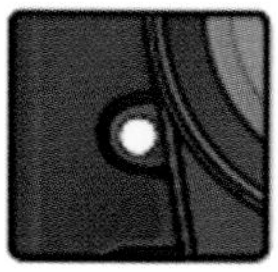

To exit without measuring a new value for white balance, press the **WB** button.

Figure 3.17

Menu choices for custom white balance. © Nikon

This is very similar to the white balancing used in video cameras. It sets the color in the camera with a relatively high degree of accuracy. The only difficulty with this method is that if your lighting changes, you have to accept inaccurate color or re-calibrate the camera again.

Choosing a File Type

Each camera has a number of built-in options for saving your image files. There are three major types: those that always use file compression and locked-in exposure and color settings, those that do not use file compression but still treat exposure and color the same way, and last, types that can be changed in every respect after the image is taken.

The first category is known as JPEGs, which is a standardized file format read by most cameras and computers. It uses a built-in method of compressing, or squeezing the file, into a smaller space. This saves time and money because it costs less to build a camera with smaller capacity.

JPEGs lock in color and exposure values as well—this means that extensive editing is needed in an image editor if you want to change them later.

The next level of quality and flexibility is TIFF, which stands for Tagged Image File Format. Recall from Chapter 2 that TIFFs are kind of the jack of all trades in digital image files. TIFFs can be saved in varying bit depths, unlike JPEGs.

Hardware Settings and Pre-Programming Your Capture Workflow

The five elements outlined in Table 3.2 combine to determine the success or failure of your image. Ideally, maximizing quality in each category provides enormous leverage to make your image pixels as much like your original vision as possible—and make your image more satisfying and competitive!

Table 3.2 Five Elements Combine to Determine Image Use and Quality

Category	Quality		
Color Space	sRGB =1	A 98 = 2	PP = 3
Exposure Controls	Low = 1	Med = 2	High = 3
File Type	JPEG = 1	TIFF = 2	RAW = 3
Sensor Resolution	Low = 1	Med = 2	High = 3
Camera Profile—White Balance	Auto = 1	In Camera = 2	Custom = 3

For high-level (professional or serious amateur) use in print or displays, you want to have a score of 12 or higher. Scores of 11 to 9 will result in images that are more limited in use, and scores of less than 9 are generally suitable for consumers only.

An example of image scoring would be color space Adobe RGB (1998) (2), moderately accurate exposure control (2), RAW file (3), high sensor resolution (3), and custom white balance (3) equals a total score of 13. A consumer-level digital point and shoot would probably score 1 or 2 in each category, providing a score of 5 to 10.

Example of Workflow

This is an example of my workflow in a recent commercial/product shoot:

Category	Specification or Tool
Lighting	5500K strobes
ISO Setting	50
Color Space	Uncompressed Native/RAW (processed to ProPhoto RGB)
Sensor Resolution	22 MP
Camera Profile—Custom WB	Calibrated to white or gray card or GMB color checker
Exposure	Metered within 1/10 stop for highlight and shadow detail
Process	Capture One Pro software for initial editing, contrast and color correction, and processing of RAW files. No sharpening.
Processed File Output	16-bit TIFF, ProPhoto RGB, 127MB
Editing	Adobe Photoshop CS2, 16-bit, ProPhoto color space
File Output to Client	16-bit TIFF or Photoshop file, converted to Adobe RGB (1998) RGB at native size, 300 px/inch

In a recent photo shoot for an electronics manufacturer, I met with the marketing manager to discuss goals and objectives. As always, being able to set up properly in advance is a critical element to success.

As this shoot involved a mix of smaller and larger products, we decided that we needed at least three sets to handle the job. Each set needed adequate electrical power, control of lighting, room for table setups for the product and computer equipment, and so on.

We also needed to control overhead lighting in the work area, as it was a mix of halogen and fluorescent bulbs, throwing shadows and introducing unwanted color variations.

We set up using studio flash units, driven by Calumet power packs. For the most part, we mounted soft boxes on each light and did not add color gels—so we were shooting at 5500K. If we needed a color accent, we added a smaller light, with the desired colored gel. All the overhead lights in the rooms were turned off for the photo shoots. A radio trigger was connected to the camera and the power pack and was used to fire the strobes.

My assistant and I built up each set one light at a time and metered the lights as we test fired them. This was done for each light individually as they were set up, and finally in combination. This ensured that even small areas of the product were lit correctly, whether dark or light in color, and that key details were visible to customers—no blown-out highlights or deep black shadows allowed.

As we started the shoot, we photographed a white card and a gray card to help us with color correction. In fact, the software provides a tool that allows you to set color balance with a test shot and apply that color balance to each subsequent shot as the work progresses. Very powerful.

If the lighting is changed, we shoot the gray or white card again and reset basic color correction in the Phase One software.

I used a Hasselblad H1 with a Phase One P25 digital back. This was tethered to a Mac G5, so we could see the small details of each shot as we worked. We used the Phase One Capture One software to edit images on-the-fly, inspecting critical image areas for color fidelity and detail, performing basic cropping, and so on. The Apple Cinema display would show each shot in about 1–2 seconds after the shutter was tripped.

One of the great things about seeing the shots in real-time is that you can make sure that trademarked colors are accurate, that labels are clearly visible, and that dust and dirt are kept to a minimum.

As we worked, we marked the best images for export to the client's in-house computer network. When each stage of the shoot was completed, we transferred the RAW images to a second computer, started processing the RAW files, and exported them as 16-bit TIFFs in ProPhoto RGB to the client's network.

The art department began sending layouts, including proof prints in accurate color to management within a couple of days.

Additional Thoughts

Digital capture offers an important difference from film—you can change the relative sensitivity, or "speed," of the sensor at any time. Within the limits of the hardware and firmware built into the camera, you can change from relatively slow ISO of 50 or 100 to relatively fast ISO of 400 to 800.

If you are shooting using RAW file format, ISO is one of the few things you cannot change in post-production. Like overall sharpness, ISO is locked in once the image is captured.

Somewhat like film, lower ISO capture in digital will result in less apparent grain or artifact. Higher ISO settings will result in higher grain.

There is also controversy over the effect higher ISO has on color. This is connected in some ways to the type of light you are shooting in, in addition to the settings on the camera.

There are three important factors to consider in types of lighting and ISO settings in digital: the range of color, the overall color temperature, and the mix of colors in the light.

- Range of color, as the phrase is used here, indicates the breadth of colors—is it full breadth of color or partial? Are you photographing a bouquet of red roses or a mix of brightly hued spring flowers?
- Overall color temperature refers to how "warm" or "cool" (yellow or blue) the overall image appears.
- Mix of colors refers to the balance between red, green, and blue in the lighting used.

In virtually every digital camera I have used, there is a significant difference in image appearance and quality when shooting at high ISO (400 and higher) and non-daylight balanced lighting. A good example of this is a high-contrast portrait shot in available incandescent lighting. Another is an image taken for commercial use, that includes brightly colored products.

Not only is noise increased, but in most cases color artifact's in the mid-tones and shadow areas will also increase. This is noticeable in relatively short-duration exposures and is more noticeable in longer exposures.

This is different than grain in film—film grain is not color oriented. It is the footprint of the physical artifact of the individual elements that make up the emulsion coating on the film base.

What can you do about this?

First, and always first, shoot a gray card before you get deep into your session. This will help you color balance the images in post-production. This is an essential habit for a photographer.

Shooting a gray card will help you balance the color in the image. For example, an image taken using digital capture in incandescent light might have the look of a red, yellow, or orange color cast. Caucasian skin tones might look yellow or red without use of this tool or in-camera automatic white balance.

You can, as an alternative, set the camera for the overall color tone of your lighting —fluorescent, incandescent, and so on. I prefer the control that a gray card provides. If the light changes, shoot another gray card.

If you can, avoid non-daylight-balanced lighting when you are shooting higher ISO captures. This will increase noise even more, particularly in the shadows. Can you retouch this in post-production? Yes, but it's a time-consuming, expensive problem. I think that most of us, given the choice, would avoid being cornered in this way.

One solution is to use analog technology to shoot digital. Use a color-correcting gel on your lighting—if you are shooting using an incandescent spotlight for example, use a blue gel, as shown in Figure 3.18. (It helps greatly if you have a color meter to measure the result.) Gel values from ? to full can be used and will of course change color temperature accordingly.

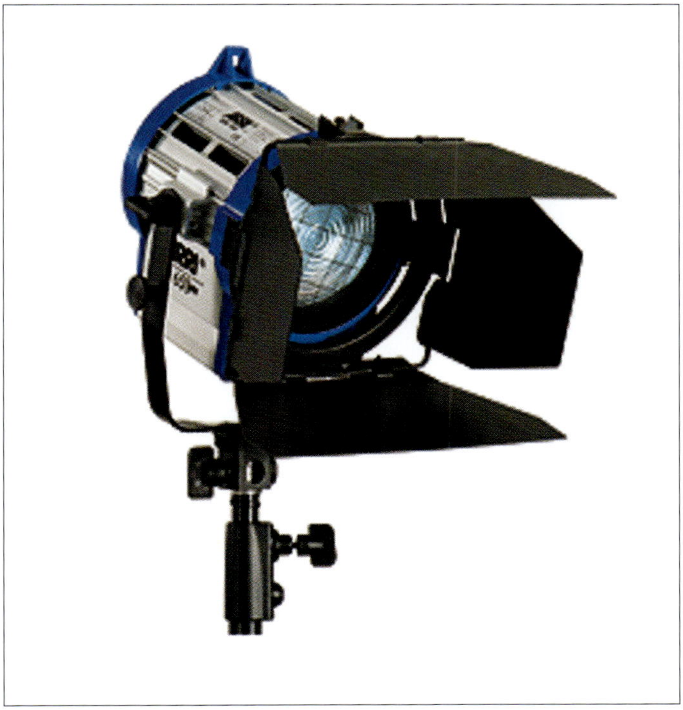

Figure 3.18

Arri hot light with blue gel corrects color temperature from 3500K to 5500K.

Along with this, keep in mind that most DSLR digital camera sensors produce increased noise in the image with longer exposures. This is one of the big differences between high-end DSLRs and medium format digital backs. The medium format backs have better software and cooling. My Phase One P-25, for example, can make images up to several minutes in length at ISO 50 with very little, if any, apparent noise.

Summary

This chapter, although it gets into the details of using the technology, is really about getting *results*: quickly, accurately, and at reasonable cost.

It is important that you understand the strengths and weaknesses of each tool so that you can pick the ones you need and get your work done. And if you have brought all of these tools together in the right way, you'll find that you've reduced the amount of work you have to do after the shoot—a lot!

In fact, if there's one important thing to remember from this chapter—learn to use the tools to get it right in the camera, as this will help you save time and make money in the long run.

4

Production Guide for Photographers

This chapter outlines a production guide for photographers. In some ways, the fundamentals of using film or a digital sensor for production in photography are quite similar. This chapter also takes the approach of a cookbook, or "favorite recipe," rather than reviewing the full range of options available. The recipe can be broken down into a number of key ingredients—and they do have one thing in common: Each involves managing color to maximize quality and produce the best image possible. The following outline provides the main points covered in the chapter:

- Begin with the end in mind—visualizing the final image to drive a successful work plan.
- The "master image" concept—working toward creating an image that can be used to maximum benefit; in many cases, this includes using an image in multiple placements and multiple formats.

- Planning and managing image capture—film, digital, and hybrid (scan film to digital).
- Color management—a key component of success.
- Processing digital image files.
- Editing.
- Output.

Begin with the End in Mind

Visualizing how the final image should look and is in intended to communicate to the viewer can be enormously useful in helping you plan your work—camera, lenses, color management, processing, and more. For example, I will in some instances plan a shoot knowing what color palette the customer wants to use, and I'll choose capture tools, lighting, processing, and output options with these criteria in mind.

I recently completed a stock image project, that included a number of vivid landscape shots—these were large-scale scenes, with lots of visual depth. One of the requirements of the project was that the output size was going to be at least 24×30 inches—which meant that I would need to use a medium format camera and pro film (or a digital back) or a top-of-the-line pro-level DSLR.

For many of the shots, I used Fuji Velvia 100 as it renders the greens and blues present in these scenes so vividly, scanned selected frames using a Minolta Multi-Scan Pro at 3600 dpi using Digital Ice, no automatic color correction, multi-pass scan to reduce noise, and no sharpening. Prints were output on the HP Designjet 130, a pro-level inkjet printer that has a broad, vivid color palette, or gamut. In some situations in the same project where the light was very high in contrast, I used Fuji Astia, which tolerates those conditions well and has a lower likelihood of losing detail in high contrast or highly color saturated areas.

The point is that I chose these tools because when they are used together effectively, they produce the look and feel in the images that met the customer's needs.

For another project, involving on-site photography in an industrial setting, I used a Hasselblad H1 and a Phase One P25 digital back and multiple studio strobes. Everything was lit to 5500K color temperature, as we wanted to keep the customer's product colors as true as possible. Because post-production time was limited, we shot in Adobe 1998 (RGB) and edited and output the files in this same TIFF format on-the-fly. These went straight to the art department, and then the print house for a catalog run.

Tip

In commercial photography, an important part of pre-visualization is collaboration with the marketing manager or art director. This collaboration can include everything from the emotional impact of the image to where and how the image will be placed and the results the final image is expected to achieve. Style, color themes, backgrounds, level of saturation (vivid or understated), and other considerations can and should be part of "begin with the end in mind."

Using Your Tools Effectively

The tools you choose must work together in harmony. In a perfect world, manufacturers would cooperate, and the cameras, scanners, displays, and other tools would work together—in other words, real "plug and play," *not* "plug and pray."

Not to be pessimistic, but when this kind of integration is not in place, the image creation process can slow down and become more expensive. "We'll fix it in post-production in Photoshop" is a dangerous phrase. I've learned how dangerous it can be through personal experience; weak pre-planning has resulted in long, tedious post-production editing—something I plan to never repeat again!

For example, some digital cameras default to capturing images as medium-resolution JPEGs, using sRGB. Others default to capturing only RAW files. Among 35mm DSLRs, there are no standards used in the controls of color saturation, contrast, or sharpening. Some image editing software defaults to and or expects sRGB, some leave it completely up to the user specification.

It is up to you, as the photographer, to understand what tools should be in your toolbox, when and when not to use a particular tool or tools, how to use those tools in combination effectively, to pre-plan your work, and to obtain the best result possible.

Tip

Whether you use film or digital capture, getting it right in the camera is the key to keeping costs down and clients happy. A few minutes spent getting lighting and exposure correct, putting your composition right, and shooting a gray or other color checker card will noticeably improve your image quality *and* save you time and money in post-production.

The automatic controls, such as exposure, automatic white balance, and default color space, built into most digital devices will only get you part of the way to the finish. They are designed for taking average photographs in average situations. I believe that, in a competitive world, you can't keep up with customer demands for exceptional images when using them in any significant degree.

For example, consider that the majority of image information in a digital capture is contained in the brightest stop. If your in-camera meter averages the scene and over-exposes the highlights, you could lose important color accuracy and image detail—and that kind of error is difficult or impossible to repair in post-production.

In fact, going back to the landscape images I referred to earlier in this chapter, I found that an average in-camera meter reading for the scene was at least a third of a stop too high to hold details in the highlights—and these highlights included some brilliant yellow wildflowers. When I used a hand-held meter in the portion of the scene that had the flowers in it, I discovered that I had to adjust the camera exposure.

Start with your vision for final image, and then create a "master image." In the next section, you'll explore how you can integrate color space, image quality, digital or film processing, and editing and manage it all so that the image can be used in a variety of scenarios or media.

Figure 4.1 shows an example of a work plan that can help you achieve your goals.

The "Master Image"

The best images, made by the best photographers, are the product of experience, talent, vision, and planning. Top photographers, when asked how they do their best work, will inevitably talk about the idea of visualizing what they want in advance and using their tools to make the image real.

It is hard enough to make such a high-quality image and even harder to get the recognition deserved for it. A "master image" is not just one that stands out from the crowd but an image that is useful, that becomes "money in the bank" for its creator.

Almost any good carpenter will tell you "measure twice and cut once." Managing image quality and color is similar to this, in the sense that any image can be edited down in quality, but rarely, if ever, "edited up." So what does this mean in a practical sense? A master image is one that can be used for many purposes. It is rich in color and detail—the total information in the image is the best you can make it. It has enough quality, size, and resolution to be used in the most demanding environments, including exhibitions or galleries, print advertising, trade show displays, on the Web, and in catalogs and brochures.

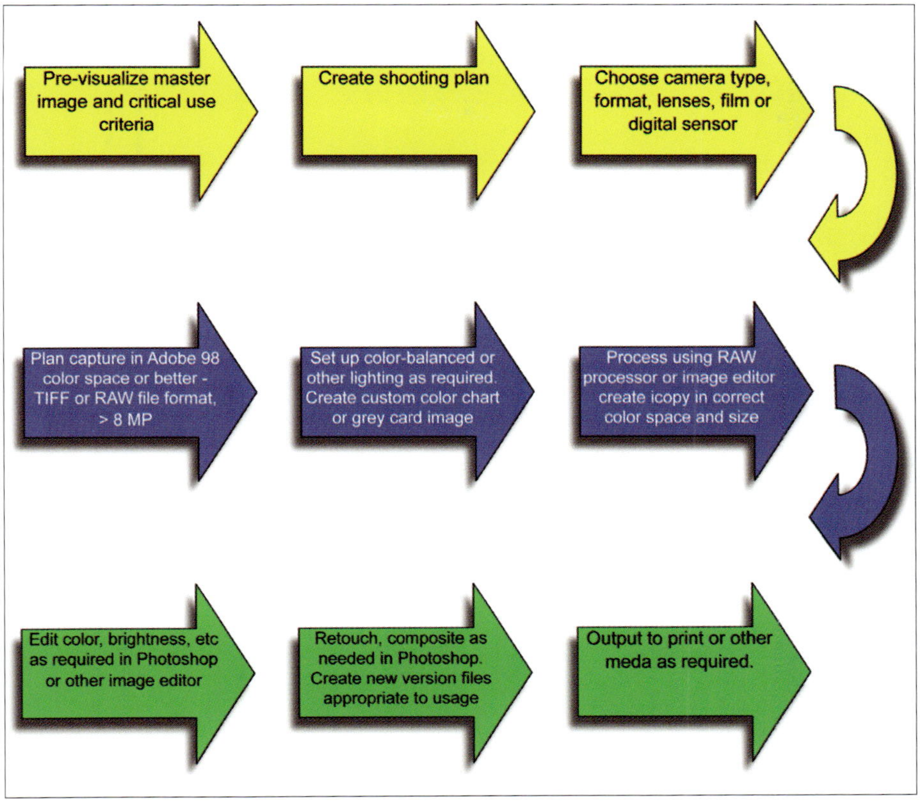

Figure 4.1

An example of the major steps involved in successfully planning and creating a winning image.

From a marketing standpoint, it has the potential to be a major part of a brand, appearing again and again in a campaign. A master image is truly like money in the bank!

Let's say that you've given yourself an assignment, and you've been shooting stock around a particular lifestyles theme, based on a good consultation with your favorite art director. You've been using 35mm transparency film, and the images look okay on the light table. You've made your selections, and you're getting ready to scan them to digital.

You can scan the images to thumbnails, or smaller files, and save time and computer storage space. Using a dedicated film scanner, you might save a couple of minutes per scan.

Or you can scan with the master image concept in mind, which will take you a few minutes more per image. However, once that scan is completed, it's very unlikely you'll have to handle that piece of film again. Put it in your archival file, make a backup copy of the scan file, and you're done.

As a last note, imagine that you've made the smaller scan, and that art director calls and says, "We've got a deal on that beach image; it is going to be the theme image on a new client's campaign for their new product on…" Well, you'll have to retrieve the slide from storage, set up the computer again, make sure you've duplicated the scanner settings you used the first time, and rescan to maximum size for all those brochure covers. And if you edited the image file from the first, smaller scan, you might have to edit the image over again, as well.

So make sure you "measure twice, and cut once." If the image is worth scanning in the first place, use the best tool for the job. If you're using a digital camera, match the camera's abilities to the master image concept, too. There's more detail on camera selection later in this chapter.

Planning and Managing Image Capture

Keeping all this in mind, you can now move forward to consider planning and managing image capture.

Because you now know in advance what your image should look like and what it will be used for, you can choose a camera that fits the job.

Selecting a Digital Camera for a Project

Table 4.1 compares some digital cameras in terms of important specifications.

> **Tip**
>
> I also believe that there is one more measurement, which although very important, is also difficult to quantify. It is the issue of noise generated in the digital image, either from using higher ISO settings or making longer exposures. Some cameras, such as the Canon 1DS Mark II, seem to give superb results in controlling noise, at least when shooting at higher ISO. The medium format digital backs, such as the Leaf Aptus or Phase One P-series, are superb at controlling noise in longer exposures.
>
> Noise can become an issue in color management—in digital capture, this is particularly true in the darker, or shadow, areas of an image.
>
> If you are a photographer who requires above-average noise management, be sure you understand the camera's performance before you commit to shooting a project.

Table 4.1 Scoring Digital Cameras

Features	Camera Specifications/Capability		
Color space	sRGB =1	sRGB and A 98 = 2	sRGB and A 98 ProPhoto = 3
Megapixels	5MP or less = 1	6-8 MP = 2	> 8 MP = 3
File types available	JPEG only = 1	JPEG and TIFF = 2	RAW, JPEG, and TIFF = 3
Camera and lens types and quality	Consumer = 1	Prosumer = 2	Professional = 3
Camera controls	Auto only = 1	Menu of control presets = 2	Custom, manual, and auto = 3

In this evaluation, a typical consumer-level point and shoot would receive a score of 5, and a pro-level model such as the Nikon D2X or the Canon 1DS Mark II would score between 13 and 15 points.

You can also match final use against potential digital capture quality, as shown in Table 4.2.

Table 4.2 Intended Image Usage versus Digital Capture Quality

Example of Usage	Score In Points
Web/Internet	5 and up
Print, size ranging from 1×2 inches up to 4×6 inches	8 and up
Full or ¾ page magazine publication	10-12 and up
Trade show displays, outdoor advertising, and signage	13-15 and up

If you are shooting extreme close-ups or macro images, such as jewelry or precision electronics, consider using the next level up (that is, if you are targeting a ¾ page print advertisement, use a score of 13–15).

In an ideal world, we would all know exactly how every image would be used, all the time. The fact is that a good image can be re-used, or re-purposed, many times, as long as it has the range of color, resolution, and details. Compare this to a small image, created in a small color space—it is not likely to be a good candidate for re-purposing. Think of it as stretching a rubber band—it will only go so far before it snaps.

Selecting Film

This section provides a checklist similar to the one I use when I'm deciding which film to use for a shoot:

- Pro-level film only; this includes expiration date stamp and controlled temperature storage
- Major manufacturer, such as Kodak or Fuji
- Lowest ISO rating suitable for the job
- What I call inherent contrast—some films render greater contrast, others are less punchy
- Neutral rendering point—what color temperature lighting is needed for the film to produce neutral color
- Enhanced color for special projects
- What I call "scan-ability," in other words, is the film relatively easy to scan

Film that I personally tend to use when I want fairly neutral color rendering and high resolution includes Fuji Provia 100F, Fuji Astia 100, and Kodak E100S. Of these, my personal experience shows the Astia to be the most "scan-able" of the bunch, requiring little in terms of correction or manipulation, giving a very pleasing scanned image that has neutral color and good detail. Astia is the transparency film I use most for product and portrait work.

For enhanced color for special projects, I strongly favor Fuji Velvia, now available in ISO 100. It has an enduring reputation for its vivid rendering of color, particularly in outdoor scenes. This film is high in contrast, so very accurate exposure is required. It is one of the most scan-able films I have used.

For black and white negative film, I've found that Kodak TMAX-100 gives a very good combination of contrast, low grain, and scan-ability. Scala, the only black and white transparency film available, is rated by the manufacturer at ISO 200 and is very contrasty and very scan-able. Fuji Neopan 1600 is one of the better high-speed black and white films, but the quality of its scans is hampered by relatively strong grain.

Scanning

If you are using film, and you know that you will need to bring the image into the digital world, you will have to scan your images. This subject is covered in significant detail in Chapter 2, in the section "From the Camera to the Computer"

There are significant differences between scanners available on the market. Some are multiuse and can be utilized to scan reflective materials, prints, and film.

Others are dedicated film scanners and can be used only on transparency or negative film media.

It is important to note that what you scan is as important as how you scan. Professional-level film stock provides excellent stability and color balance, even from lot to lot and from year to year. Also, film can be matched to lighting conditions and color temperature, the simplest example of which is the use of tungsten or daylight-balanced film.

Again, you can score scanner performance as a predictor of quality in final use, as illustrated in Table 4.3. I assume that the film stock and exposure used in the original image are appropriate to intended usage.

Table 4.3 Evaluating Film Scanning Quality

Category	Criteria		
Scanner type	Multiuse flatbed = 1	Dedicated film scanner = 2	Drum or virtual drum scanner = 3
Color space	sRGB =1	Adobe RGB (1998) = 2	ProPhoto RGB, Ekta, or Wide Gamut RGB = 3
Resolution	2000 dpi or less = 1	3000-3800 dpi = 2	> 3800 dpi = 3
Density range	< 3.5 = .5	3.5—3.9 = 1	4.0 and up = 3
Color depth—bits	8 bits = 1	Up to 14 bits = 2	16 bits = 3

In selecting a scanner, look for a combination of density range, ability to scan in higher bit-depth, and so on. I feel that a total score of 12 or higher is required for serious amateurs and professional photographers.

Note that total scan size is not as big a factor as some service bureaus would have you believe. Most price their product by the megabyte, which is fine as far as it goes.

But a 50MB scan in sRGB and 8 bits will almost always lose out to a same-size scan, in pixel size, that is created in Adobe RGB (1998) and 16-bit color depth. Your post-production editing will take less time, be more successful, and render better color if you use the latter, rather than the former. As a general rule, density range of 4.0 and higher is recommended. For more information on scanning, bit-depth, and density range, see Chapter 2.

If I were paying an outside vendor for a scan, and I wanted it for anything other than indexing or the Web, I would want to get a file that was produced on a scanner that yielded a score of 12 points or more on Table 4.3. Similarly, if I was scanning film on my own scanner, I would want to scan as close to 16 bits as I could get, at the highest resolution possible, in Adobe RGB (1998) or better.

A 16-bit scan provides much more information in your image over an 8-bit file. File size is doubled; more importantly, 16-bit files perform better during editing—the incidence of color distortion, banding, posterization, and other color defects is greatly reduced.

The classic example of this is seen when printing an image that includes an expanse of smooth, intense color such as the sky. An 8-bit scan that has been edited and then printed will frequently show alternating bands of light and dark blue in the sky (called banding). This is much less common when using a 16-bit scan.

Tip

A final note on scanning: Different operators have conflicting opinions on the value of creating a custom profile for a scanner. I have personally found that making a "raw" scan, to Adobe RGB (1998), and exporting the scan to Photoshop as a 16-bit TIFF gives the most consistent results. In the scan, I make sure that the full range of tones, color and highlight detail, and color are present—and stop there. Make further adjustments in a more robust image editor, such as Photoshop.

The Importance of Color Space and Profiling

In my view, good color management is one of the key building blocks of image quality management—even if you are shooting black and white! Good color management, for example, can maximize visible detail in an image—whether in high contrast situations, highly saturated colors, finely detailed fabrics, or still life subjects.

Most digital cameras default to a color space called sRGB. Originally intended for use on computer displays and the Internet, sRGB has a much narrower range of color in it than other options available to you. Adobe RGB (1998) and ProPhoto RGB are much broader and contain more image information than sRGB, as shown in Figure 4.2.

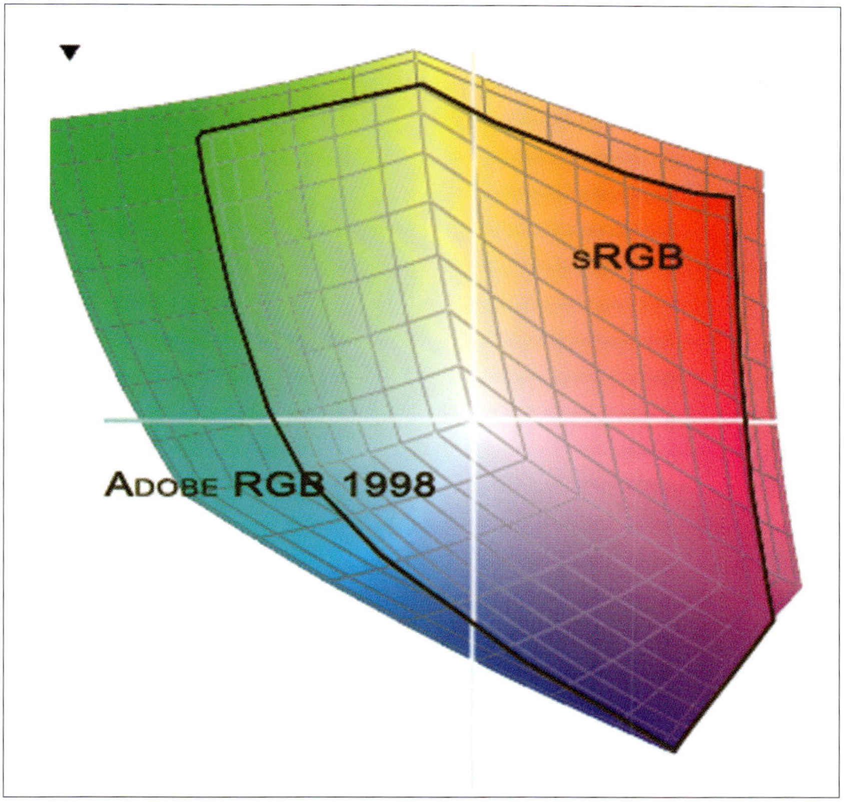

Figure 4.2

Comparing color space—size/coverage.

Digital sensors are also limited in respect to the range of highlight and shadow detail they can record. In a way, if you allow the default color settings to control image capture, you have two strikes against you—first, a limited color space, and second, the physical limits of the digital sensor. (Please refer to Chapter 2 for more information on digital sensors.)

Another reason to get as much image information while you can, when you can, is that every adjustment, edit, file save, data transfer, or other maneuver results in some loss of image quality. Believe it or not, computers and the software that runs on them make errors in arithmetic or otherwise toss some of your information out the window every time you use them. Ever had a digital file go bad and become unreadable? On some level, this happens because the information lost becomes too much for recovery.

Using Gray Cards

You should consider using a gray card or even a custom camera profile (see Chapter 7, "Color Quality Control," for details on custom camera profiling). A gray card should be considered to be the minimum that you use.

Gray cards are made by a number of companies in a variety of configurations. Although in the past they were fashioned out of a thick piece of paper or cardboard, they are now made from rigid plastic, fabric, and other materials—see Figure 4.3. My personal preference now is a card that is made from fabric, such as those manufactured by Lastolite and Wescott. The older cardboard cards were designed for use with film and in some cases have an undesirable color cast.

When shooting a gray card for color management purposes, first set your camera to the correct exposure in the same light you'll be using for your project. Then, capture one or more frames in which the gray card fills the majority of the frame in your viewfinder.

Interestingly, if you are using a digital camera that provides a histogram, or you look at the histogram in Photoshop, you will see a graph that looks like Figure 4.4.

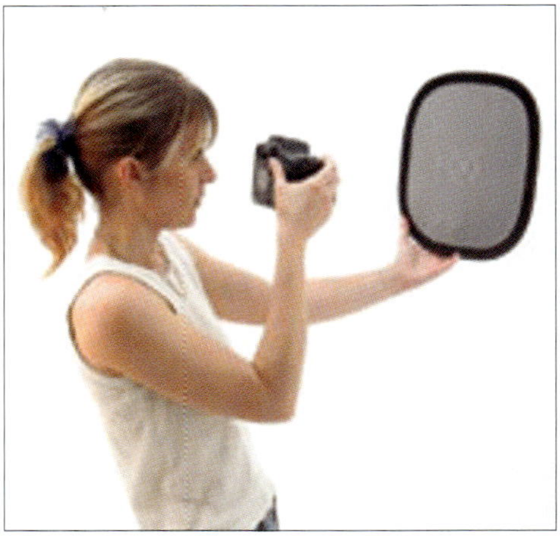

Figure 4.3

When shooting a gray card, be sure to use the same lighting as you would for the remainder of the shoot and fill the frame in your viewfinder with the gray card. © Lastolite Corporation

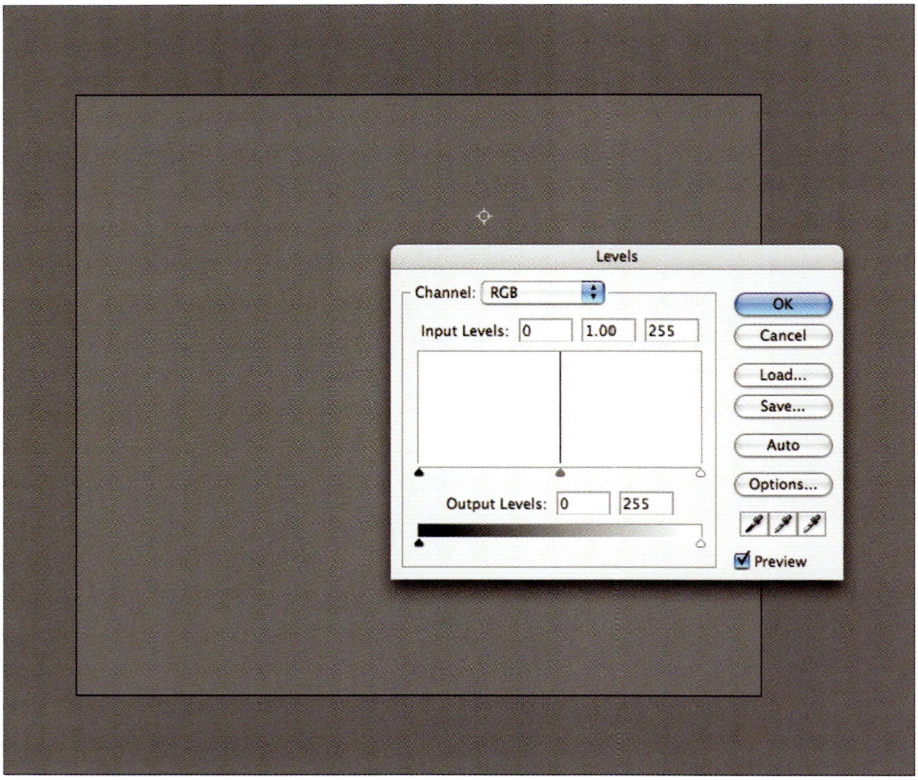

Figure 4.4

A histogram (shown in the Levels dialog box) produced when using a gray card. Note that because the image has only one tone, gray, the histogram simply shows a narrow spike in the center.

Second, once you are back in the studio and you are processing and editing your images, you can use the gray card image to color correct all of your other images. In Photoshop, choose Image>Adjustments>Curves, or Image>Adjustments>Levels, and use the gray eyedropper to color correct your gray card image. The gray eyedropper is the middle of the three in either dialog box.

Once you have used the gray eyedropper to calibrate your gray card image, leave the Curves or Levels dialog box that you are using open. Click Save, and an additional dialog box will open, prompting you to save the current gray adjustment setting. Give it a name, for example photoshoot1.acv, and click Save again. Now this adjustment setting can be recalled and used on other images from the same shoot.

If you don't have a suitable gray card image, you can still use the gray eyedropper technique—just click on an area in the image that has a suitable gray tone. In landscapes, I find that rocks and trees frequently provide the right target; in portraits, clothing or room furnishings can be helpful.

Judging Gray Tones

If you want to evaluate the tone or color of a particular area in an image, first choose Window>Info in Photoshop. The Info palette will appear on your screen. Note that in the upper-left corner of the palette, you'll see a small eyedropper icon and the letters R, G, and B. If you hover over the image with whatever tool or cursor you are using at the moment, you will see numbers appear next to the RGB indicators. Pure white, for example, will show as 255, 255, 255, pure black as 0,0,0. An area in the image that shows 128, 128, 128 (or within a few points of these numbers) is mid-gray and might be suitable for image correction.

See Chapter 7 for details about in-process and production color controls.

Processing Digital Image Files

Let's go back to digital image capture and production. You have captured a digital image. You know it's likely to look great, because the composition, lighting set, and capture were well planned and well executed. Now what?

JPEG or TIFF

If you have captured a JPEG or a TIFF file, you can open it directly in Adobe Photoshop or another image editor. There is a long list of editors available, including image editors provided by camera and printer manufacturers, including but not limited to Canon, HP, Nikon, Corel, Adobe, and Apple. The cost of these ranges from free, or nearly so, up to several hundred dollars.

JPEG images take up less storage space in the camera and on the computer; they are quick and convenient on the image capture side of the process.

On the downside, the JPEG 8-bit image file has less built-in information and is less tolerant of image editing, particularly when you are dealing with color issues. A JPEG can be likened to older Polaroid technology—in most cases, the image, once taken, is difficult to change.

Table 4.4 shows a comparison of what you can expect to be able to do after a photo shoot with a JPEG versus a RAW capture. Degree of difficulty is rated from 1= easy, to 5 = difficult.

Table 4.4 Comparing JPEG and RAW File Formats

	JPEG/TIFF	RAW
Color Balance	4	1
Color Temperature	5	1
Correct Single Color Cast	4	2
Correct Multiple Color Cast	5	3
Selective Color Adjustment	4	2
Exposure	4	1
Contrast/Levels	5	2

An easy way to see what can happen when you edit a JPEG or other 8-bit file is through a Levels adjustment. In Figure 4.5, you can see the photograph before a Levels adjustment. Note how the histogram rises from the left, peaks in the middle, and falls off to the right. The histogram is a graph of the amount of shadow, midtones, and highlight information in the image.

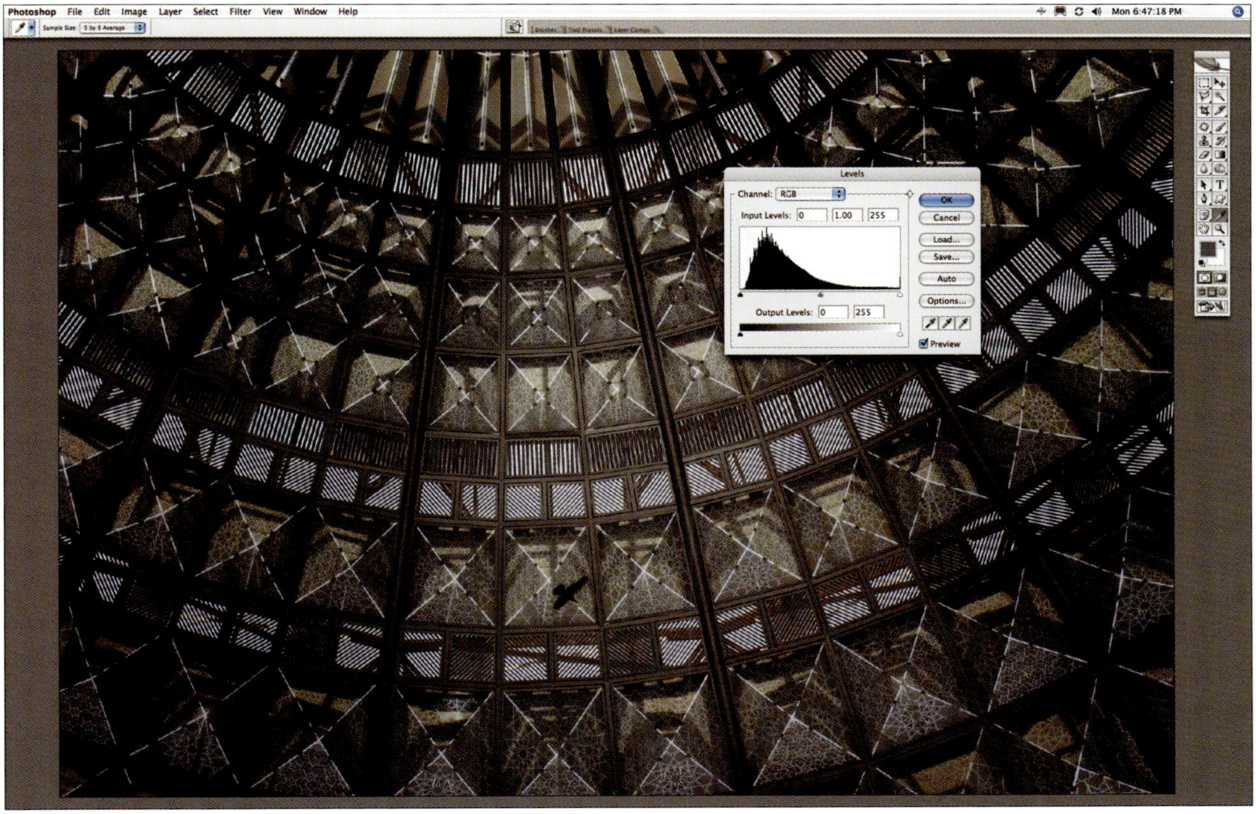

Figure 4.5

This histogram is smooth and even and has no gaps. © Cynthia Saffir

Next, look at what happens to the histogram when you make a basic Levels adjustment by moving the shadow and highlight markers toward the center (see Figure 4.6). In this type of image, it stretches the image information and creates banding or gaps. In many cases, when the image is printed later on in the work process, you will see color artifacts, color bands, or posterization in different areas of the image.

Damage created by "stretching" limited image information is cumulative. Every adjustment in color, contrast, brightness, and the like takes the image downhill, by small or large amounts. Once the information is lost, it is difficult or impossible to restore it. A higher-quality capture is more resilient and tolerates the insults of image editing more easily.

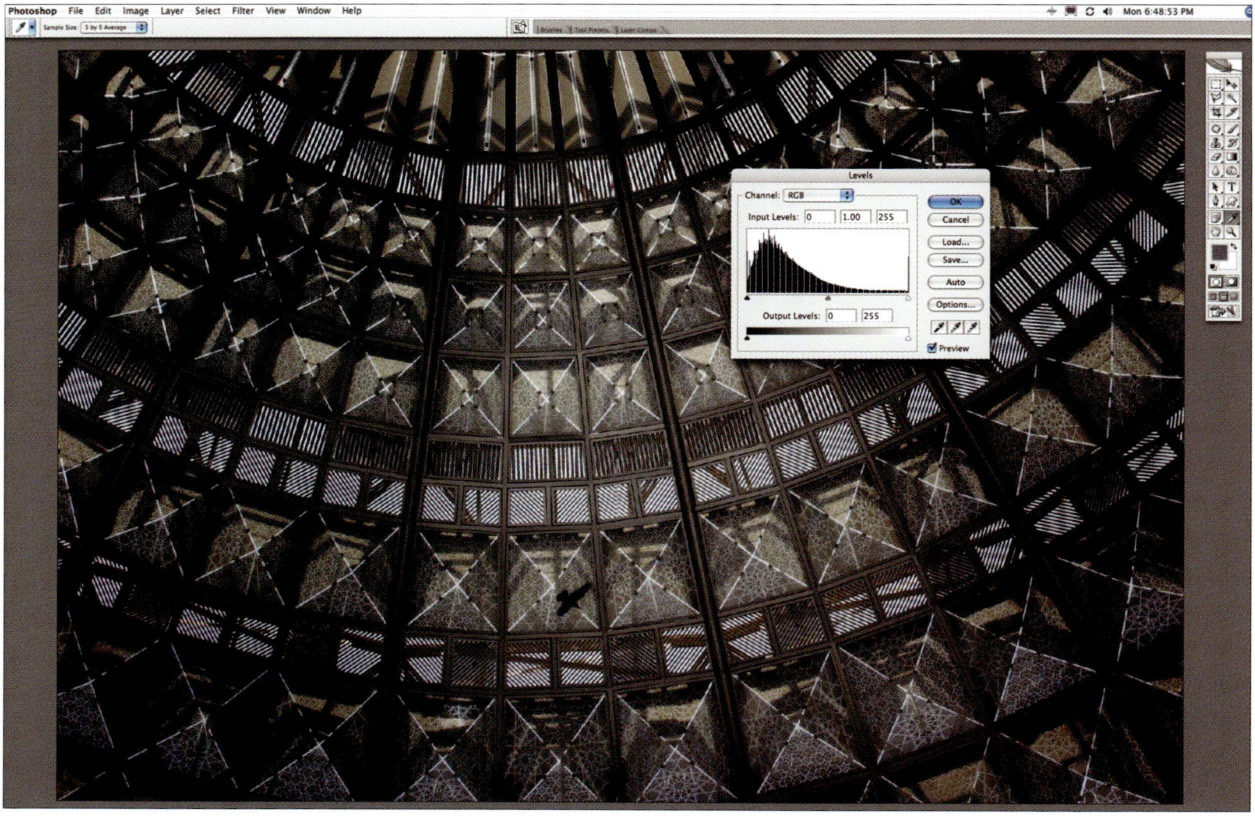

Figure 4.6

This histogram has white gaps across its width—this defect can lead to color distortions or posterization. © Cynthia Saffir

Cooking RAW Files to Perfection

If you have created a RAW file, you need a RAW image processor that is provided by the camera manufacturer or a third-party supplier. Examples of these include Adobe Camera RAW, Capture One by Phase One, Bibble, or Capture Ten by Leaf.

Let's start with RAW conversion, as it provides you with your best chance of top image quality in the digital world. Images may be output as 12-, 14-, or 16-bit large color space images, and they leave your original digital "negative" untouched.

RAW conversion software looks and behaves a lot like higher-end scanner software. Figure 4.7 shows screen shots of Adobe Camera RAW, Apple's Aperture software, and Phase One Capture One.

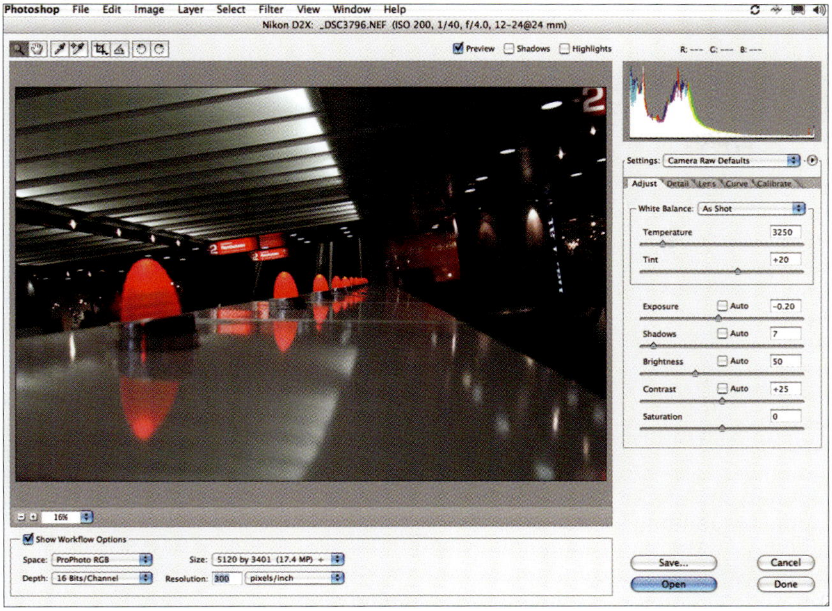

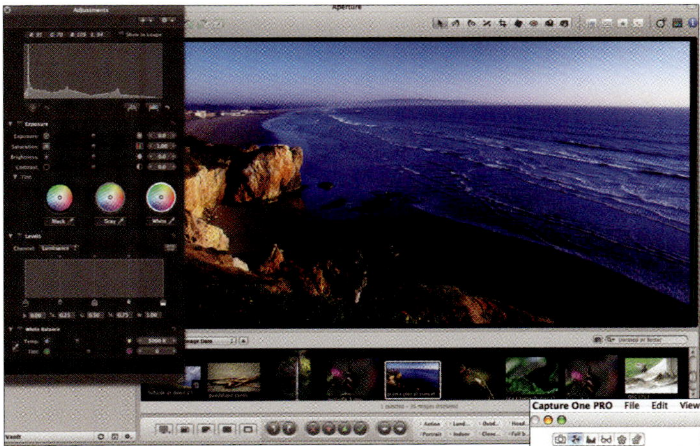

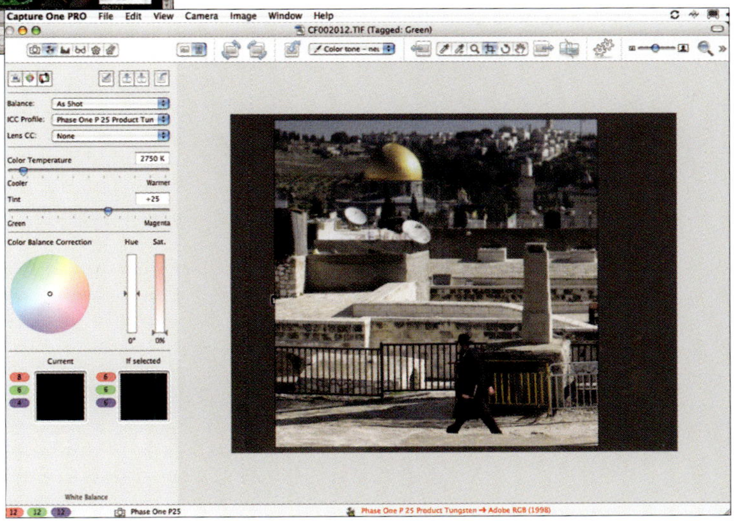

Figure 4.7

Screen shots of Adobe Camera RAW, Apple's Aperture software, and Phase One Capture One.

RAW Processing Recipe

I recommend the following workflow when capturing and then processing RAW files. This scenario assumes that your lighting setup is in place and can be controlled within reasonable limits, and that you are capturing and working in RGB color space:

Part A:

- Specify processing color space in-camera (Adobe 98 RGB or ProPhoto RGB).
- Select bit depth in-camera (12- 16-bit is best).
- Use lowest appropriate ISO setting in-camera (100 and lower is best).
- Perform metering via in-camera or hand-held meter.
- Make an image of your digital gray card, GMB color checker chart, or similar device (repeat this step every time you make a lighting change).
- Make test exposure(s) of your subject.
- Whenever practical, examine test exposure using computer and a large, color accurate, and calibrated display—use RAW converter software to view curves, levels, highlight/shadow warnings, and verify color fidelity. This practice beats using Polaroid tests every time.
- In-computer: Adjust custom curves, color temperature/color balance, shadows/contrast. If appropriate, use the color checker or digital gray card to color-balance the test image.
- At this stage, some software applications will do a better job if they are color balanced using a white point, and others using a gray point. Adobe Camera RAW is best using a white sampling tool; Capture One can use either a white or gray sampler equally well.
- Make appropriate lighting and lighting color adjustments. In most editing/conversion software, you can now set these adjustments as defaults for subsequent captures in your work sessions.
- Make second test exposure(s).
- Lather, rinse, repeat!!
- At this point, you should have complete control of color, clarity, contrast, and composition in your images.
- You are in a perfect position—if while shooting you discover that a particularly combination of factors is working well or not working well, you can act on it immediately.

Part B:

- If you are shooting tethered to a computer, ensure that the cable you are using is within specifications—for example, keep Firewire cables under 14 feet in length. Longer cables can affect image quality—which of course includes color.
- If you are saving images to internal camera storage, transfer images from the camera to the computer—use a Firewire or high-speed USB reader. Do not transfer files directly via camera-computer cable—this is slow and risks image transfer errors.
- Do not erase, write to, or format the card when it is inserted in the card reader. Always re-format the card in the same camera you intend to use it in. Doing otherwise risks loss of image data or even ruining the memory card.
- Ensure that images are saved into a separate directory, on a hard drive separate from the root drive, and on a drive that is connected to the base computer in use. I do not recommend sending original files over a network to a primary storage device.
- Copy the directory, or folder, of the original images to a separate hard drive, and specify this as your "working" folder. If you are obsessive like I am, you might also want to copy one of these directories to another hard drive or to writable media like a CD.
- Many RAW converter software packages, and also Adobe Lightroom and Apple's Aperture, require that you import the working folder images into the application. This takes a few minutes.

Part C:

Now that your images are up and running in the image converter or editor of your choice, I suggest that you:

- Set preferences in your RAW converter or other software application to the following:

  Adobe 98 color space or ProPhoto color space. I do not recommend sRGB or ColorMatch unless your output is going directly to an outside print service provider that requires it.

  If color temperature is set to auto, reset it to custom or manual.

  Use 16-bit depth for higher-end work. For Web work, 8-bit depth is plenty.

  Set the software for 300 dpi image resolution. In some cases, you can also try enlarging the file size or pixel dimensions at the same time.

  Enable the highlight/shadow warning. This helps warn you when your adjustments are damaging important details.

If there are preset curves adjustments, use the medium-contrast or mid-range curve to start.

Keep sharpening and noise reduction at minimum or, even better, turned off. It's almost always best to perform sharpening tasks on a layer in Photoshop or other image editor that supports layers.

Save these as your defaults for jobs that involve anything other than basic snapshots.

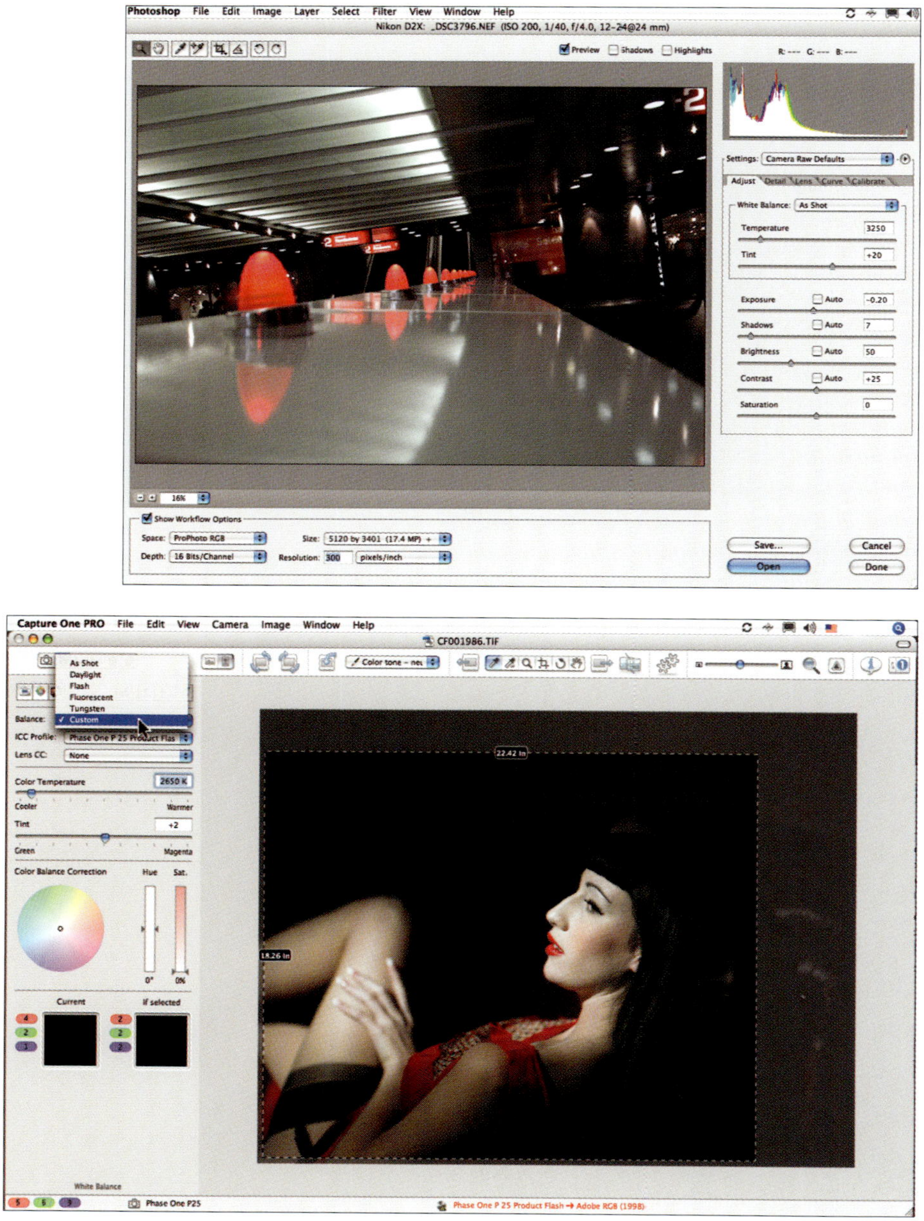

Figure 4.8

Adobe Camera RAW and Phase One Capture One main screens.

- Examine each image as a thumbnail. You checklist should include:

  Total exposure

  Overall color and color temperature

  Highlight and shadow detail

  Spot or selective area color accuracy

  Sharp and non-sharp image elements

- Pre-sort and eliminate unacceptable images, but only in your working directory. (Leave all the originals in the source directory alone! These are your digital gold mine.) These pre-sorts can include over- or under-exposed frames, poor posing or set element positioning, image out of focus, lighting failures, and the like.
- Next, make first-pass edits to the first few acceptable frames of the shoot. A good way to do this is to alternate between small adjustments to global color temperature and global exposure. Go back and forth, and use the exposure, shadow, and highlight warning tools to identify adjustments that will create an unacceptable image. If your display is a decent one, and it is calibrated, your changes will be accurate and appropriate.
- Some image editors provide tools for a basic Levels adjustment. You can consider this; however, I recommend that these adjustments be done in Photoshop, where the original image can be better protected through use of a more robust color engine and multiple adjustment layers.
- If you need to manage overall color cast or tint, this is the time to make minor changes. The tools differ between applications, but all accomplish the same thing.
- If your image software has the tools (most do), make small adjustments to color noise reduction, sharpening, and so on. Again, I reserve time later in production for most of these changes—Photoshop usually does a better job.
- You can try the auto, or "as shot" settings and see if the color is satisfactory. In my opinion, this works best in highly controlled, standardized lighting set to daylight temperature (around 5500K). In mixed lighting, or in variable, changing lighting, you are probably better off using a standardized digital white or gray card to color correct.
- Now, save your adjustment settings for this shoot or group of images. Using Adobe Camera RAW, for example, you can open an entire folder of images, adjust the first one, and synchronize all the other images to match it. In Phase One Capture One, you can adjust your first image and tell the software to make the same adjustments to every new capture—automatically.

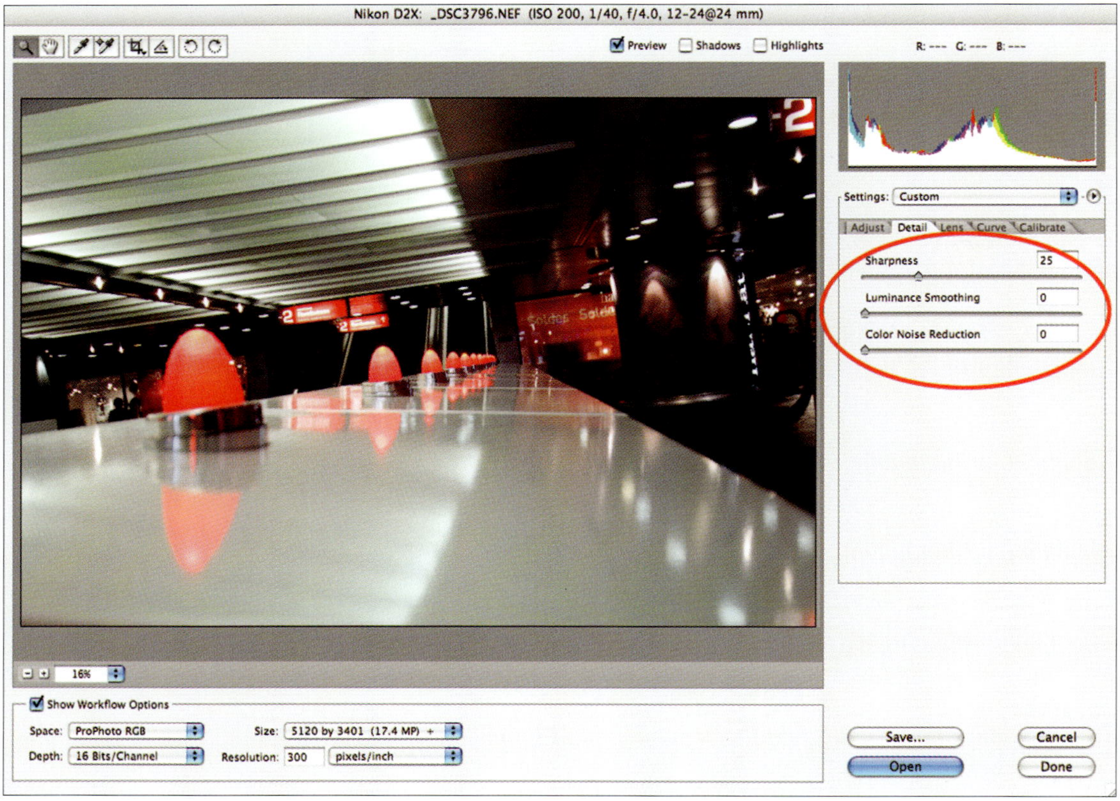

Figure 4.9

This figure shows sharpening and other adjustments available in Adobe Camera RAW.

- You have several options at this stage. You can keep the RAW file in its current home, and the software will remember the adjustments and tweaks you have made. You can batch process the RAW files and resave them as TIFF or JPEGs in another directory.
- In Adobe Camera RAW, for example, you can tell the application that you are finished by clicking Done, which will close the RAW editing window and save your settings, or you can save the image as an Adobe DNG (digital negative), RAW, TIFF, or JPEG. You can also choose to open the image in Photoshop.

You should now be the proud creator of a pre-sorted, pre-edited folder of top-notch images—images that are ready for a quick, efficient post-production process.

Note that most of the really hard work is already complete—you will have to do little, if anything, in post-production before you hand off these images to your client.

Editing

Once your RAW or other files are transferred into your computer system, you're ready to go forward and begin to edit all or part of the images.

Before you open an image in Photoshop, you should begin by double-checking your Photoshop default settings. Make sure your color space defaults to Adobe RGB (1998) or to ProPhoto RGB. Look under the Edit>Color Settings in Adobe Photoshop CS2.

The simplest and most trouble-free color space to use in your workflow is Adobe RGB (1998). In many respects, ProPhoto RGB is a specialized tool and has its uses in situations where contrast or color saturation is very high, or the appearance of final output involving skin tones is critical.

One situation in which ProPhoto RGB can be very useful is when you are sending image files to be output on film—for example, onto transparency for projection or archiving. This is a highly specialized activity and is beyond the scope of this book.

Please keep in mind that while I feel that ProPhoto RGB has advantages for image editing, it is not necessarily ideal for printing via inkjet or other processes. In my own work, I usually will edit the image in Photoshop using ProPhoto RGB as my working space, and then when that work is completed, save a duplicate file for printing use that has been converted to Adobe RGB (1998). As a parting shot, feel free to give this alternative a try; your mileage may vary.

Keep in mind that it is better in terms of efficiency and effective color management to first make adjustments to the image as a whole and progress to selected large areas, and finally perform small retouching tasks.

Your initial checklist for image editing should include:

- Make sure that the folder of original images is duplicated for editing. Even better, duplicate those images on a separate hard drive.
- When you first open an image for editing or revision, immediately save it under a new file name. I recommend that each major revision be given a unique file name, such as Rev 2.tiff.
- Actual image editing works best if you start with the broad changes and work your way down to the smaller ones. (See Chapter 2 for details of image-editing techniques.)
- I recommend that you make any major adjustment on a separate layer, or an adjustment layer. You can create a new layer by choosing Layer>New>Layer Via Copy. Or you can create an adjustment layer by choosing Layer>New Adjustment Layer and specifying whether you want a Curves, Levels, or other adjustment.

- First, evaluate the image for overall color balance or the presence of a color cast. The easiest way to do this is 1) use a color-calibrated display, 2) examine the image to see any obvious color problems, and 3) use the Info Palette to measure the mix of red, green, and blue in a relatively neutral area of the image.

Now that you have successfully completed your first pass of presorts and basic image edits, you have a folder full of images ready for editing. This outline provides a recipe for image editing. I will start at the global or macro level and work down to the local or micro level:

- Ensure that you understand the intended final output before you begin editing any image. Generally, I edit images as though they are master files, intended for re-purposing for anything from a two-page four color magazine spread down to a Web thumbnail.
- This means that you will usually be editing images in Adobe 98 color space or better. You can always narrow a color space, for example from Adobe 98 to sRGB, but you can't remake the color space back to Adobe 98 once the conversion is complete.
- You should understand and be able to use soft-proofing for on-screen color correction. This will enable you to see the impact of your edits in real-time as they will appear in final output. Enable gamut warning in the View menu drop-down so you can see if your output media can duplicate your color and other edits.

Editing Global Contrast

Open an image in Photoshop or other high-end image editor and make a duplicate layer on top of the original background layer. Make a basic Levels adjustment on this layer. This involves moving the shadow point and white point a small amount toward the center of the histogram. General limits on the values these are set to are 6-8 on the shadow side and 240-245 on the highlight side.

This type of adjustment will often introduce a warming color cast to your image. If this is not desired, you can choose Edit>Fade Levels, and change the blending mode to Luminosity. You also have the option of setting the Layer Blend mode to Luminosity.

If you see that you need additional edits, create another new layer.

The Levels Histogram Is Your Friend

A histogram is similar to a bar chart. It shows the darkest tones on the left and the brightest tones on the right. The height of the chart above the baseline shows the intensity, or amount, of light recorded in the image in that tonal range.

For example, a smooth, rounded mountain-like histogram indicates an image that has a balanced exposure from dark to light. A histogram that's heavily weighted to the left is probably underexposed, and in this case shadow detail will suffer. A histogram that leans far to the right is probably overexposed, endangering highlight detail.

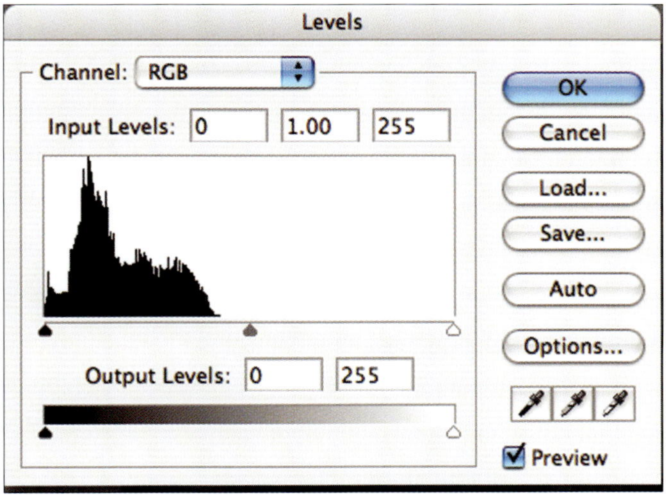

Figure 4.10

An underexposed image.

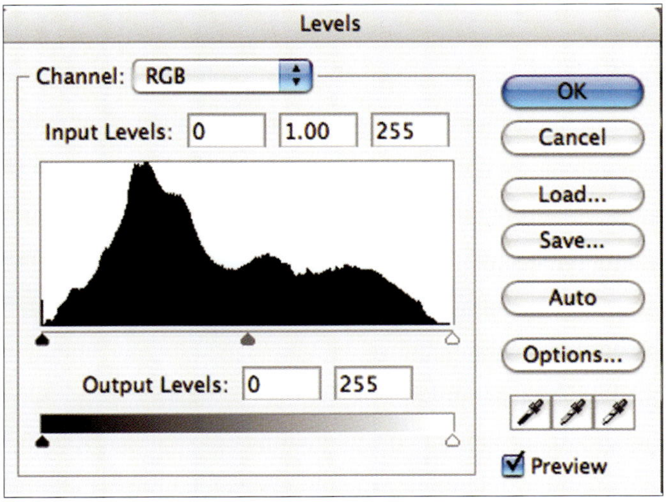

Figure 4.11

A properly exposed image.

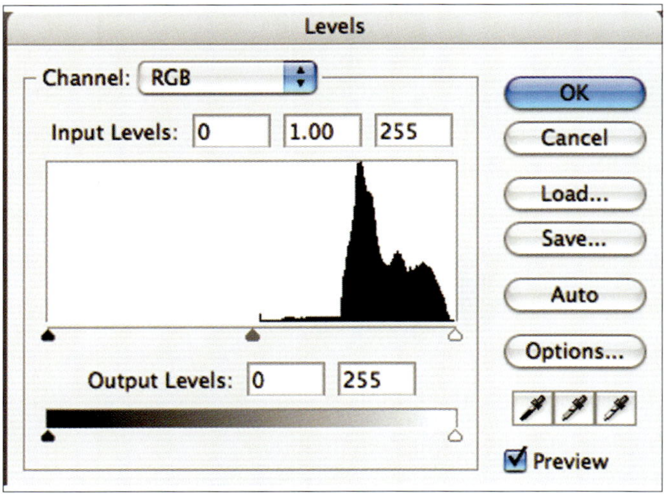

Figure 4.12

An overexposed image.

You can also use a histogram to help evaluate a color cast in your image. An unbalanced histogram in a particular color channel is also a useful tool. For example, in the Photoshop Histogram window, you can expand the histogram window via the drop-down menu (see the red arrow) and then choose All Channels View and Show Channels in Color.

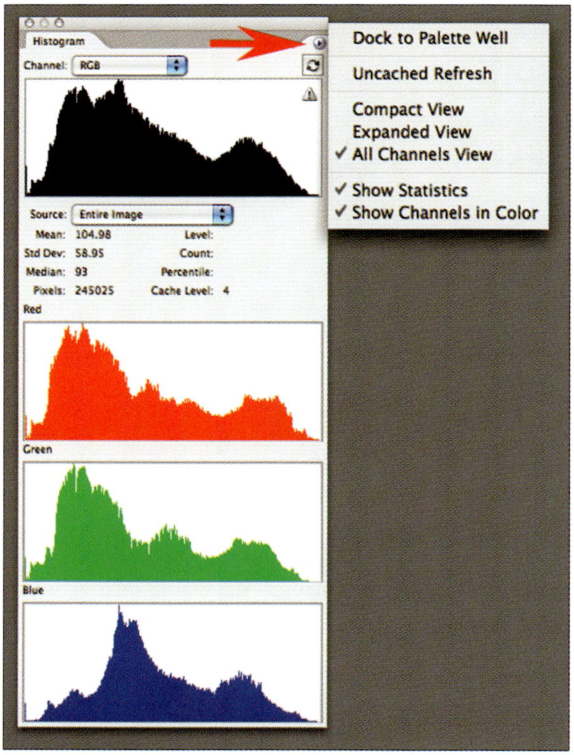

Figure 4.13

You can use histograms to evaluate the color cast of your image as well.

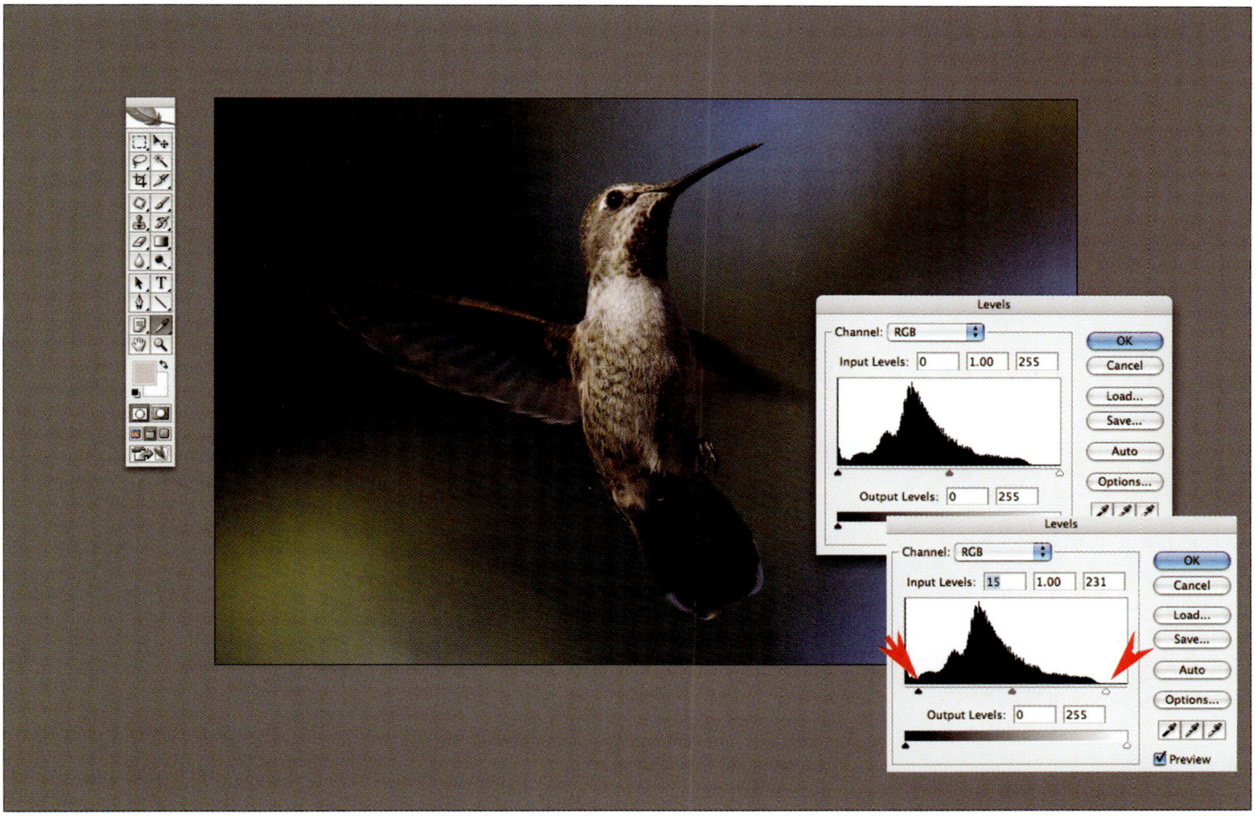

Figure 4.14

Making Levels adjustments.

Editing Color Using White and Gray Point Balancing

If the image color needs adjusting, you can use the following procedure:

- Choose Image>Adjustment>Auto Color (this is usually far from ideal and is not recommended).
- Choose Image>Adjustment>Levels and use the white or gray dropper tool on a strong highlight or neutral gray area in the image (better).
- Choose Image>Adjustment>Levels and use the white or gray dropper tool on a standard white or gray card included in the image (much better).
- At a more advanced level, you can use the preset color profiles provided by software manufacturer or camera manufacturer as a starting point for your color correction. These are generally oriented around the type of the most dominant lighting source, such as tungsten, fluorescent, or daylight. In most cases, I still wind up using a white or gray eyedropper anyway.

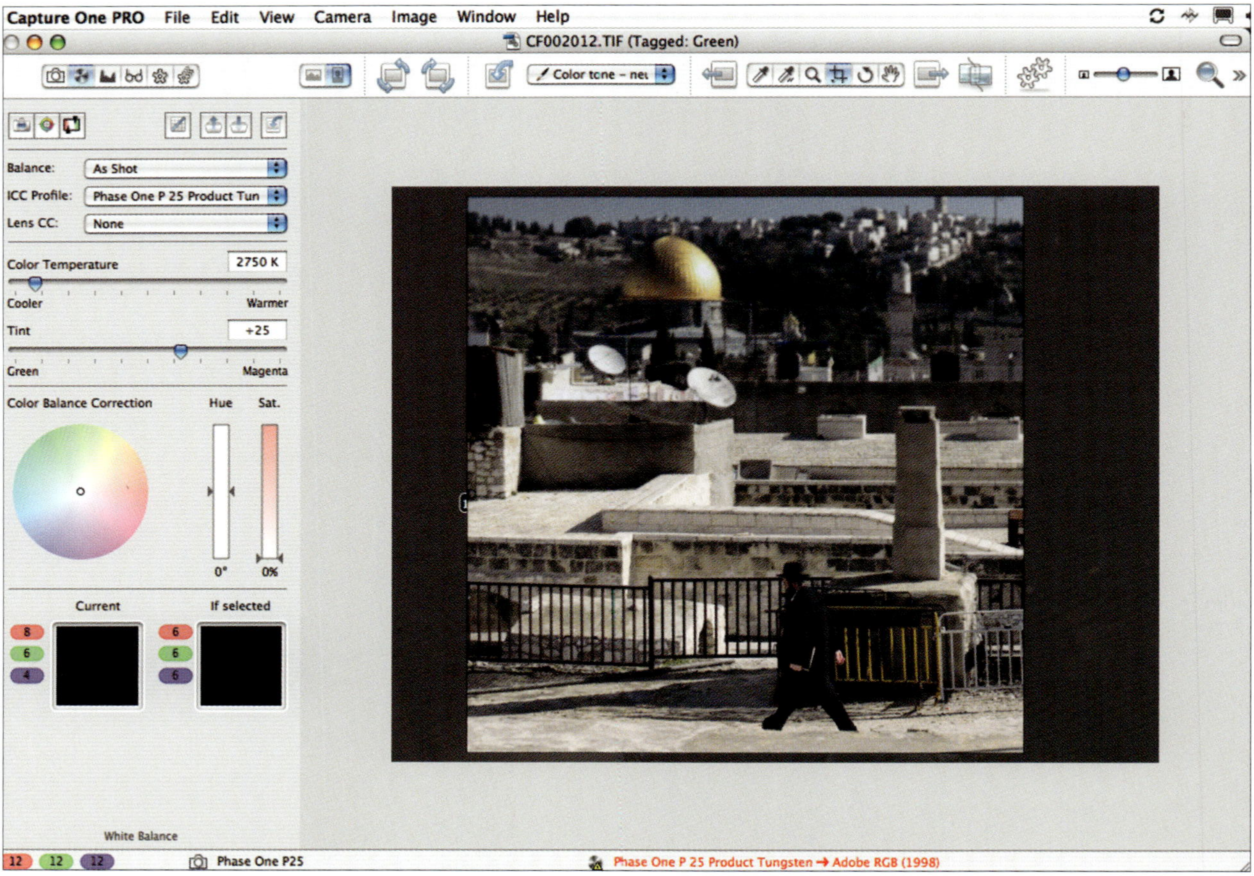

Figure 4.15

Phase One Capture One color temperature presets.

Be sure to save your work periodically. I make it a practice to have plenty of hard drive space available—cost is under $1/GB right now and still dropping. If I make a major change to an image, I will then save it as a separate file with a revision name. So, for example, the name will change from image1.tiff to image1_revision_2.tiff, and later to image1_revision_3.tiff.

In the next step, I frequently make a global Curves adjustment. Most digital images are a bit flat in contrast, and this adjustment will make the image color and contrast pop nicely. Normally I do this on a new layer or adjustment layer. Choose Image>Adjustments>Curves. There are two basic curves adjustments that I use—these cover about 90% of the images that photographers make, as illustrated in Figures 4.16 through 4.18.

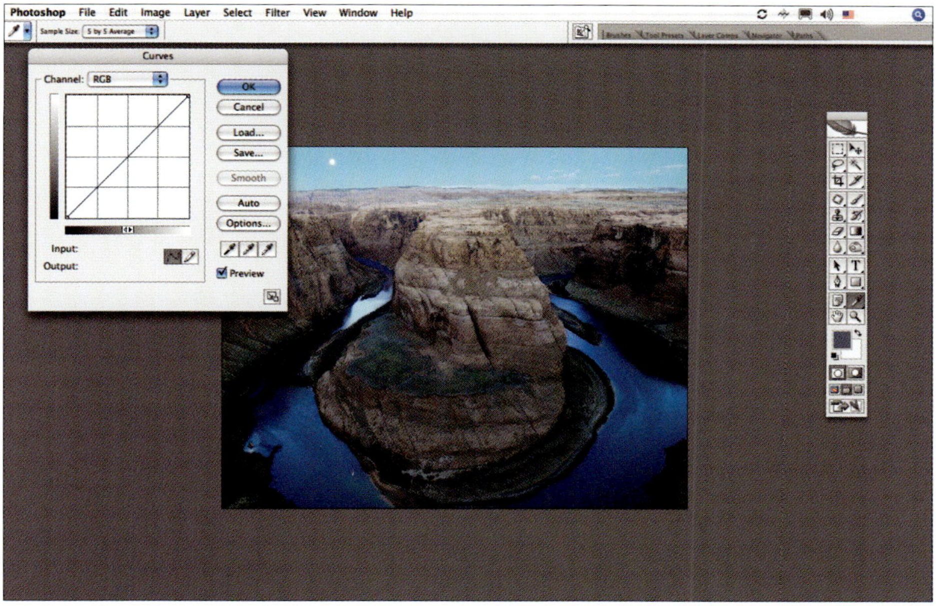

Figure 4.16

Curve before adjustment: This is an unadjusted Curves dialog box.

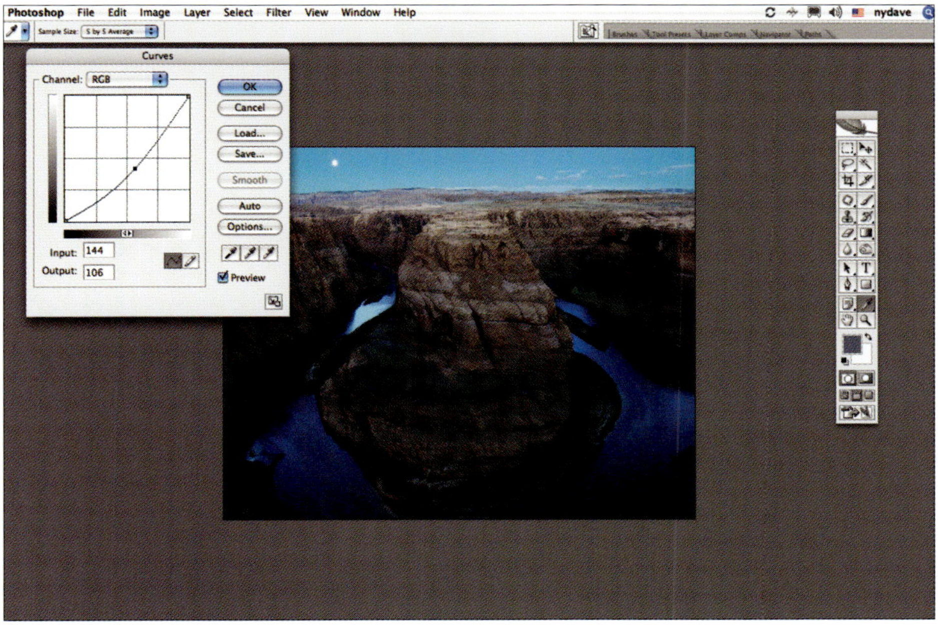

Figure 4.17

Curve adjustment option one: In the Curves dialog box, left-click and hold with your mouse at the center point of the ramp. If the image looks a bit bright and flat overall, drag this down and to the right until the curve looks like this. If the image is a bit too dark, drag the point up and to the left a small amount.

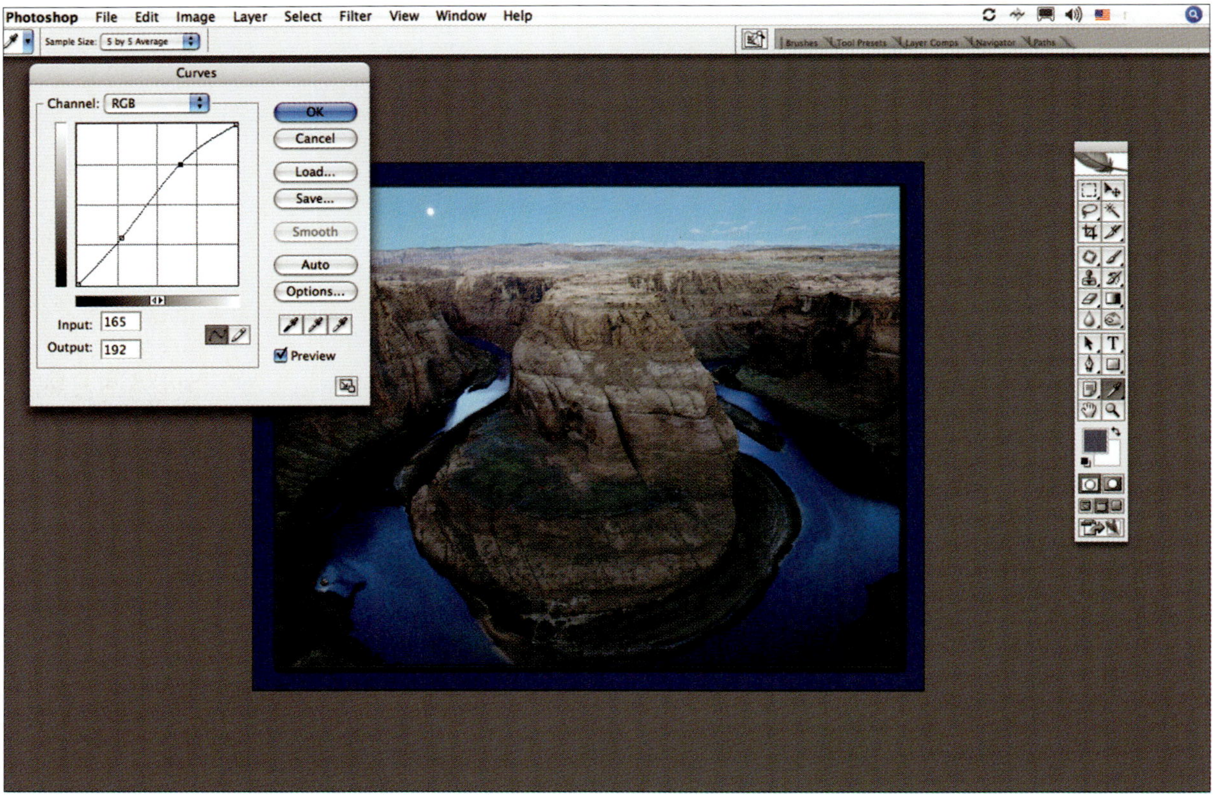

Figure 4.18

Curve adjustment option two: In the Curves dialog box, left-click and hold at point A and drag the spot down a short distance. Left-click and hold at Point B, and drag up a short distance.

Note that this type of Curves adjustment also affects color. If you prefer the warm tone this almost always introduces, you can leave it alone. Otherwise, choose the Edit, Fade Curves command and change blending to Luminosity. Or change the Layer Blend mode to luminosity.

You can also use the Curves command to correct a general color cast in an image or to create an overall color cast to satisfy creative specifications. The Curves adjustment uses a basic color wheel as its starting point. Open the Curves dialog box (see Figure 4.19). At the top of the box, you will see the Channel drop-down menu, which should say RGB.

This adjustment is directly related to the well-known color wheel. To correct an overall blue color cast, you want to add yellow. To correct a green color cast, you want to add magenta. To correct a red color cast, add cyan—and of course, you can switch these around as needed.

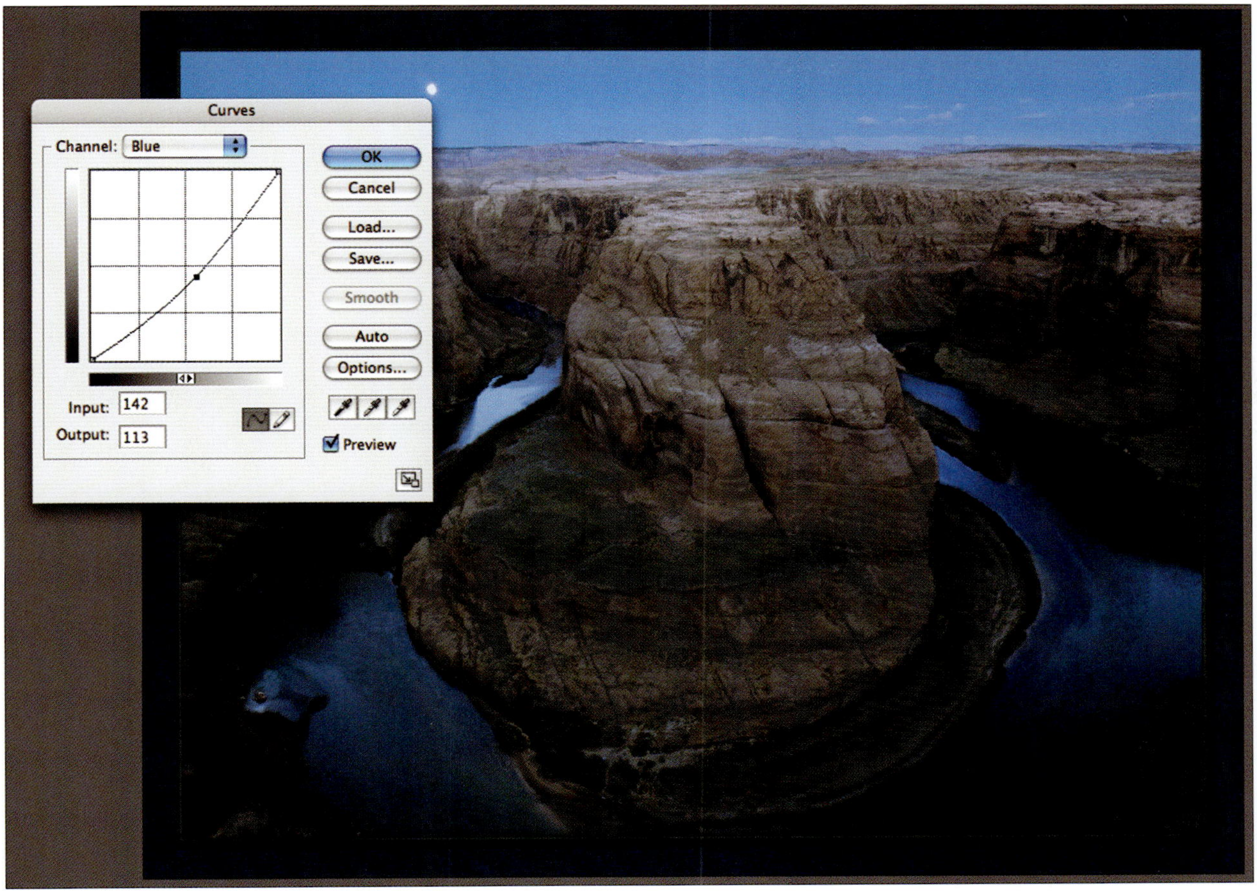

Figure 4.19

Curves adjustments made to individual color channels are an easy and efficient way to correct simple color casts.

Add a new layer, and make a Curves adjustment on that layer or add an Adjustment layer using the command Layer>New Adjustment Layer>Curves. To do this, first select the color channel that corresponds to the color cast. In this case, we want to balance out some blue, so we select the Blue channel in the Curves dialog box.

You can start by left-clicking on the center of the line and dragging it down to reduce blue and add yellow. In this case, "less is more"; try a little at a time. You can do this with any image and add or subtract a global color cast. Just select a color channel, Red, Green, or Blue, and experiment with moving the curve up and down.

Editing Global Color Using CS2 Hue/Saturation

Remember that editing changes pixels in your image. So wherever possible, create a new layer (Command/Ctrl+J) so that your editing will be non-destructive and can be adjusted at a later time.

One of the simplest ways to adjust color in the overall image is to adjust total saturation. Choose Image>Adjustments>Hue/Saturation (or Command/Ctrl+U). You'll see the Hue/Saturation dialog box pop up. Note that at the top of the box, you'll see the Master drop-down menu. This indicates that any change you make will affect all colors in the image you are working on.

Use the middle slider, and move it to the left 2 to 8 points, to see a significant change in the overall color saturation of the image. Click OK to complete this step.

Next, let's assume that you want to change only the red tones in the image. Again, press Command+U and, on the Master drop-down menu, click on Red. Now, using the saturation slider, you can reduce or increase the vibrancy and saturation of the red tones in your image.

The lightness slider provides some adjustment in the brightness of the color tone you are focusing on, but I rarely use it—it's just too drastic.

In a later chapter, I will explore the use of selective color adjustments, which are more precise but also more time consuming. In most of my product and portrait photography, I use global adjustments and rarely resort to selective adjustments of any kind.

Editing Global Color Using CS2 Color Balance

Color balance is an extremely useful tool. I find that its primary use in photography is in correcting small to moderate color casts in an image; in many cases, those result from mixed lighting in location shooting.

To use the Color Balance dialog box, press Command/Ctrl+B (Image>Adjustments >Color Balance). You'll see a dialog box pop up that has three sliders in it, as shown in Figure 4.20.

Note that each slider has a color specified on the right and left. These are colors that are opposites on the color wheel we are all familiar with. If you move the slider toward yellow, blue is diminished, and yellow is increased in the image. If you move the slider away from green and toward magenta, you can in many cases correct a green color cast in your image.

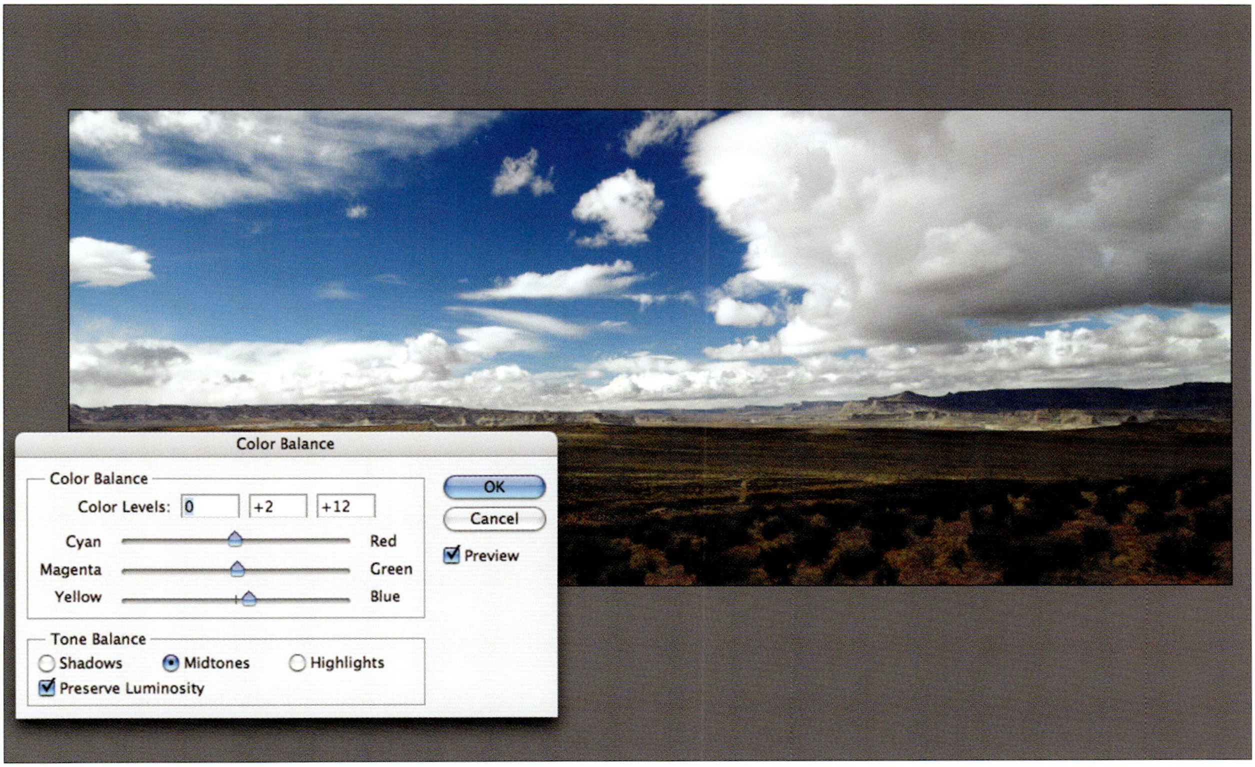

Figure 4.20

The Color Balance dialog box is based on the standard color wheel. So, for example, to balance a blue color cast in an image, move the yellow/blue slider toward yellow until the desired effect is achieved.

I have found that in most cases it is best to use the sliders only on the midtones in the images; adjustments in the highlights or shadows are too extreme. So just click on the Midtones selection and choose Preserve Luminosity. I also suggest that you make color adjustments on layers, preserving underlying image information.

Editing Global Color Using CS2 Photo Filter Tool

One of the coolest tools introduced in Photoshop recently is the Photo Filter adjustment tool. In many ways, it simulates using a filter on your camera—with one important difference. You can change the filter in post-production or combine filter effects in ways that are difficult, if not impossible, on the camera.

Another benefit of using the Photo Filter adjustment is that it does not "rob" you of light while you are photographing. Most photo filters used on cameras absorb some light, requiring you to use a slower shutter speed or larger aperture, making it more difficult to stop action or control depth of field.

You can apply a photo filter directly on the image or via a new layer. To make the adjustment directly, choose Image>Adjustment>Photo Filter. In the dialog box that appears, you'll see that Photoshop defaults to a warm yellow filter. In fact, Adobe provides the old photography filter number (85) as a guide for you. If you click on this drop-down menu, you'll see a whole list of filters that you can experiment with.

Another method you can use is to create a photo filter adjustment layer. Choose Layer>New Adjustment Layer>Photo Filter, and you'll see this dialog box.

This is similar to the tool described just above, with two important differences: It creates a new layer, and the opacity and blending mode of that layer are changeable. This gives you quite a range of options in adjusting color.

In my own work, I use the #85 warming filter on portraits quite a bit, adjusted from 10-20%, as it gives a very pleasing glow to skin tones and fabrics. This is particularly true on indoor and studio shots. In outdoor shots, I frequently use the #80 blue filter, reduced to about 10% opacity, to bring some snap into skies and water.

Retouching techniques:

- Create a new layer, duplicating the original, to work on for retouching.
- Zoom in to at least 100%.
- As much as possible, work within areas that have common tone and color first.
- Retouch areas on the margins of highlight/shadow later in your workflow.

You will find that, in particular, this systematic workflow is kind to skin tones or other delicate texture areas in an image. With practice, you'll see an improvement in your images, particularly in print.

Finishing Up

Well You are not done yet. A few important points for your adjusted master images:

- Save your files as you go along. Don't work for long stretches forgetting to save your work. Save them as high-bit TIFF, Photoshop (PSD), or DNG files. Don't downsize these or use JPEG file format for archiving! If you make a significant change in an image, consider saving it under a modified file name, such as xyz-Revision 2. Keep layers intact, within reasonable file sizes.

  You will use these images, with their major adjustments, for fine-tuning or other work later. These will include portrait retouching, using image elements in compositing, resizing for Web pages, and more.

- Make it your practice to back up image files, even work in progress, to another drive or to CD/DVD.
- Last, an important reminder about screen calibration: None of this color work will be very effective if you are using a computer display right out of the box. A color-calibration tool, used at least twice a month, is key to your success in managing your RAW files and your edited output.

Some tips for image editing and retouching that will help you control and preserve color:

- Keep your image in 16-bit color as long as you can. In Photoshop CS2, nearly all editing tools are available in 16-bit, but some are not. If possible, save these for later, and switch to 8-bit only when you have no other choice.
- Keep your image in Adobe RGB (1998) or ProPhoto RGB as long as you can. Drop down to sRGB only if you feel you must—for example to send work out to a lab that requires it or to repurpose a master image for the Web. Remember, once you drop down to sRGB, you can't go back to Adobe RGB (1998). The color information was eliminated, and it is gone forever.
- If you make an adjustment in Levels and Curves, you will find that these will shift your color in (usually) surprising directions. This can be eliminated by changing the Layer Blending mode to Luminosity or by choosing Edit>Fade (levels or curves) and then choosing Luminosity from the drop-down menu.
- Stay away from extremes in large-scale image editing if possible. Generally, Levels adjustments in the shadows higher than 10 are rarely very useful; adjustments above 245 in highlights are pretty much the same.

Getting the Best Output

There are a number of choices in output:

- Output only to a file, used for electronic or video display.
- Output to an in-house printer, such as an inkjet.
- Output using an outside print service provider (PSP).

Some general rules for each of these options:

- I recommend that you save the master image file using the same color space that you used for your working space. If you used Adobe RGB (1998), leave it that way.

- Some inkjet printers use 300 ppi, others 360 ppi (pixels per inch). You will find that you can squeeze out a small improvement from your larger prints if you match the image file resolution in ppi to the printer. (For example, Epson printers do best on a diet of 360 ppi images, and HP Designjet printers do best on a diet of 300 ppi.)
- I do not recommend that you convert the color space of the image to the intended print output color space (for example, Epson Premium Glossy on the Epson 2400 printer). This is what is called a "destructive" edit and will limit printing the image to that one printer-ink-paper combination. (See the sidebar "Successful Printing from Photoshop.")

Successful Printing from Photoshop

Printing from Photoshop is not as easy as I'd like it to be. First, the Photoshop default settings are not really suitable for high-quality photographic output. I recommend that you use the following steps to obtain improved results:

1. First, get it right in the camera! There's no substitute for a good image.
2. Next, make sure that you capture and edit the image in Adobe RGB (1998) working space, at minimum.
3. Set up your image resolution to match that of the printer—in Epson, 360 ppi is best, in HP, 300 ppi.
4. It doesn't matter much as far as print quality is concerned if your image is in 8-bit or 16-bit format. I do recommend that your master image be kept in 16-bit for major editing and archiving, but there's nothing wrong with printing from an 8-bit file.
5. Although there are many good alternatives available on the market, I still recommend that you use the manufacturer's ink and paper for your prints, at least until you feel as though you completely understand the behavior of the printer and the way it renders your images. Once you have mastered that, feel free to experiment.

Assuming you will be using the manufacturer's inks and papers and that you've set up the printer according to the manufacturer's instructions, we'll move on to printing your image from Photoshop using the printer driver.

1. First, with the image open in Photoshop, choose File>Page Setup. Choose the correct printer, paper size, and whether you want landscape or portrait orientation (see Figure 4.21).

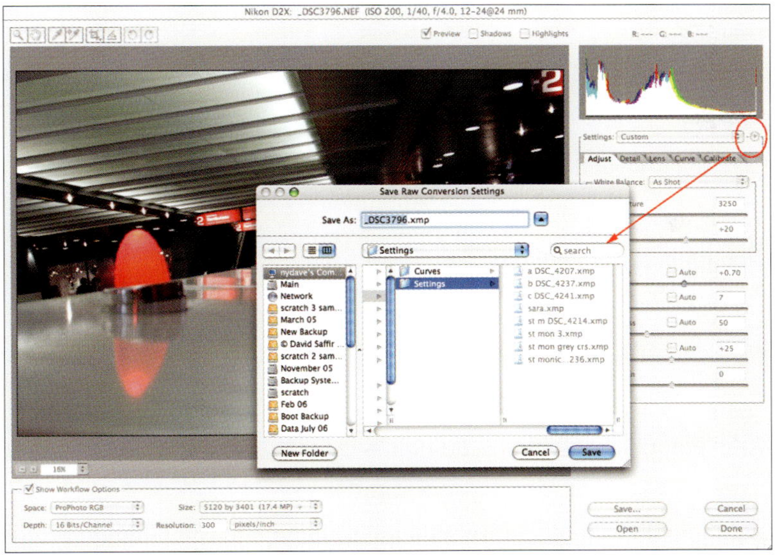

Figure 4.21

This dialog box manages basic settings such as which printer you are using and the paper size.

2. Next, choose File>Print with Preview. This opens a new dialog box that looks like Figure 4.22.

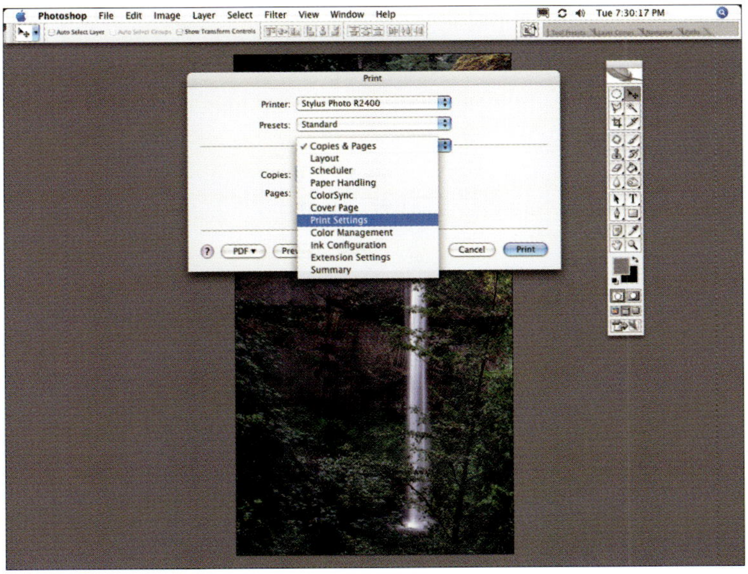

Figure 4.22

The Print with Preview dialog box is your primary gateway to producing good color in your prints.

3. On the upper-left corner of this dialog box, you'll see a thumbnail preview of the image you want to print. (Please keep in mind that this preview is not color corrected and should not be used to predict color rendering in your print.) Immediately below this is a drop-down menu that offers you the choice of Color Management or Output. Choose Color Management.
4. Next, immediately below this, you will see a section of the dialog box that is titled Options. It contains three drop-down menus: Color Handling, Printer Profile, and Rendering Intent. Your settings should be:

   Color Handling: Let Photoshop Determine Color

   Printer Profile: Choose your specific printer/paper combination (for example: HP PS 8700, Premium Photo Paper, or the Epson Stylus 2400—Premium Glossy). These printer profiles were loaded into your system when you installed the printer driver.

   Rendering Intent: In most cases, use Perceptual. You can experiment with the other rendering intents, but 99 times out of 100 you'll find Perceptual gets the job done.
5. Be sure you scale the image to the output size you want. This part of the dialog box is located dead center and is pretty straightforward to use.
6. Click Print, which will take you to the dialog box shown in Figure 4.23. At the top of this dialog box, you'll see the Printer drop-down menu, and just below it, the Presets drop-down menu.

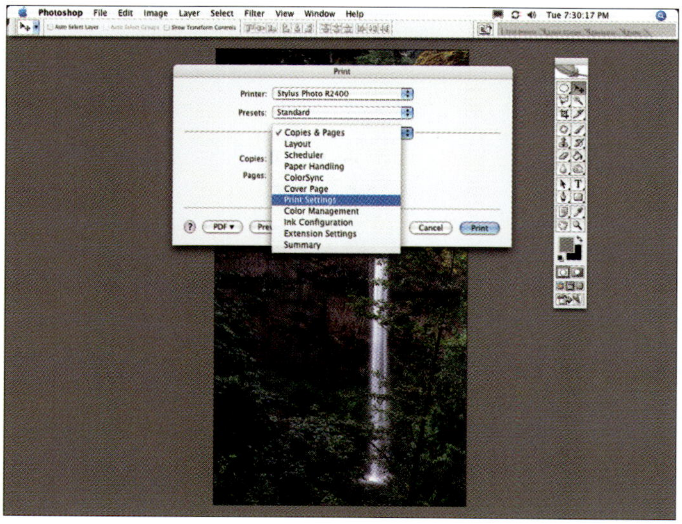

Figure 4.23

Choosing preset driver choices.

7. If you click on the Presets drop-down menu, you'll see the a list of driver choices. Mouse down to Print Settings, and the dialog box will change to what is shown in Figure 4.24.

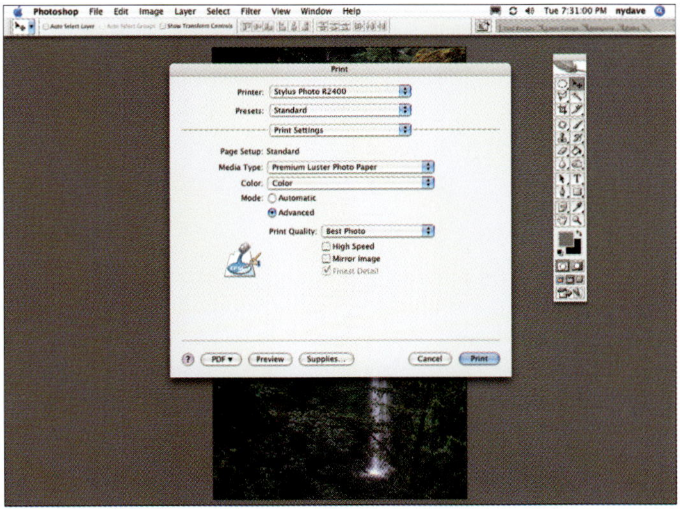

Figure 4.24

Choosing your print settings.

8. Under Media Type, choose the paper you are using—be sure to match the name the manufacturer gives the paper you are using. An incorrect setting here will cause your print color to look distorted.
9. Under the Color drop-down menu, choose Color. Under Mode, choose Advanced.
10. Under Print Quality, choose Best Photo. Disable High Speed, as this setting can degrade print quality.
11. Now, go back up to the top of the dialog box, and in the Print Settings drop-down menu, click and hold—the drop-down menu will reappear—choose Color Management. You'll see a new dialog box that appears in Figure 4.25.
12. Now, just choose Color Controls Off.
13. Now, to make sure that you can use these settings again, click on the Presets drop-down menu, mouse down until you see Save As, and save these settings for future use.
14. Click Print, and voila!!

A last note—there are some small differences between choices available in the printer driver that's installed with Epson printers, HP, or Canon. Don't let that throw you—the menu choices are close enough that you're sure to get it right.

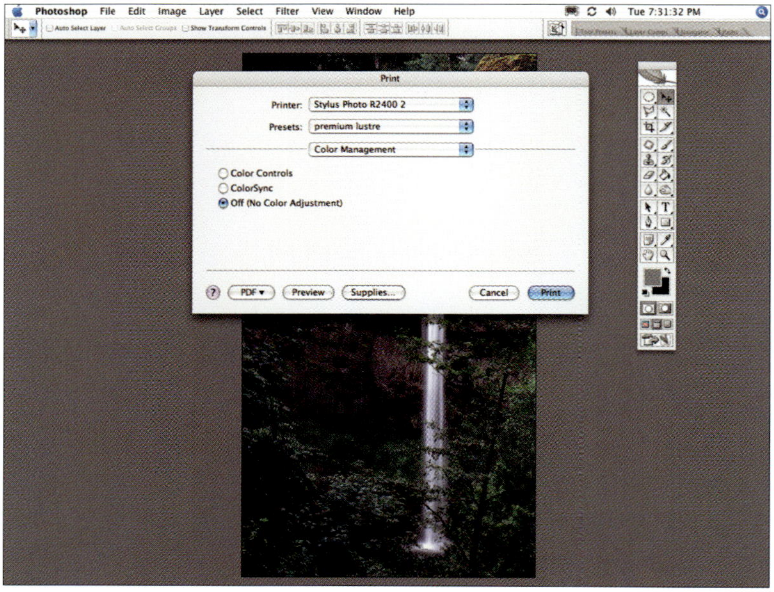

Figure 4.25

The Color Management options.

- Although sharpening is not necessarily a part of color management, it can affect color—if it is overused, it affects color by generating unwanted distortions or artifacts in the image. Sharpening is in many ways a subjective thing, in that it can be a matter of personal taste just how much sharpening you use. Generally, I apply sharpening on an additional layer, set to Luminosity blending mode.

  For example, when setting up a medium sized 16×20 print, I set the Unsharp Mask filter apply a fairly high percentage (150-300%), a small radius (usually around 0.3), and a threshold of 3-8. (To access the Unsharp Mask filter, choose Filter>Sharpen>Unsharp Mask.) Once the Unsharp Mask is applied, you can change the opacity of the Sharpening layer from 100% down to desired intensity.

- If you are printing via a third-party print service provider, many require that you use sRGB. It's a good idea to ask them if they want you to apply sharpening, or if they will do it themselves. You certainly don't want a situation in which both parties apply sharpening, as this will probably ruin the print.

Digital printing is an activity that takes practice—no different, in this respect, than working in the darkroom. Making a truly great print is an iterative process—frequently nothing more complex than trial and error. Sometimes a print can go from good to great just by using a different kind of paper—or a small change in your image editing process can give big dividends in the print.

It is also important to keep in mind that different printers have different "looks," just as film and digital sensors do. If you're not satisfied with one option, please go forward and try something new—there's a world of choices now, so take advantage of them.

Working with a Print Service Provider

Working with a third-party print service provider can be a joy or a headache. This sidebar assumes that the photographer or artist is working with a provider that is focused on photographic printing. (For more information on fine art printing, see Chapter 6, "Production Guide for Artists.")

There's one real key to success, and that's good communication. I use the following recipe when dealing with a new or established print service provider. Some of these are questions to ask, and some are recommendations for implementation:

- How often do you work with my kind of photographer (wedding, stock, events, portrait, or other)?
- What is your color-management process?
- Can you provide me with sample prints made from my image files?
- What is your printing process? Which papers and chemicals do you use? Are these archivally rated materials (in other words, print life of at least 50 years, preferably 75-100)? Do you notify customers if this changes?
- What arrangements can be made for the printer to provide proof prints for important jobs?
- Can the printing service provide a printer profile (ICC profile) that allows the photographer to soft proof the images before they are sent to the printing service?

- What is the range of sizes and print finish options (glossy, luster) that you offer?
- What specialty media can you print on, such as canvas?
- What are the specifications that you require when I send you an image file, such as size, file format (JPEG/TIFF/other), resolution, color space, and so on?
- Do you provide software and training for me to submit images to you for printing? Is it free? What is the cost?
- How do I upload images to you?
- How do you manage the printing process? Does the printing operator sit at the machine and inspect and adjust incoming image files, and inspect outgoing prints?
- What is your average turn-around time for a job? Is there any time of the year that this turn-around time changes?

I've found enormous variation between one provider and another. In addition to good communication, good customer service and problem solving are very important to your success.

Summary

There are a lot of recipes in this chapter. Most if not all of them were developed through the counsel and advice of colleagues and friends—and some really tough trial and error development on my part. I sincerely believe that there is always room for improvement in efficiency and quality in photographic processes—so treat this as a good head start, and then improve on it.

Keep in mind that there's always room for growth—and for realizing your unique vision in your images!

5

Color Management Policies for Photographers

I admit that I use the word "policies" with some reservations—on one hand, I've learned through painful experience that it pays to have a methodical approach to generating top-quality images via digital capture and output. It's simply a matter of time and money. I want to minimize my chair time and still focus on results and produce the highest quality images possible.

The goal of this chapter is to help you do that—but keep in mind that as time goes on, you'll still have to keep up to date with the latest tools and customer requirements and adapt your workflow as you go along. Flexibility and adaptability are important components of success in modern photography.

I recommend that you use a workflow that is appropriate to your intended use of your images. I'm also suggesting that you construct your image creation process with more than that in mind—that you consider that, down the road, having the highest possible, in-depth quality will keep your options open and your business going strong. Keep your options open because you *will* discover new opportunities. A strong parallel is taking care of your negatives and transparencies —because as you continue to grow as an artist and photographer, you'll find new ways to use them.

You'll be in better shape as an artist and professional if you put a little extra time and effort into creating a body of work that has sustainable depth and breadth, that will keep its quality for many years to come. This means that we have to leverage the tools we have now to create the best images possible. Don't accept compromises for the sake of short-term convenience.

If you were a watercolorist, I assume you would purchase the finest paper, brushes, and watercolors you could afford, knowing that they will render color as you wish it, and that your finished work will last well into the future. Using shortcuts in digital capture can be likened to purchasing your watercolor media strictly on the basis of price, or using materials that have been tucked away in storage for a long time and as such have faded or are otherwise damaged.

Color management is a term that probably falls short in capturing all of the aspects we're going to cover in this chapter. This list should help you understand the scope of the major issues and topics covered here:

- Impact of color space choices in-camera on image quality and color
- Use of color space and file type in-camera and its effect on your post-production process
- Setting up Adobe Photoshop to maximize control, quality, and productivity
- Managing scanning film to digital
- Basics of RAW file processing
- Impact of computer display choices on your work
- Calibrating your display and using soft proofing
- Maximizing quality in print output—inkjet printers

Impact of In-Camera Color Space

A fundamental theme is repeated several times in this chapter: Color quality can be maintained only if you protect it like you would protect your bank account. Once color quality is downgraded, it is very difficult to restore it without doing much of your work over again—if it is possible at all. It's hard to put the pennies back in the piggy bank once it's been broken, as Figure 5.1 shows.

In the world of photography, several choices are available to you in controlling in-camera color space. Examples of your choices include, from smallest to largest: sRGB, Adobe RGB (1998), and ProPhoto RGB.

I recommend that you set up your camera to shoot in Adobe RGB (1998) color space, unless you plan on using your images only on the Web or you have all of your images printed by an outside vendor that uses only sRGB.

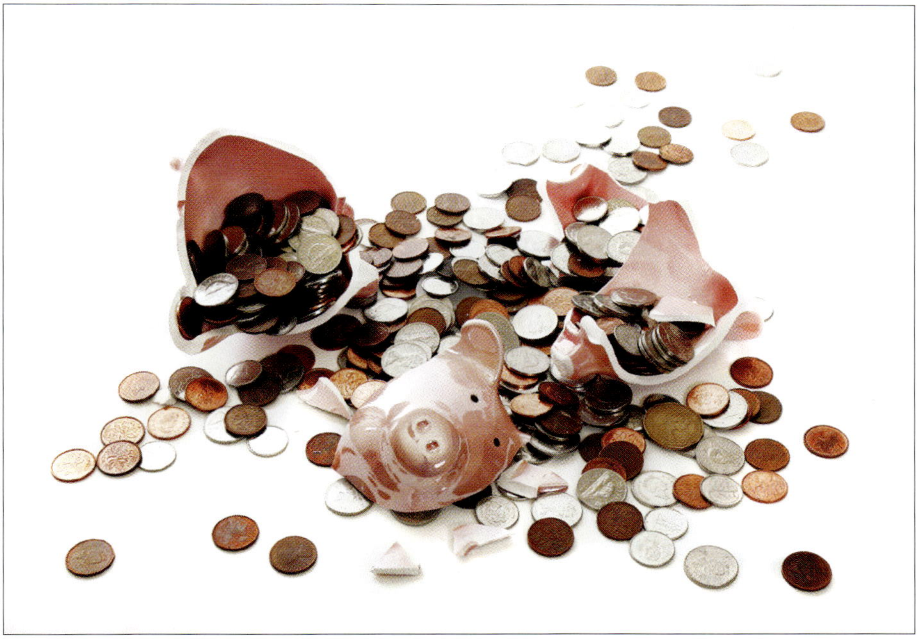

Figure 5.1

A broken piggy bank is hard to put back together. So is color quality in a degraded image. (Image licensed from istockphoto.)

Why do I say this? Simply put, you will over time see improvements in shadow and highlight detail, better smoothness in continuous tone areas such as blue skies, and in transitions from highlight to shadow areas such as a shadow on a model's skin.

A large color space, such as Adobe RGB (1998) RGB, is significantly bigger than its cousin, sRGB. If you capture your image using a smaller color space, or you convert an image file from a larger space to a smaller one, you discard a significant amount of image information. The camera or the computer calculates how the original color can be squeezed into the color space you choose. In many cases, the hardware and software substitute a compromise color for the original. You also have little or no control over how this substitution may, or may not, take place.

The sRGB color space was originally designed for use on computer displays. It looks great on a nice, bright screen, but sRGB cuts off, or clips, many of the colors found in its larger siblings. Adobe RGB (1998) was, in part, designed to cover the range of colors that can be printed using a four color (CMYK) printing press and is far better suited to modern digital printing than sRGB. The sRGB color space encompasses about one-third of the color we can see; Adobe RGB (1998) covers about one half. Also, Adobe RGB (1998) provides greater coverage in the shadows, midtones, and highlights. Figure 5.2 shows that Adobe RGB (1998) is significantly larger than sRGB.

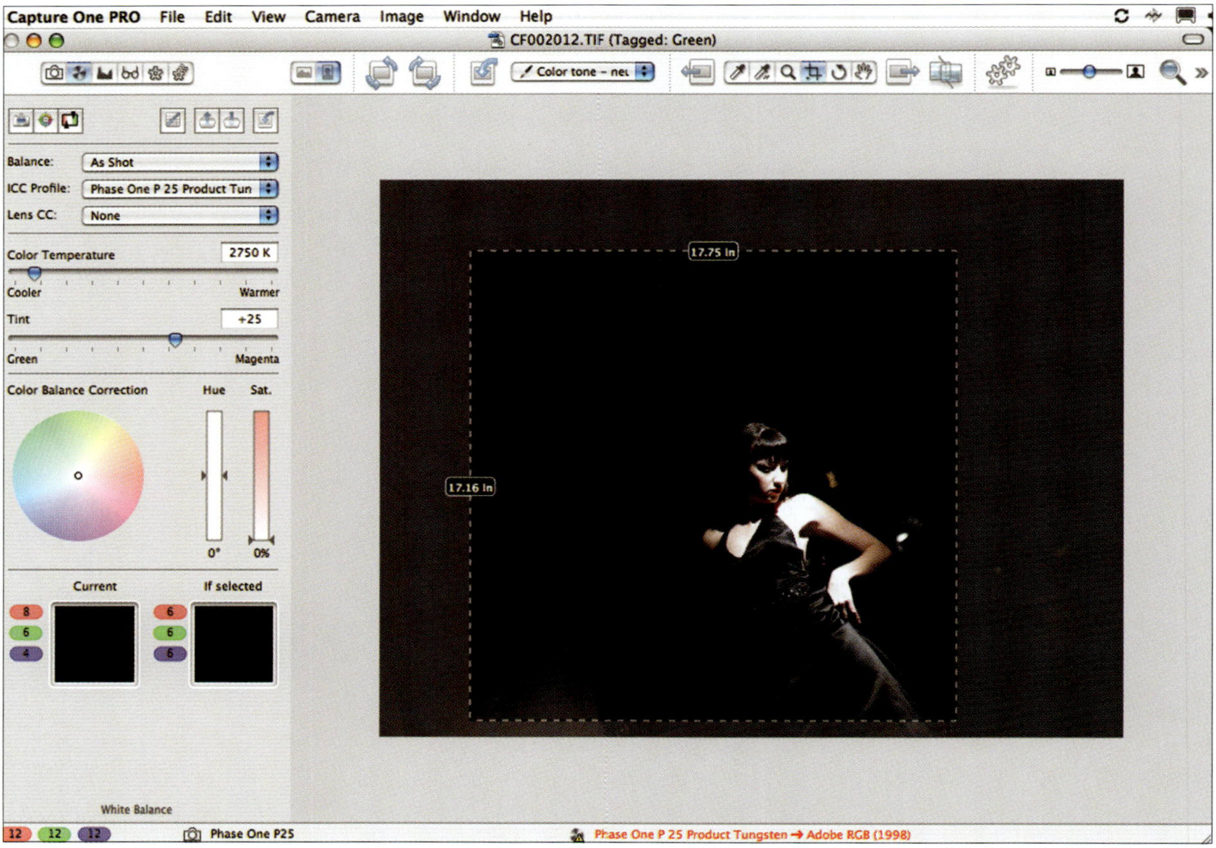

Figure 5.2

Adobe RGB (1998) is significantly larger than sRGB.

Using a larger color space also allows you to leverage the capabilities of the latest, improved inkjet printers. Their wider gamut and more accurate rendering of color give you the opportunity to make more vibrant prints, and become more competitive in a crowded market.

There are now printers with eight inks, and some on the way that have 12 inks. (More on this later in this chapter.) It makes sense to be able to take advantage of these innovations.

In-Camera Color Space and File Type Decisions

Using a smaller color space can sometimes make image editing a headache. I have found that in many cases it takes me more time to get skin tones to look good in an sRGB JPEG than it does in an Adobe RGB (1998) RAW or TIFF file.

I think you can see the reason for this if you compare the information available in an 8-bit JPEG to a 16-bit RAW or TIFF file, as shown in Figure 5.3.

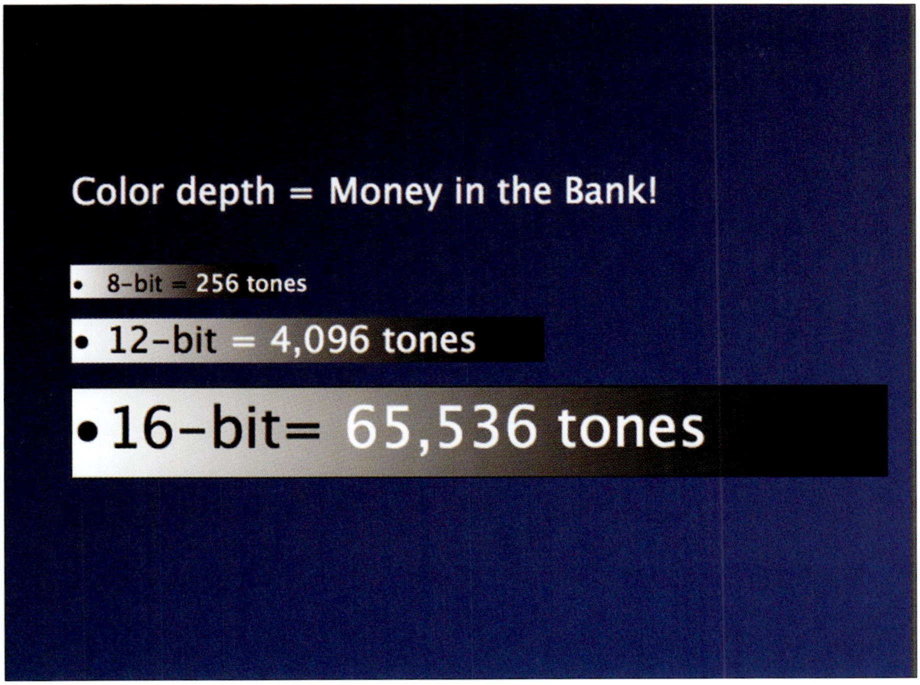

Figure 5.3

Example of 256 tones in 8-bit JPEG versus over 65,000 tones available in a 16-bit RAW or TIFF image file.

In some ways, the deck is stacked against photographers. Here are just a few examples of how small changes can combine in degrading image quality:

- In digital photography, the majority of the information in the image is contained in the brightest stop of the exposure. If you assume that there are six stops of information in the image file, (medium format digital backs have more), one stop equals about 15% of the total. *That stop contains roughly 50% of the information in the image.*
- Given that the brightest stop contains 50% of your image information, imagine what happens to image quality if you over-expose the photograph, even by a fraction of a stop. In fact, digital exposure is even less forgiving than shooting transparency film. Missing exposure by even 1/10 of a stop will often have significant effects on image details and color. Highlights, once lost, can't be regained.
- In most cameras, underexposure will increase noise, particularly in shadow areas. This includes increased luminance noise and color noise.

- Every image alteration that you perform, whether it is a Levels adjustment, correcting color, adding a photo filter, or the like, alters the information in your image. Most of these changes require the software to process the pixels, and in the course of doing this there are calculations and compromises.
- If you are scanning film to digital, remember that you are introducing at least one production stage that can degrade image quality in between capture and final production. No scan is perfect; some image quality is lost along the way. Scan to a small color space, and you give up even more of the range the film provides to begin with. Scan using major changes in color, tone, or contrast and you risk the same thing.

Given all these issues, the best way to control color in the digital world is to start with the best quality image you can and protect it every step of the way—which means that you should understand the tools you are using as well as what using those tools does to the color and details in your image.

Color Management and Studio Strobe/Flash Lighting

There are complete books on this subject, of course. The following list includes some tips about studio lighting that can help you keep your color under control:

- Studio lighting quality varies from manufacturer to manufacturer. Some are very consistent in color temperature, others are not. Examples of good, consistent studio lighting include, but are not limited to, Broncolor, Prophoto, Hensel, and Elinchrome. I also find the studio strobes sold by Calumet to be very reliable.
- For the best level of color control using studio strobes, borrow or acquire a color meter. These measure the color temperature of your lighting, making it much easier to keep color consistent.
- One issue that can come up with studio strobes is consistency and repeatability. Some units will be very consistent, flash after flash. Others, as they warm up, may change color temperature up or down. Flash tubes may change color temperature as they age.
- You can also mix studio strobe with so-called hot lights, incandescent studio lights that are continuously lit. Their color temperature varies from 3500K on up. Many people use these for color accents, particularly in portrait work as a hair light or kicker—they give a nice warm glow to the edges of your portrait subject.

Setting Up Adobe Photoshop Color Options

Adobe Photoshop, like many other image editing software packages, comes to you with default settings intended for the basics. It is a very powerful image editor, and you can get a great deal of mileage out of it with a few tweaks and adjustments.

Figure 5.4 shows the color management and color policy settings built into Photoshop as it ships from the manufacturer:

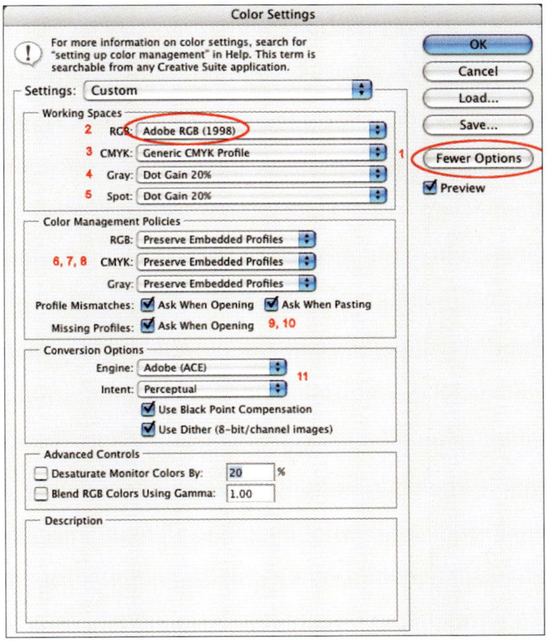

Figure 5.4

The color management and color policy settings built into Photoshop.

Note the numbered features (shown in red on the figure):

1. On the upper right, the default setting is Fewer Options. Click on this so you can see all choices available.
2. Working Space default is sRGB. This should be changed to Adobe RGB (1998) for photographers.

3, 4, 5. Leave these settings as they are.

6, 7, 8. Change these three to preserve embedded profiles.

9. Profile mismatches: enable ask when opening, ask when pasting.
10. Missing profiles: ask when opening.
11. Under conversion options, choose Adobe ACE, and for photographers, choose Perceptual.

After you make these changes, you'll find that when you open an image that has an embedded profile, Photoshop will ask you if you want to keep it that way or convert it to a different color space. Now you are in the driver's seat, and Photoshop will no longer make changes that you are not aware of. Keep in mind that some people don't like to have that little pop-up reminder—but personally, I feel more comfortable knowing what I'm getting into.

Managing Scanning Film to Digital

Interestingly, using a scanner and its software is much like using a RAW file converter. The controls and the steps employed in using them are quite similar.

Here's one important thing to keep in mind when scanning film: It pays to be conservative in scanner settings because once the scan is made, you are locked into your choices—unless you want to do the work over again. Personally, I prefer to get it as close to 100% as I can on the first try.

So unlike using Photoshop for image editing, which allows you to create non-destructive layer adjustments, a scan is a one-time deal (almost). Whatever is in the scan is pretty much locked in or, at minimum, will be difficult to change.

Here's what I recommend:

- I recommend dedicated film scanners for most photographers and artists, particularly if you plan to make prints 8×10 and larger. They are reasonably priced and give excellent results on 35mm and medium format film. Make sure that the film holder keeps the film as flat as possible. Clean the film before scanning using standard methods. (There are cream-of-the-crop flatbed scanners available that deliver amazing results, but at a high cost.)
- If you are scanning film that's larger than 6×9, a desktop film scanner may have difficulty keeping the film flat enough to give a sharp scan. In this case, it is probably best to use a drum scanner or the highest-quality flatbed scanners.
- Scan to Adobe RGB (1998) or larger color space. Don't use any automated color management tricks or tweaks.
- If you plan to edit and print the image later, scan to 16-bit TIFF format. This takes more time, but it is worth it.
- Make a pre-scan of the image before taking the time for a full-size high-resolution version. Look carefully at the histogram and make sure there is balanced exposure with no clipping. Make sure you look at the Red, Green, and Blue channels separately!

- If there is a gross colorcast, you can try to use the white or gray point tool in the scanner software to bring overall color back in line. I usually find that automated color correction will not get the job done.
- If available, use dust/scratch removal software. (Of course, the cleaner the film is, the better the scan will be.) One leading brand of this type of software is called Digital ICE. It is difficult to recommend exact settings for this, as each scanner differs somewhat. I recommend that you make a few trial scans, starting with low settings and working your way up. Watch for the balance between dust removal and loss of sharpness and details in your image.
- Keep your Levels and Curves adjustments to a minimum. For example, in Levels, I recommend that you start by moving the left (black) slider to the right between zero and five points. On the right (white) side, move the slider to the left between zero and five points. Examine the effect on the image, and in particular watch for loss of detail in the shadows (sometimes called "blocking up" the shadows) and loss of details in the highlights—for example, look for loss of texture in brightly lit, light-colored areas.

Figure 5.5 shows the Imacon Flextight scanner.

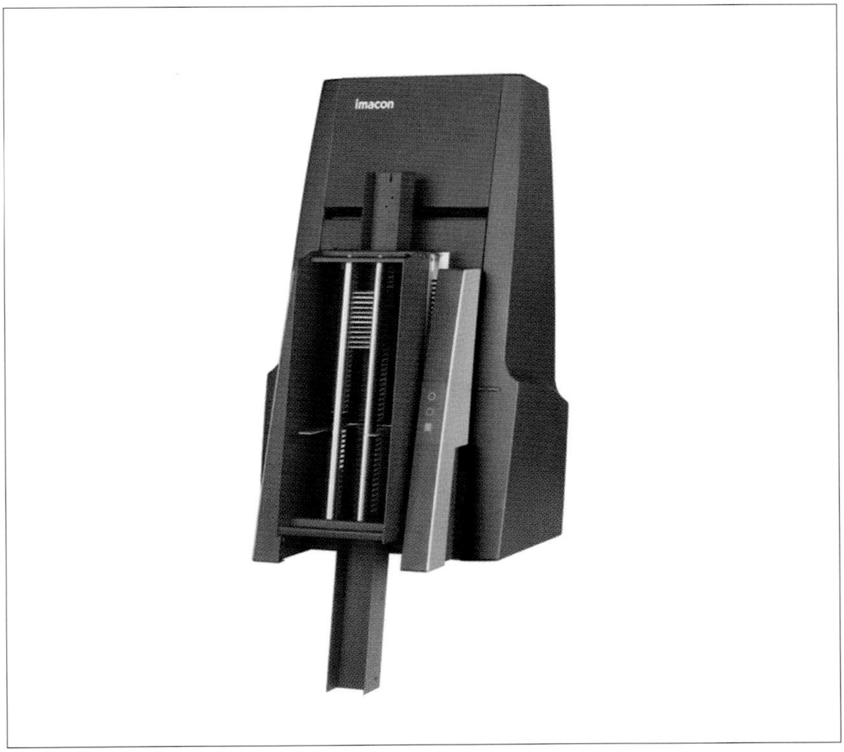

Figure 5.5

The Imacon Flextight Scanner line can handle a wide range of film sizes. © Imacon

Once your scan is complete, you can treat it like any other digital image file. I recommend that you edit in Photoshop or other high-end image editor and make your changes and edits using a layer-based workflow. Always save your images in TIFF or PSD format, not JPEG. This gives you the most control and protects your pixels from permanent damage.

In some cases, you will want to profile your scanner, or in other words, create a custom software description of how your scanner behaves when rendering color. Companies like GretagMacbeth and X-Rite sell color scanner targets and the software needed to convert the target scan into a usable profile. These work well with transparency scans, but not as well with negative film.

As a final note, in many cases the scanner operating software provided by the manufacturer is not as powerful as some aftermarket software packages, such as SilverFast. (One of the features I like about SilverFast is its powerful handling of color profiles and its built-in feature for calibrating the scanner using a standardized color target.) Although they can be expensive, trying a demo version of one of these software alternatives is a good idea if you plan to do a lot of scanning.

Basics of RAW File Processing

It's been said that RAW capture will let you change anything you wish in post-production. Well, that's not completely true. Some of the things you can't really change are the ISO (speed) rating and noise generated by the sensor. It's usually impossible to restore highlights lost through overexposure. And, as a practical matter, it *always* costs less in time and money to get it right in the camera, rather than in post-production.

For the most part, RAW processing is straightforward, particularly if it is being used as part of a color managed system. Please see Chapter 4, "Production Guide for Photographer" for more information on RAW image capture and file processing.

Many of the same caveats apply to RAW processing as to film scanning. However, one thing that is rarely discussed, if ever, is the issue of the quality of RAW converter software.

I have had the opportunity to use several RAW processing packages. Table 5.1 summarizes my opinions on their usefulness.

Table 5.1 Selected RAW Processing Software

Criteria/Type	Adobe Camera RAW	Phase One Capture One Pro	Apple Aperture	Adobe Lightroom	Canon Digital	Nikon Capture NX
Overall ease of use	4	4	3	3	2	3
Speed	4	3	3	3	3	2
Overall image quality	3	5	3	3	3	4
Noise control	2	5	3	3	3	3
Color correction	3	4	4	4	3	4
Lens distortion correction	2	2	2	2	3	3
Total	**18**	**23**	**18**	**18**	**17**	**19**

Note: A score of 1 is lowest; a score of 5 is highest.

Adobe Camera RAW is a good choice for general photography. It is provided with Photoshop at no extra cost, and it works with many cameras. However, for the best results in processing RAW images, I still can't find a software package that outruns Phase One Capture One. The user interface takes a little time to learn, but once you are past that, the software in my opinion produces the cleanest images from the widest variety of cameras. The Phase One software is available bundled with their digital camera backs or can be purchased separately. And, as good as the batch processing utility is in Adobe products, the Phase One software is easier to use—although processing large files takes more time, the result is worth the wait.

In processing RAW files, use the same basic strategies as you would with scanned film. Keep your changes modest, and save your high-powered image editing for a software program that allows you to use layers. Output your images as 16-bit TIFF or PSD files.

One special note: It is always best when converting a RAW file to leave sharpening off or at minimum levels. In many images, sharpening creates color aliasing or artifacts on high-contrast edges. You are better off using a selective sharpening technique in an image editor that allows you to use layers.

Recommended RAW processing workflow:

1. In camera controls set to Adobe RGB (1998) RGB or larger color space, use the RAW file format.
2. Copy images from a separate card reader connected to the computer. Do not format the memory card in the computer, only in the camera. Formatting the memory card in the computer can cause the card to have data errors.
3. Once images are copied to a folder on the computer, make a backup master copy on a physically separate hard drive, DVD, or CD. Do not rely on camera memory cards for storage.
4. Open the image using your RAW converter of choice. Pre-set your RAW converter to open images in the same color space they were captured in.
5. The first rough correction is usually exposure. Look at the histogram, and see if it is balanced. Adjust exposure accordingly. Note: If you find that you routinely have to make exposure adjustments of more than ½ stop, you should reconsider your metering and shooting policies.
6. Make your first global color adjustment. There are two main ways to do this: use a white balance preset built into the software (that is, daylight, tungsten, fluorescent, shade, and so on), or use an eyedropper tool to set a white or gray point. Shooting a white or gray card is always useful in color correction.
7. Look at the overall color, contrast, and detail of your image preview. Compare this overall appearance to the histogram. If your software allows it, look at the histogram for each color channel, Red, Green, and Blue. Ensure that there is no clipping in any channel, and that you have a balanced histogram across the board.
8. Specify your output file type and size. It is usually best to turn sharpening off or to minimize it.

The Impact of Computer Display Choices On Your Work

That low-priced flat-screen monitor that you saw advertised may not be the bargain it appears to be. Your display is an important link between your image capture and output. Here's an example of how important your display can be: A customer of mine asked me to calibrate a new display for her. (*Calibration* refers to adjusting the monitor so that it displays colors as accurately as possible.) I arrived at her studio and saw that she also had a brand-new computer, a printer, and a gleaming LCD flat-screen monitor.

Once I had performed the calibration cycle with my GretagMacbeth iOne, I found that the range of tones that the display could show us was limited—so limited in fact, that I couldn't see much of the details in image shadow areas. If she kept the display, it would be very difficult, or impossible, to see all the details in the image and to edit accurately. Luckily, she was able to exchange that monitor for a better one.

Some of the things that you should look for in your image editing display include:

- Brand—Is the display made by a major or second-level manufacturer? First-level manufacturers include, but are not limited to, Mitsubishi, NEC, Apple, Dell, LaCie, and Eizo.
- Nearly all monitors manufactured now are flat-panel LCD designs. The old CRT (Cathode Ray Tube) models are no longer manufactured, as far as I know.
- Is it an entry-level monitor, or is it a more robust design? If you look closely at the product description, you may see language like "pro" or the like. Price can be a reasonable indicator, most of the time. You usually get what you pay for.
- Generally, better monitors have a wide angle of view—in other words, color appearance and visible details don't change when your eyes move off-center. Most manufacturers claim a wide angle of view (170 degrees horizontally or vertically), but it is a good idea to see a monitor set up and running and see for yourself.
- Some monitors, such as the 30" Apple Cinema Display, may require an upgrade in the computer graphics card installed in your computer. This can be an additional expense.
- Many manufacturers make claims that their screen is very bright, and values stated in some cases are 400 cd/m^2 (candelas per square meter—which is a standardized measurement of luminance). That is much too bright for editing photographs; my Apple Cinema display is adjusted to around 90-100 cd/m^2.
- It's essential that the monitor design is flexible enough that it can be calibrated using a device called a *colorimeter*—more on this in the next section in this chapter—calibration failure indicates that a monitor is defective or too old for use in photographic editing.
- When considering any flat-panel display, insist on seeing it in operation, in a room lighting situation that is similar to your studio. Turn it on, and let it warm up for 15-30 minutes. Look closely at the screen—is the brightness of the screen even top to bottom and corner to corner? Some monitors have dark areas on the sides or in the corners. Are there bad pixels—a misbehaving pixel is one that is black or white all the time, or even a steady bright color.

Some of the monitors that you should consider include, but are not limited to, the following:

- Apple Cinema Display 23" and 30"
- LaCie 321
- Eizo CG 221

Of these, the Eizo is the clear leader, but the cost—well, the cost is very high as compared to the others. In terms of performance, it is very hard to beat. This kind of decision is best made after seeing the monitors in action—I even suggest you use some of your images that you are familiar with that will also challenge the equipment. It is a big investment, and one that you'll have to live with every day.

Note

I have not seen a laptop screen that can equal the color performance of a desktop display. I try to avoid doing serious image editing on my laptop for this reason.

Working conditions are an important part of the formula for success. I suggest that you work in a room that has low or gentle lighting. Strong glare from a window or light fixture will make it difficult for you to see the image on the screen. I don't like wearing light, bright colored clothing when I'm working because the reflections bother me—but this is a personal preference, and some people don't seem to notice this.

One last tip—I find that I see subtle differences in color best when I am rested and I have had an hour or so to become accustomed to the light levels in the studio. For me, prime time for color editing is in the mornings and early afternoons—and I find that image editing late at night is frequently a waste of time.

Calibrating Your Display

Most monitors come out of the box ready for use in a typical office environment, usually with business software, such as word processing and e-mail programs. The screens are very bright, and the color temperature and contrast are set high. Great for a lot of things, but not for image editing—so the first thing to do is to adjust and calibrate it.

Calibration is a word that scares some people, but it simply means that your display will show you colors that match an accepted standard. The display adjustment utilities that are provided with both Windows and Mac operating systems are adequate for most purposes, but they are just not as good as true hardware-software calibration.

The benefit is simple: first, you will be able to make image edits that are accurate—you should be able to see the results onscreen. Second, you should be able to use the monitor to preview your image as it will appear when you print it—this is called *soft proofing*. Soft proofing is an essential tool in color management.

A color-accurate display, properly calibrated, and using soft proofing will save you time and money. It will be much easier for you to see what your prints will look like before they are actually produced.

Several manufacturers provide display calibration products that you can buy separately. In a few cases, the display manufacturer will bundle the calibration tool with the display. Third-party manufacturers of display calibration tools include GretagMacbeth, X-Rite, Colorvision, and Pantone.

At a typical cost of a couple of hundred dollars or less, these devices are an essential part of your toolkit. They all include software that guides you through the calibration process. CRT monitors used for serious color editing should be calibrated every week and flat-screen LCDs once a month. See Figure 5.6 for an example of a calibration device mounted on a computer display.

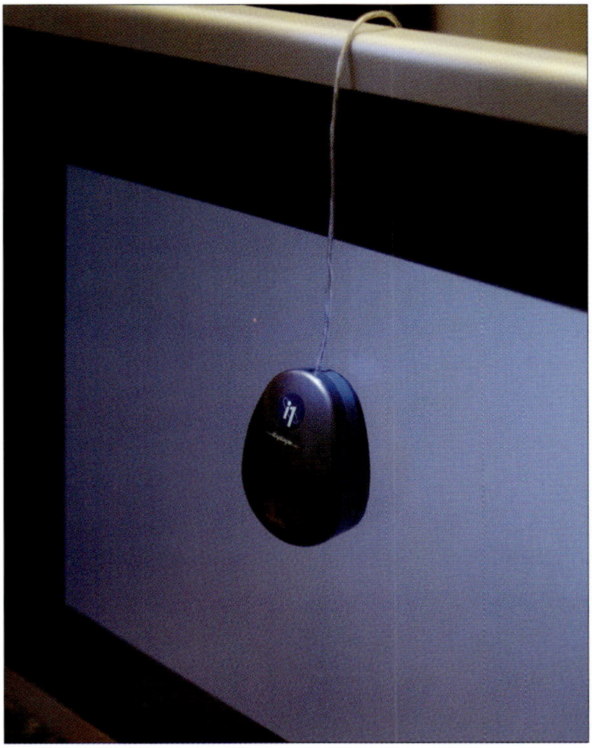

Figure 5.6

This is the iOne display calibration device, shown with the 30" Apple Cinema Display. I have both this device and the X-Rite Pulse system in my studio.

This is a brief summary of the calibration process, using the X-Rite system:

- Following the manufacturer's instructions, install the software on your computer.
- Most display calibration devices connect via USB cable. Use a USB port mounted on the computer, not on a keyboard or other accessory.
- Place the colorimeter on the screen according to the manufacturer's instructions. LCD screens are vulnerable to scratches and other damage, so take appropriate precautions.
- When you start up the display calibration software, the step-by-step instructions are very clear and easy to follow. Figures 5.7 through 5.11 show selected examples of the process.
- The software, when finished, will notify you that the calibration cycle has been successful. It will also show you a summary of the current display settings, and you will be asked to save the calibration settings. Save these settings to the directory the software designates for you.
- There's some debate in the literature about gamma settings (related to brightness), color temperature, and luminance. My personal preferences are 2.0 or 2.2 gamma, color temperature of 5500K, and luminance of about 90-100 cd/m^2. I find this allows me to edit comfortably for long periods and to easily compare a print to the image on the screen. Having said this, most people will tell you to set a Windows display to 2.2 gamma and a Mac to 1.8.

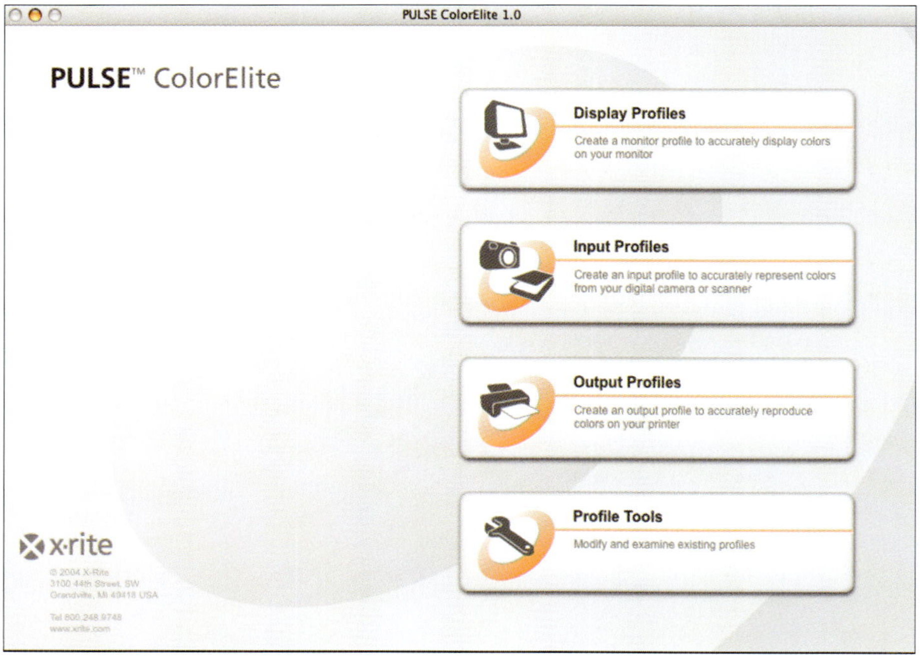

Figure 5.7

When you start up the display calibration software, you'll see this screen. Select Display Profiles.

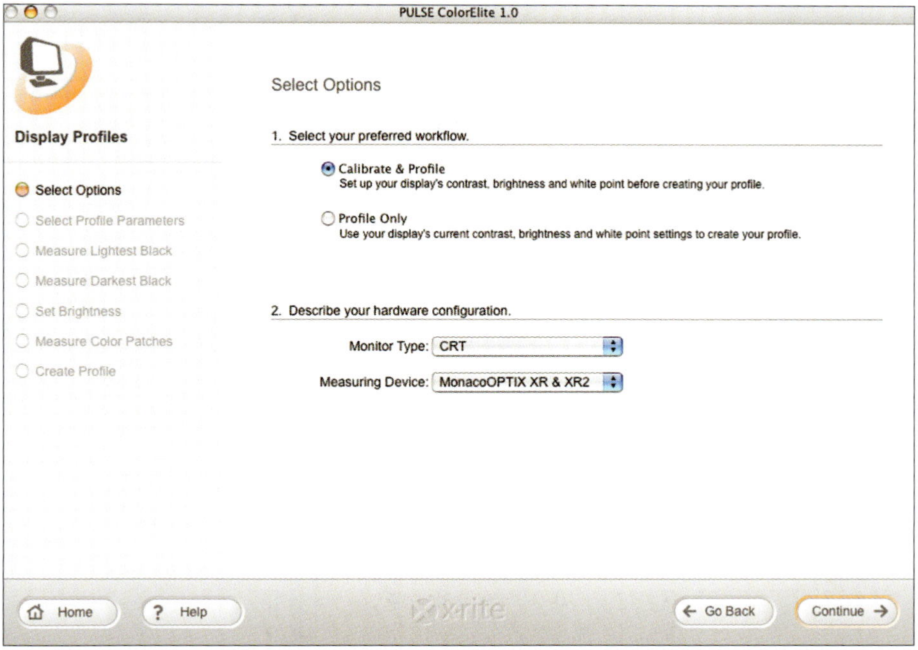

Figure 5.8

This screen allows you to choose Calibrate and Profile or Profile only. Choose Calibrate and Profile and your monitor type—CRT or LCD (flat screen).

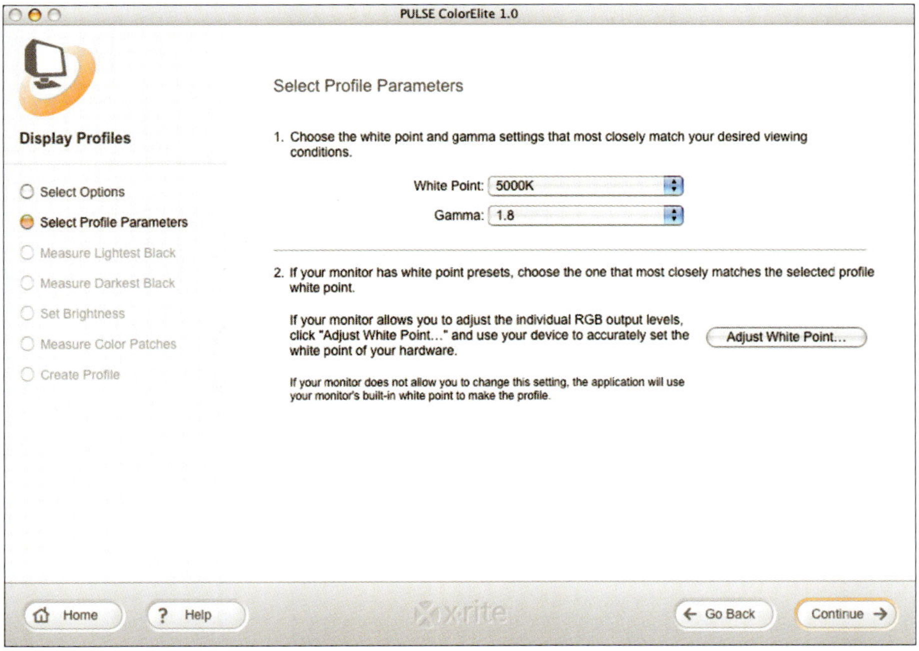

Figure 5.9

This screen provides choice of white point and gamma.

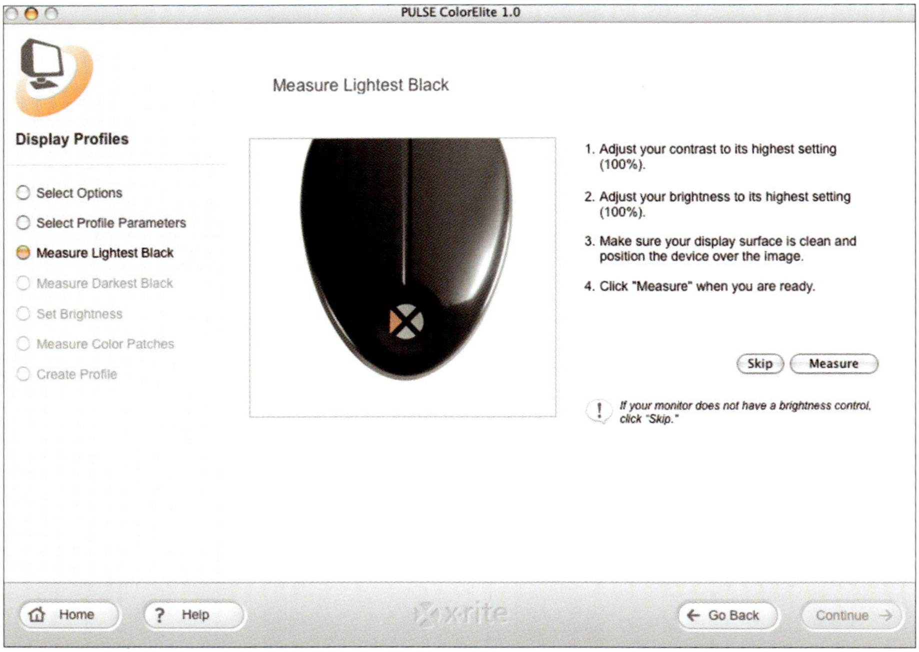

Figure 5.10

This screen walks you through adjusting contrast and brightness.

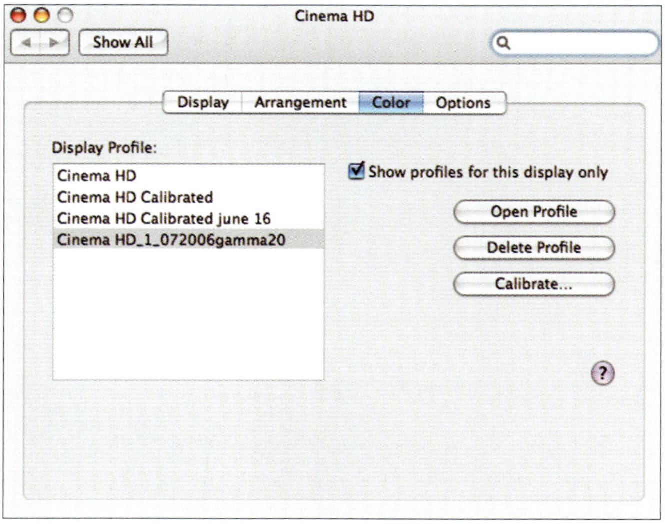

Figure 5.11

Your computer's operating system will allow you to change your display profile for different purposes. If you want, you can make small adjustments and try variations of settings in your studio until you find a combination that works for you.

Maximizing Quality Using Inkjet Printers

This topic has been the subject of a number of articles and books, among them *Mastering Digital Printing*, by Harald Johnson. In the remainder of this chapter, I provide selected topics relevant to photographers and artists when printing their own work. Also see the sidebar in Chapter 4, "Successful Printing from Photoshop."

One of the most important things to recognize is that a good print is the product of a chain of events that the photographer or artist has managed successfully. It's like building a house brick by brick—the bricks have to line up right and stick together to make the house strong.

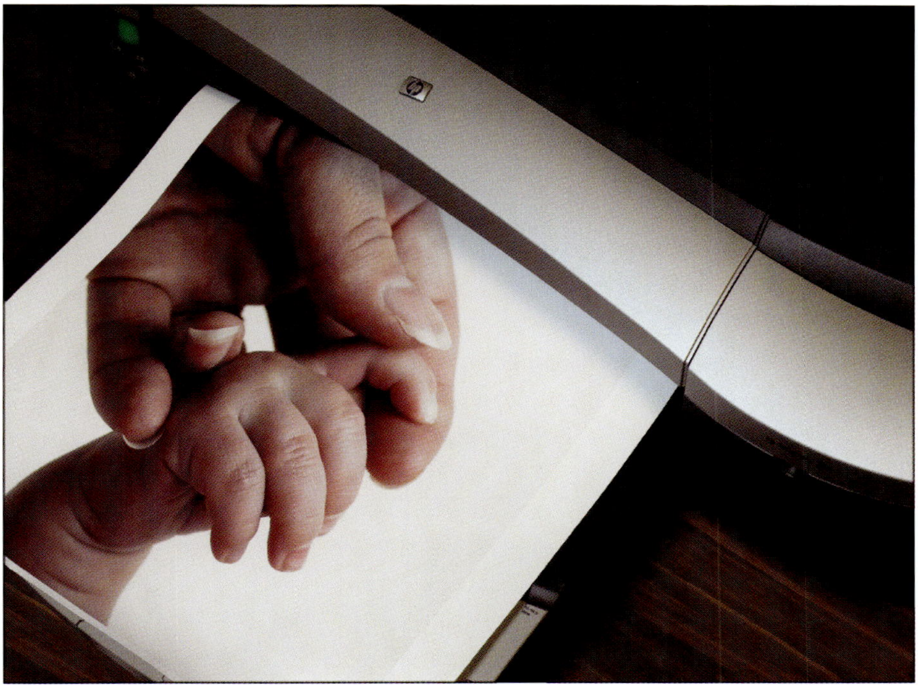

Figure 5.12

The HP Designjet 130 Printer produces archival-quality prints.

Color-management policies for printing, therefore, are partly based on the foundation you've built in image capture and processing. Reviewing that chain of logic in brief:

- Understanding the image capture and editing tools you use should improve the quality of your final product and increase efficiency as well.
- Generally, it is a good idea to plan image capture and processing with the end result in mind. Your choice of tools may be governed by the anticipated use of your image or artwork.
- It's good policy to keep your options open. By this, I mean that the more information and color that is present in your master image, the more potential it has for adaptation to new ideas or usage.
- Capture your images in a robust color space such as Adobe RGB (1998) and in high-bit format. If possible, keep the image in this state throughout the editing process and when archiving.

- Use a color-calibrated display while editing your image. This helps ensure that the colors you see on-screen are accurate.
- Use soft proofing in your image editor. Photoshop, for example, has excellent tools for this.
- In Photoshop or another image editor, send your image to the printer using the application-managed controls in the print driver, and use an accurate printer profile. See the sidebar called "Successful Printing from Photoshop" in Chapter 4.
- I recommend that most people use the printer manufacturer's inks and papers for final prints. You can use third-party papers for proofs and such, but it is best to stay away from so-called generic inks you can buy at many office-supply stores—they are inexpensive, but their quality and use in terms of serious art and photography are questionable.
- Having said this, there are specialty inks for use in printing black and white and other applications that are quite good; one example is the Lyson Quadtone inkset.

Soft Proofing

Once you have your display calibrated, and you have installed printer profiles on your computer, you can take advantage of one of Photoshop's (and other image editors') strongest features——soft proofing. Soft proofing is the ability to accurately view color, tones, and shadow and highlight detail on your computer display before you print. This means that you should be able to see what your print will look like, before you make it!

Soft proofing is intended to show you what your print will look like given the printer, paper, and ink combination you have chosen. This discussion assumes that you are using Photoshop for this work. Once you have opened an image (using the correct color space, of course), choose View>Proof Setup>Custom. You'll see a dialog box that looks like Figure 5.13.

The dialog box title is Customize Proof Condition. If you click on Device to Simulate in this dialog box, you'll see the drop-down menu that contains of all the profiles available that you've installed on your computer (this assumes they are in a folder that's proper and accessible for your chosen image editing application). If you choose one of these profiles, your display will probably change its appearance, and you'll see a difference in contrast and color in your image. If you turn the Preview option off, the image will change back again.

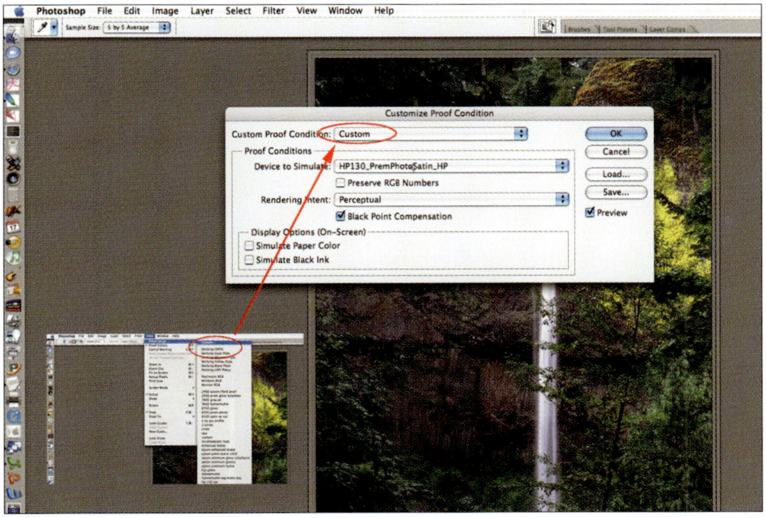

Figure 5.13

The Customize Proof Condition dialog box in Photoshop.

Generally for photography and digital printing you will want to leave Preserve RGB Numbers off and use Perceptual Rendering Intent. Next, you can save your custom profile settings for future use by clicking on Save. You'll see the dialog box shown in Figure 5.14 next.

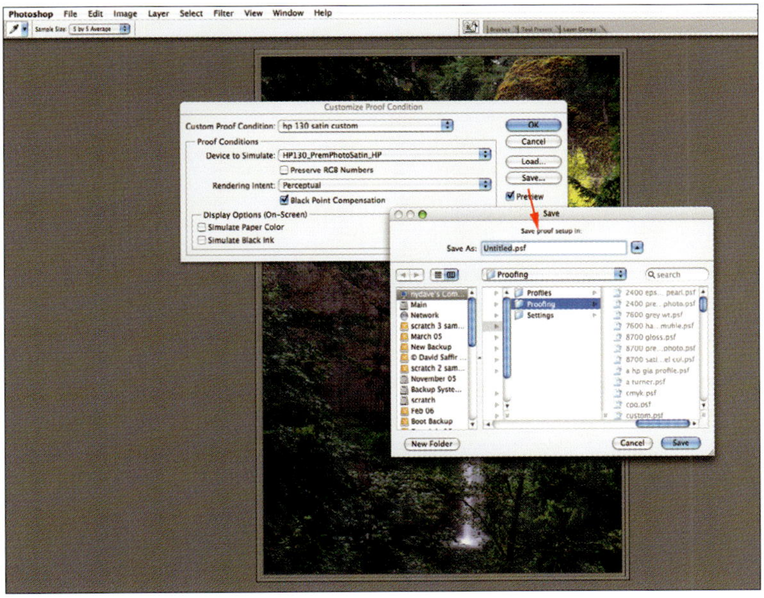

Figure 5.14

Save your settings with a name that you can remember so that you can use it in the future to preview and soft proof your image.

Another great feature of soft proofing is called gamut warning, shown in Figure 5.15. This will show you colors in your image that your chosen printer/ink/paper combination can't print accurately. After you have enabled soft proofing, you just choose View>Gamut Warning. By default, Photoshop will indicate the colors that are out of gamut (read: out of range) in gray.

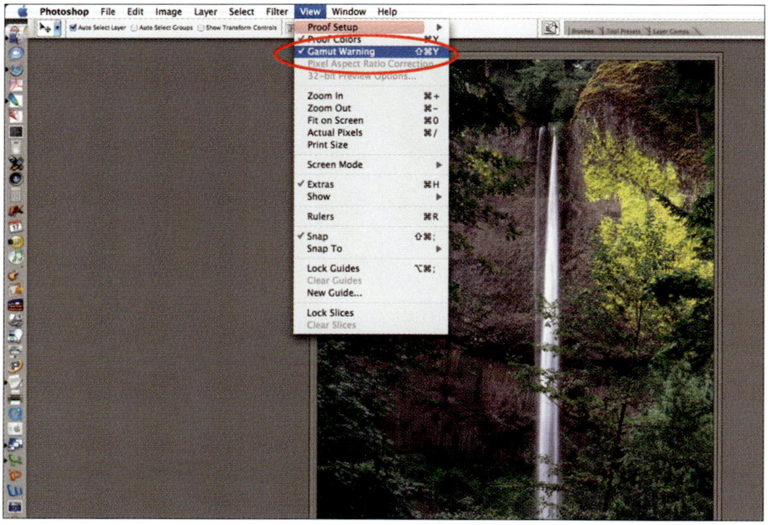

Figure 5.15

Photoshop indicates the colors that are out of gamut. Default settings show the out-of-gamut areas grayed out. You can set out-of-gamut warning to any color you want in Photoshop Preferences.

My personal settings change this warning color to bright magenta, which is a color you rarely see in the real world. To do this, go to Photoshop>Preferences>Transparency and Gamut Warnings. Change the color to anything you like. I've made a radical adjustment to the image, so you can see what happens when some colors are out of gamut, shown in Figure 5.16.

If you are using a good quality monitor and reasonably good profiles, you should be able to save quite a bit of time and money using soft proofing. You can see the impact of image adjustments in real-time, evaluate the "look" of one printing option versus another. This can easily reduce the number of proof prints you have to make. In my case, I have reduced the number of proof prints from 3-4 per image to just one or none. At over $1 a square foot, that adds up fast.

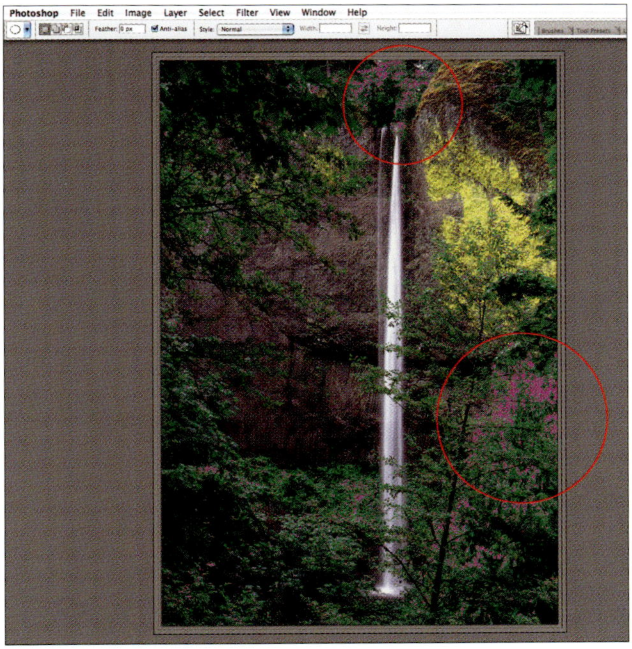

Figure 5.16

Note the colors out of gamut, as indicated by the magenta areas (also circled).

Viewing Inkjet Prints During the Production Process

The color appearance of inkjet prints sometimes changes with lighting conditions. For example, a good old-fashioned incandescent bulb is very warm in color temperature and can make a print look red, yellow, or orange in tone. Incandescent lighting, found in most offices, can make an inkjet print look green or magenta.

One straightforward but inconvenient way to help solve this problem is to take the print over to a window that provides indirect daylight. However, color temperature of light coming through a window can be inconsistent, depending on time of day, weather, surface light might be reflected from, and so on.

The best solution is a color viewing station. This is a frame that allows display of prints or other artwork under controlled color temperature. Basic models are set up to provide color balanced light at 5500K; more complex models can provide multiple light sources and color temperatures. Suppliers include GTI and GretagMacbeth.

Viewing stations are typically very bright, much brighter than your display. If your budget can support it, I suggest that you acquire a viewing station that has a dimmer switch on it. If you can only afford a basic model, you can place a neutral density gel over the lighting fixture to cut the luminance by a stop or two.

A color-corrected viewing station really helps streamline the production process. Some people I've worked with who didn't want to take the trouble to go with soft proofing, largely because of their studio lighting, changed their minds after they got their hands on a professional-level viewing station.

A fairly good substitute for a viewing station is a daylight-corrected desk lamp. These involve some compromise, as they are not originally intended for this kind of color critical work.

Color corrected bulbs have a finite service life; color accuracy may diminish over time. The manufacturer will specify the number of hours bulbs can be used before they should be replaced.

Viewing Inkjet Prints On Display

This can really be a headache for an artist or photographer. I've had plenty of experiences where my work was put on display in a room where the lighting made the prints look great, and other situations where the lighting made the color look quite strange.

The solution is color managed studio and gallery lighting. One company that provides a wide range of products for this purpose is Solux (see www.solux.net). They offer bulbs set to different color temperatures, and their products are used to display art, jewelry, and in other color-critical applications. Portable and permanent fixtures are available; quite a few artists and photographers I know use portable color-corrected lighting at art shows and other venues.

Specialized Software for Inkjet Printing

The best solution for color-managed inkjet printing is to use specialized software called RIP (Raster Image Processor). It lets you incorporate all of the other color policies you've implemented into one printing application—and RIPs allow you to save your custom settings to make it easy to consistently produce high-quality prints.

Most RIPs operate separately from image-editing software. Unlike printer drivers, RIPs have the following benefits:

- They can lay out multiple images for you on one sheet of paper or in a group on roll paper.

- Many RIPs feature drag-and-drop layout changes to these groupings, along with on-screen resizing.
- RIPs typically use custom print profiles. Like their cousins, the printer profiles provided by manufacturers, these profiles fine-tune and adjust the printer to render the most accurate, controlled color possible. The big difference is that a custom profile is tuned to just one specific printer—using a selected paper and ink set.
- Use of a RIP and a professional-level printer profile will enable you to get more out of some of your images. Images that include a wide range of tones and/or highly saturated colors will frequently show smoother tone transitions, better detail in highlights and/or shadows, and better color accuracy. In some images, you will see smoother colors and elimination of banding—for example, in blue skies.
- Additionally, many RIP software applications are better at making enlargements than the basic printer driver, particularly in sizes over 8×10 inches. There's no need to up-size in Photoshop.

Obtaining Custom Printer Profiles

There are a couple of ways you can obtain a custom printer profile: You can purchase one from a third-party vendor, or you can purchase the equipment to make it yourself. Unless you plan to use a very wide range of papers, I suggest that it is more cost-effective to have someone make your profiles for you. If you insist on doing this yourself, check out the GretagMacbeth website or the X-Rite website, and look at their spectrophotometer products.

A third-party vendor will make a profile for you in a few easy steps. First, they will have you download an image file to your computer. This is a series of color patches. They will ask you to print that target using specific settings for your printer driver or RIP. Then, you will mail that printed target to them, and they will scan it with their equipment. You'll receive the printer profile via e-mail, with instructions on how and where to install it on your computer.

Custom profiles typically cost $60-$100 each; by comparison, a spectrophotometer system can cost anywhere from $800-$3,000, or more.

Custom printer profiles are well worth the effort. They are almost always superior to the "canned" profiles supplied with the printer driver.

RIPS are provided by many companies, including some of the major inkjet printer manufacturers. Some of the better-known names in RIP software include but are not limited to Fiery RIP, Onyx, Colorburst, Colorbyte (ImagePrint), Caldera, and Wasatch.

The next section will show you the basics of working with a RIP; for this example, I've chosen ImagePrint, which in my opinion is one of the better RIPs for use by photographers. I prefer it because of its relative ease of use, decent graphic user interface, custom controls, and a wide range of printer profiles that are created by the manufacturer.

The ImagePrint RIP, shown in Figure 5.17, provides tools for multiple-image layouts on single sheets or roll paper.

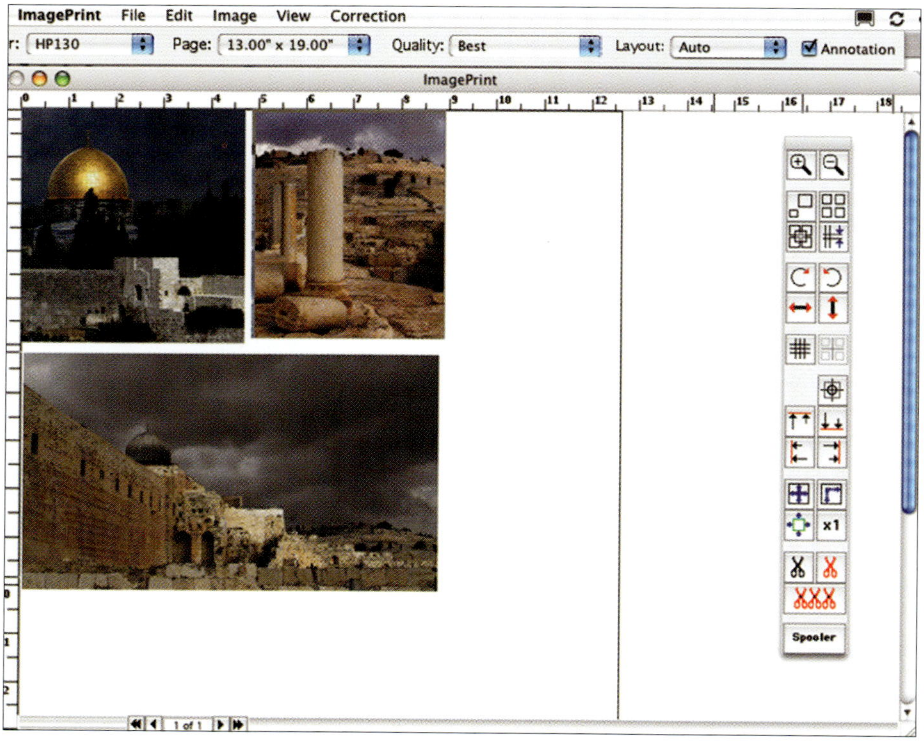

Figure 5.17

The ImagePrint editing screen with three images in a combined layout.

Figure 5.18 shows two dialog boxes accessible from the ImagePrint main menu. The upper dialog box contains controls for layout, margins, repeating images, and the like. The bottom dialog box is particularly important, as it contains the controls over which printer profiles will be used. Figure 5.19 shows the list of available profiles in the drop-down menu.

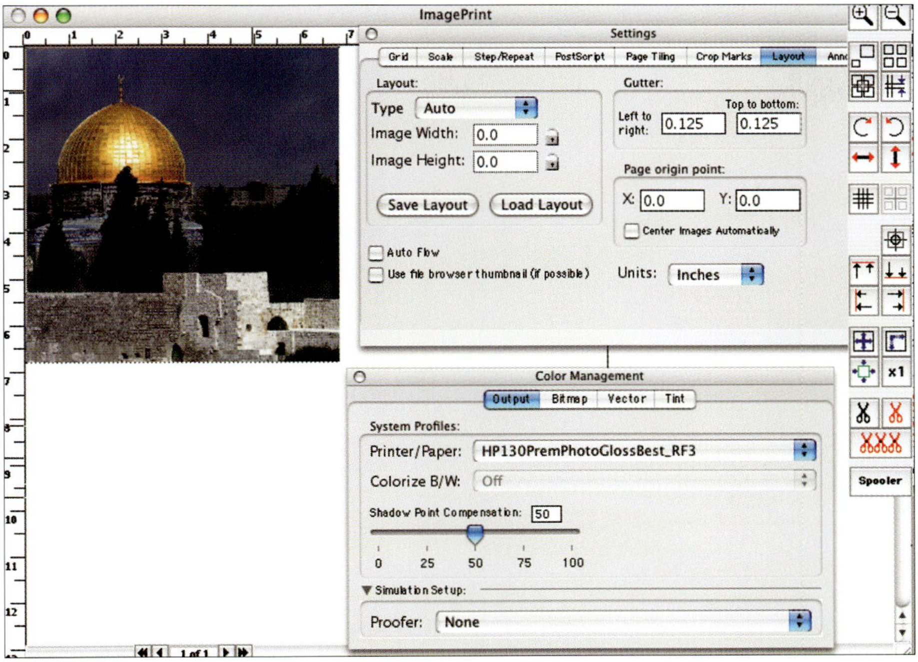

Figure 5.18

ImagePrint offers printer profiles for a wide range of printers and media combinations.

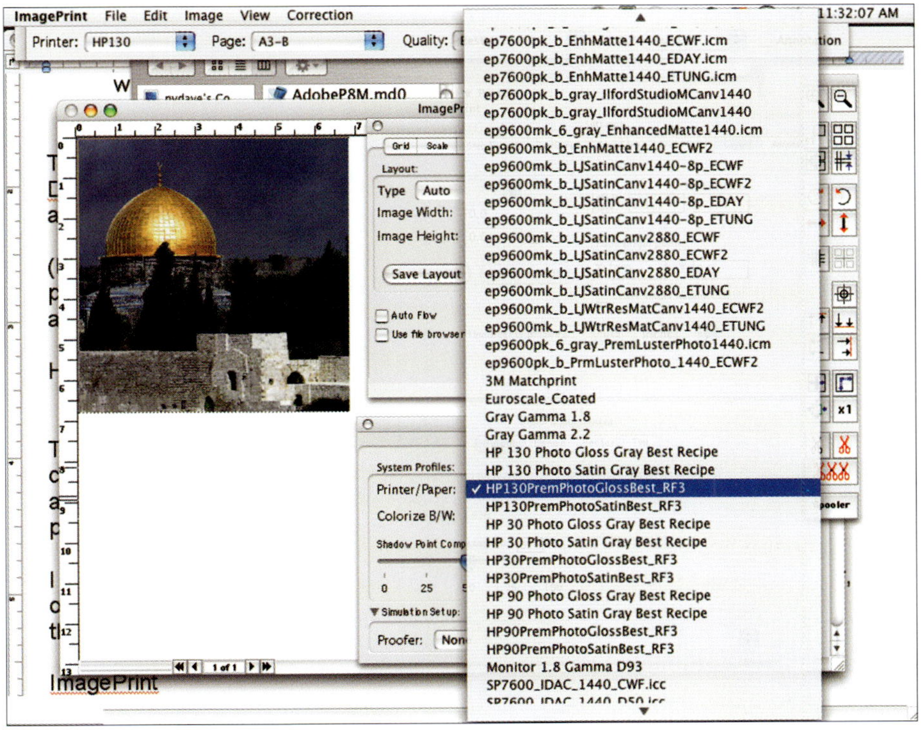

Figure 5.19

ImagePrint has a long list of available profiles.

ImagePrint includes curves and levels adjustments, along with sophisticated color tint and color correction tools. I normally make these corrections on a layer in Photoshop, but last minute tweaks are fine via ImagePrint. Figure 5.20 shows the Curves Adjustment dialog box. ImagePrint also includes soft proofing abilities.

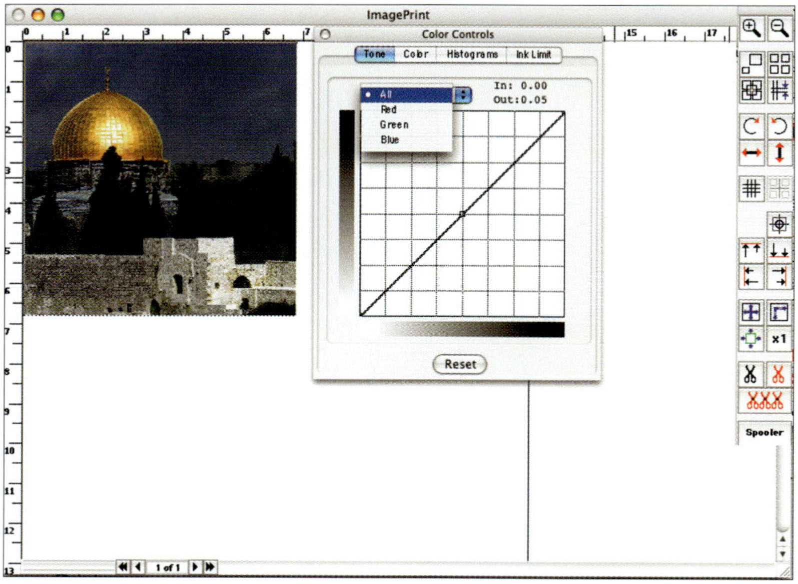

Figure 5.20

The ImagePrint Curves Adjustment dialog box.

Going back to the RIPs you might choose from, I recommend that you look for the following features and benefits: a good, easy-to-use menu system, flexibility in using different printer hardware platforms, ease of changing media types, ability to resize images, ability to place more than one image on a page and preview that layout, and quick and effective technical support.

Summary

This chapter reviewed the fundamentals of good color policies for photographers and artists. It is a building process, with a discrete beginning, middle, and an end. It does take some time and patience to dial everything in to fit your work and style.

As you move forward, look to the manufacturers and suppliers of these tools for training in the fine details and support. During your own product evaluations, insist on a live demo from a trained representative or a detailed training video so that you can really understand what you're investing in.

The next chapter is intended for photographers and artists who want to reproduce their artwork—and for those who want to do this work themselves or work through an outside print service provider.

6

Production Guide for Artists

This chapter speaks to several groups of people: It offers guidelines for photographers, fine art printmakers, and artists who want to reproduce paintings, drawings, or other types of flat art. These "specialists" may also be working together to produce a top-quality reproduction.

There are a number of advantages to reproducing artwork via digital technology. A few examples of these advantages include:

- Preservation of the original and its color, with reduced physical handling and no exposure to pressure, heat, or chemicals.
- Minimal risk in transportation or in exhibition.
- Tight control over color in the reproduction and, in some cases, a broader color palette than in the past.
- Availability of a wide range of papers, from canvas, to glossy, to fine art rag papers.
- Print-on-demand: In other words, there are no minimum or maximum quantities. There is no need to commit to making more than a few prints.
- Current high-quality printers are rated for fade resistance for 80-200 years, when framed and displayed properly.
- Last, and certainly not least, the artist can choose to keep or sell the original, confident that he or she can choose to continue to market and sell the artwork printed in a variety of sizes.

A marketable artist who was previously held back by financial constraints or a normal unwillingness to part with an original work is now able to choose to be competitive in the art world—even, perhaps, become profitable.

This chapter assumes that you:

- Are working from an original piece of flat art or a photographic print
- Have access to a high-quality digital or film camera or scanner and controlled lighting
- Have access to a high-quality film scanner (if you are using film) or appropriate flatbed scanner for larger art pieces
- Have consistent and accurate color controls from capture through printing
- Have access to a high-quality inkjet printer
- Have access to a print-making studio or shop that can provide the above

Expectations Are Everything

Most artists I have spoken with who want to create reproductions of their work have hopes that the original and the copy will be nearly indistinguishable.

It is important to recognize that a reproduction can only closely resemble but not really duplicate an original piece. As good as current cameras, scanners, and printers are, it is nearly impossible to make an exact copy of an original. There will always be some small differences between the original and the print.

Some of the things that can't easily be duplicated from the original include the full palette of available color and textures. Oils, for example, photograph or scan very well, but of course the depth and texture of brush strokes can't be duplicated on paper. You'll see the textures, of course, but highly textured prints may still look a bit "flattened" when displayed side by side with the original.

On the other hand, the contrast and color of many water color images can often be increased in reproduction, particularly if the capture, processing, and output stages are well integrated and the right paper is used for the final print. Figure 6.1 shows a reproduction of a watercolor painting from artist Greg Wilsey.

Note in Figure 6.1 that the original watercolor, which is a superb rendering of a Victorian-style house, shows very subtle colors and tonal ranges. The reproduction shows higher contrast and increased color saturation, which the artist requested. He's had significant sales since he decided to make limited editions of his work.

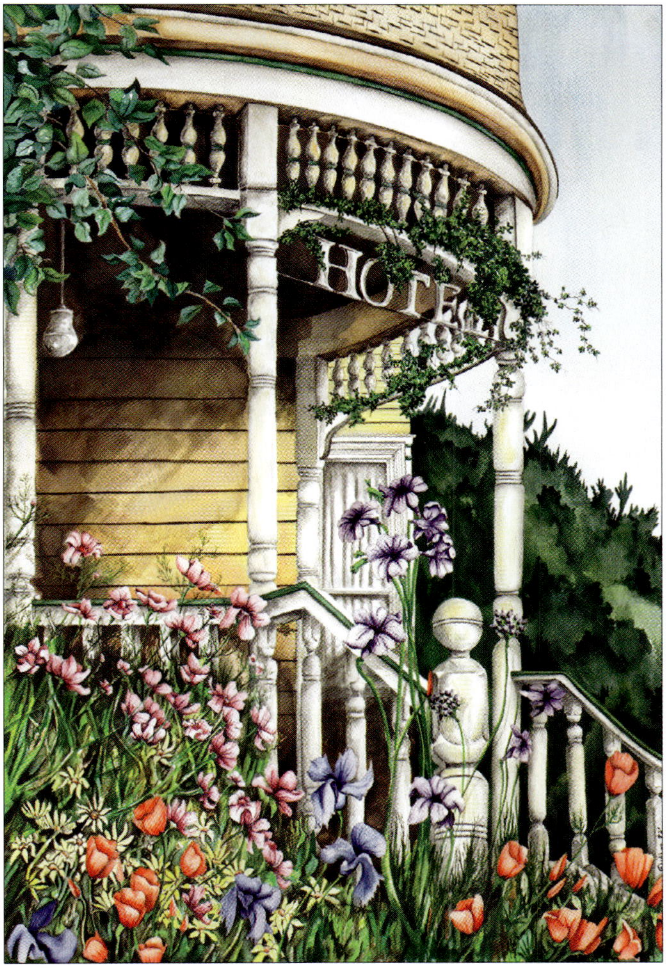

Figure 6.1

Watercolor by Greg Wilsey
© 2003, by permission.

So before you begin a work cycle, ensure that you have a clear idea of what you want from the end product, and understand media types, color fidelity, adjustments to color, contrast, and details. It is very important to recognize that there are some colors available to the artist that cannot be exactly reproduced via a reproduction printing process. A classic example is cobalt blue. If I'm talking to an artist about making prints, I point out that the print cannot exactly match the original.

In fact, it is my practice to have the artist view the original using a daylight corrected light source when they first arrive. Next, when the proof print is ready, I have the artist look at the proof under the same controlled lighting, before we compare the original to the proof. Last, we examine the two prints side-by-side. This helps the artist become accustomed to the changes, large or small, that may result from the process of capturing and printing an image.

The following steps outline the work process that can help you with this issue. This list assumes you are doing the work yourself. If not, please keep in mind that face-to-face meetings between artist and printmaker can be very useful:

- Decide who your target market is and what type of product you want to sell to them.
- Review media types available. Review examples of other reproductions of artwork on the same media, preferably from the same art category (watercolor, pastels, and so on).
- Understand where and how the reproduction will be displayed—overall lighting, light intensity, light color temperature, and so on. It is best to adjust the final print to optimize appearance of the reproduction under display conditions.
- Photograph or scan the artwork, process the image, and make a color-corrected proof for review.
- If you are working with a printmaker, be sure to schedule a face-to-face meeting to review the proof. Artist decides that proof is acceptable, in either case, and approves proof for color accuracy, correct media, range of tones, and detail.
- Repeat previous cycle if required.
- Final print or prints made. Proof print should be kept on file for reference when making additional prints.

Making an Image of Your Art: Options and Actions

There are a number of options available to you when capturing an image of your artwork. These include scanning, digital photography, and film photography.

Any of these will work well, provided the technology is top notch and the skill of the photographer or scanner operator matches the job.

Table 6.1 lists the different methods you can use to make images of your art.

Table 6.1 Image Capture for Artwork: Comparison of Methods

Capture Method	Pros	Cons
Flatbed scanning	Highly accurate; creates first generation image file	Cost, number of qualified operators relatively low.
Digital photography	Very accurate; moderate cost; creates first generation image file	Number of photographers with expertise and equipment relatively low.
Film photography	Probably most accessible technology	Scans create second generation image, production costs are probably highest of all.

Table 6.2 will help in setting up the job and making a successful reproduction.

Table 6.2 Details, Image Capture for Artwork

Method	Size of Capture	Bit Depth (if Applicable)	Film Stock	Final Output File Type	Color Space
Flatbed scanning	At least 300 dpi	16-bit	N/A	16-bit TIFF 16-bit PSD IRIS Graphics or equivalent	Adobe RGB (1998) or ProPhoto RGB
Digital photography	Medium format chip 6×4.5 22MP single shot sensor	16-bit	N/A		Adobe RGB (1998) or ProPhoto RGB
Film photography	Minimum is 6×4.5 (medium format), optimum is 4×5	Scan via Tango or equivalent to minimum 3000 ppi and 16 bits	Film w/ good neutral rendering point, such as Fuji Astia		Adobe RGB (1998) or ProPhoto RGB or Deke color space

Photographing Your Artwork

There are many issues to consider when photographing your artwork, including the lighting used, the camera and film used, and more. This section discusses these issues and how you can control them and make them work best for you.

Lighting

Artwork should be photographed using professional-level studio lighting. Some photographers endorse the use of continuous lighting, or so-called *hot lights.* Hot lights are tungsten or halogen based lights that resemble stage or theater lights. I recommend that the lighting used be professional level strobes that operate at 5500 Kelvin, such as the stand shown in Figure 6.2. Note that this is set up with a 35mm camera, and that larger stands are available for medium format cameras, and so on. See Chapter 7, "Color Quality Control," for more information on choosing a studio lighting setup.

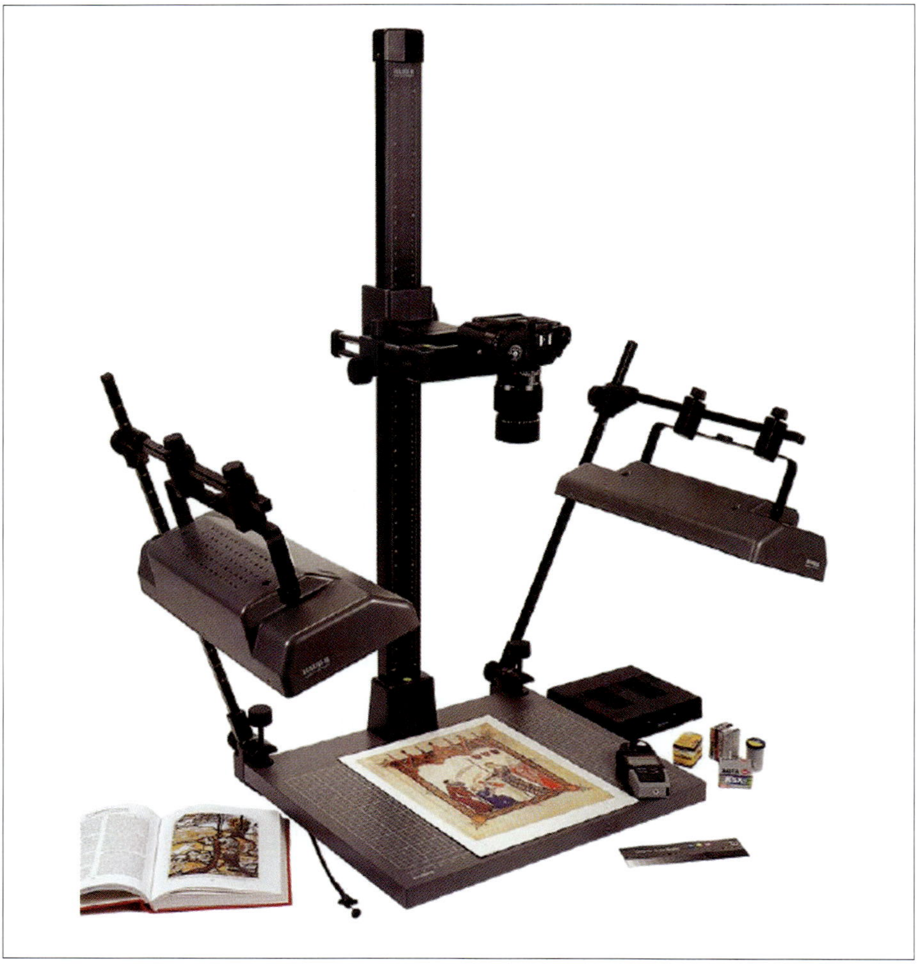

Figure 6.2

The Kaiser repro stand creates professional-level studio lighting best for photographing artwork. Photo © Kaiser Corporation.

In fact, I also recommend that strobe lighting color temperature be calibrated using a dedicated color meter, such as those made by Broncolor, Minolta, or Gossen. Studio lighting color temperature varies from manufacturer to manufacturer. Color temperature may change as the lighting equipment ages.

Lighting should be controlled so that the entire surface of the artwork is illuminated evenly and so that the lighting does not expose the artwork to excessive heat. Even illumination requires use of an accurate digital exposure meter, such as the Sekonic 358 or equivalent.

Figure 6.3 shows a schematic of a four-light setup for flat art reproduction. The four lights are set up at equal distances from the corners of the artwork and are aimed downward at the artwork at an angle of 45 degrees. Illumination is measured with an exposure meter. Exposure should be even across the entire surface within 1/10 of an exposure stop as indicated by the meter.

When you are metering during a project like this, be sure that you don't stand between one of the lights and the artwork. Even a small shadow can throw off your preparations.

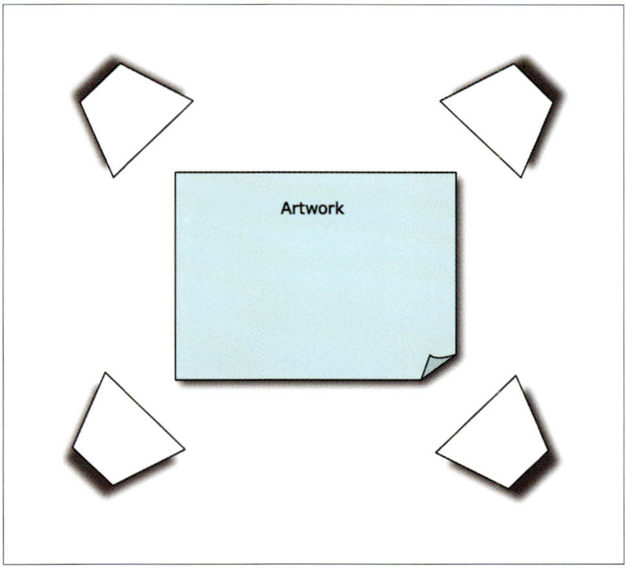

Figure 6.3

Schematic drawing of a four-light copying setup for flat art reproduction.

You can use two lights as well. They should be placed opposite one another, firing across the artwork. It is helpful to increase the distance between the lights and artwork in this circumstance, as it will help keep illumination even.

Measure the exposure of the artwork every few inches, top to bottom, corner to corner. I strongly recommend that there be no more than 1/10 of a stop exposure difference between any two points. Most flaws in exposure occur in the corners or on the edges of the piece. Variances in exposure, whether you are using digital or film capture, can cause distortions in color or loss of detail in the reproduction.

If your exposure is off in one area, adjust the lights. Remember that lights can be adjusted by electronic controls or just by moving the angle or distance of the light from the subject. Move or adjust one light at a time, and re-check with your exposure meter. If you think you will need to do a lot of this work, consider setting up the lights and photographing a number of pieces in one work session. If the pieces are roughly the same size and in the same category (watercolor, oils, and so on), the lighting will need only small adjustments during the session.

It is very helpful to shoot a gray card or a color checker card for color management purposes. This is also the type of work that can benefit from use of a color checker card. The color checker card has standardized white, gray, and black patches. You can measure either the gray card or the color checker card in Photoshop or another image editor using an Eyedropper tool or equivalent. The RGB values will appear on your screen in the Info window or equivalent.

The RGB value of pure white is Red 255, Green 255, Blue 255. The value of neutral gray is 128, 128, 128. Pure black is 0,0,0. If the RGB values are out of balance, there is a color cast in your image. If the Blue values are higher than the Red and Green values, you have a blue color cast.

The most straightforward way to calibrate the image to neutral is to choose Image>Adjustment>Curves and use the middle eyedropper (for gray) to click on the gray card and color-balance the image. There are many other ways to do this; see Chapter 4 for details.

Tip

One useful trick that you can use to help gauge exposure is to photograph the artwork on top of a sheet of white paper or mat board, the whiter the better (in other words, bright white, with little or no gray or other tints). Use the white background to create a white border around the image. Once you have imported the image into Photoshop, use the Eyedropper tool and mouse around the white edges of your image. If the exposure is correct, the values in the Info palette will be stable and will change very little. Try this yourself—look at the RGB or LAB values. (By the way, this is not a good way to color balance an image—use a standard gray card or color checker card!)

Cameras and Film

If you are capturing to digital, I recommend a 22MP, medium format digital camera, set for 16-bit RAW capture, using Adobe RGB (1998) or larger color space.

I do not recommend using any 35mm digital camera for creating captures of artwork that will be reproduced above 8×10 inches in size. Also, use of JPEG-type files in capture risks significant loss of image detail and color in the reproduction.

If you are capturing to film, I recommend using at least a medium-format camera using 6×6 film or larger. For all but the smallest size original artwork, use of a 4×5 large format camera with a high-quality lens will give the best results with film, provided that you capture to color transparency film that has a neutral color rendering point. One such film is Fuji Astia, which also scans well. Kodak and other major film companies also provide excellent films for this purpose.

You can use a 35mm camera with slide film to make slides for submissions to juried shows. This is an inexpensive alternative to the high-end captures described here. However, I don't recommend that you use these slides for reproducing your artwork—they just don't have the size to make anything other than small prints.

Photographers should, at minimum, use a gray or white card exposed at the beginning of a session and again any time lighting is adjusted in any way. This image can be used in Photoshop or other image-processing software to provide basic color correction.

In Photoshop, choose Image>Adjustments>Curves (see Figure 6.4), and then use the gray or white eyedropper to create basic color correction for your photo shoot.

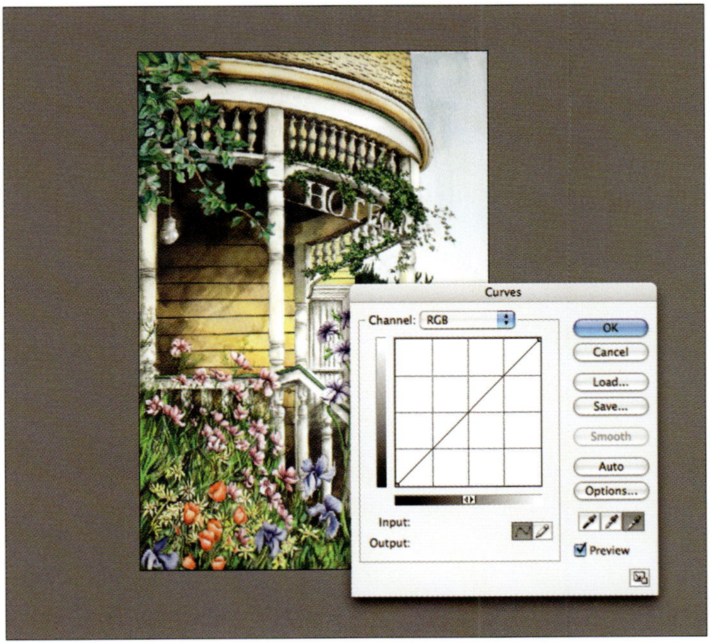

Figure 6.4

The Photoshop Curves dialog box.

Ideally, photographers will create custom color profiles for their camera and each lighting setup when creating images for high-quality reproductions. See Chapter 7 for more details on use of the color checker card in creating camera profiles (see Figure 6.5). (If you are photographing using film, use of the color checker chart is still recommended.)

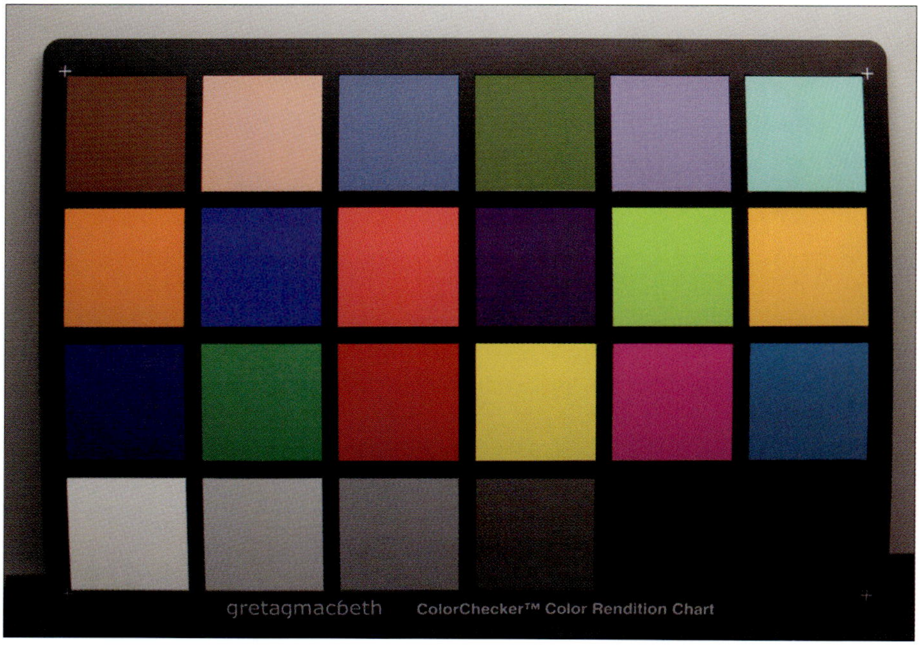

Figure 6.5

A color checker card.

Of course, film must be scanned. This creates a second-generation digital file, which must be carefully managed to preserve both color and detail in the image. See the following websites for additional information: www.nikon.com, www.canonusa.com, www.gretagmacbeth.com, www.xrite.com, www.phaseone.com, and www.imacon.com.

Scanning Your Artwork

It is possible to use a flatbed scanner to create digital images of flat artwork. Although it is far from ideal, even a small desktop scanner can be adapted to the task.

For example, you can scan a printed photograph on a flatbed scanner. It is possible to scan an even larger piece of work by scanning it in overlapping segments. The simplest way to do this is to have one or two assistants and hold the artwork over the scanner. They can then be stitched together in Photoshop.

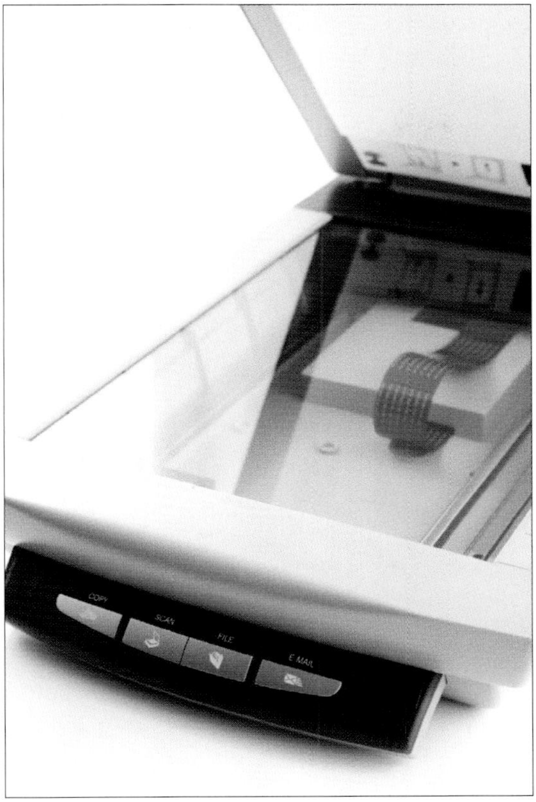

Figure 6.6

A flatbed scanner can be used for printed photographs, artwork, and printed documents. Some models are capable of scanning film. (Photo licensed from istockphoto.)

Dedicated, larger scanners will usually do a better job. Houses such as ArtScan (see www.artscans.com) use a custom-built scanner that automates the process of scanning a large item, creating highly detailed and precisely color-managed image files. Art scans can scan original artwork up to 44×50 inches in size. They can also scan larger pieces in segments and stitch the files together.

In any scanning, it is vital to understand that you should have to make one good scan. Make a master file for use now and in the future, of a size that is matched to the largest print you ever expect to make. Quality suffers, in color and the details, when a digital image file is "upsized" by adding pixels to a significant degree. Scanned files should be color managed as described earlier in this chapter. Basic image editing of the completed scan, as described in Chapter 4, is also required.

Generally speaking, this will result in very large image files. There is some inconvenience and expense involved in creating files of this size. However, the overall cost is much less than when you have to repeat a scan of a popular piece of art simply because you want to create a new edition at a larger size.

Successful Printing from Photoshop

Printing from Photoshop is not as easy as I'd like it to be. First, the Photoshop default settings are not really suitable for high-quality photographic output. I recommend that you use the following steps to obtain improved results:

1. First, get it right in the camera! There's no substitute for a good image.
2. Next, make sure that you capture and edit the image in Adobe RGB (1998) working space, at minimum.
3. Set up your image resolution to match that of the printer—if Epson, 360 ppi is best, if HP, 300 ppi.
4. It doesn't matter much as far as print quality is concerned if your image is in 8-bit or 16-bit format. I do recommend that your master image be kept in 16-bit for major editing and archiving, but there's nothing wrong with printing from an 8-bit file.
5. Although there are many good alternatives available on the market, I still recommend that you use the manufacturer's ink and paper for your prints, at least until you feel as though you completely understand the behavior of the printer and the way it renders your images. Once you have mastered that, feel free to experiment.

Assuming you will be using the manufacturer's inks and papers and that you've set up the printer according to the manufacturer's instructions, we'll move on to printing your image from Photoshop, using the printer driver.

1. First, with the image open in Photoshop, choose File>Page Setup. Choose the correct printer, paper size, and whether you want landscape or portrait orientation.
2. Next, choose File>Print with Preview. This opens a new dialog box that looks like Figure 6.7.
3. On the upper-left corner of this dialog box, you'll see a thumbnail preview of the image you want to print. (Please keep in mind that this preview is not color corrected and should not be used to predict color rendering in your print.) Immediately below this is a drop-down menu that offers you the choice of Color Management or Output. Choose Color Management.

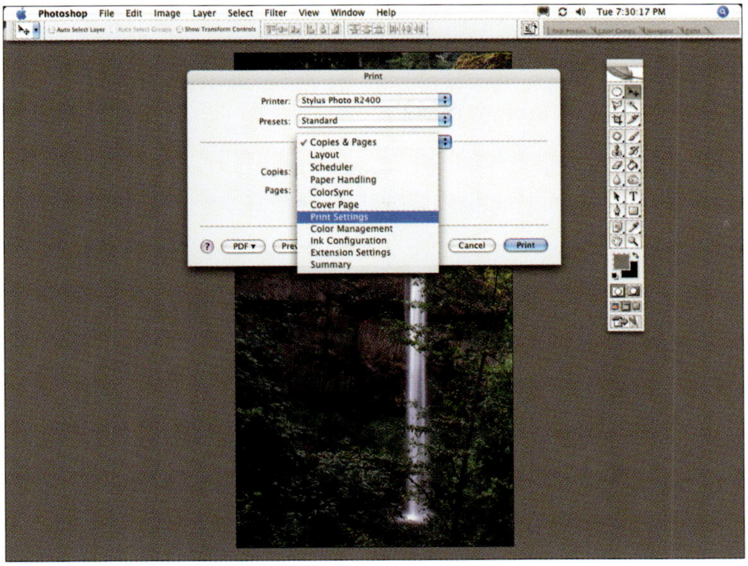

Figure 6.7

The Print with Preview dialog box is your primary gateway to producing good color in your prints.

4. Next, immediately below this, you will see a section of the dialog box that is titled Options. It contains three drop-down menus: Color Handling, Printer Profile, and Rendering Intent. Your settings should be:

   Color Handling: Let Photoshop Determine Color

   Printer Profile: Choose your specific printer/paper combination (for example: HP PS 8700, Premium Photo Paper, or the Epson Stylus 2400—Premium Glossy). These printer profiles were loaded into your system when you installed the printer driver.

   Rendering Intent: In most cases, use Perceptual. You can experiment with the other rendering intents, but 99 times out of 100 you'll find Perceptual gets the job done.

5. Be sure you scale the image to the output size you want. This part of the dialog box is located dead center and is pretty straightforward to use.

6. Click Print, which will take you to a new dialog box. At the top of this dialog box, you'll see the Printer drop-down menu, and just below it, the Presets drop-down menu.

7. If you click on the Presets drop-down menu, you'll see the a list of driver choices. Mouse down to Print Settings, and the dialog box will change to what is shown in Figure 6.8.

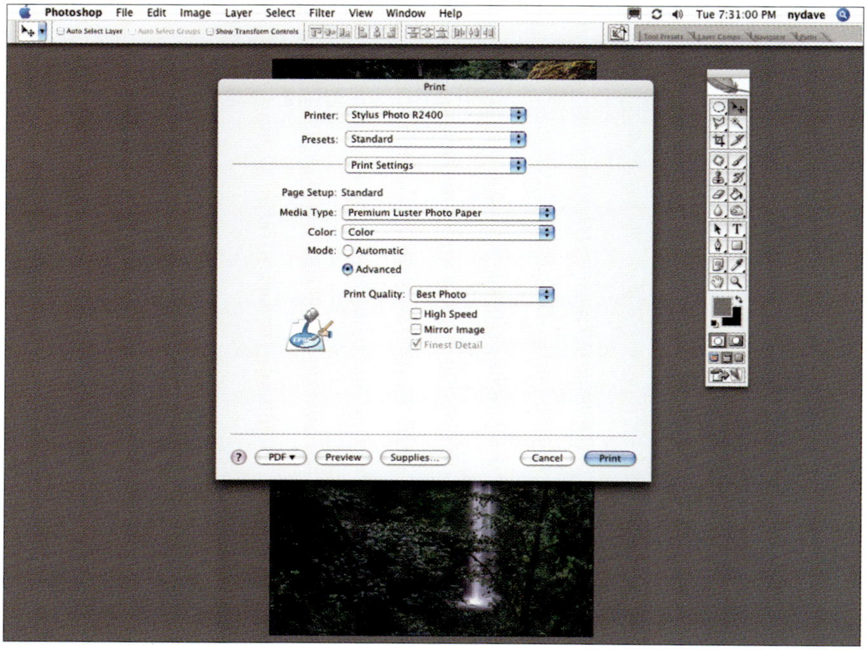

Figure 6.8

Choosing your print settings.

8. Under Media Type, choose the paper you are using—be sure to match the name the manufacturer gives the paper you are using. An incorrect setting here will cause your print color to look distorted.

9. Under the Color drop-down menu, choose Color. Under Mode, choose Advanced.

10. Under Print Quality, choose Best Photo. Disable High Speed, as this setting can degrade print quality.

11. Now, go back up to the top of the dialog box, and in the Print Settings drop-down menu, click and hold—the drop-down menu will reappear—choose Color Management.

12. Now, just choose Color Controls Off.

13. Now, to make sure that you can use these settings again, click on the Presets drop-down menu, mouse down until you see Save As, and save these settings for future use.
14. Click Print, and voila!!

A last note—there are some small differences between choices available in the printer driver that's installed with Epson printers, HP, or Canon. Don't let that throw you—the menu choices are close enough that you're sure to get it right.

Note

A few notes on printing: this book is not intended to be a how-to guide for printing. I strongly recommend that artists, photographers, and printmakers use paper/ink/printer combinations that have been professionally rated for color fastness (see **http://www.wilhelm-research.com/**) and a color-managed image-editing and printing system.

For more information, see Chapters 4 and 5 in this book. Also, see *Mastering Digital Printing, Second Edition*, by Harald Johnson.

Evaluating and Managing Quality

Quality management is one of the more important parts of the process of art reproduction. It involves two major activities: managing quality of the image capture and managing quality of the final print.

The following sections provide summary checklists of issues related to managing color quality in image capture and printing, respectively.

Quality Issues when Capturing Images

The following list provides a review of key issues relevant to capturing your artwork:

- Is the digital sensor at least 17MP, and preferably 22MP+? Is it mounted in a medium-format or large-format camera?
- Is the photographer using top-quality lenses, such as Zeiss, Fuji, Schneider, or an equivalent?

- Is the created image free of visual defects, such as lens distortion (barreling or pincushion), color shifts or color fringing, or vignetting (darkening in the corners)?
- Are there any hot spots, or areas that are too bright on the image? Is the image too dark overall (underexposed) or too bright (overexposed) as compared to the original? See Figure 6.9.

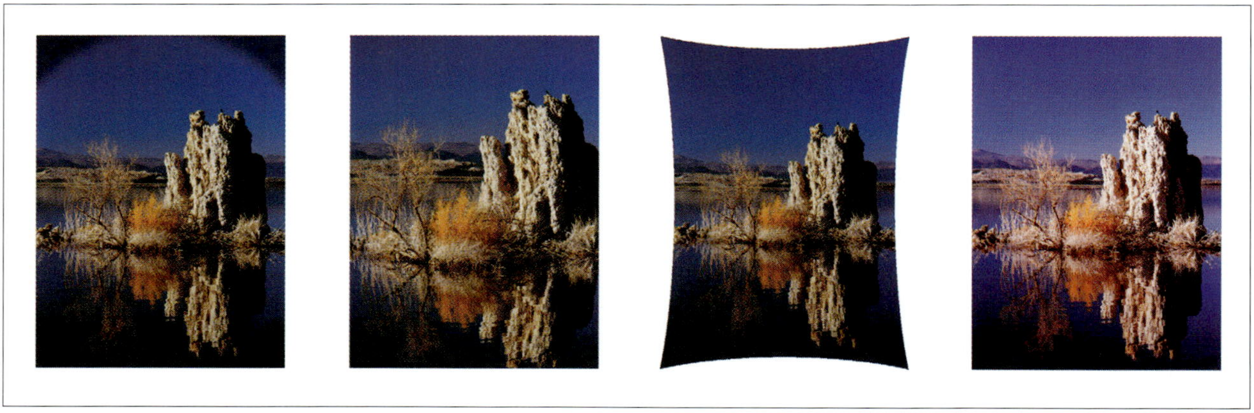

Figure 6.9

From left, this collection shows vignetting (darkening in the corners), barreling (bulging), pincushion (pinching), and uneven exposure with color shift toward magenta.

- Is the created image clean? Is it in focus from corner to corner, overall color neutral, and the like? Viewed in neutral daylight or in a color-controlled light table or display, are the colors pleasing to the eye and reasonably accurate?
- Is the photographer using a mainstream film manufacturer's product, that has a valid date stamp and has been stored in temperature-controlled conditions?
- Is the scanner used for film a drum scanner or virtual drum scanner manufactured in the past five years? Is the scanner operator a skilled professional with experience in scanning film intended for art reproduction?
- Is the created image file stored in 16-bit format, Adobe RGB (1998) or better?
- Is the capture process color managed? In other words, does the photographer or scanner operator use color charts and/or custom profiles for the camera or scanner?
- Does the transparency, or the image viewed on a color-calibrated display, provide a color palette and range of tones very close to the original artwork?
- Special areas to check: skin tones, blue sky colors, foliage, any edge or corner, and areas of high contrast (light color next to dark colors).

Quality Issues when Printing Images

The following list provides a review of key issues relevant to printing your artwork:

- If you are using an outside print provider, does the person controlling the printing have a working environment that provides a color-calibrated display, custom profiles for each ink/paper/printer combination, and the capability to provide both on-screen proofing and proof prints on the paper to be used on the final print?
- Do you have access to a variety of media, such as high-quality inkjet canvas or art paper?
- Does the printer you are using, along with the media/paper, provide print life of at least 50 years, and preferably 75 years or more? Is this print life validated by an organization separate from the ink/paper manufacturer?
- Is the paper of recent manufacture, within the past 6-12 months? Has it been stored in a light and temperature controlled environment? Just like photographic papers, inkjet papers will deteriorate in high temperatures.
- On inspecting the print, look for dust spots, scratches, or irregularities in the image or the paper, uneven or distorted color, overall sharpness, and good contrast. For example, check high-contrast areas, such as adjacent dark and light tones. See Figure 6.10.

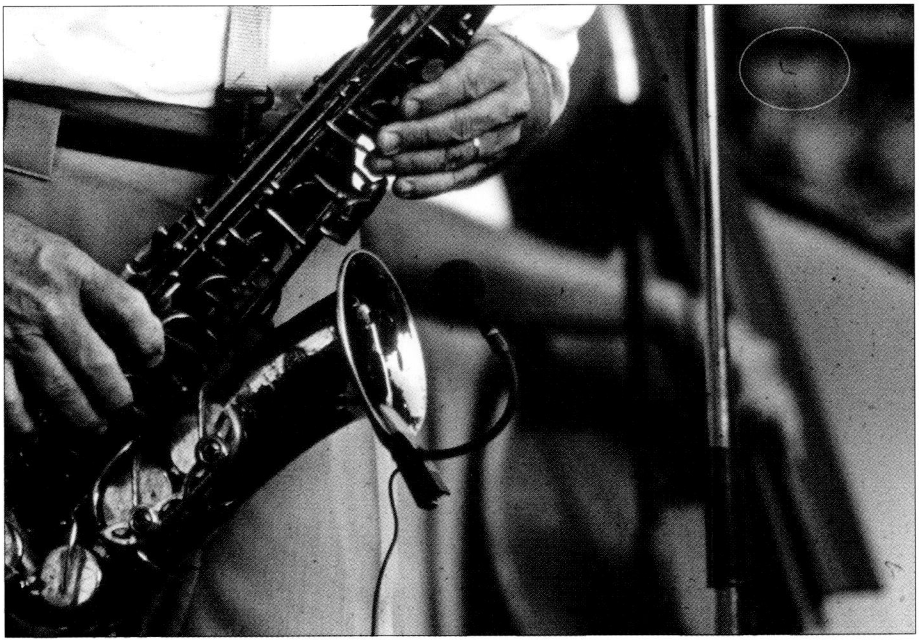

Figure 6.10

An example of dust spots on a scan of black-and-white film.

- Check large areas of color, such as images of sky or water, for smooth color tones. Inspect for color banding, or "stair-stepping," and uneven color across these areas. See Figure 6.11.

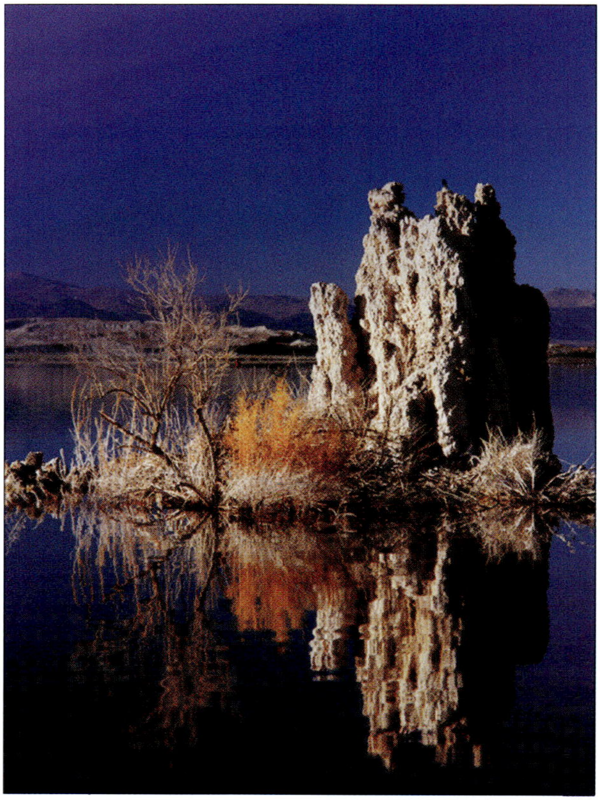

Figure 6.11

This is an example of banding in the sky. Also notice the color distortion in the blue tones.

- Key areas to check for color fidelity include known color values, such as skin tones, blue sky, green foliage, and white objects. See Figure 6.12.

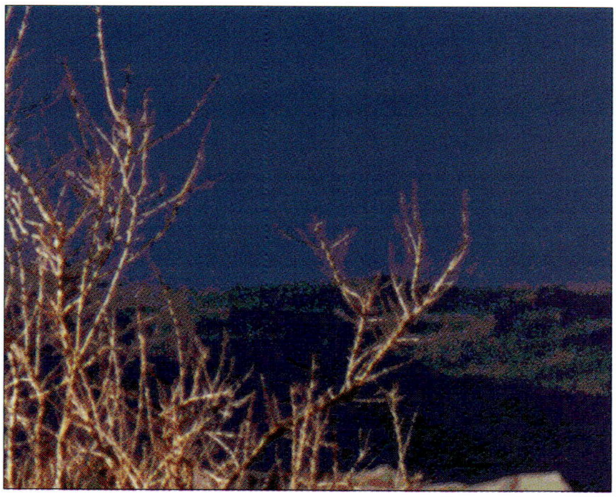

Figure 6.12

This is an example of posterization and color fringing. Notice the color changes in the sky around the tree branches.

Printing On Demand

Unlike previously available reproduction systems, digital printing allows for what I call "print-on-demand." This means that you can make just one print at a time, and in a color-controlled work environment, come back a year later and make a print that is, for all practical purposes, identical to the first reproduction.

In the past, the cost of reproduction printing setup and related work was so costly that it made economic sense to make dozens or even hundreds of prints in a first edition. That is no longer necessary. If you want one print or a hundred, this should be possible using current materials, capture technology, and color management systems.

Put another way, the cost of making high-quality reproductions of artwork has now fallen from thousands of dollars to a few hundred dollars. Combine this with the extension of practical print life, and we have an art market that's in some ways more accessible to the emerging artist.

However, to ensure consistent quality, you should use the same image file, color controlled workspace, ink, paper, and printer type. Ideally, use of the same physical machine will help, too.

One thing to keep in mind is that, although print-on-demand offers almost unlimited access to any size edition of your prints, the market price of your art reproductions is strongly connected to how many printed reproductions are available, or will become available.

For example, some artists will price the first prints in an edition at what they feel is marketable level. They also announce that as the print sells, and the edition becomes more popular, they will raise the price. This encourages new buyers, as they may feel that their investment will grow as the edition sells.

Other artists may announce that the edition is composed of a specified number of prints, at a specified price. The prints will go up in price only if they are resold, or if the bidding is enthusiastic enough to encourage the galleries to raise the pricing.

The big benefit of print-on-demand is that the artist can begin an edition at a much lower cost than was previously possible; in the past, printing technology and the cost associated with it dictated that it was more cost effective to make a large quantity of prints. This happened because setting up a press was very time consuming and expensive, and the cost of media for a large number of prints was comparatively insignificant. Now, inkjet printing allows artists to make prints almost any time, in smaller quantities.

Legal Issues Related to Art Reproduction

In some states, such as New York and California, the law requires disclosure of key information about any artist's release of reproductions, including photographers. Examples of requirements include:

- The name of the artist
- Whether the artist is alive or deceased
- Whether each reproduction is identified by the artist's signature or a stamp
- The printing process used
- The year in which the edition is first published
- The number of prints intended for the reproduction

This is not a complete list. There are many resources and publications on this topic. Examples include the Art Publishers Association at http://pmai.org/apa/standards.html and "Fine Art Limited Edition Print Disclosure Laws" by Joshua Kaufman at http://www.jjkaufman.com.

Storing Digital Images

There is a great deal of debate over storing digital images over time. Although this is not a pure color-management issue, loss of the digital master file is very much like destroying a film transparency or negative.

There is one important difference between physical storage of a transparency or negative and a digital file. Film may deteriorate, and colors degrade over time. If they do suffer some losses, in many cases restoration is possible. Digital files, however, are pretty much intolerant of abuse. Even small data loss can cause a digital file to become unusable. So, this is not just a matter of color control—it is a matter of preserving the entire image.

Issues related to this include:

- Physical storage of the file. There is disagreement among experts about how to store the file and which media to use. We can choose between traditional film storage, copying digital files to CD or DVD, or to magnetic storage on disk or tape.
- Only a small minority of currently made CD and DVDs will protect digital data for more than a few years. So-called hard storage, such as digital memory cards, are rated only for a few years.

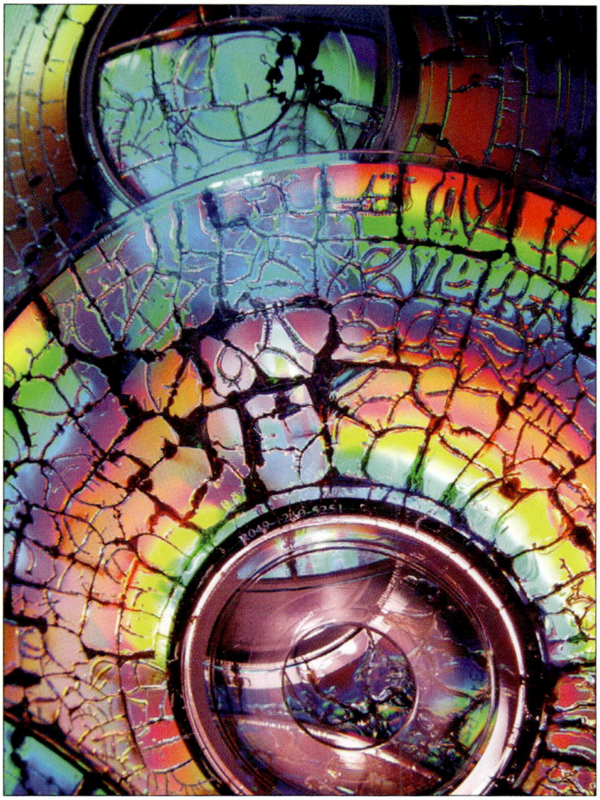

Figure 6.13

This is a CD that has been exposed to high temperatures. (Photo licensed from istockphoto.)

- Some plastic cases manufactured for storing CD and DVDs are made from non-archival petroleum-based plastics, which out-gas in a way that destroys the disk over time.
- Digital file formats are changing constantly. Many have become obsolete, and new technologies are being developed every day. Some experts are concerned that some digital images, stored using older file formats, will soon become so outdated that they are unusable.

The best protection is a multi-layered plan. I suggest that you archive important digital images just as you would other critical data:

- Store duplicate data in two physically separated locations.
- Physical storage locations should be protected in the usual ways, from theft, fire, water, and other threats. Ideally, the storage environment is dark, cool, and dry.
- Use at least two digital file formats. In my opinion, at least one of these should be TIFF file format. Proprietary RAW file formats carry some risk of becoming obsolete and unusable.

- Use at least two digital storage media. I currently use archivally rated CDs for critical image storage, duplicated on at least one or two portable hard drives. In other words, there are at least three copies of each critical image.

This is a relatively expensive, labor-intensive requirement. However, I feel that my critical images are like cash—I put them in a safe place, and I provide reasonable protection against loss.

Tip

When saving your digital master file, please do save it without permanently embedding an output profile in the image. In other words, it is fine to save these images in Adobe RGB (1998) or other large color space. However, converting the file permanently to an output color profile for a particular output device, such as printer/paper combination, potentially locks you out of using some output options in the future. Save the file as TIFF or other mainstream file format, and store copies in more than one physical location.

Archiving and Storing Digital Images and Prints

Modern digital prints should last for generations. Printers recently released by major printer manufacturers such as Canon, Epson, and HP have expected print lives/color fastness running from 80-200+ years (see the manufacturers' websites for more information). See Figure 6.14.

Printing technology and print life expectations have reached the point that, as a practical matter, digital print life and fade-resistance is unequaled in the world of art publishing.

Even so, protecting the color and physical integrity of your prints is a challenging task. Some of the things that can degrade the color and quality of a print include:

- High temperatures (over 70-75 degrees F)
- High humidity
- Atmospheric pollution, including smog and ozone
- High light levels, or light that includes a strong presence of ultraviolet (UV) radiation

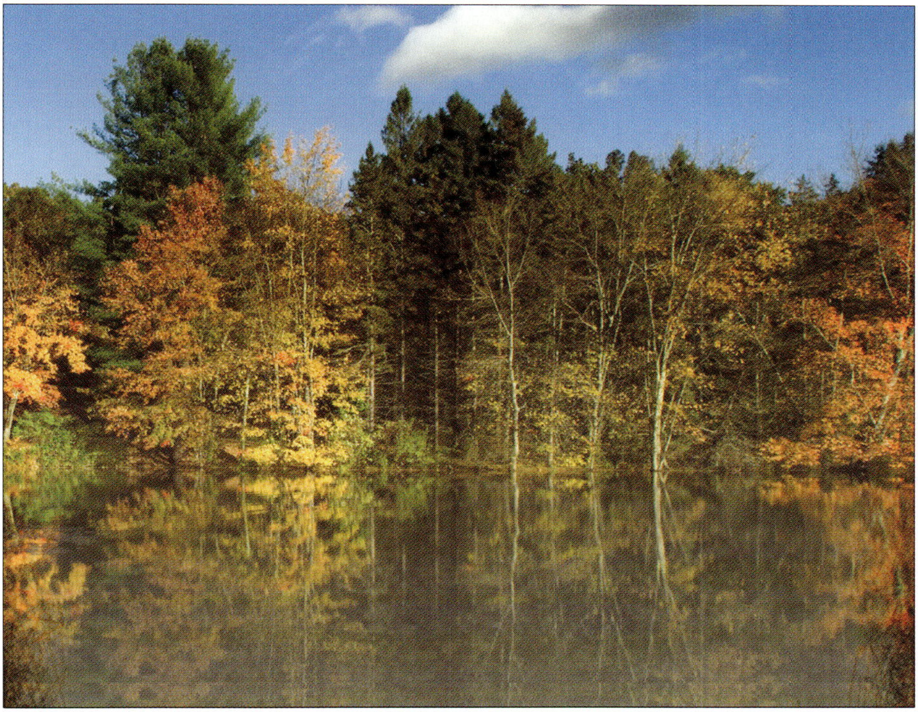

Figure 6.14

This is an example of a print that has been badly damaged by improper storage.

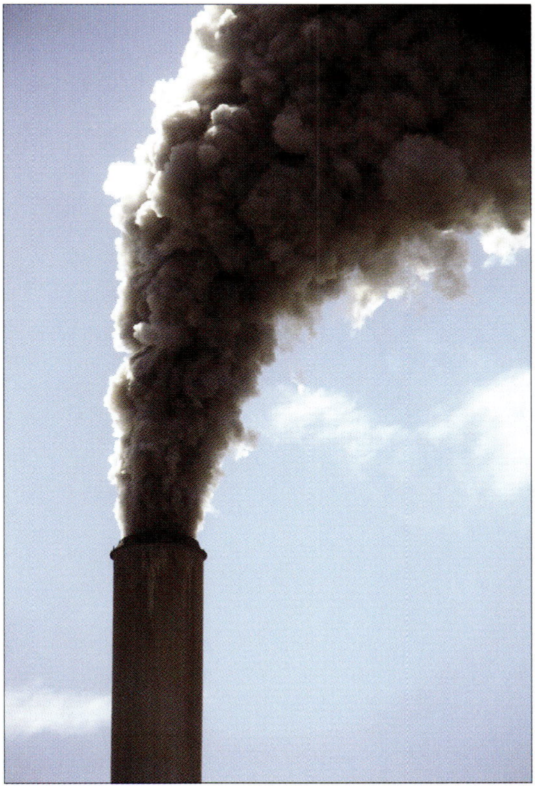

Figure 6.15

Air pollution can also damage your printed images. (Photo licensed from istockphoto.)

Dark storage (in other words, in a vault) that's both temperature and atmosphere controlled will give the longest print life. Major museums use this extensively and rotate artwork of all types through dark storage and open display to extend the life of the work they own.

However, this is rarely practical for galleries or individuals. Instead, artists and photographers should use archival methods and materials for mounting, framing, and displaying their images. These include, but are not limited to:

- Using acid-free mounting and matting materials.
- Mounting the print under UV protective glass and using an archivally rated mat to separate the surface of the print from the glass. If the print touches the glass, it will over time adhere to the surface of the glass.
- If mounting a print on a mat for framing, the method that preserves the print longest is called a hinge mount, as shown in Figure 6.16.

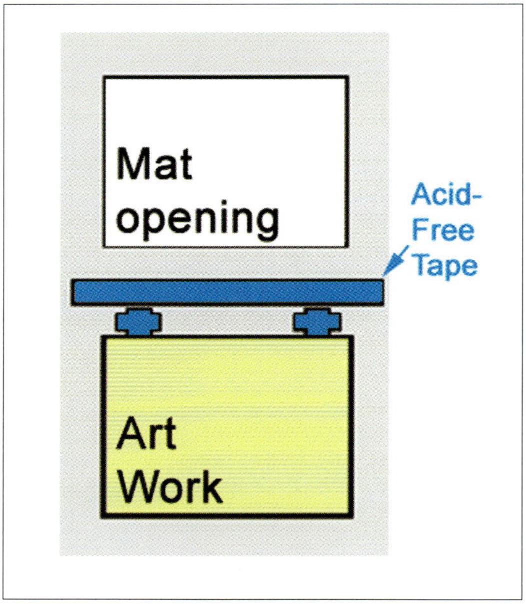

Figure 6.16

This is a schematic drawing of hinge mounted artwork.

- If a digital print must be mounted fully on a mat, you can use an archivally rated adhesive method. A dry-mount system is also okay, although these systems use heat to activate the mounting tissue. Ensure that mounting press temperatures are low. In the opinion of some experts, temperatures under 180 degrees F are required. Higher temperatures risk "cooking" the print, causing early color distortions or fading.

- Display the print in controlled lighting, preferably non-UV indoor lighting. Exposure to bright daylight, even indirect daylight, can shorten print life.
- Prints can be stored in an archivally constructed box, if they are separated by correct interleaving or tissue. For more guidance on this, see websites such as **www.lightimpressionsdirect.com**.

When saving your digital master file, remember to save it without permanently embedding an output profile in the image. In other words, it is fine to save these images in Adobe RGB (1998) or other large color space. However, converting the file permanently to an output color profile for a particular output device, such as printer/paper combination, potentially locks you out of using some output options in the future. Save the file as TIFF or other mainstream file format, and store copies in more than one physical location.

Summary

Making reproductions of your artwork is easier now than it ever has been. Please don't let yourself be intimated by the idea—given recent developments in cameras, scanners, and color management, it's less expensive and time consuming now than even a year or two ago.

Personally, I like the idea of artists having greater freedom to distribute their work and the quality control that we can get from our digital toolbox.

7

Color Quality Control

Quality control in digital color management is an essential and demanding task. The rewards are great, as success in this area can improve the final result and save time and money.

Color quality control is a chain of cause-and-effect; it is nearly impossible to bypass any significant step and not suffer the consequences.

There are a number of checkpoints or milestones that you have to keep in mind. Managing and integrating these important steps may seem like additional work, but on a project-by-project basis, integrated quality control and color management will save you time and money and give you a better chance to get the results you need.

In part, this involves getting away from automated color controls, understanding the options available to you, and using them in an efficient and effective workflow. You'll also want to know how to check your work at each major stage, so you can keep your quality on track.

This workflow process can be broken into three major categories:

- Capture and lighting controls
- In-process controls
- Post-production controls

Each of these areas involves some essential steps or elements, as shown in Table 7.1.

Table 7.1 Color Quality Control Steps and Actions

Steps/Actions

Capture	Lighting intensity and color temperature controls.	Standardized lighting color temperature and color rendering index used.	Sensor/film standardization on color, size, resolution, and manufacturing standards.		Color space/gamut standardization.	Digital file type available (RAW).
In-Process	Color-controlled work environment.	Software processing for RAW file conversion, basic global color management.	Color calibrated display for viewing and editing.	Standardized lighting color temperature and color rendering index used.	Professional-level processing software and controls available.	
Post-Production	Color-controlled work environment, image-editing software that contains high-quality customizable tools. Soft proofing, or accurate on-screen review of images intended for publication, is available.		Press or printer profiling available and used at site of production—quality control oversight of incoming media—ink and paper.		Appropriate and timely maintenance and calibration.	

Capture and Lighting Controls

Color control during image capture is dependent on a number of variables. This section covers the control you may exert on these variables and coping strategies for partially uncontrolled models.

Lighting, for example, might not be under the control of the artist or photographer. For example, you may be photographing under a mix of daylight, artificial lighting, and studio lights—Figure 7.1 illustrates this.

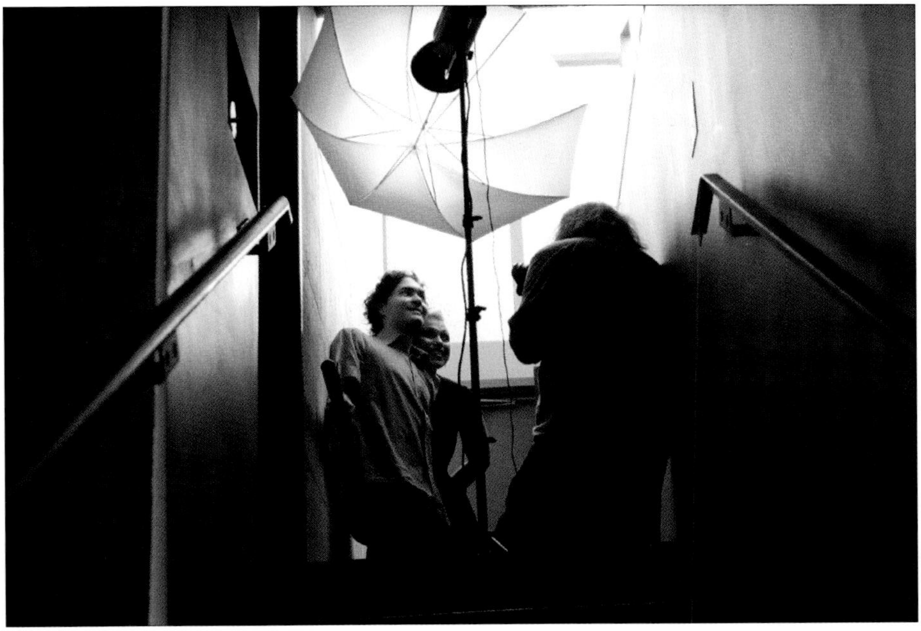

Figure 7.1

An example of photography using mixed lighting—daylight, indoor, and strobe.

Let's consider a couple of scenarios in photography in which a mixed lighting model is used:

- Outdoor photography in which general lighting conditions are changing, including shifting cloud cover and normal changes in the direction of sunlight.
- Indoor photography in which lighting in the structure is composed mainly of halogen overheads, but strobe or flash is needed to fill in or stop action.

In the first scenario, you might manage color using the following strategies:

- Ensure that film, if used, is matched to daylight color temperatures.
- If you are using a digital camera, I strongly recommend that you set the white balance to match the color temperature you are shooting in. Using the "auto" setting on the camera will result in each image being slightly different in color, as the camera calculates individualized settings. This means that in post-production you may have to color adjust each image *individually*.
- Use a gray card, or a GretagMacbeth color checker card. Photograph a frame including this color management tool whenever there is a significant change in lighting levels or location of the photo shoot. This card can be used in post-production to help color balance the images.

- Add additional artificial lighting that complements the available daylight, and correct the lighting to a temperature that blends with the ambient light or complements it.
- Make sure that your exposure is accurate. Inaccurate exposures will adversely affect color quality.
- It is very helpful to use a color meter to measure the color temperature of the available lighting. These are available from Broncolor, Minolta, and others. The color temperature of incandescent/halogen indoor lighting may range from 2500K to 4000K. Fluorescent lighting is usually much cooler (bluer) than incandescent or halogen, but also contains some very strange color casts, including magenta and green.
- If you are shooting on film, and the lighting is predominantly fluorescent or tungsten, it may be best to use an on-camera filter to provide color correction, if no additional lighting is used. Also, tungsten-balanced film is still available, although purchase and processing costs are higher than conventional film.

Tip

Most cameras are delivered to their owners set to capture images as JPEGs, in sRGB. Here's a tip that will instantly improve your image quality and color fidelity: Learn how to use your camera shooting in RAW mode, and set your color for Adobe (1998) RGB. Photoshop now provides a plug-in called RAW Converter that makes processing these files pretty easy—and the quality will easily exceed anything you can get in a sRGB JPEG. Remember, Adobe RGB (1998) provides a color space that's about 40% larger than sRGB.

If you are using additional lighting in the studio or on location, I recommend that you use either color-corrected strobes calibrated to 5500K or continuous lighting calibrated to the same temperature.

Warmer color temperature "hot lights" can be used for color accents and the like, but in my opinion these are usually less suitable for main lights in still digital photography. If you must use these, use a color correcting gel to change the lighting temperature to near-daylight values; digital camera sensors are designed for this and may deliver lesser quality in uncorrected tungsten lighting.

It is possible to control lighting and color indoors or outdoors or in mixed situations with only a few inexpensive tools. These can include lighting gels, different lighting sources, on-camera filters, and colored reflectors to bounce light onto your subject. It's well worth the effort.

Using a Color Checker Card

Using a color checker card, such as the one manufactured by GretagMacbeth, is a bit similar to using a color target to calibrate your scanner. Under controlled conditions, and with automated color management software turned off, you expose the camera sensor to the card. The image file is then imported into the profile/calibration software and analyzed, and a color profile is generated.

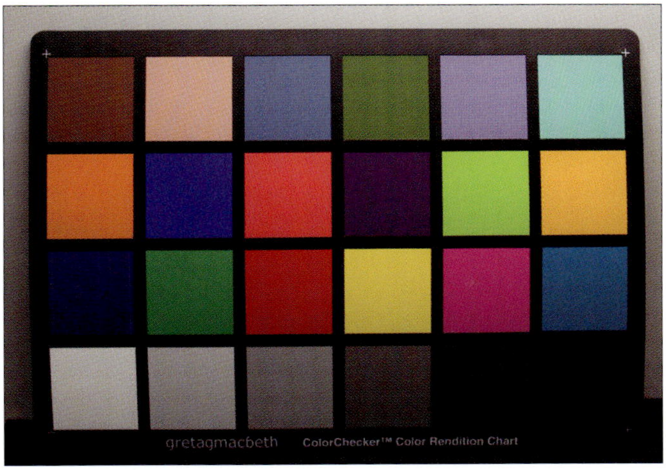

Figure 7.2

A typical color checker card.

These color profiles are very accurate. They can be used to adjust color in your RAW image processor, for example.

There are some important details to keep in mind: The profile you create is valid only for the exact lighting and exposure settings in place at the time the shot is taken. If you change the lighting, you should re-shoot the card and recalculate the profile.

In my photography, I use the color checker card and camera profiling only for really critical color management issues. One of the reasons is that much of my shooting is on location, and in those circumstances I usually don't have complete control of lighting. I find that using a gray or white card for general color correction and using a color checker card for reference is most useful.

Software provided by a number of manufacturers can process the image file to create your profile. X-Rite and GretagMacbeth are among the leaders.

Solving a Real-World Lighting Problem

Recently, when photographing in a church, I found that the dominant ambient lighting was provided by quartz-halogen spotlights, which the color meter measured to an average color temperature of 3800K. I also needed to use an on-camera flash to provide additional light to stop action, as people were moving from place to place in the church.

The problem was that the ambient lighting and the flash were at least 1000K in color temperature apart—this means that parts of the image illuminated by the flash looked daylight-balanced (white dresses looked white), but areas less well-illuminated by the flash looked much warmer, or yellow. Messy, at best.

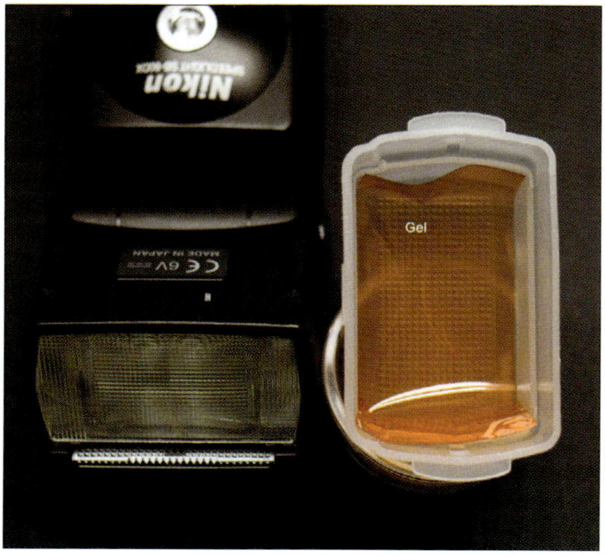

Figure 7.3

A color-correcting gel on the front of on-camera flash.

The solution? I taped a color-correcting gel to the front of the on-camera flash and matched the color temperature of the flash to the color temperature inside the church. Next, I adjusted the camera so that it would assume that all the lighting was incandescent color temperature, and... voila! I had perfectly exposed and color-balanced photographs that showed no sign of sickly yellow indoor lighting. My customers loved it, and I loved it too—there was literally no post-production color tweaking needed, which saved many, many computer hours.

Interestingly, I was shooting this using 800 ISO (high sensitivity film), and I expected to see significant grain and color noise in the images. I discovered in post-production that this was greatly reduced in the color-balanced images—as compared to images taken in another location, using an uncorrected strobe in an mixed indoor-lighting environment.

Tip

An issue that goes hand-in-hand with color management is understanding the quality of the lens you are using. Briefly, all lenses use glass that's coated with a thin layer of material designed to reduce reflections, color shifts, and the like.

A high-quality lens will show little, if any, color distortions, and an average-quality lens may show quite a bit. This can become very noticeable when combining an older lens with a modern, high-end digital camera—it exaggerates the flaws in the lens. Some software programs, such as Adobe Camera RAW, provide for adjusting flaws in these types of images.

Choosing Lighting Equipment

A wide range of lighting equipment is available, ranging from low cost to high and poor quality to superb. Here are a few things to consider when putting together a lighting ensemble for a particular job or for your studio:

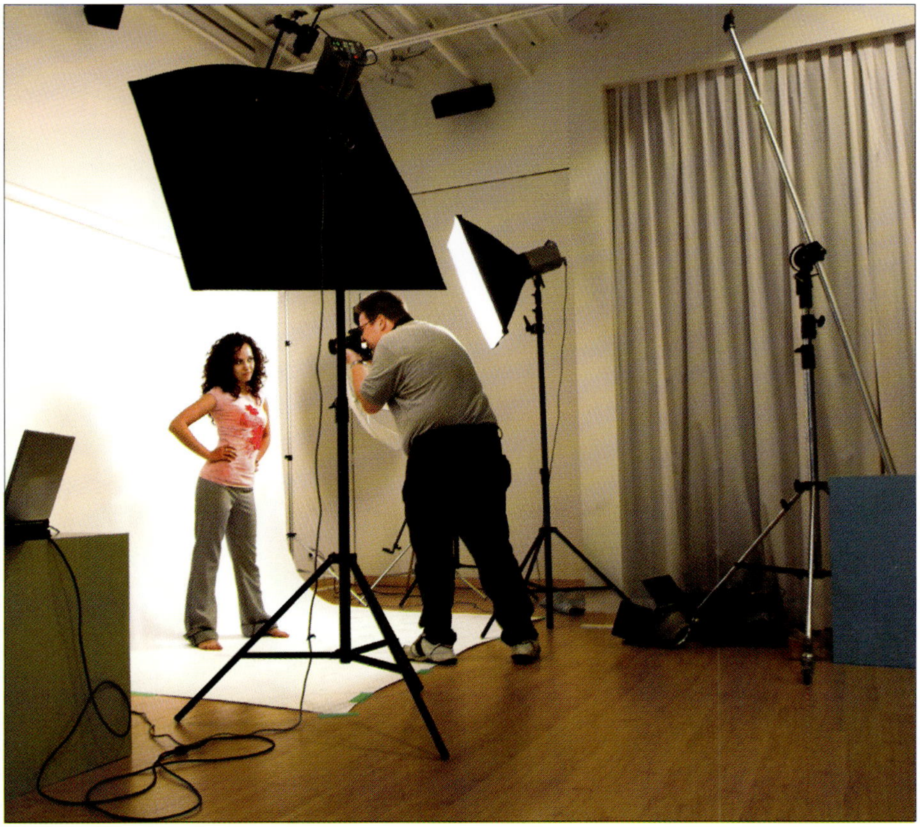

Figure 7.4

A typical studio portrait setup. Note that the intensity of the strobes should overpower any color cast from existing room lighting. (Photo licensed from istockphoto.)

- Consistency of color temperature: Top quality strobes will go all day long and vary little if at all. Color temperature is one of the first things to drift in a system where engineers or manufacturers have cut corners. A good color meter will help you identify how good your lighting equipment is.
- As flash tubes and power packs age, it is a good idea to re-check their performance with a color meter.
- This is also true as regards light intensity; some manufacturers' units will produce light at very consistent levels from one lamp head to another, and others will vary.
- Quality of accessories, particularly in regard to diffusers, reflectors, and related items. Inner coatings must be absolutely consistent in color and density; imperfections will result in unwanted variations in color.

Some of the lighting manufacturers I've used and found to deliver consistently top quality include, but are not limited to, Broncolor, Profoto, Hensel, Calumet Elite, and Elinchrome (check out sinarbron.com, profoto-usa.com, henselusa.com, calumetphoto.com, www.elinchrom.com). Please see Chapter 5, "Color Management Policies for Photographers," for more information on lighting.

Color Space and Color Control

Most digital cameras provide color adjustments for the photographer. These can include color space, overall color temperature, in-camera processing of color, image file type, and more.

Table 7.2 provides recommendations for best color in different types of digital cameras.

Table 7.2 Color Spaces for Digital Cameras

	Color Space	ISO	Contrast	File Type	Color	Sharpening Enhancement
Consumer-level camera	sRGB	100	Low	JPEG	Low or medium	Low
Professional-level camera	Adobe (1998) RGB or ProPhoto RGB	50-100	Low	RAW	Low or off	Low or Off

The color space that you decide to use in digital capture is one of the most important choices you have in digital photography. A broader color space, such as Adobe RGB (1998), gives you many advantages, including reduced color distortion during processing and better color fidelity after processing. Similarly, RAW files contain more image information than their JPEG counterparts; use of RAW usually results in better quality images down the road. Figure 7.5 shows the ProPhoto RGB color space.

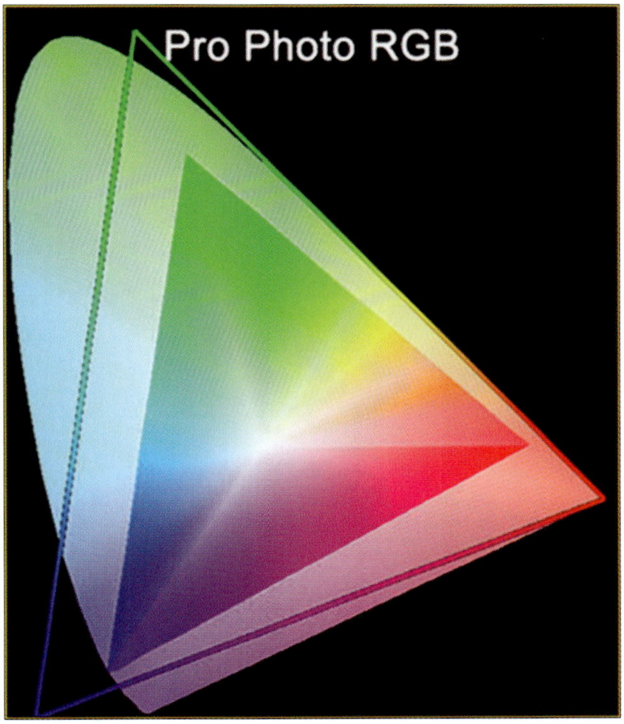

Figure 7.5

The ProPhoto RGB color space.

Contrast control is built into most cameras; it too can be heavy handed, and you are better off making most contrast adjustments in Photoshop.

Please note that sharpening, or too much use of sharpening, is a legitimate concern in color management. In digital photography, *sharpening* refers to image manipulation tools that actually increase contrast on the edges of things in an image. This gives the illusion of making an image appear to be sharper, or clearer, to the viewer.

Most cameras' built-in sharpening is aggressive, and it can adversely affect color in high-contrast areas of the image. It is best to sharpen an image in post-production, using Photoshop or other image editor.

Exposure Management and Color Control

One of the most important factors in color control in photography is exposure. Although this is less true when you use negative film, it is critical when making digital exposures.

An underexposure or overexposure will significantly affect image quality and color fidelity.

Digital camera capture, unlike film, is linear in recording light. Another way to express this is that the brighter the light, the more energy the camera sensor pixel records at that point. In fact, a typical digital image capture contains at least six stops of information. Also, the majority of the information in the image is contained in the brightest stop of the capture, as illustrated in Figure 7.6.

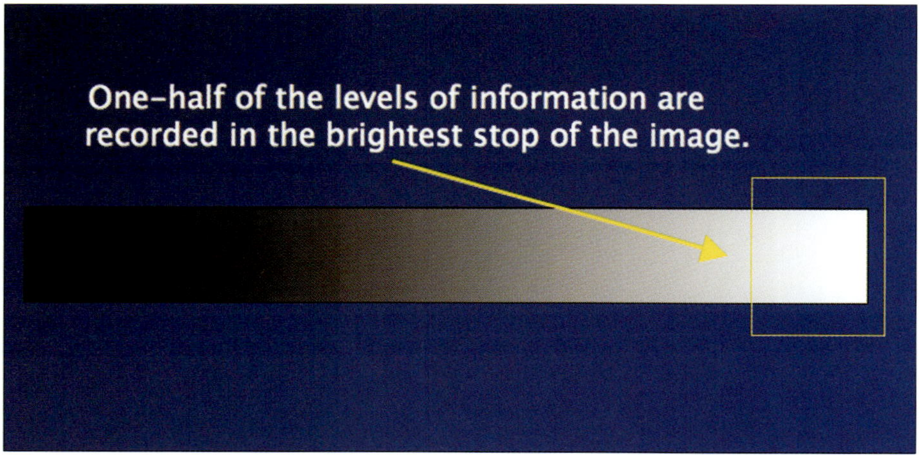

Figure 7.6

Note that half of the information in a digital image capture is recorded at the brightest stop.

As a practical matter, an overexposed digital capture will not include a lot of important image detail and color information. Practically speaking, exposure latitude in digital is even less than in transparency. Generally, digital captures have a +1/3 stop overexposure, and a -2/3 stop underexposure.

Metering to Manage Color

Here are a couple of tips that can save you time and money in getting your color right:

- Get a modern, well-made exposure meter. Gossen and Sekonic are unequaled in build quality and accuracy. My Sekonic meter has been mistreated so badly, so often by a long line of photo assistants (and me!) that I'm amazed it still works at all. I hope it lasts forever. See Figure 7.7 for an example of an exposure meter.

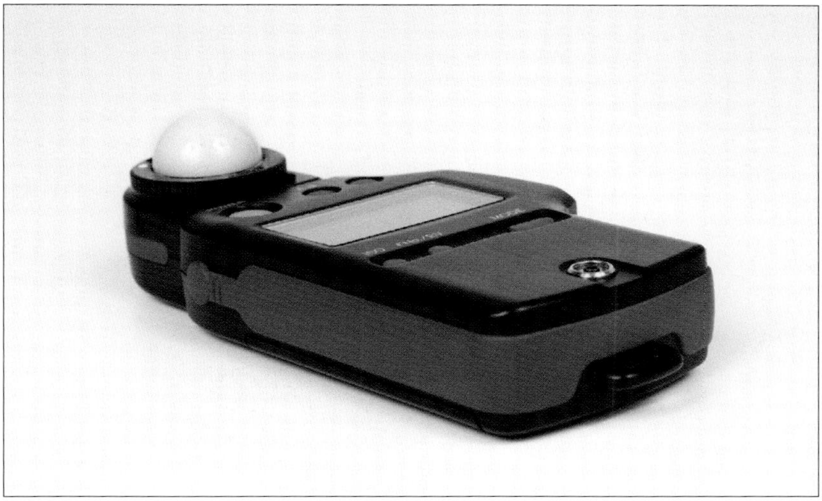

Figure 7.7

An exposure meter is an indispensable tool for photographers. (Photo licensed from istockphoto.)

- Keep the meter battery fresh. Sounds obvious, but....
- It is a very good idea to calibrate your meter. One of the easiest ways to do this is to compare it side-by-side with another meter, or even three together. You can also make a full-frame exposure of a gray card and examine the histogram—if there is a spike dead center in the histogram, the exposure is correct for middle gray—Figure 7.8 shows what I mean.
- Learn to use your meter correctly. Some photographers will insist that you point the meter into the light you are measuring. This will in most circumstances result in inaccurate measurements. Point the axis of the meter into the axis of the lens. The meter is designed to be used this way.

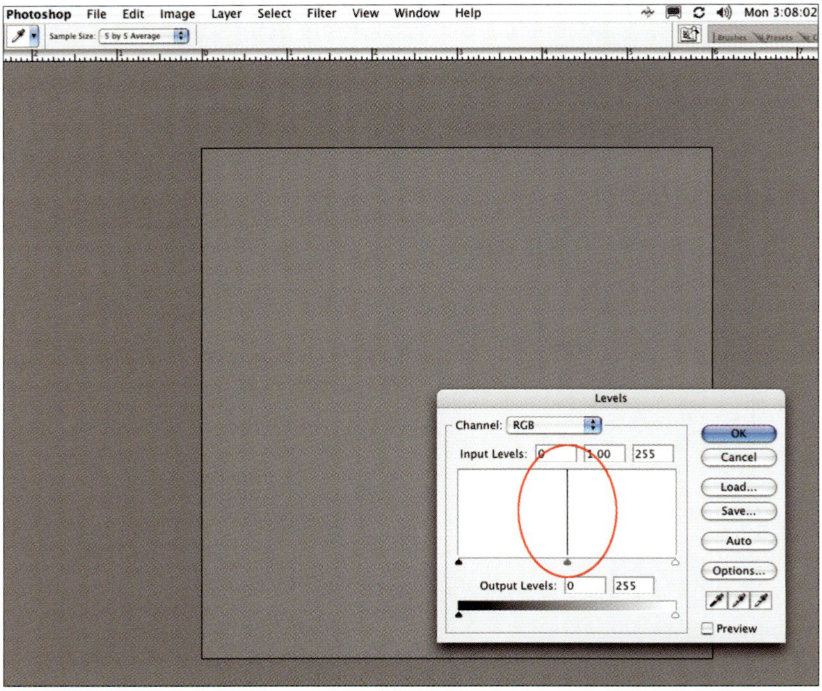

Figure 7.8

Gray card histogram.

- As with film, the rated ISO of a particular digital camera might not be accurate. Once you've metered your subject, take a test shot and look at the histogram. The LCD on the back of the camera, or even a tethered computer monitor, will usually not show you an accurate image. Check the histogram!
- When metering, build your lighting setup one light at a time. Meter each light separately and then as an ensemble. Each light should be providing exposure within 1/10 stop of what you need, individually and collectively.
- If you are shooting for commercial work, consider whether you should incorporate use of a calibrated gray or white card and a color checker card into your work.

In the case of overexposure, the lost image detail and color are gone and cannot be recovered. Some photographers, therefore, advocate underexposing all images and using image editing software to adjust the photograph in post-production.

The difficulty here is an underexposed image does not retain detail in the shadows as negative film does. Remember THE linear capture model? A small minority of the image information is contained in the darkest stops of the capture, and so underexposed shadow areas block up, losing detail. Attempting to brighten these areas through image manipulation usually results in a significant increase in color noise and color distortion.

The key is to make your exposures with a very high degree of accuracy. My suggested standard is to keep all critical areas of an image within 1/10 stop in the brightest details and 1/10 of a stop in shadow areas where I want to preserve detail.

Additionally, inspect the histogram after each shot. The histogram is your friend! Figure 7.9 shows three histograms side by side. The histogram shown on the left indicates an underexposed image, the one in the middle is a correct exposure, and the one on the right is overexposed.

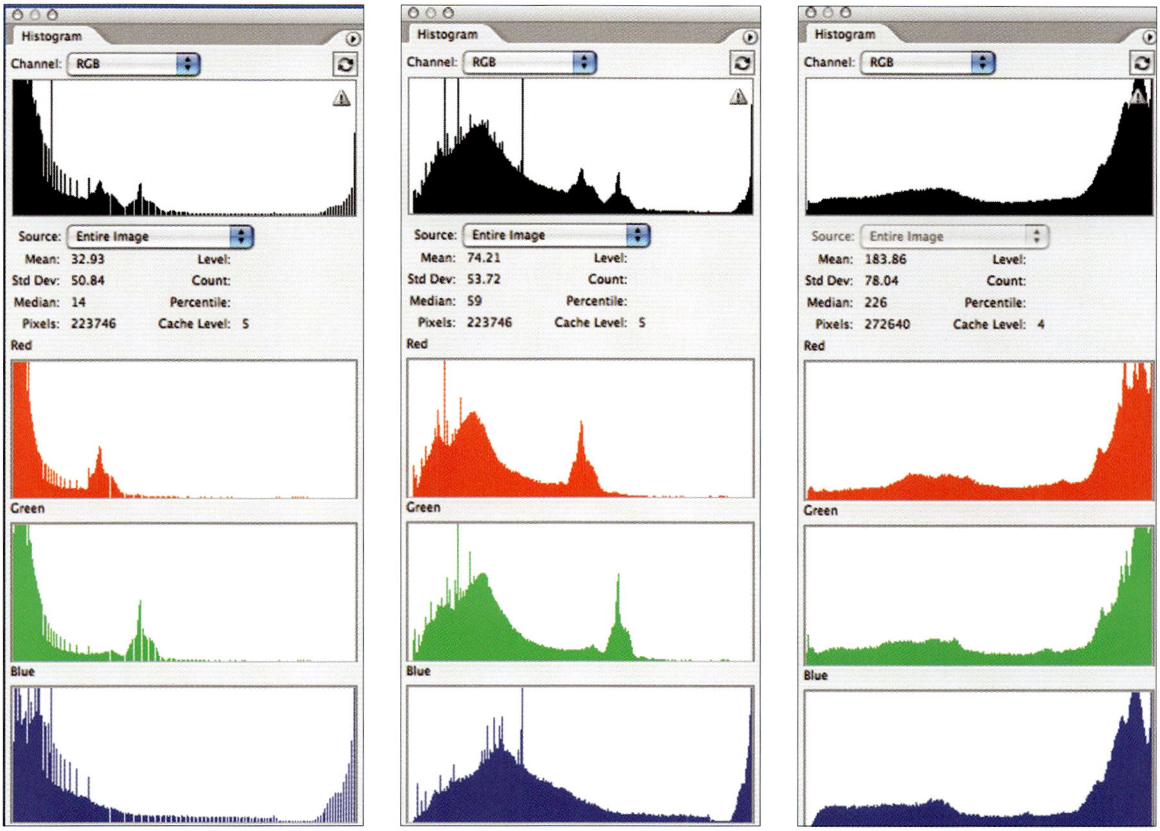

Figure 7.9

The histogram shown on the left indicates an underexposed image, the one in the middle is a correct exposure, and the one on the right is overexposed.

Note the red arrow pointing to the left side of the left-most histogram. The graph spikes at that point and also bleeds off the left side of the graph. This shows loss of image detail, sometimes called *clipping*, in the darkest tones and potential loss of color information in these areas.

The histogram in the middle does not show spikes on either end and so indicates that you have saved as much information as possible for later use.

The histogram on the right includes a red arrow on the right side, which points to clipping in the highlights and loss of image and color information in that area.

Last, when using film there are issues related to length of exposure that can affect color. Sometimes called the *reciprocity effect* or *reciprocity failure*, this involves changes in color recorded by the film when exposure is very short or is very long. Manufacturers provide information on this in the film packaging, or on the website.

ISO (film speed or sensor sensitivity) is also a consideration. In most cameras, high ISO settings will create visible grain and color "noise," or fine color speckling. This is most visible in darker or shadow areas of the image. Keep your ISO settings as low as you can, provided your shutter speed stays fast enough to stop the action and prevent blurry images.

Color Enhancement

Some cameras and some consumer-level image editors have automated "color-enhancement" features. These usually increase color saturation and contrast in the image, and they may be useful in some types of landscape or outdoor photography, as shown in Figure 7.10. Sometimes marketed as "one-click" adjustments, they are erratic in the results delivered.

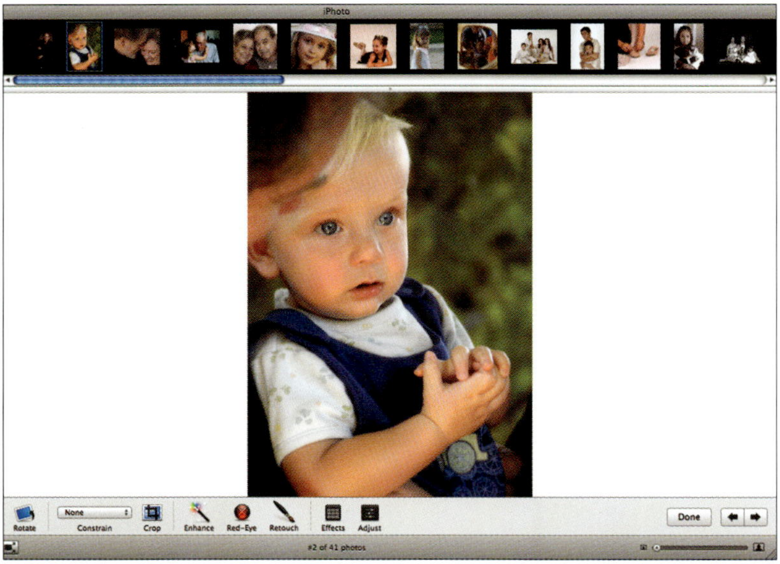

Figure 7.10

Some consumer-level image editors have automated "color-enhancement" features, but the results can be erratic.

Reciprocity Failure

Reciprocity failure on film usually occurs during long exposures—it is the result of exposing the film to light in a way that it was not engineered to handle. It frequently results in increased color saturation and in most cases a shift in color balance.

Reciprocity failure can also refer to the light sensitivity of film to fall off, or decrease, when exposure times exceed those recommended by the manufacturer. This means that total exposure time may have to be increased beyond the values indicated by your meter.

Some photographers and artists like this otherwordly look, and some don't—so please experiment a bit and gain some experience with long exposures before committing to a major project. Two photographers whose time-lapse photographic work I respect include Dwight Blemker (www.timesculpturephotography.com) and Michael Frye (www.michaelfrye.com).

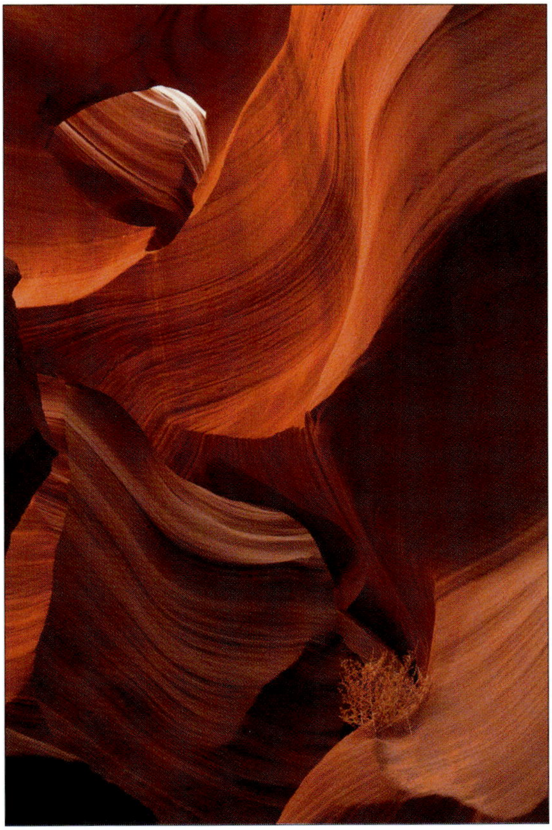

Figure 7.11

Antelope Valley Image—© Dwight Blemker, photographer, by permission.

However, in most cases you are better off in avoiding these automated software features, either in the camera or in your image editor.

Additionally, one may place color-adjusting filters on both digital and film camera lenses—for example, a filter that has a slight yellow or orange tint may be used to brighten a landscape or to "warm up" skin tones.

In-Process Controls

In-process controls include transferring images from the camera to computer (or scanning film and storing files on the computer), selecting software to process your image files, and ensuring that your work environment, computer display, and print viewing areas are all color managed.

It might sound strange, but one aspect of managing color quality is ensuring that image files are transferred as-is from your camera to your computer or other storage device. Some manufacturers provide image transfer and image editing software in the box with the camera; unfortunately, some of these tools include automated processing or pre-sets that alter the image enroute.

Instead, purchase an inexpensive digital card reader, and always transfer images using this, rather than a direct computer-to-camera cable. In Windows or Mac, a card reader that has a card in it will show up on your desktop as new removable media or drive. Simply drag or copy files in the card to a separate folder on your computer. When this task is complete, eject the card reader via Explorer or Finder. (If you just "pull the plug," you could damage the card reader or the card.) Other benefits of owning a card reader include saving camera battery life and reducing wear and tear on the camera cable connection.

I recommend that you also copy the image files to a second folder on another hard drive connected to your computer or on your network. This way, you can work on editing your images in one folder and leave the "originals" untouched in the other.

Once you have a folder with your images safely on your computer, the next thing to do is to burn a backup CD or DVD and store it in a safe place, preferably a cool, dry physical location separate from the computer. If you do label the disk with a soft-tip marking pen, be sure that the pen is rated for use on CDs. Ordinary marking pens contain solvents that damage CDs and can make them unreadable.

Digital Storage Cards

When you have ejected the card from the computer card reader, I suggest you store it temporarily and insert a fresh card in the camera. On a few occasions, access to the original card and its saved images has saved me from an unexpected computer problem. Also, always re-format a digital storage card in the camera, never in the computer. Formatting a digital card in the computer can damage it.

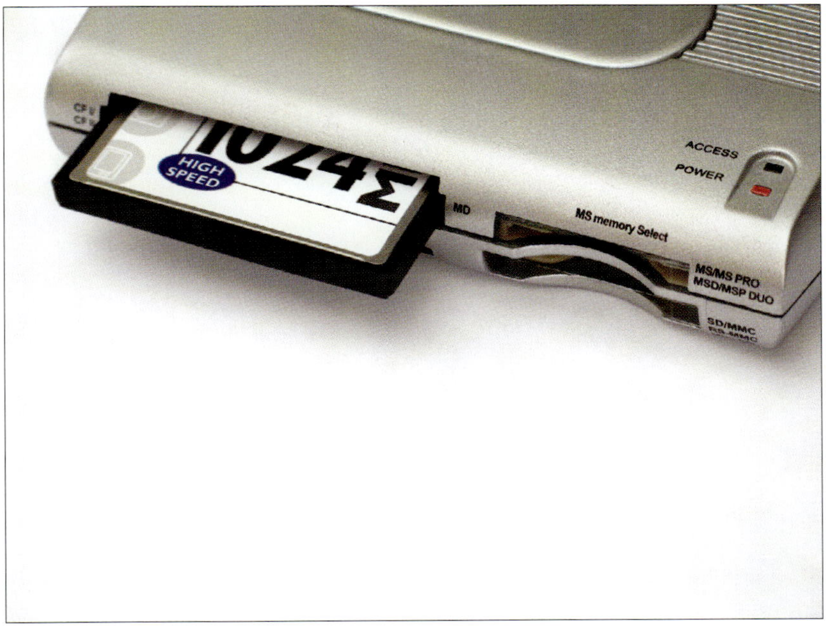

Figure 7.12

A card reader in use. (Photo licensed from istockphoto.)

Work Environment

Your work environment will strongly affect your perception of color. A vividly painted room, let's imagine blue, will make everything in the room have a bluish tinge to it. Instead, use a room that is painted a neutral white or middle gray.

Strong overhead lighting, found in most offices, makes color perception and color management much more difficult. Much of this office lighting is standard fluorescent, which introduces a wide range of color tints and color casts, depending on the age of the tube, the manufacturer, quality of the ballast, and so on. If you can, replace the old bulbs with daylight-corrected ones.

Although an artist appreciates a day lit studio, a photographer reviewing film or digital images needs a color-managed environment. For transparencies, a daylight color lightbox is an essential tool. If you are viewing prints, a color corrected viewing station, such as those made by GTI, is required.

I recommend that a photographer's or artist's workroom for image editing minimize or eliminate outside light sources, such as direct window light, and indoor lighting fixtures using conventional bulbs. Color-balanced lighting, such as that offered by Solux (www.solux.net) can be used. A high-end, color calibrated computer display is also required. Although in the past CRT type monitors delivered the best color and highlight/shadow detail, LCDs have caught up fast and have literally taken over the market.

As monitors age, their color accuracy declines. Any CRT monitor over three years old is likely to be a candidate for replacement.

Here are a few recommendations for LCD monitors:

- Apple Cinema Display
- Eizo Color Edge
- LaCie 321

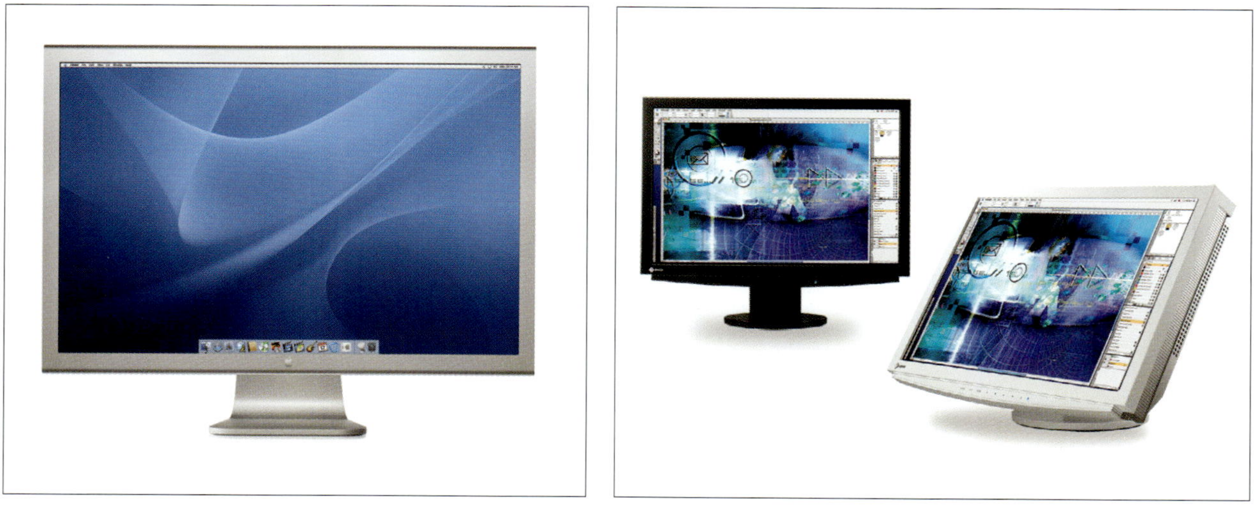

Figure 7.13

These monitors are suitable for image editing.

You really cannot go wrong with the Eizo Color Edge, but you'll need to have deep pockets. They are expensive, but they are very, very hard to beat in color-critical work. Any of the others mentioned in the sidebar are also very good and should work quite well. But as this is written, if you have the budget, go for the Eizo.

Tip

A quick tip: Regardless of the type of monitor you are using, turn it on and let it warm up and stabilize for 30-60 minutes before performing a calibration cycle or doing any serious color work.

One thing I do hope that LCD manufacturers do is to include Red/Green/Blue individual adjustments in all models of monitors intended for image editing.

Some of the things you'll want in an LCD monitor are a broad color palette (range of visible color), adjustable brightness and contrast that allows you to see the widest range of tones from highlights to shadows, an adjustable stand, and built-in USB and Firewire ports to help reduce desktop clutter.

Controlling Your Monitor

Nearly every monitor is shipped to you or the store you purchased it from with pre-sets designed for word processing and using the Internet. These pre-sets are very bright (remember the overhead office lighting) and very blue. This is far from ideal for color quality control.

Both Windows and Mac operating systems include a bare-bones monitor adjustment utility program. However, I do not recommend using these for anything other than casual work. What's the reason? They depend on the human eye, which works great overall but is notoriously unreliable in judging color on a computer.

Here's an experiment you can try: Next time you go out of your home or office, take a look around at the room, and note your perception of colors in different places in it. Then, go out into the daylight, and don't wear your sunglasses. Take note of how colors appear different when you return—usually less vibrant and lower contrast, at least for a minute or two. The effect fades, of course, at different rates for different people. Fact is, your as-issued eyeball is too often inconsistent.

Invest $80-200 in a decent quality display calibration device, sometimes called a *colorimeter.* It is provided with a software disk and a small gadget that looks a bit like a computer mouse.

The color management software and the device will painlessly adjust your monitor from its basic, and largely unusable, settings to a heavenly combination of optimal brightness, contrast, color, and highlight and shadow detail.

An additional benefit to having a color-managed display is that you will spend less time squinting at it, trying to see details and subtle changes in color. And you have an excellent chance of creating a system in which the color on your screen matches your prints.

The Human Factor

Human fatigue plays a role in color management. Your work area can help or hinder you in this activity. Workstation ergonomics are similar to those for other computer applications: A good chair, correct desk height, and elimination of inappropriate office lighting are all important. Believe me, if you get too tired, your perception of color will be affected.

In fact, I recommend to all of my clients that they plan to do their color-critical work at the time of day where they are most rested and most energetic. It has happened to me more than once, working on a color adjustment late in the day just isn't working—and when I come back to it in the morning, I can solve the problem in a minute or two and move on.

Display Calibration Devices

Display calibration devices made by any of the major manufacturers, including GretagMacbeth, X-Rite, and Colorvision, are all good products. You can purchase devices that provide only automated calibration, such as the Huey, or more expensive devices that will either automate or allow manual control of just about every variable. Follow the directions provided by the manufacturer, and all will be well. For more details, see Chapter 5.

Software for Processing

Digital images need processing, just as film does. Interestingly, there is a wide variety of programs available for this purpose—ranging from bare-bones consumer level to top-quality pro software.

Sometimes digital image processing is very simple, involving nothing more than an adjustment in contrast, resizing for a particular purpose, and storage on a CD, DVD, or hard drive.

Image processing software can convert RAW files into TIFFs or JPEGs, re-set or assign a color space, adjust color or contrast, provide sharpening, and more. Some packages are nearly fully automated, and others completely customizable.

One of the most commonly known image processing programs available is packaged with Photoshop CS2—it is called Adobe Camera RAW.

Table 7.3 compares the selected digital image processors.

Table 7.3 Digital Image Processors, Compared

Processor	Ease of Use	Automation	Customizable	Color Space Controls	Color Controls	Cost	Version
Adobe Camera RAW	Intermediate	Yes	Good	Yes	Good	Ships w/ Photoshop CS2; $500 total	Final
Apple iPhoto	Basic	Yes; dominates	Minimal	No	Fair	Packaged w/ some Macs	Final
Adobe Lightroom	Intermediate	Yes	Good	Yes	Good	No charge as Beta Ver. (Beta 4 Fall 06)	Beta
Leaf Capture 10	Advanced	Yes	Excellent	Yes	Excellent	Ships w/ Leaf Camera Back	Final
Phase One Capture One Pro	Advanced	Yes	Excellent	Yes	Excellent	Ships w/ Phase One Camera Back—or separately ~ $500	Final
Apple Aperture	Moderate	Yes	Good	Yes	Good	$299	Beta

Of these products, I use and recommend Phase One Capture One Pro and Adobe Camera RAW (ACR). Here are a few reasons why, from a color control and color management point of view:

- The Phase One and ACR software handles a wide range of digital camera files (see www.phaseone.com or www.adobe.com for a list). These camera model lists are being upgraded nearly every month.
- Both packages provide a wide range of controls, including exposure, color temperature, contrast, saturation, chromatic aberration, tint, curves, and more.

- Also, both packages provide for processing multiple images in the background, sometimes called *batch processing*. Images that need similar adjustments and enhancements can be processed in a queue and saved as TIFF or JPEG digital files. This kind of productivity tool is essential for photographers who need to process on a large scale, after a wedding or event, for example.
- I've found that the RAW image processing offered by the Phase One software is hard to beat. It does take a bit longer to process the image from RAW to TIFF, but the result is worth the effort.

Post-Production Controls: Soft Proofing

Once you have your display calibrated and you have installed printer profiles on your computer, you can take advantage of one of Photoshop's (and other image editors') strongest features—soft proofing.

Soft proofing is the ability to accurately view color, tones, and shadow and highlight detail on your computer display before you print. This means that you should be able to see what your print will look like before you make it!

Soft proofing is intended to show you what your print will look like given the printer, paper, and ink combination you have chosen.

Most manufacturers now provide, at little or no charge, accurate profiles that can be added into the appropriate folders on your computer system, making them available to applications like Photoshop. Virtually all the inkjet printer manufacturers, third-party distributors like Lexjet, and software manufacturers like Colorbyte and Colorburst provide these profiles. This discussion assumes that you are using Photoshop for this work. Once you have opened an image (using the correct color space, of course), click on View>Proof Setup>Custom, as shown in Figure 7.14.

Tip

You can use Apple+Y on a Mac or Ctrl+Y on a PC to toggle between soft proofing and the normal display mode.

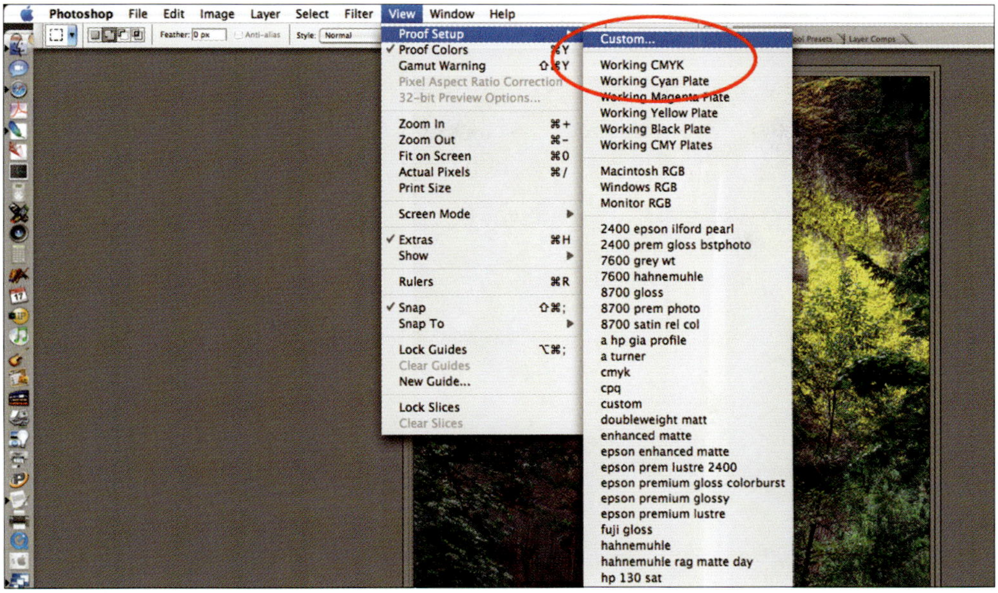

Figure 7.14

In Photoshop, choose View>Proof Setup>Custom.

Next, you'll see a dialog box that looks like Figure 7.15.

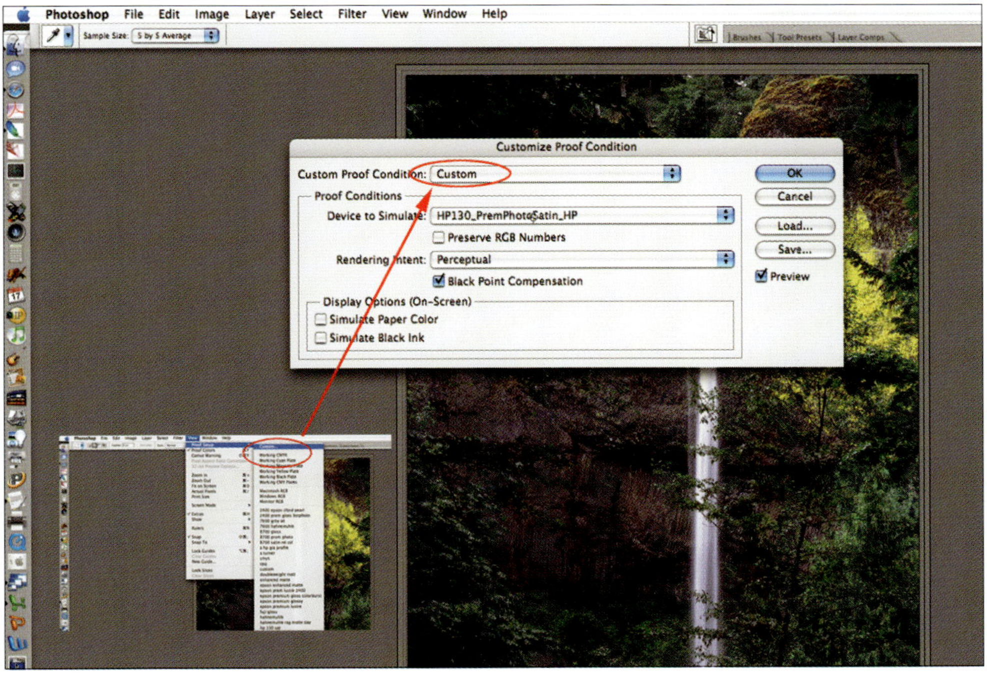

Figure 7.15

The Customize Proof Condition dialog box in Photoshop.

If you click on Device to Simulate in this dialog box, you'll see the drop-down menu shown in Figure 7.16.

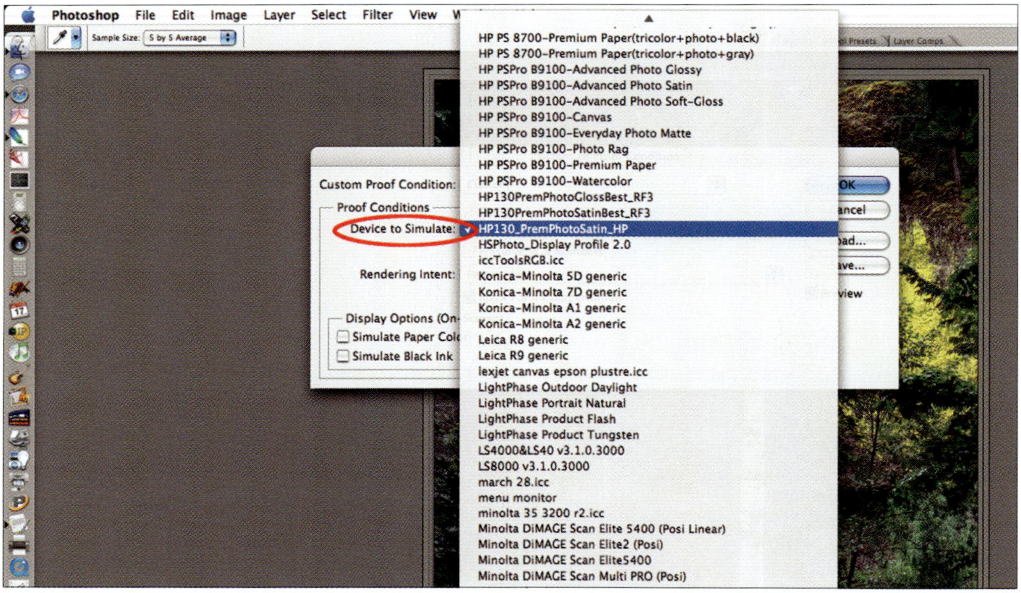

Figure 7.16

This drop-down list contains all the profiles you've installed on your computer (assuming they are in a folder that's proper and accessible for your chosen image editing application).

If you choose one of these profiles, your display will probably change its appearance, and you'll see a difference in contrast and color in your image. If you turn the Preview option off, the image will change back again.

Generally for photography and digital printing you will want to leave Preserve RGB Numbers off and use Perceptual Rendering Intent.

Next, you can save your custom profile settings for future use by clicking on Save. You'll see the dialog box shown in Figure 7.17.

Another great feature of soft proofing is called *gamut warning*, shown in Figure 7.18. Simply put, this will show you colors in your image that your chosen printer/ink/paper combination can't render accurately. After you have enabled Soft Proofing, you just click View>Gamut Warning. By default, Photoshop will indicate the colors that are out of gamut (read: out of range) in gray.

My personal settings change this warning color to bright magenta, which is a color you rarely see in the real world. To do this, go to Photoshop>Preferences>Transparency and Gamut Warnings. Change the color to anything you like.

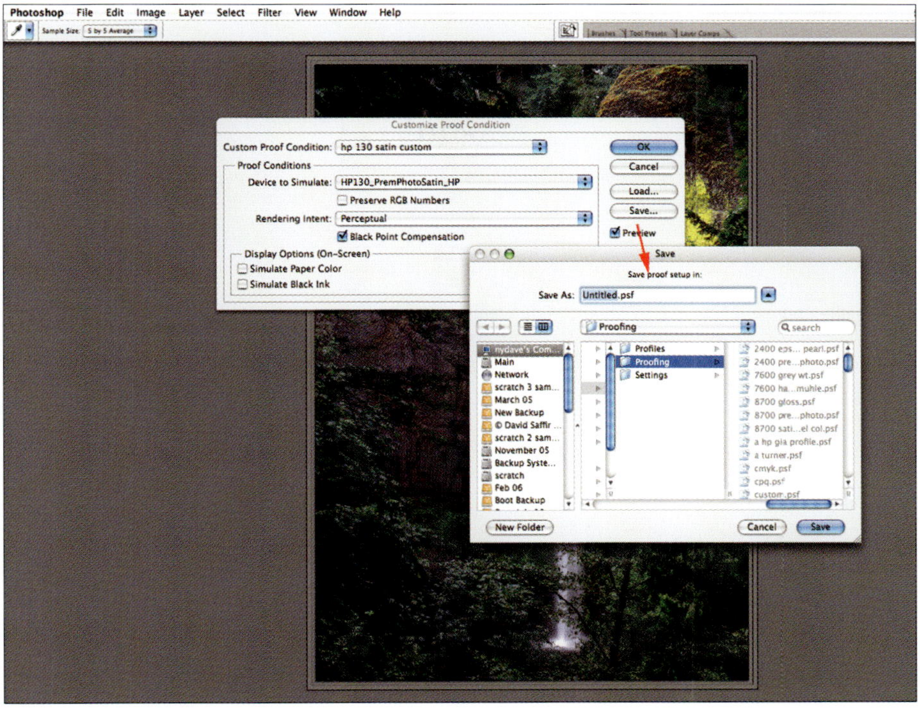

Figure 7.17

Save your settings with a name that you can remember easily so you can use it in the future to preview and soft proof your image.

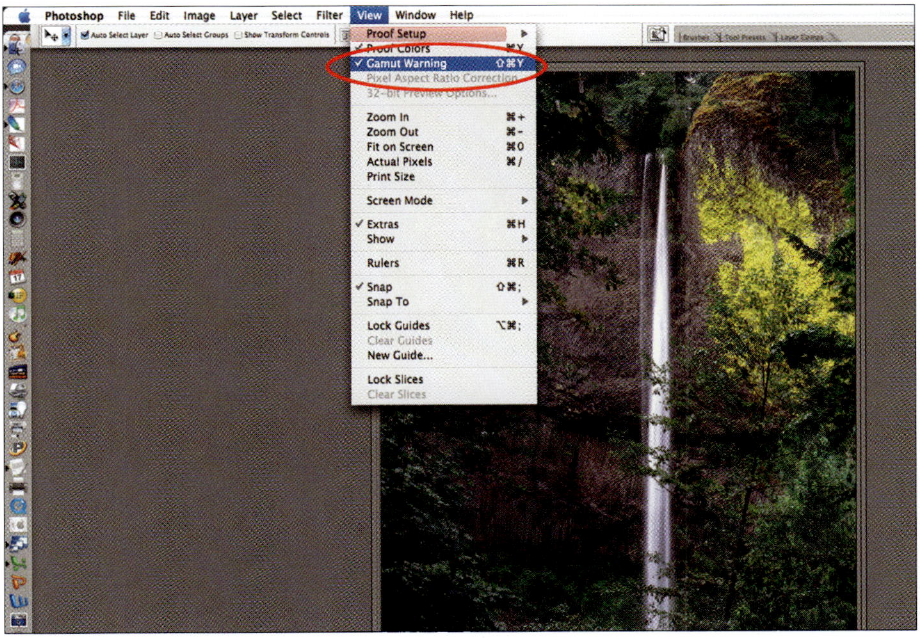

Figure 7.18

When you use Gamut Warning, Photoshop indicates the colors that are out of gamut.

I've made a radical adjustment to the image, so you can see what happens when some colors are out of gamut, shown in Figure 7.19.

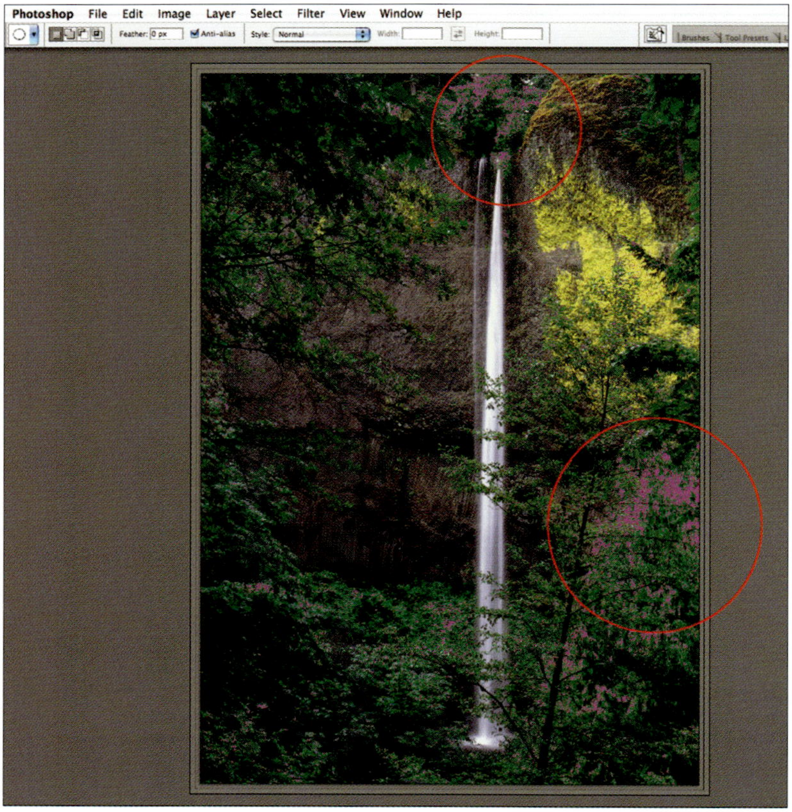

Figure 7.19

Note the colors out of gamut, as indicated by the magenta areas (also circled).

If you are using a good quality monitor and reasonably good profiles, you should be able to save quite a bit of time and money using soft proofing. You can see the impact of image adjustments in real time, evaluate the "look" of one printing option versus another, and reduce the number of proof prints you make. In my case, I've reduced the number of proof prints from 3-4 per image, to just one, or none. At over $1 a square foot, that adds up fast.

Post-Production Controls: Evaluating Output Quality

One part of evaluating output or printing color can be handled pretty simply. You should view any prints, film or digital based, in a professional-level workstation. Office lighting, home table lamps, and the like will introduce errors in color perception. It is also important to keep lighting brightness moderate—light that is too bright or too dim will likely affect your perception of the quality of the print.

A color-corrected booth, such as those offered by GTI, will get the job done. These color-controlled workstations provide daylight-balanced, even lighting and will not introduce unwanted color casts or tints that will interfere with your evaluation.

Once you have a controlled viewing environment in place, how do you evaluate a print and determine the quality you are getting?

The checklist provided here can be used for evaluating print quality and color for most photographic work. I feel that most experienced photographers will want to add criteria to the list or perhaps modify a few. Artists who are having reproductions made of original work will use many of the same criteria in evaluating their prints:

- One very good way to evaluate the overall color fidelity of a print is to compare it to the original transparency or chrome, if you have one. This assumes that the transparency is viewed on a daylight-corrected lightbox, and the print in a daylight-corrected viewing station.
- Another way to validate color from capture through processing and output is to create an image or two of a standardized gray card or white card, a GretagMacbeth color checker card, or equivalent. One thought—the old Kodak gray card used for film is no longer suitable for use in digital imaging—obtain a gray or white card that is made with digital capture in mind.
- Common objects can provide a starting point for your print review. Is foliage the green you expect to see? Red cars? Yellow lines on a highway? Is white clothing white?
- Examine broad areas of color, such as open sky, for smoothness and absence of patches of lighter or darker tones.
- Look at clouds in the sky. Do they look neutral in color, or do you see patches of inappropriate color, particularly in transition areas from bright to dark?
- Look in sections of the image that have strong transitions in contrast, such as trees against a bright sky. Do you see any inappropriate colors on the edges of leaves or other sharply defined objects? Do you see a purple (or other) fringe?
- Accuracy of skin tones, of whatever group of people, can be very telling when evaluating effectiveness of your color management process.
- When evaluating prints, examine skin tones in what are called highlight-to-shadow transitions. Are the changing tones nice and smooth, or do they show evidence of patchiness, graininess, muddiness, or color noise?
- Can you see the details in the image in particularly bright or dark areas? Do bright areas tend to take on a color cast or just lose detail completely? Do shadow areas look muddy and vague?

- In areas of intense color, can you see etching, or so-called *gloss differential*? This may be an indication of inaccurate ink and color management during printing. In these same areas, do the details hold up, or are they submerged in a blob of overwhelming color?
- Are the midtones appropriate to the level of the highlights and the levels of the shadows?
- Check overall sharpness and color separation without bleeding or contamination from one color area across another.
- Check the overall uniform weight and density of the color.

In general, if you find one or more of these problems, you will have to backtrack and diagnose the cause. Color management is a chain that is as strong as its weakest link—so assuming that the original image is not fatally flawed, the first thing to do is to implement a quick overview of the production process to date. That overview will usually uncover an issue that can be addressed.

Actual viewing distance can be very important. A rough rule of thumb can be to measure the diagonal of the print from the upper-left corner to lower right, and double or triple that measurement to determine correct viewing distance. In evaluating print quality, take the time to look at the image up close and also simulate normal viewing conditions.

A good print, one that is the product of a well-controlled system, will show good highlight and shadow detail, subtle textures in fabrics and skin tones, and rich smooth color without visible artifact, even in high contrast areas.

Summary

As indicated at the beginning of this chapter, color quality control is a chain of cause and effect. It's difficult, if not impossible, to take shortcuts and get the best results. It is really worthwhile to invest a small amount of time in nailing down quality—it saves time and money down the road.

Certainly in my own work I've learned the hard way that this kind of work can't be rushed—one of the worst projects I ever tackled a few years ago was one where we said at the beginning "we'll fix it in Photoshop!"

In the next chapter, you'll explore the toughest color management issue of all—producing top-quality black and white images in the digital world.

8

Black and White Imaging in the Digital World

Black-and-white imaging in the modern world can involve many options. Just a few examples: You can shoot digital in color and "convert" later to black and white, or you can create an image on black-and-white film and scan it to digital. Some digital cameras provide custom settings that facilitate original capture in black and white.

Place this in the context of the "traditional" world of silver-halide, palladium, platinum, and other black-and-white printing processes, and you start to see complexity in every corner.

In fact, in my own photographic work, I've returned to capturing images for black-and-white output on film and scanning to digital. Nothing else I've tried gives quite the same range of tones and subtle transitions that I prefer in an image. Neil Snape, a professional photographer based in Paris, recently indicated to me that he is doing much the same.

Both of the images, which I made a few years ago, shown in Figure 8.1 have won several awards between them. The image of the woman was captured on a Nikon D100, and the image of the old sailing ship was captured on Fuji 800 color film and scanned to digital.

Interestingly, color management is in many ways more challenging in this segment than in printing full-color images. Current digital printing technology is, with a few exceptions, set up to deal with color—from software to final print.

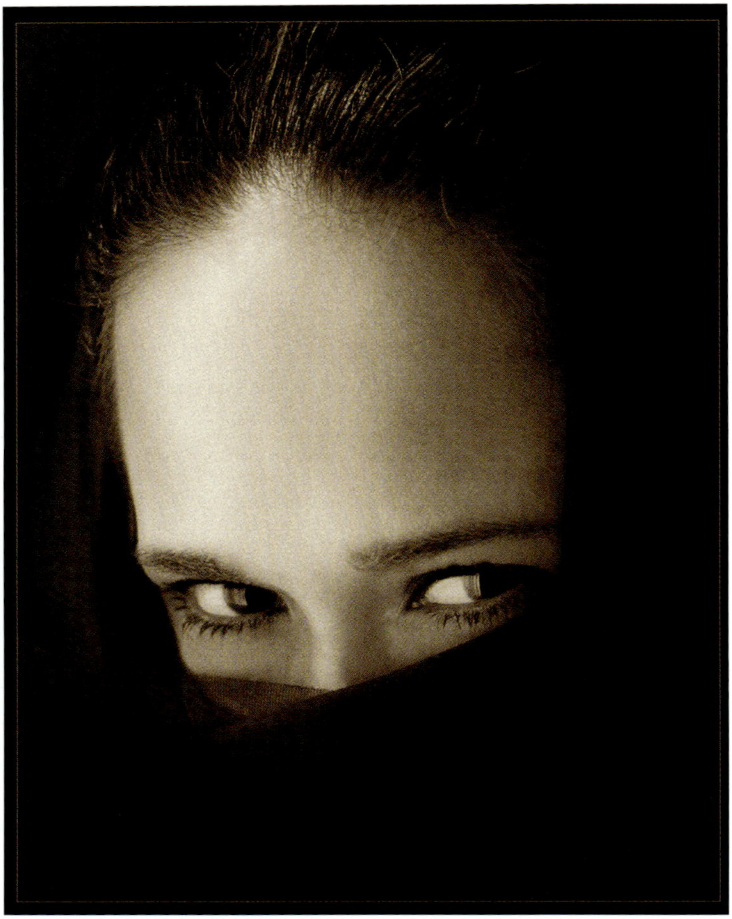

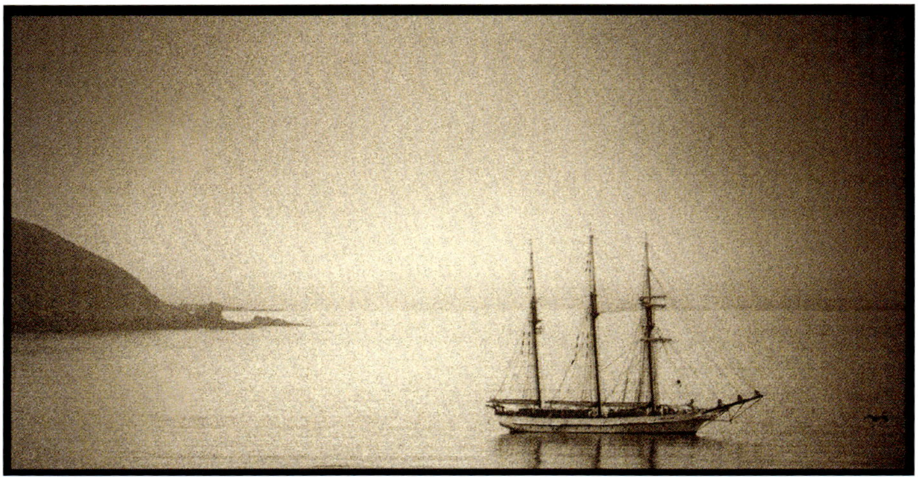

Figure 8.1

Black-and-white images provide a wonderful range of tones and subtle transitions.

Here's the issue: Many digital printing processes do not print in black and white, they print in "color"; that is, they use many, or all, of the colors available in their palette to create a grayscale, duotone, or similar print. In a work environment where most of the color rendering will be to neutral tones, any flaws in color management are glaringly obvious.

It's very useful to outline examples of alternative workflows. In this instance, I assume that you are using desktop scanners for dealing with film, such as dedicated film or flatbed devices.

Table 8.1 Workflows for Black-and-White Production

Black-and-White Negative or Positive Film	**Color Film or Transparency**	**Photograph in Color Using a Digital Camera**	**Photograph in Black and White Using a Digital Camera**
Scan to Adobe RGB 16-bit TIFF	Scan to Adobe RGB 16-bit TIFF	Set camera to capture in RAW format, Adobe 98 RGB or better.	Set camera to capture in black and white
Import to image editor	Import to image editor	Import to image editor	Import to image editor
Major image contrast and tone adjustments	Major image contrast and tone adjustments	Major image contrast and tone adjustments	Major image contrast and tone adjustments
Manual dust and scratch removal	Automated dust and scratch removal	Retouching	Retouching
Retouching	Retouching	Choose method to convert to black and white	Output to master file or print
Output to master file	Choose method to convert to black and white	Output to master file or print	
Output to print	Output to master file or print		
Pros: Wide range available film media; superb rendering of tones	***Pros:*** Wide range available film media; good rendering of tones when converted to grayscale	***Pros:*** Convenience and low cost/unit of digital capture; availability of a variety of custom adjustments and appearances	***Pros:*** Convenience and low cost/unit of digital capture; some cameras offer custom in-camera B&W processing
Cons: Expensive workflow, in media cost and post-production time; particularly dust and scratch removal	***Cons:*** Expensive workflow in media cost and post-production time, but not as expensive as shooting black-and-white film, as color film allows automated dust and scratch removal	***Cons:*** Conversion from color to black and white still does not exactly match appearance and tonal range of black-and-white film capture	***Cons:*** Initial capture in black and white discards image information as compared to color capture, which limits options in image editing in post-production

Choosing a method to convert from color to black and white may involve using an image editor to desaturate the image, create a grayscale or duotone mask over the image, using third-party conversion software, and so on. (Recently, Alien Skin released a software add-on called Exposure for Photoshop that converts color images to resemble black-and-white film. I have limited experience with this, but so far it is very interesting. Other companies, such as Nik, also make very good conversion add-ons and plug-ins.)

Figure 8.2 shows an original color image. Figure 8.3 shows the image converted to black and white using Alien Skin's Exposure, and Figure 8.4 shows the image converted to black and white using Nik Color Efex Pro. In Figure 8.4, note the spectrum slider, which allows you to apply a color filter to the black-and-white image—this gives an effect similar to using a color filter on the camera, such as a red or green filter.

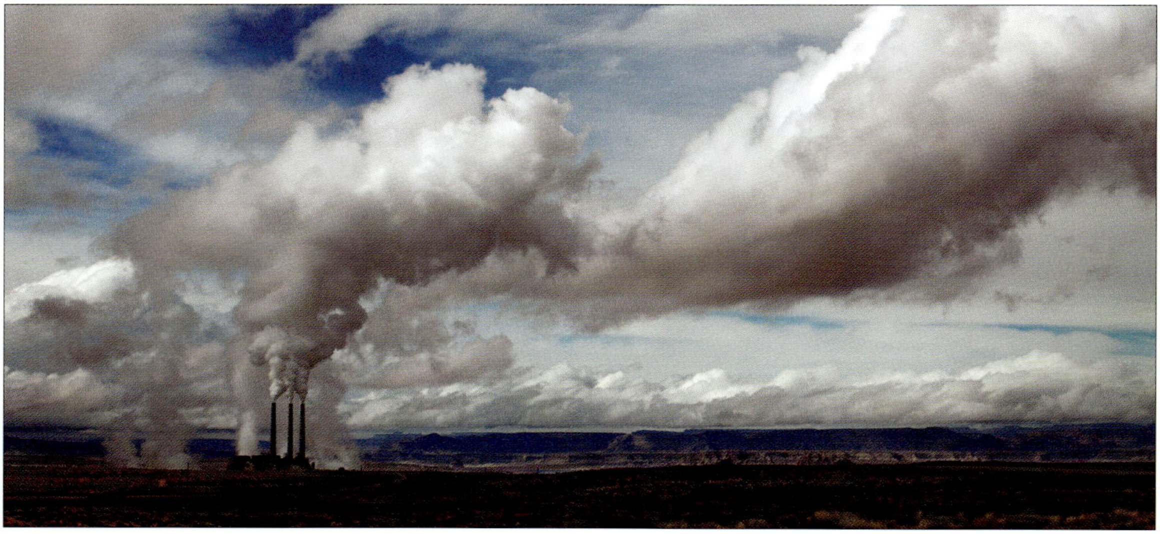

Figure 8.2

The image in color (digital capture).

At present, most of the time I choose to shoot black-and-white images on film, accepting the cost of manual dust and scratch removal or the cost of using a high-end drum scanning process utilizing *wet mount,* or *fluid mounting.* (Wet or fluid mounting employs a non-destructive clear liquid coating over the film, which fills in scratches and smoothes over dust spots. It is removed after scanning.)

Recently, Epson released a new flatbed scanner that incorporates an accessory wet mount film holder. I have not had a chance to try this—but it holds promise for making this scanning technology available at a more reasonable cost than a drum scanner.

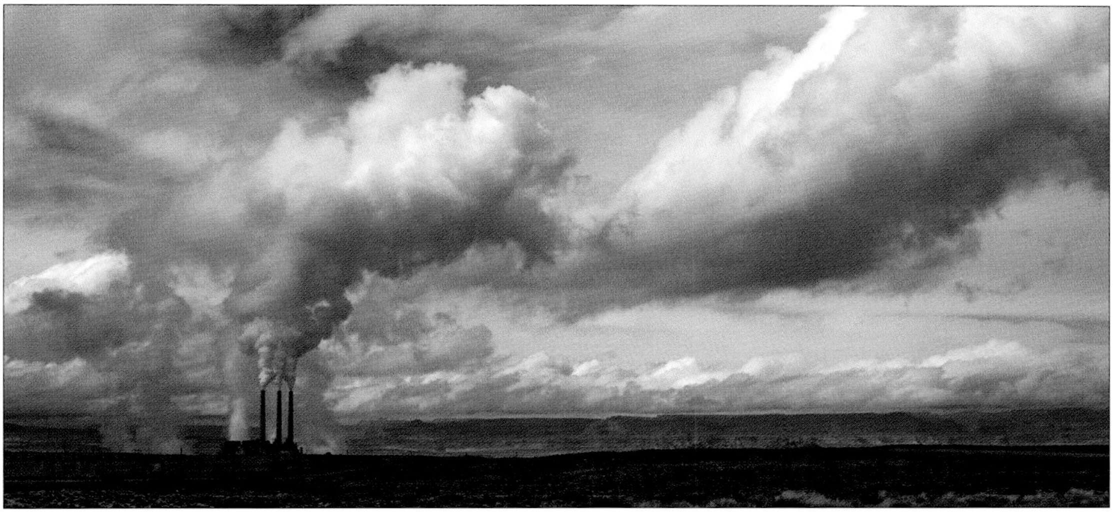

Figure 8.3

The image converted to black and white using Alien Skin Exposure.

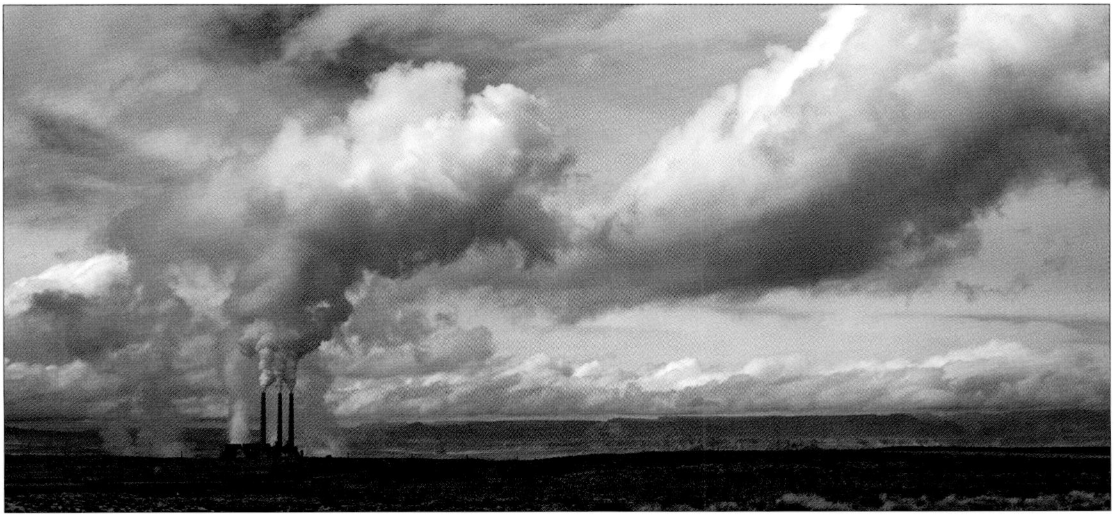

Figure 8.4

A color to black-and-white conversion using Nik Color Efex Pro software plug-in for Photoshop.

Note

There are a number of ways to manually remove dust and scratches from an image. It is of course important to use a method that protects image quality. The scope of this book doesn't really include that part of Photoshop techniques; I suggest that you follow up with a Photoshop guru such as Russel Brown at www.russellbrown.com.

Converting a Color Image to Black and White

One thing is certain: It is a pain in the neck to remove dust and scratches manually, no matter how good you are. Be prepared to spend 20 to 60 minutes on each image to get it right. If I do convert a digital color image to black and white, I use one of several techniques.

- I still begin with a high-bit capture, in a large color space. Editing of the image in Photoshop begins in color, and the black-and-white conversion is performed using Layers, plus a Photoshop filter or a third-party plug-in.
- Using layers also provides the option of adding in the appearance of color toning, such as platinum or selenium.

Here is an example of conversion of a color image to black and white: In Photoshop, go Layer>New Adjustment Layer>Channel Mixer. The first dialog box you'll see is unimportant, so just click OK and continue. Figure 8.5 shows the dialog box that comes up next.

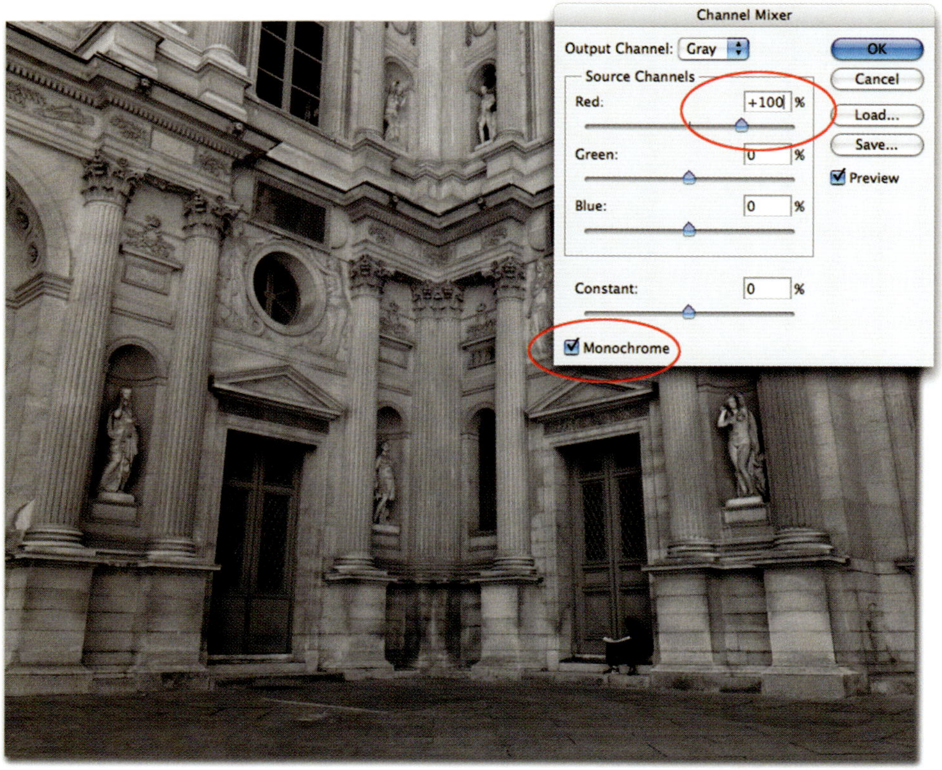

Figure 8.5

The Channel Mixer in Photoshop is an option for conversion to black and white.

When the dialog box shown in Figure 8.2 first appears, Photoshop assumes that you'll want to use the Red channel. Note that this option appears on the upper right, and that the Red channel is set to 100%.

Also note that I have checked the Monochrome box, which causes Photoshop to convert the image to black and white. The interesting thing about the Channel Mixer dialog box is that you can blend the channels, as I have done in the next example, shown in Figure 8.6.

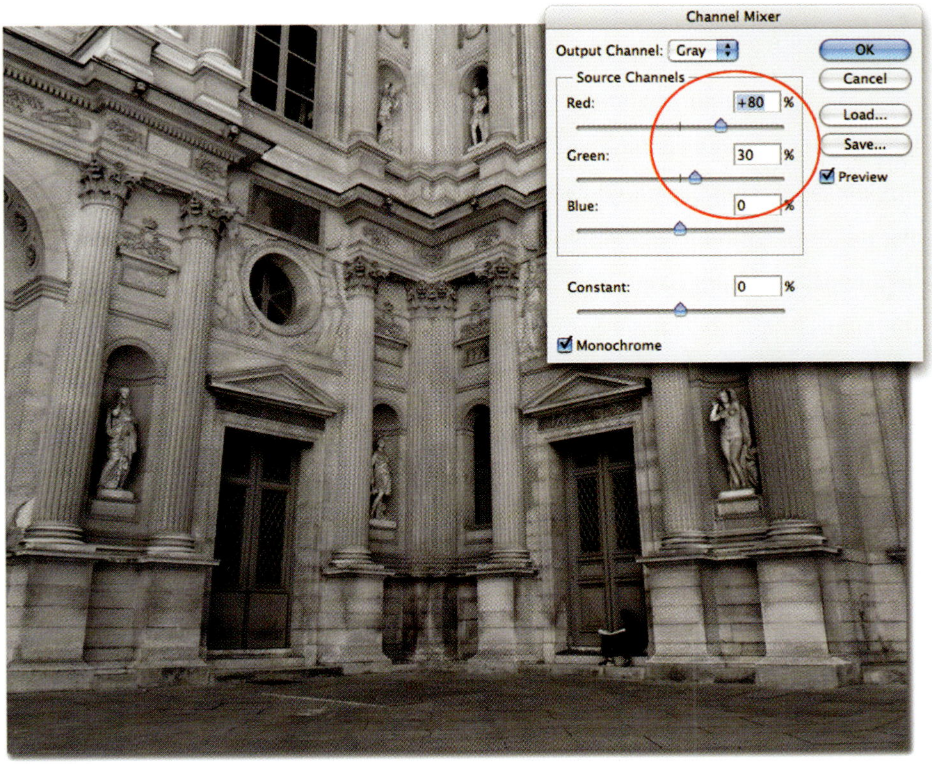

Figure 8.6

Blending the channels using the Channel Mixer.

Note the changed blending of the different color channels. This can be done to whatever degree you want, but please keep in mind that excessive change will result in strange looking images, loss of shadow or highlight detail, and so on. I suggest that whatever settings you choose, you keep the total contribution of the three color channels near 100%.

As you are working with an adjustment layer, you can go back at any time and rearrange these settings to alter the appearance of the image.

Another option is use of the Nik Color Efex Pro filters for Photoshop, which includes a Black and White conversion filter. I also apply this filter to a new layer, although it cannot be re-adjusted as a Photoshop adjustment layer can. Note that there are a number of slider controls, which you can use to adjust the image. Of particular interest is the Spectrum slider, which allows you to simulate use of a colored filter on camera.

There are other methods available to perform color conversions. Some software applications, standalones and plug-ins, do a reasonably good job and are worth investigating. Please note that I discourage use of Photoshop conversions to grayscale, where you click Image>Mode>Grayscale. This method dumps a lot of image information and in my view does not give a good result. In most cases, this method flattens out the image, making mush out of a big portion of the midtones. Figure 8.7 shows three versions of the same image and how Photoshop's conversion to grayscale is not as effective as conversion to black and white using the Channel Mixer palette in Photoshop.

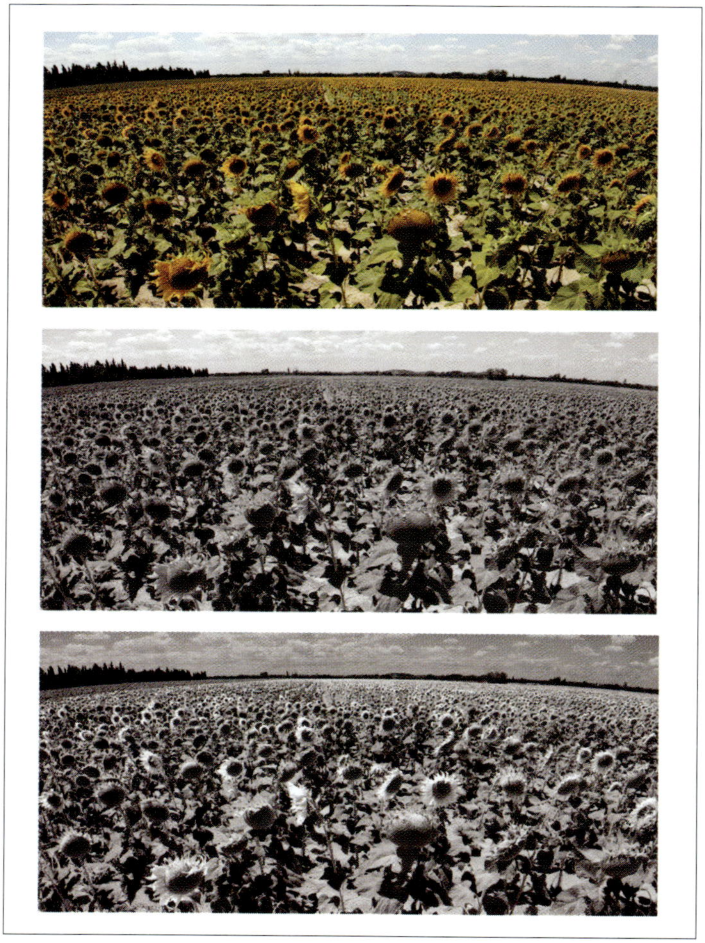

Figure 8.7

This is three versions of the same image. The top image, of a field of sunflowers in France, is in color. Immediately below is the same image converted directly to grayscale in Photoshop. Note the flat, muddy appearance. The version at the bottom was converted using the Channel Mixer palette in Photoshop. Note the improved snap and contrast of the conversion through Channel Mixer.

Some of the proprietary RAW image processing software also includes black and white conversion capability. Apple's Aperture for example, provides black-and-white conversion and color toning as well. Figure 8.8 shows Apple's Aperture; note the red circle indicating the tone controls and the red arrow pointing to the selection on the colorization wheel.

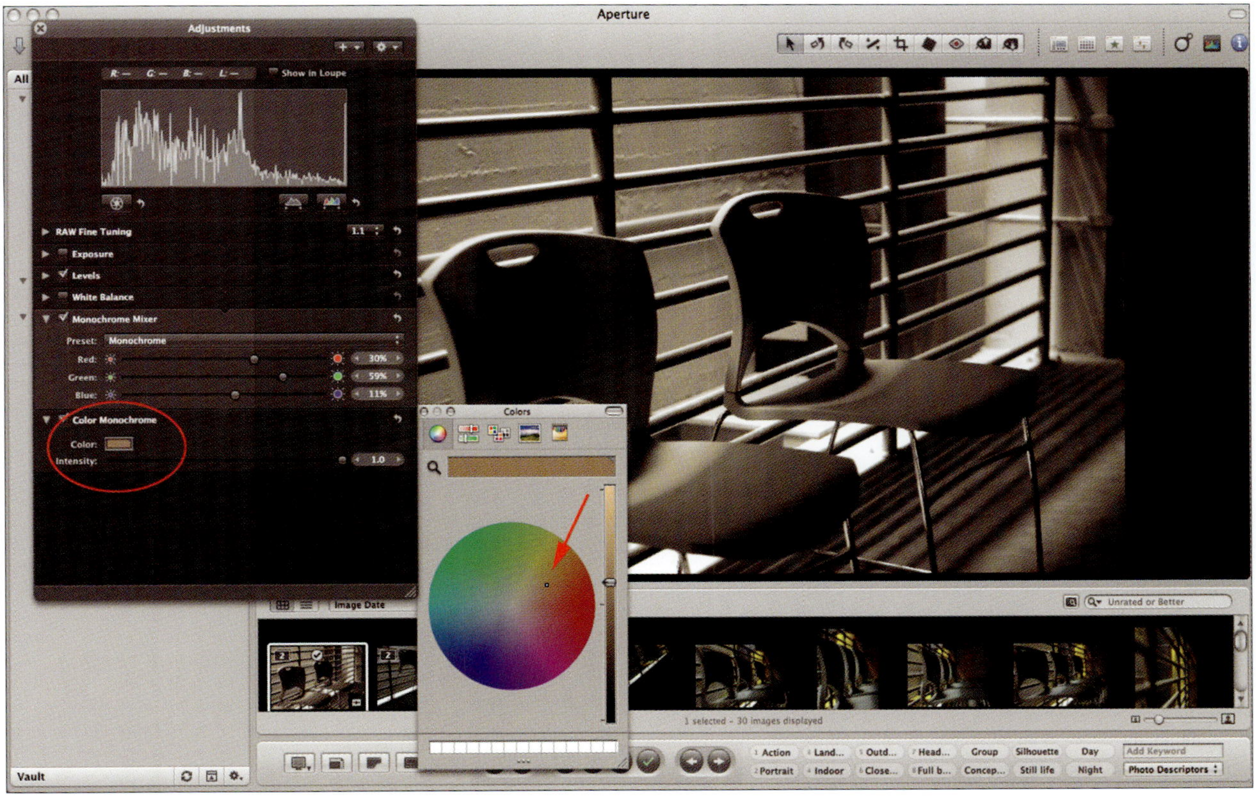

Figure 8.8

Apple's Aperture provides a black-and-white conversion, plus toning.

Adobe Lightroom offers a different interface, as shown in Figure 8.9. One interesting feature is the availability of a number of presets for different film "looks," in addition to manual controls.

Aperture and Lightroom are relatively new products. They are difficult to classify, as they are a mix of image organizer, image editor, and other features. I think it is fair to say, given the frequent updates of the software by both companies, that we will see continuing additions and improvements in these applications in the near future.

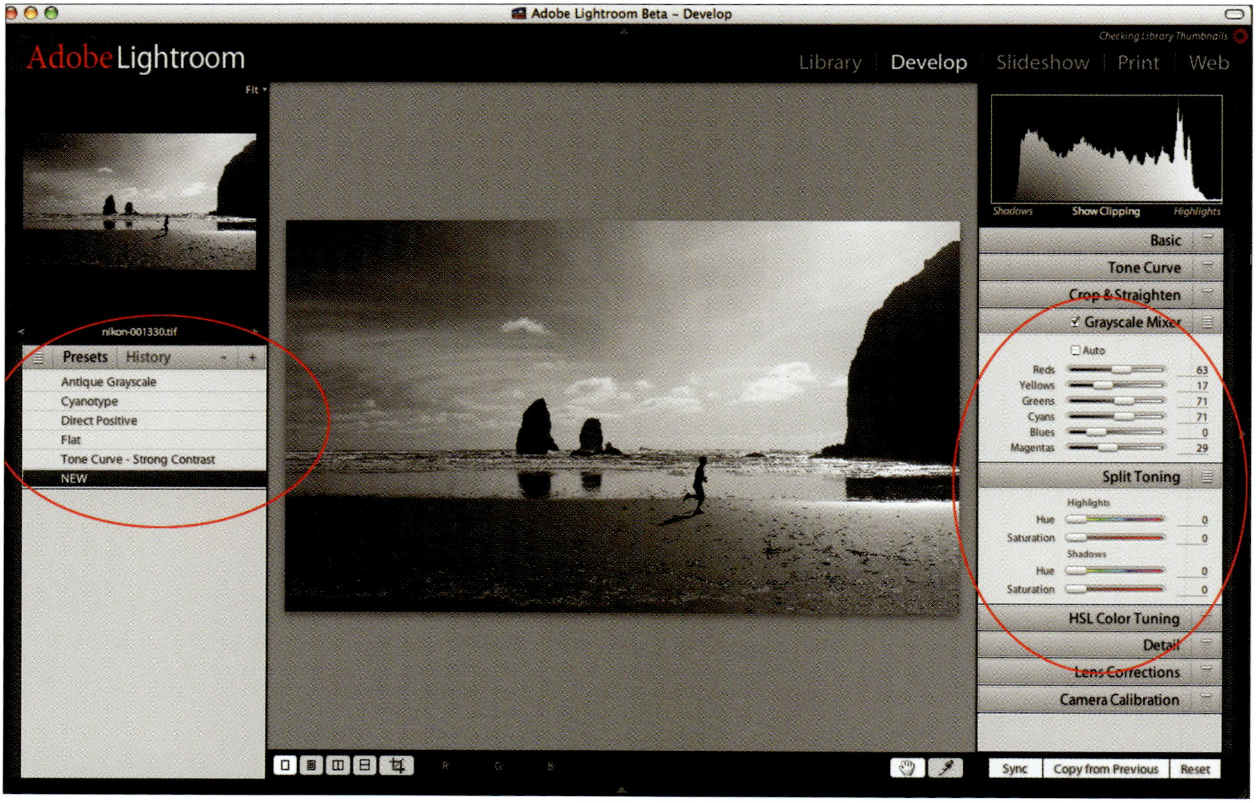

Figure 8.9

Note the controls in Adobe Lightroom for Grayscale mixer, split toning, and film appearance presets.

They both have some amazingly powerful features, including a number of presets for changing image appearance, color balance, and more. At present, however, I still recommend Photoshop as the image editor of choice—although its competitors can do some things better than Photoshop, Photoshop still has the upper hand in breadth and depth of functionality and features.

Printing in Black and White

One of the most difficult parts of this production cycle is making a black-and-white print, particularly on an inkjet printer. In fact, up until about a year ago, most inkjet printers available were quite difficult to use in making black-and-white prints. One almost always would see a green or magenta color cast in all or part of the printed image.

One of the reasons for this is that most printers use all the colors available (typically six or more) to create a grayscale image. For the moment, at least, let's bypass the issue of secondary-market black-only inksets.

One partially successful workaround (if you didn't have access to custom print profiles) was to make adjustments to the individual color ink levels in the printer driver. This is time consuming at best and inaccurate at worst. If you see a particular color cast, you would add a small amount of additional color from the opposite side of the color wheel.

To reduce a red color cast, add some cyan, and vice-versa. Same thing for Magenta-Green and Yellow-Blue. See Figure 8.10.

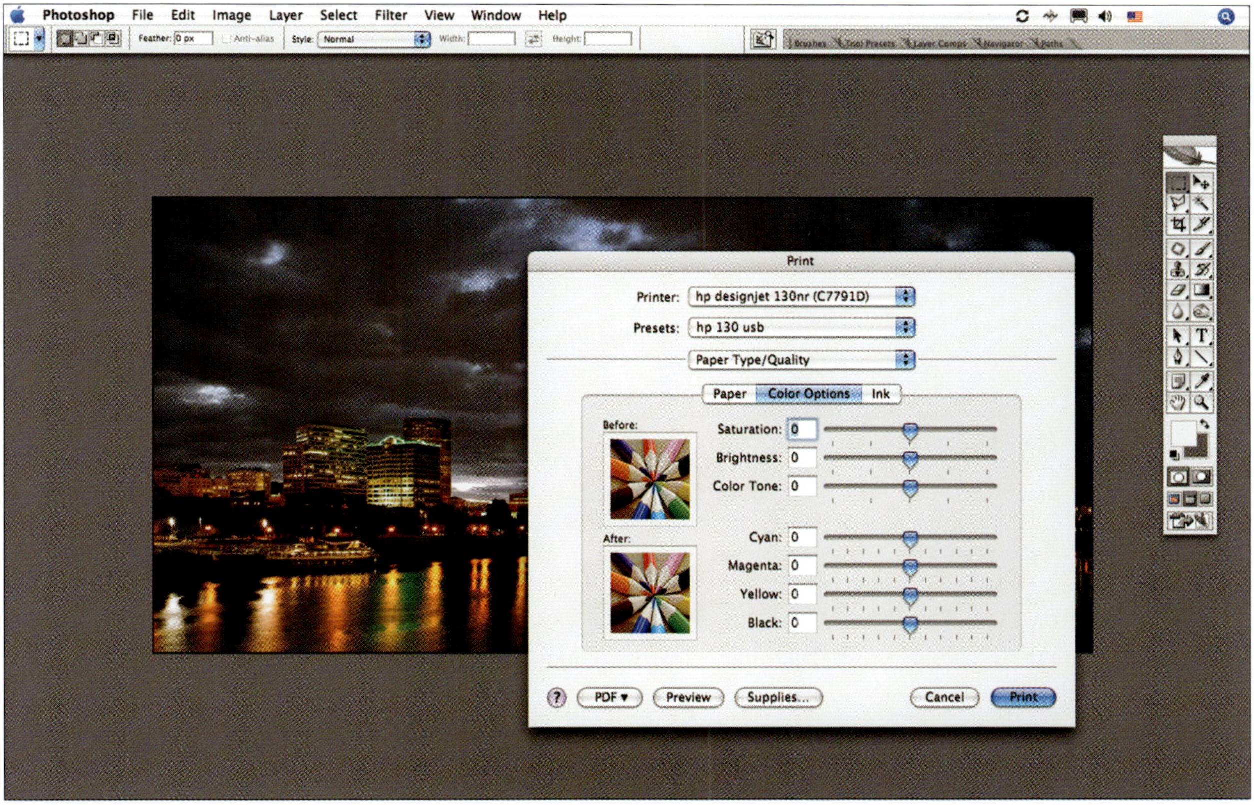

Figure 8.10

Ink controls are useful but difficult to work with.

Improved Printer Drivers

Presently, major printer manufacturers have begun to include greatly improved controls for black-and-white printing. These are contained in the printer drivers, usually several levels down in the dialog boxes or menus. (*Printer drivers* are the basic software tools provided by each manufacturer to run the printer.)

These are great improvements over previously available options in the printer drivers; the quality of the black-and-white prints produced is greatly improved, and color casts and metamerism are greatly reduced, if not eliminated. (Metamerism refers to apparent shifts or changes in color in a print, when it is viewed in different lighting conditions. It can be quite annoying—an image that looks fine in one viewing situation looks quite different, or worse, in another location.)

An example of this software modification (from Epson) is shown in Figure 8.11; it is by no means the only one available, nor does it necessarily render the best rendition of black and white available.

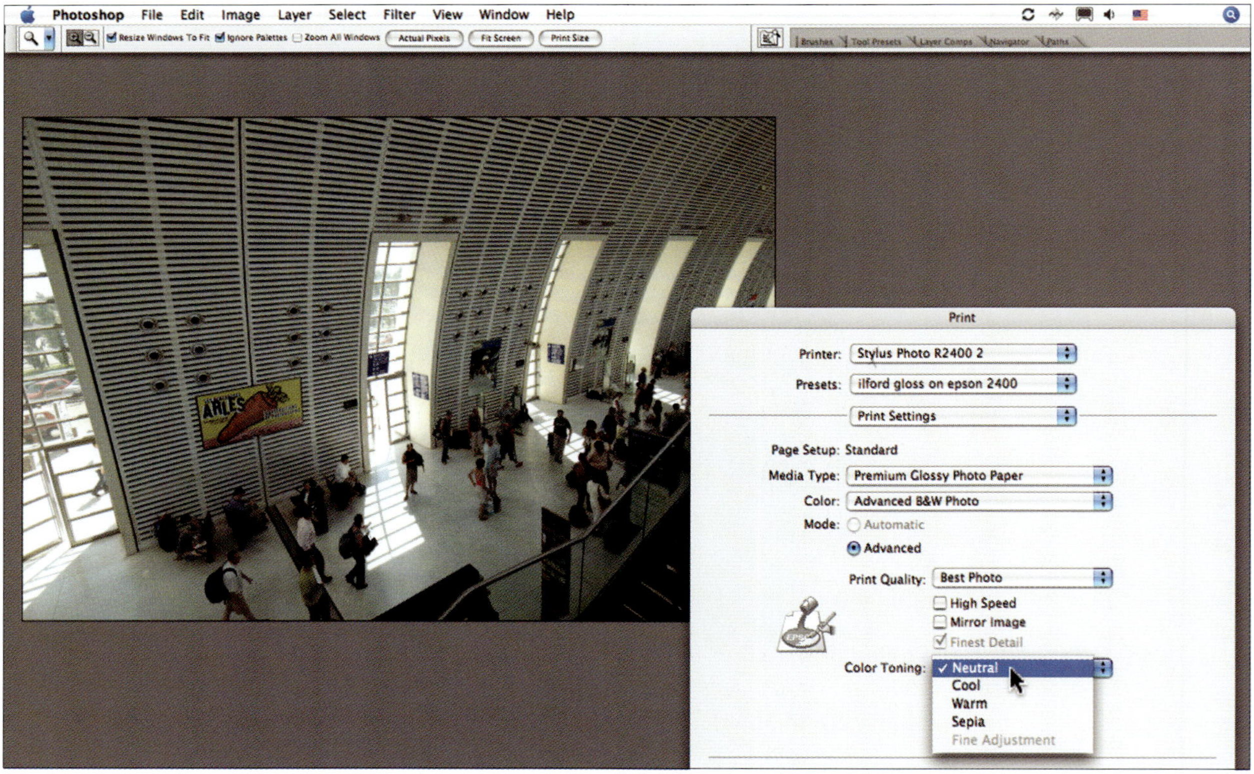

Figure 8.11

The Epson black and white printer driver.

Note that in Figure 8.11, you can use presets to add color toning to your black-and-white print.

Also, Epson provides a color wheel-color picker tool in the next dialog box, shown in Figure 8.12 (see the red arrow). Please note that Epson recommends that, when using the advanced printer driver, you refrain from attaching a printer profile. Finally, you select the paper type in the Print dialog box.

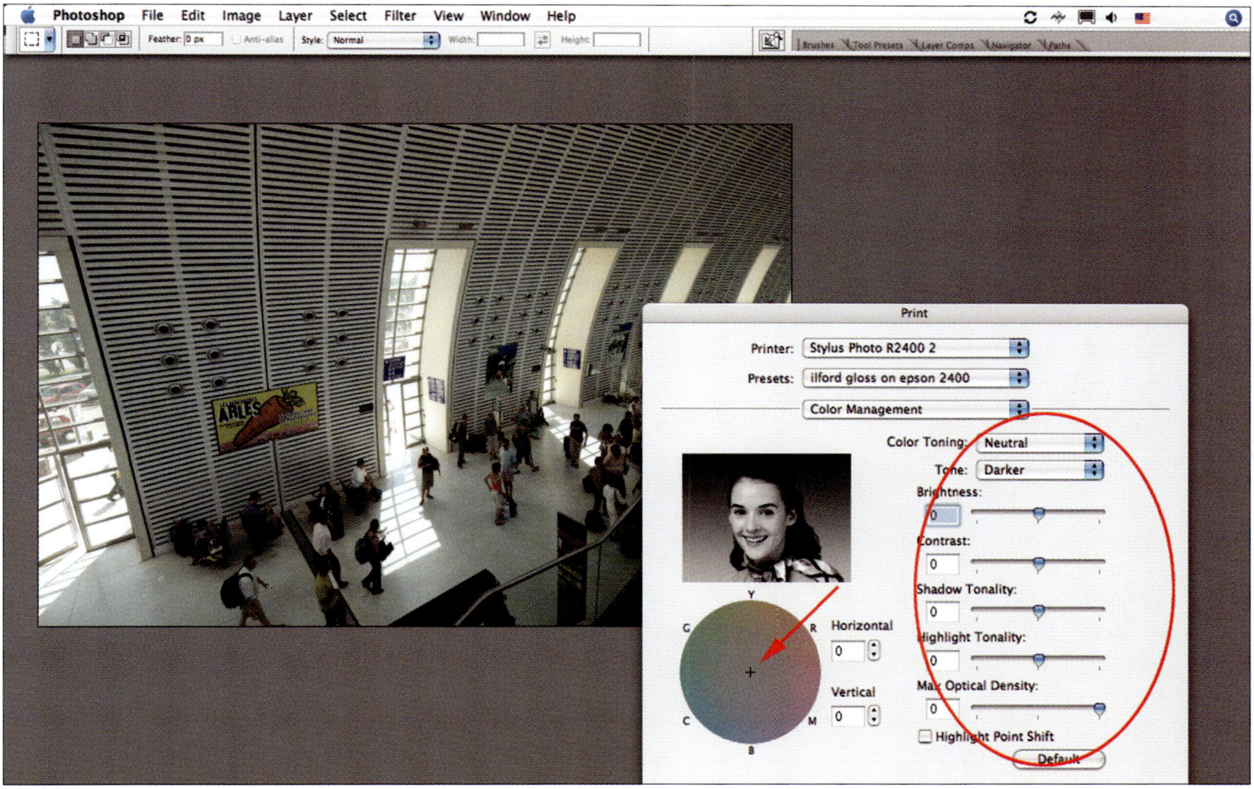

Figure 8.12

The Epson color wheel-color picker tool.

Also note the red circle shown in Figure 8.12, which shows you the range of controls available in adjusting the image. Epson does not provide a real-time preview, however.

As another example, HP offers printer-driver based grayscale printing. The results from both of these printer drivers are quite good. Prints are very neutral, and metamerism is very low to non-existent (assuming you are printing using manufacturer's inks and papers).

Custom Printer Profiles for Black and White

A printer profile is a small software add-on file that you can use to tell the printer how to handle rendering color on a particular paper. Put another way, a printer profile used correctly will usually improve the overall color, clarity, and contrast of your printed image.

To use a printer profile, first obtain the profile file (called an ICC profile) from the printer or paper manufacturer or another vendor. The profile is intended for use with a selected combination of ink, for example HP Vivera or the Epson K3 inks, and one selected paper.

For example, HP offers paper profiles for the Designjet 130 printer. They are available via the HP website at http://h41186.www4.hp.com/country/us/en/iccprofile_bw/index.html.

Note that each profile is intended to produce a slightly differently toned image. There are test files included in the downloads to assist you in determining which profile to use. Instructions on use of the HP profiles are also available on the same web page.

Epson also offers profiles on its website. From their website, go to Support> Printers and select one of the printers you want to use. An index of available files will pop up.

Quoting Adobe's online help for Photoshop CS2, the profiles should be copied to the following folders on your computer:

- In Windows, right-click a profile and select Install Profile. Alternatively, copy the profiles into the WINDOWS/system32/spool/drivers/color folder (Windows XP) or the WINNT/system32/spool/drivers/color folder (Windows 2000).
- In Mac OS, copy profiles into the /Library/Application Support/Adobe/Color/Profiles/. You can also copy profiles into the /Users/username/Library/ColorSync/Profiles folder (see Figure 8.13).

After installing color profiles, be sure to restart your computer.

Using Printer Profiles to Make Prints

Now let's consider how to use these profiles in making your prints. From the main Photoshop screen, go to File>Print with Preview. You'll see the dialog box shown in Figure 8.14. Note on the upper right there is a red arrow pointing to a button right underneath Page Setup. The normal default for Photoshop will cause this button to say More Options, and the dialog box is very small and gives you limited choices. If you click it, the dialog box expands to show you the one in Figure 8.14, and the button says Fewer Options.

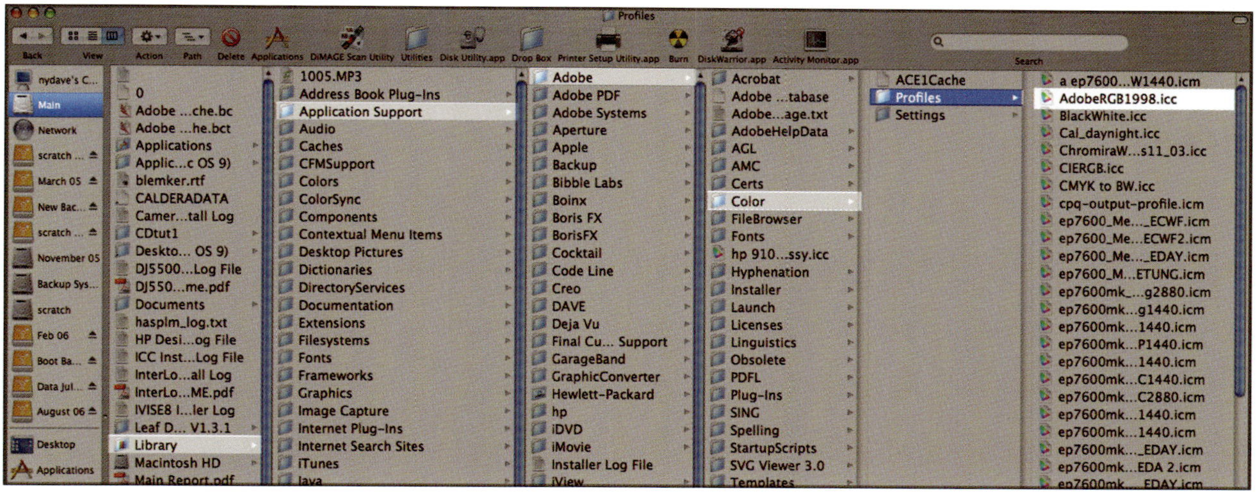

Figure 8.13

A screenshot of the Mac OS X folders for Adobe applications.

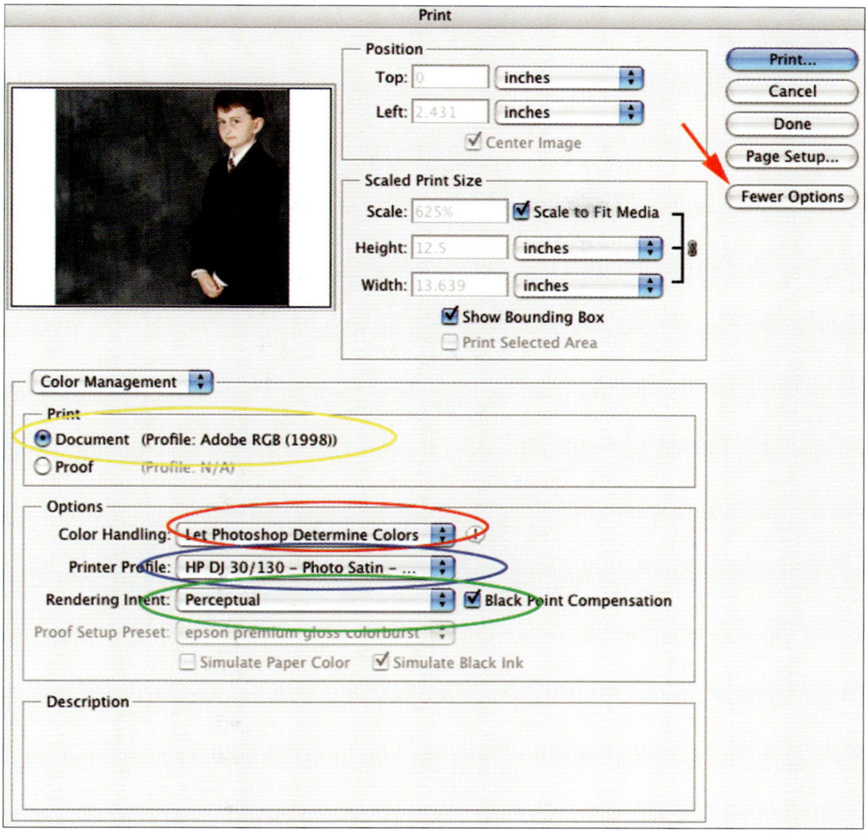

Figure 8.14

The Photoshop Print with Preview dialog box.

The drop-down Color Handling menu circled in red provides you with a number of choices, including No Color Management, Let Printer Manage Color, or Let Photoshop Manage Color (although this option might say Application Managed Color in some cases). Choose Photoshop/Application Managed Color.

The second drop-down menu, titled Printer Profile, is indicated by the blue circle. This drop-down menu will contain a list of the ICC printer profiles available on your computer. Choose the correct profile for your current printer, ink, and paper combination. (Choosing an incorrect profile will give you at best some color distortions, at worst a surreal mess on the paper.)

The third drop-down menu, titled Rendering Intent, is circled in green. Generally, for color printing you'll want to use Perceptual Rendering Intent, and for black and white you can try Absolute Colorimetric.

Next, click Print, and the dialog box shown in Figure 8.15 will appear.

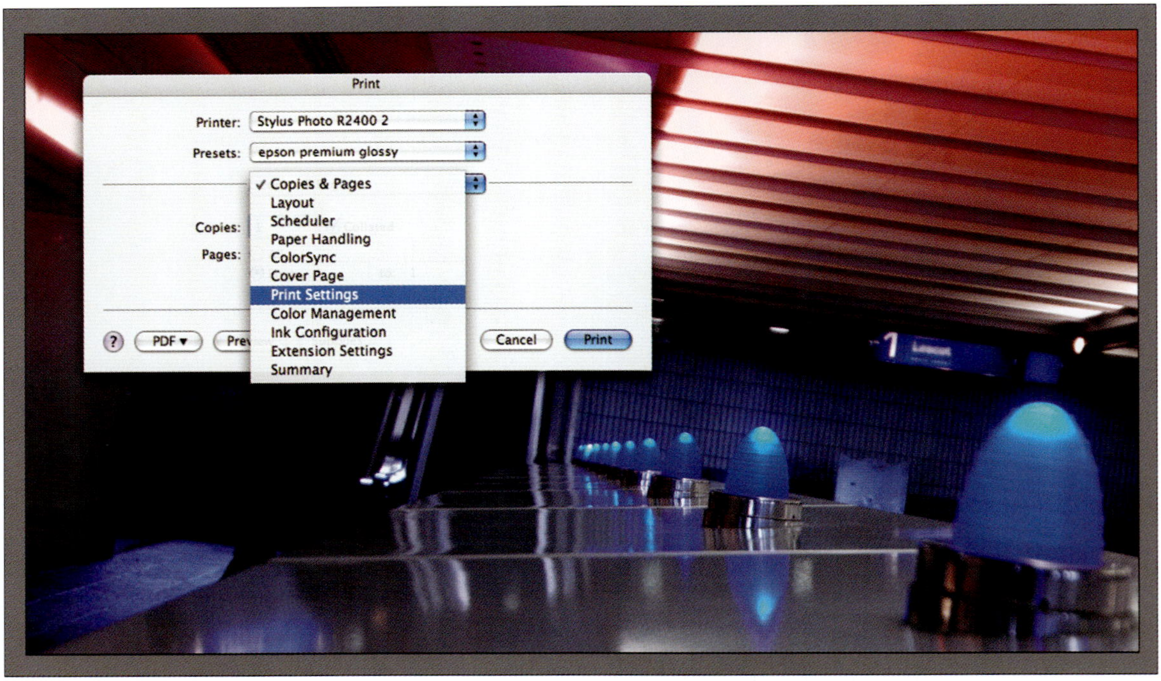

Figure 8.15

Selecting Print Settings from the drop-down menu.

Note that the drop-down menu located third from the top has been clicked and shows you a number of adjustment options. The one that's most important to this discussion is the Print Settings selection.

Next you'll see the dialog box shown in Figure 8.16.

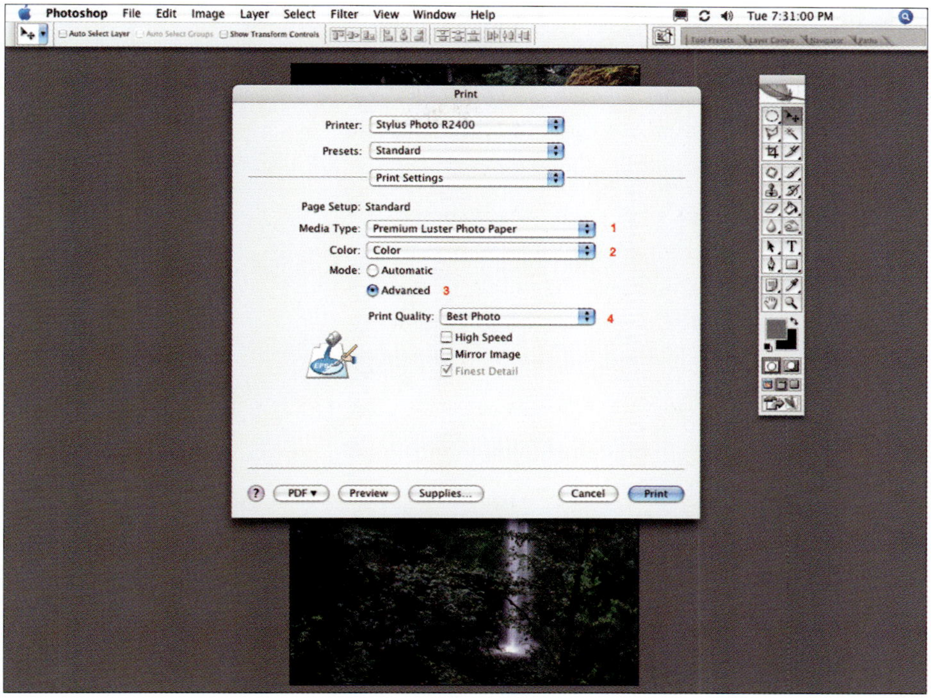

Figure 8.16

The Print dialog box provides options for color/black and white, print quality, and more.

Select paper type in the menu choice indicated by the red number 1. Select Color or Black and White in the drop-down menu indicated by number 2. Select Custom, indicated by the number 3. Next, select Best Photo, indicated by number 4. For best results, leave High Speed unchecked.

This is, obviously, more complicated than the instructions provided previously for so-called "grayscale" printing. In fact, if you are going to be involved in a significant amount of black-and-white printing, you might want to consider using a RIP software application (Raster Image Processor).

Using a RIP for Black-and-White Printing

One of the best reasons to use a RIP is black-and-white printing. Although the manufacturers' printer drivers have improved quite a bit in the last 6-12 months, RIP software still has the advantage in the level of control you have in making enlargements.

A number of companies sell RIP products that provide for black-and-white printing via inkjet. They include but are not limited to Colorbyte, Sundance, Bowhouse, and Colorburst.

Some manufacturers also sell replacement ink sets that are intended only for black-and-white printing. These are, by reputation, capable of producing very good prints. (However, I'm reluctant to set up a printer just for one type of image production—I would personally rather have a printer that can print in both color and black and white.)

For the purposes of this discussion, let's review one of the RIP products that has an outstanding reputation for both color and black-and-white printing—ImagePrint by Colorbyte Software. In my opinion, ImagePrint is one of the best RIPs available for photographers and artists—the color and black-and-white images that it renders on my printers (Epson and HP) are superb, and the image detail is excellent, as well.

For example, I get excellent results printing black-and-white images on Hahnemuhle Photo Rag, using matte inks in my Epson 7600. And, the black-and-white prints that I can make on my HP Designjet 130, using Premium Plus Photo Satin paper, are superb.

ImagePrint can be used with a number of printing platforms, including those made by Epson, Fuji, HP, and Roland. It also supports the Lyson, Cone, and MIS inksets made for Epson printers. ImagePrint has a good interface—it is, however, a little bit unusual, in that some of the toolbar icons are not as intuitive as they could be. The learning curve is pretty short though, and the results are worth the effort.

Colorbyte software provides printer profiles for a very wide range of ink/paper combinations, for color and black-and-white printing. Now, in most cases, I've found that so-called "canned" profiles are not in the same league as custom-made profiles; however, in my experience I've found the ImagePrint profiles to be as good or better than any custom profiles I have seen.

This is a big savings to you if you decide to use this application, because there's little need for purchasing additional equipment or paying for a custom printer profile.

Next, I'll review some of the more important features of the software. ImagePrint runs on both Mac and PC. When you first open the software, you'll see the screen shown in Figure 8.17.

In the vertical toolbar of the main screen, shown on the right, there are utilities for rotation, centering, flipping horizontal or vertical, filling the page, repeating the image, and more.

I've imported an image of mine, which was scanned from Kodak TMAX 100 using a Nikon Coolscan 4000 and subsequently edited in Photoshop. Note that this is a 16-bit TIFF file, which ImagePrint handles just as well as an 8-bit file. See Figure 8.18.

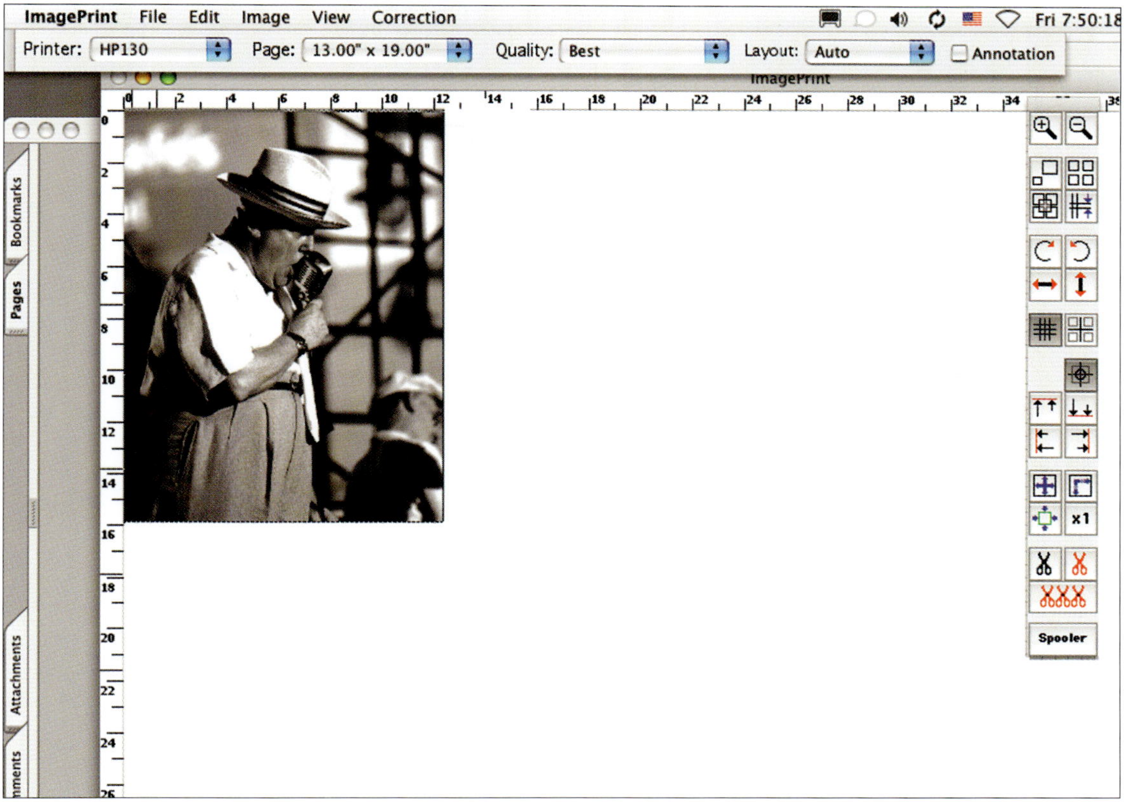

Figure 8.17

The ImagePrint main screen, where you can easily change the printer you are sending the job to, the paper size, and print quality.

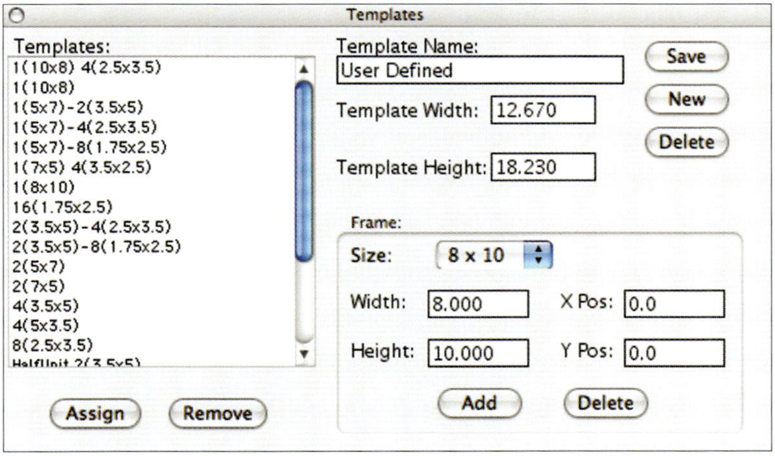

Figure 8.18

ImagePrint provides a large menu of preset templates for photo package layouts. This is a great tool for a busy photographer.

Under the main menu bar, if you choose Image>Color Management, you'll see the screen shown in Figure 8.19.

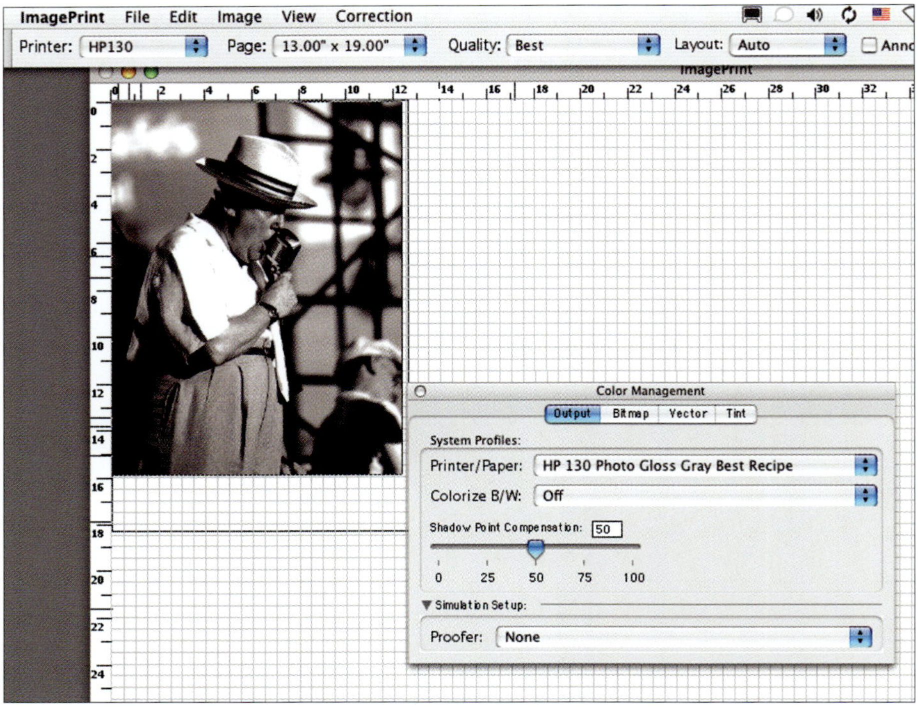

Figure 8.19

ImagePrint's color management screen provides tools for assigning printer output profiles.

The Color Management screen provides tools for assigning printer output profiles by printer and paper type used. It also provides a number of other tools, including a tab for tinting the overall print.

To begin the printing process, choose File>Print, and the Print dialog box will come up. If you click on Options, you'll see a secondary dialog box, shown in Figure 8.20.

In the case of the HP Designjet 130, this part of the software also provides an integrated color closed loop calibration cycle for the printer. This calibrates the printer to better match the profiles in the ImagePrint software (it is also available through the HP printer utility application).

Under the main menu title Corrections, you'll find a drop-down menu for color, tone, histogram, and ink limits. These are all together in one tabbed dialogue box, as shown in Figure 8.21.

The first three of these four tools you are now familiar with; the ink limit tool is a specialized utility that under most circumstances should not concern photographers or artists using an inkjet printer.

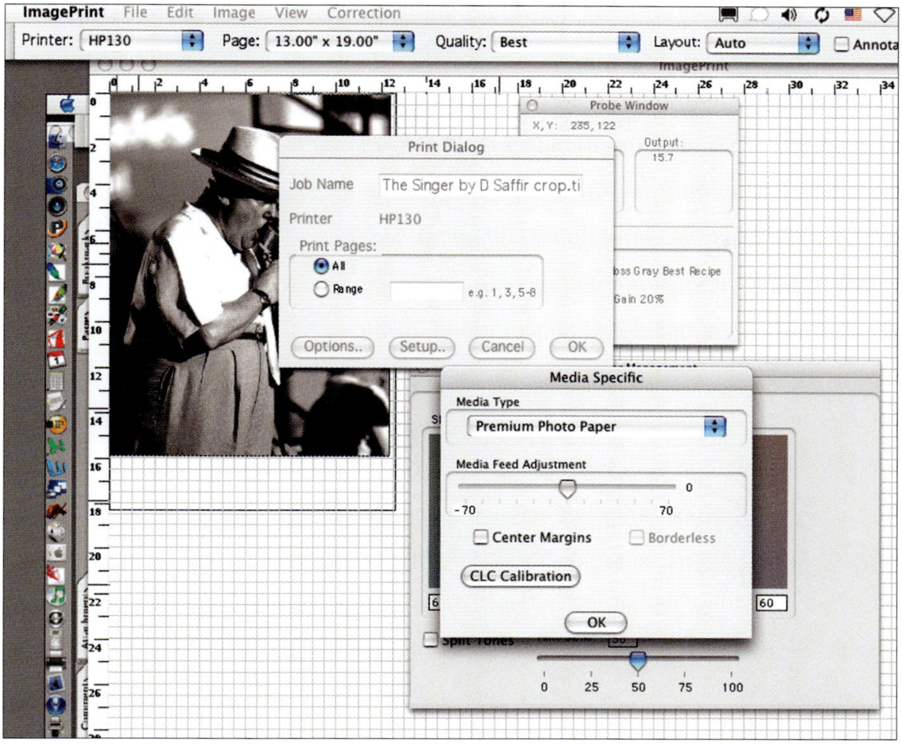

Figure 8.20

The Print Options dialog box allows you to choose paper type, center the margins, and specify a borderless print.

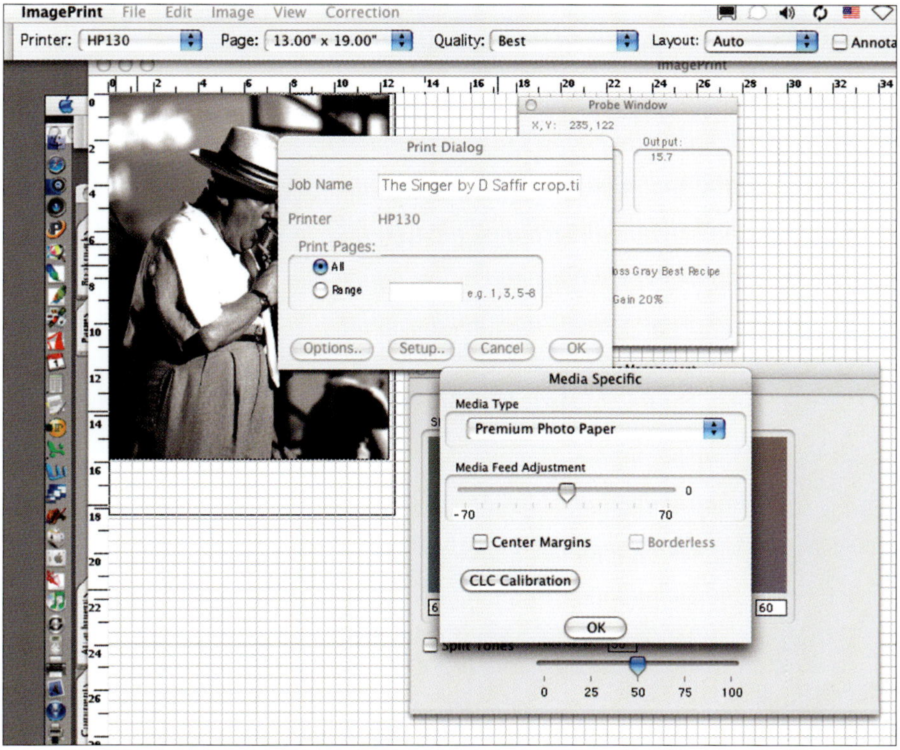

Figure 8.21

This dialog box in ImagePrint provides tools for tone, color, histogram, and ink limit. The first three of these function in a fashion similar to their counterparts in Photoshop.

From the main menu, choose Image>Settings, so you can access the dialog box, which has some very powerful tools, including a superb upsizing utility (scale), tools for repeating images, setting space between images, setting crop marks, and more.

ImagePrint also incorporates an excellent file browser, shown in Figure 8.22, that provides image previews and drag-and-drop image import.

I use ImagePrint all the time. I also use Onyx Postershop (a variant sold by Ilford Imaging) quite a bit. Both RIPs deliver outstanding performance and, in larger prints, images far better than I can get from the standard printer driver.

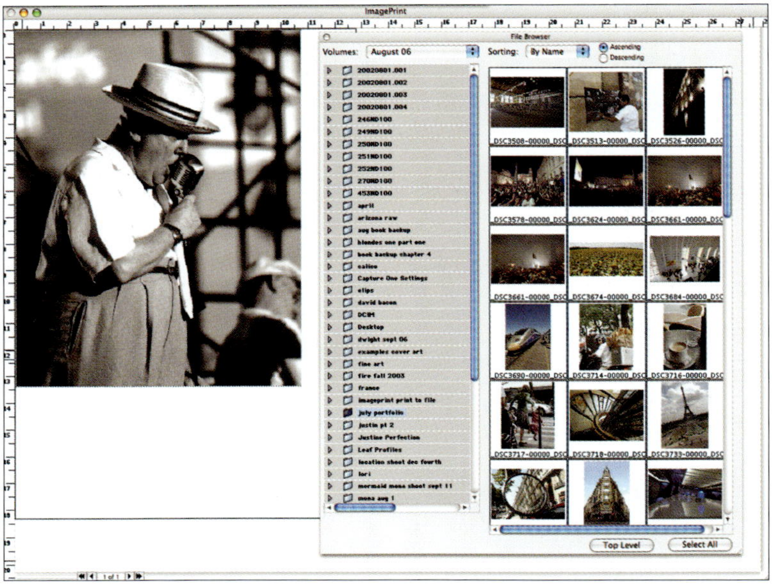

Figure 8.22

The ImagePrint file browser.

One more thought about RIPs in general: When you send a print from Photoshop through the printer driver, it ties up Photoshop for a few seconds, or a few minutes, while it is processing the image. A RIP, on the other hand, will usually generate the printer file separately from your image editing application, which allows you to keep working while your printer is running. A great benefit!

Summary

It's true that in the past, many people stayed away from trying to make black-and-white prints using digital technology. It was complicated, and too often the results were just not good enough.

Now, there isn't really any good reason not to take advantage of improvements in software and hardware. Just about any photographer or artist can make excellent, neutral-tone or controlled-tone black-and-white prints.

9

Preserving Color: Archiving and Storage

This chapter explores a number of aspects of the subject of preserving color. The primary points of view are those of the person responsible for protecting or storing artwork and the artists whose work is potentially their "bank account." In both cases, the work involves protecting color, quality, and value.

Please note that the word "archival" is one which has been defined in a multitude of ways—with much disagreement over standards and expectations. My approach to this is that a material, mounting board, matting, media, ink, display or container, or other tool used in displaying and storing my work should be able to deliver performance that supports at minimum 80 years of colorfastness.

This is very, very conservative, and most experts will tell you that it should and can be longer. For example, given improvements in technology in many areas, you can now expect print life spans exceeding 100-200 years with proper care.

Color and the Ageing Process

Different materials and color media age at different rates. Some materials, such as pigment inks, are more resistant to fading. Up until a few years ago, dye-based inks faded much more quickly, but this has changed, and dye-based inks equal or exceed the performance of their pigmented cousins—and frequently offer more lively color. Figure 9.1 shows a faded image—something you of course want to avoid!

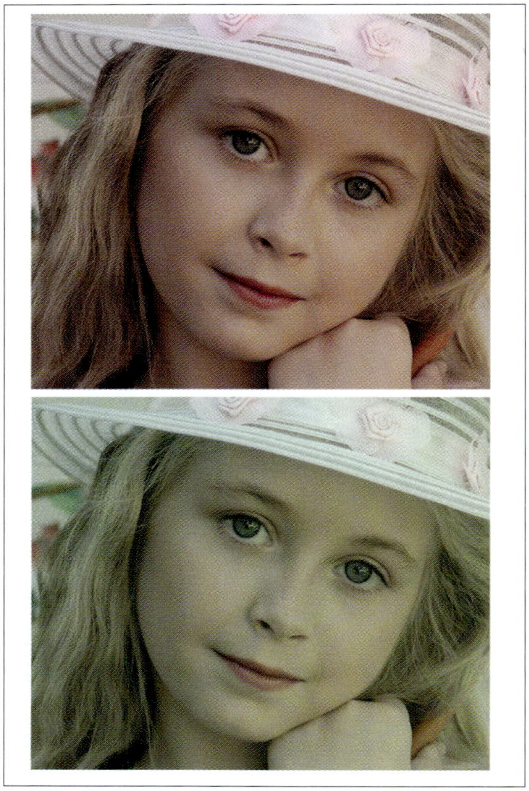

Figure 9.1

You can avoid faded images like this one by storing them in the right environment.

Printed images are exposed to different environments, in different combinations. Some of these variables that can contribute to deterioration of an image include:

- Heat
- Light
- Moisture and humidity
- Air pollution, such as ozone
- Physical handling, such as fingerprints, perspiration, and scuffing
- Gases emitted by natural and man-made materials
- Aerosol or liquid cleaners
- Dust (which may or may not contain additional contaminants)
- Mold, fungus, bacteria, and insects
- Any glue, adhesive, or paint that is not certified by the manufacturer to be harmless to fine art prints and photographs
- Some wooden cabinets, particularly those made of plywood, are not suitable for storage as the glue used in their construction outgases and affects prints

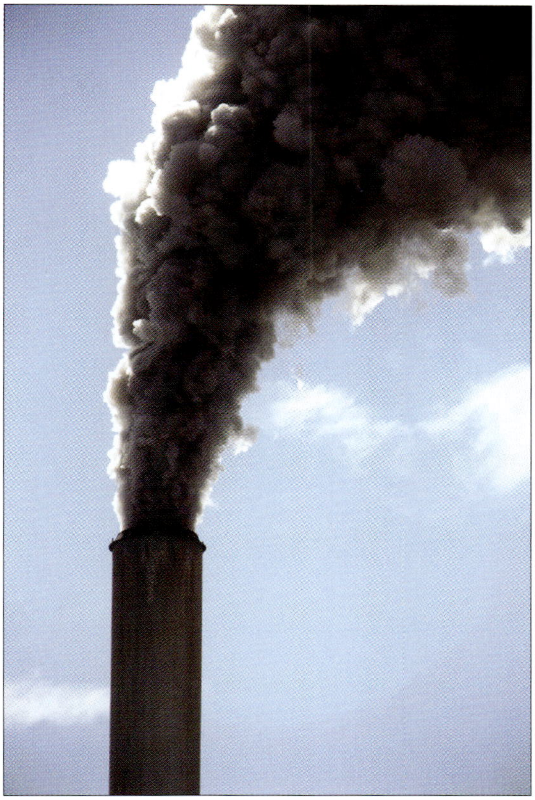

Figure 9.2

Simple air pollution can ruin your images if the exposure is long enough. (Photo licensed from istockphoto.)

The idea, of course, is to keep all of these things away from your artwork. Unfortunately, this means that the photographers, artists, printmakers, or curators must do their homework. It takes skill and work to assemble a collection and only one error to ruin it.

As you continue in this chapter, you'll explore options in creating display and storage environments that help protect critical color and your artwork.

How Can You Tell If You Have Color Troubles?

First, if you notice that the color of the frame, the mat, or the wall that the image is mounted on is graying or fading, you should consider what is causing this and perhaps relocate the image.

If a mat has a beveled edge, some mats will show discoloration on the edge that has been cut. This should be checked. Figure 9.3 shows the proper way to mount artwork to a mat.

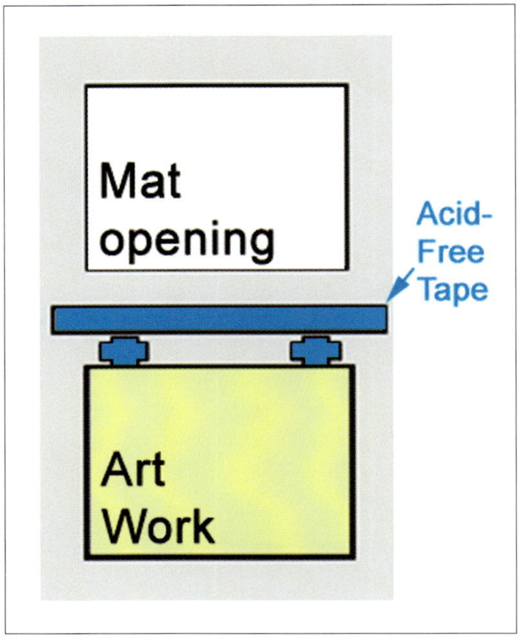

Figure 9.3

The proper way to mount artwork to a mat. Be sure to use acid-free materials all around.

Color shifts can take place over long periods of time. Skin tones, particularly in the case of light-skinned photographic subjects, will usually show first, as will areas of intense blue sky, bright green foliage, and the like. I have an image (a C-Print) of a barn that I've owned for perhaps 25 years, and I've noticed that both the red of the barn and the green fields around it just don't look as vibrant as they once did.

An increase of dust or other foreign material behind the glass is cause for concern, as are flakes of color coming off, or areas of color that are becoming mottled or uneven.

Original paintings may give you hints of adverse changes when their overall appearance seems to darken or yellow.

Note

As an anecdote, I have been told that a photographer's assistant packed a collection of large prints and shipped them to a gallery for an exhibition. During packing, some ordinary foam that one might obtain in a fabric or furniture-refinishing shop was used to pack the box. En-route, this foam was exposed to heat in the back of the shipper's truck, with the result that the edges of all the prints turned yellow and were ruined.

Storage places guaranteed to damage color:

- The attic
- The basement
- The garage
- The trunk or back seat of your car
- A closet located near a laundry room or bathroom
- Under the bed (bugs and dust!)
- In direct sunlight

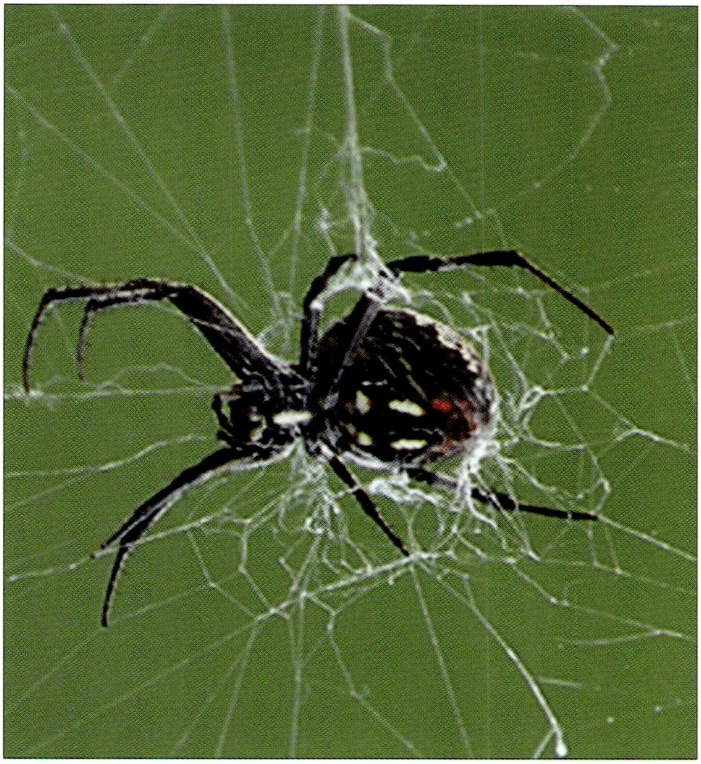

Figure 9.4

When it comes to your artwork, spiders and other insects are not your friend!

Displaying, Storing, and Archiving Your Work

One of the questions I hear all the time is "how do I display my work?" Given that most American households put many of their photographs on the refrigerator door, let's start by saying "not there."

In fact, at times it has become fashionable to display artwork suspended by clips in a wire frame or laying flat on a table. Others sandwich the image between two sheets of glass. None of these is recommended.

If you want the color of the work to last, you'll have to do more. Ideally, a photograph or piece of art should be placed in correct dark storage or framed using acid-free and chemically neutral materials designed for the purpose. Like so many things, you get what you pay for.

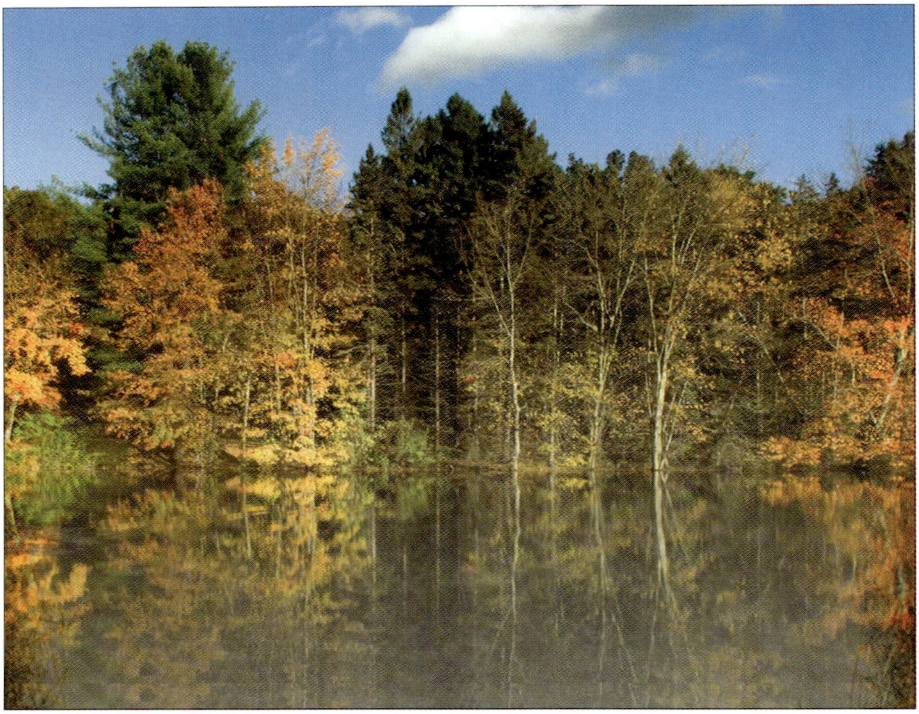

Figure 9.5

A photograph or piece of art should be placed in correct dark storage or framed using acid-free and chemically neutral materials designed for the purpose.

The frame should be designed to hold the artwork or photo away from the glass. Mount the image on suitable backing board or mat; I prefer using a hinge mount. At minimum, use UV-resistant glass on the front of the frame. On the back of the frame, it is often desirable to provide a vapor barrier covering the back opening top to bottom and side to side—particularly if you live in a humid region.

Display conditions should be cool, low in humidity, and free of air pollution such as car exhaust, cooking fumes, and the like. There is quite a bit of debate over the effect of indoor light levels over time; as a practical matter, direct sunlight is nearly lethal to color and nearly so filtered through blinds or curtains. (Some skylights are big offenders in this department.)

Stay away from standard fluorescent lighting fixtures, as these usually have high component of UV light, which is harmful. An example of this is hanging a fine art photograph in an office environment and forgetting to change the overhead lights to non-UV fluorescents.

Some traditional lighting fixtures used to illuminate photographs and other artwork are actually dangerous. A traditional incandescent light, sometimes called a "piano" light, generates quite a bit of heat, and if it is dismounted accidentally from the frame, can damage the image. See Figure 9.6.

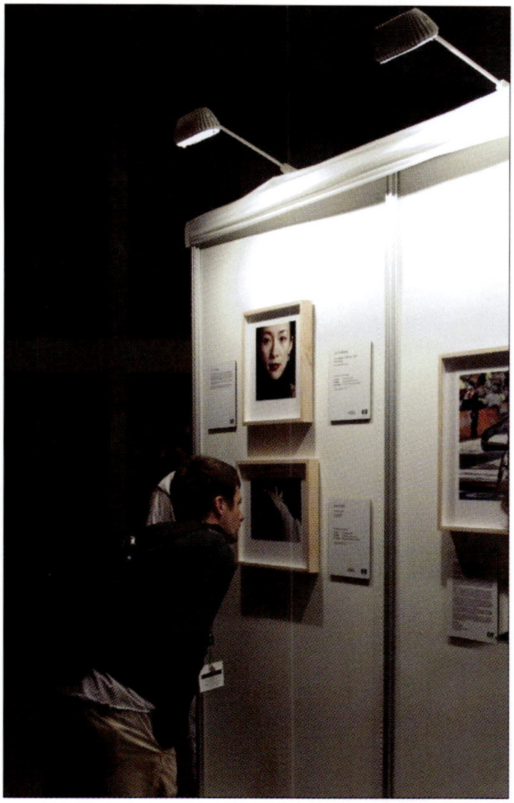

Figure 9.6

This show used a better (low-voltage) lighting environment to show the artwork.

Among the best are color-corrected track lights, sconces, and flush mounted ceiling lights. These are UV-free, usually low voltage, and very well made.

Ideally, you want to be purchasing framing and display materials from a supplier who understands this subject well, who will provide the quality you need, and who will notify you if they change suppliers, or if they make a substitution for something that is temporarily out of stock.

I have used two methods for identifying and monitoring suppliers that I use. In one case, I have spent quite a bit of time in discussions with local businesses that frame artwork, concentrating on those who others in the local art community recommend. Of course, quality of materials available varies from place to place.

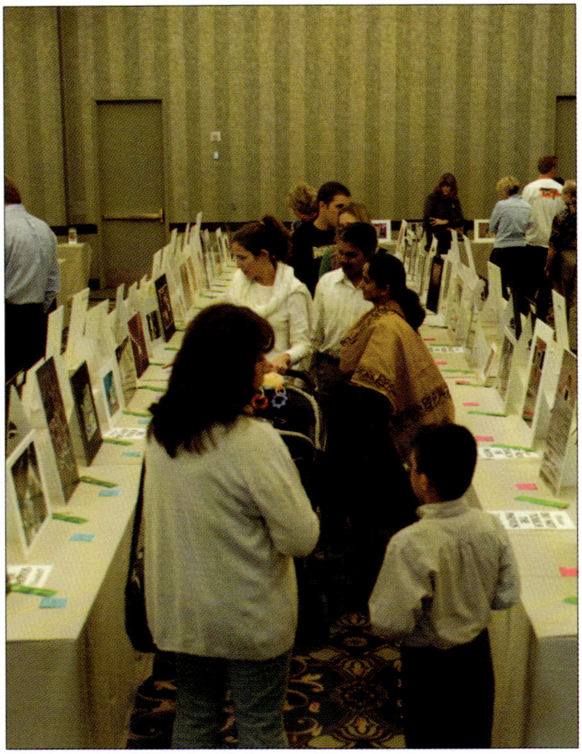

Figure 9.7

Note how the uncontrolled color of the environment lighting in this show gives everything a green/orange color cast.

I also found that, on rare occasions, I could find an owner who runs the business, who is there every day, and who will take the time to get to know the customer. With my favorite shop, I stop by every week just to ask how business is—and he keeps me up to date on all kinds of things. Combine this kind of personality with access to good materials, and you have a combination that will really keep you on top of color management issues connected with display and storage.

The other method is word-of-mouth, usually employed when I'm ordering materials from a supplier outside my region. I've tried many, and Light Impressions is among the best as far as consistency of quality of materials is concerned.

Storing Artwork

If you have an extremely important piece of art or a photograph, and preservation of color is critical, there are a number of options available to you:

- Place the original in professional-level dark storage. This is the safest arrangement and can be set up for a fee.
- You can create a reasonable level of protection storing images and prints in archivally rated boxes, using supporting materials sold by companies like Light Impressions (www.lightimpressionsdirect.com).

- If you want to be able to see the art work on a regular basis (who could blame you!), you can have a reproduction made, frame it in your home or office, and rotate different images from display to dark storage.
- Some museum curators have created standards for total light/air exposure per year to maximize the lifetime of the photograph or artwork. They show a piece for a limited time and then put it back in storage. In this way, you can still enjoy your photographs or art and maximize their life.

Last, have the right frame made, with the right materials, display it in a color-friendly place, and enjoy!

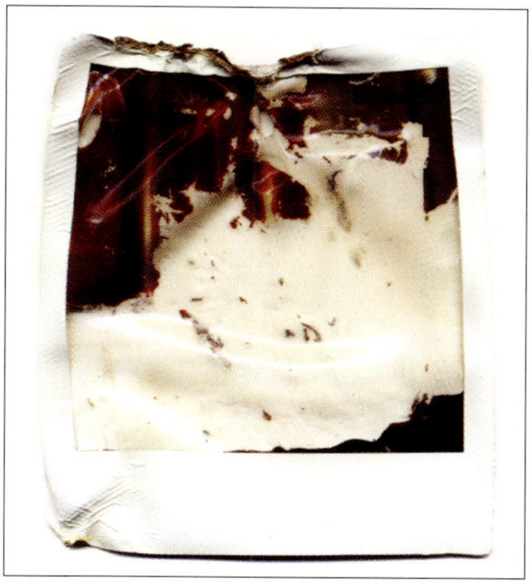

Figure 9.8
Let's hope this photo wasn't the only picture of Great Aunt Sally there ever was...

Saving and Archiving Image Files

Your digital files are a tangible asset, just like your camera, your prints, or your artwork. In a way, digital files are deceptively fragile—they look fine as they are read from a storage device or media again and again—until they won't open. It seems that systems available today are better than ever—but there's room for improvement. And, honestly, most people have their important image files stored on one computer and one hard drive, leaving them vulnerable to loss.

There's no color in an image file that's become unreadable. Seriously, in the digital world that electronic file is too easy for an image file to become damaged. Just one example: An image-recording error was discovered recently in one high-end digital camera model. If the photographer was shooting a rapid sequence, and the memory card became full while it was trying to record the last image, the card became unreadable.

It's important to have good habits to protect your work. Here are some suggestions to make your life a little easier when it comes to saving your image files and keeping control of your color:

- Have your computer connected to electrical power through a surge protector. A power surge or lighting strike can destroy an unprotected machine and your files. In fact, the power went out as I was editing this chapter, and my backup power supply allowed me to save my work and shut things down correctly.

Digital Storage Cards

When you have ejected a digital storage card from the computer card reader, I suggest you store it temporarily and insert a fresh card in the camera. On a few occasions, access to the original card and its saved images has saved me from an unexpected computer problem. Also, always re-format a digital storage card in the camera, never in the computer. Formatting a digital card in the computer can damage it.

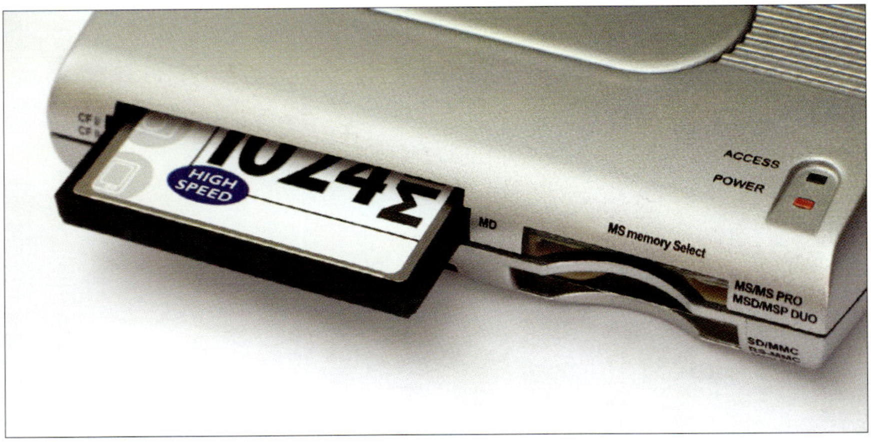

Figure 9.9

A digital storage card. (Photo licensed from istockphoto.)

- Keep your camera batteries charged. A low battery can cause problems in image file readability.
- When I return from a photo shoot, the first thing I do is put the memory cards in a card reader and copy the image files to two separate computer hard drives—located on two *separate* computers. When removing the card from the reader, I use the computer's operating system to eject the card. If you just pull the card out of the reader, you risk damaging it.
- The hard drives that I use for image storage are what I call everyday hardware. There's nothing special about them. They are not part of an array, or series of linked drives. They use the current operating system's formatting, and the files are organized into normal directories. I'm trying to keep this process uncomplicated and minimize dependence on specialized technology. I know plenty of people who have old data stored on floppy disks they can't read any more.
- Format the memory cards in the camera. Do not format the cards while they are in a card reader connected to the computer; this risks causing what I call a "digital lobotomy" to the card, making in unreadable.

- Memory card prices are pretty reasonable now, and it pays to buy a couple of extra cards. Also, avoid deleting images while the card is in the camera.
- I don't re-format the memory cards after download until the next shoot. Every once in a while, I find that being able to go back to the memory card is a lifesaver.
- At least once a week, I make backups of my new, critical images. In my studio, I copy original, and edited master image files onto a second hard drive, and I burn image files to CDs. Important backup CDs are archived in a location that is physically separate from the studio. Recently, I've begun using archivally rated CDs from Fuji. The company claims its CD-Rs can be expected to last 70-100 years. It's a good idea to stay away from low-end CDs for long-term storage—it is not known how long they will really last.

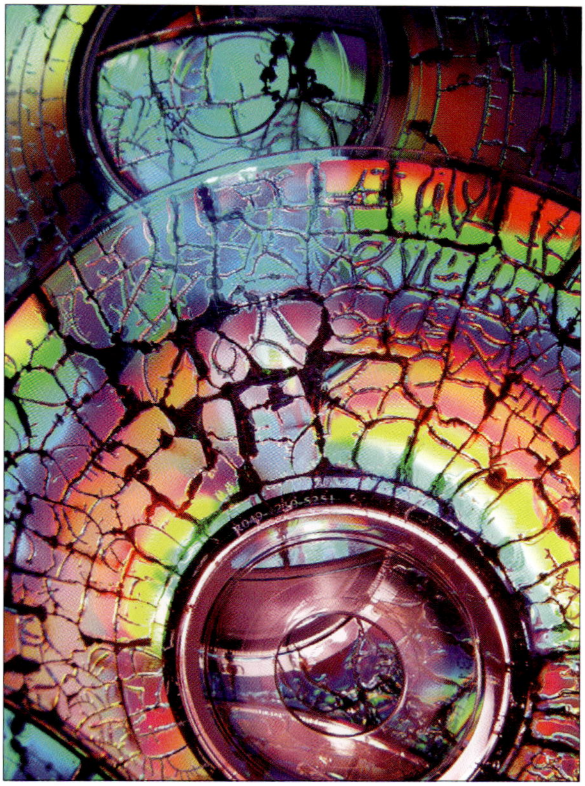

Figure 9.10

A CD doesn't have to look this fried in order to be damaged. Be sure to back up your work! (Photo licensed from istockphoto.)

- There are software applications available that will help you automate file backup tasks. Silverkeeper is only one example; there are many others.

- Use camera memory cards that are made by a major manufacturer. Sandisk and Lexar have delivered the best performance in my work. There are also other companies that make good products. Sandisk and Lexar also make really useful software that can help you recover images that are accidentally deleted. (Some reports have indicated that solid-state memory cards are not reliable for long-term image storage. I don't have any evidence one way or the other on this issue.)
- I save my image files as uncompressed TIFFs. The TIFF file format seems to be the de-facto standard that can be used by most image-editing software, using multiple editing layers, in high-bit format. Using JPEG for storage is not a good idea, it limits you to 8-bit format, and it compresses the file and discards small amounts of data.
- Using proprietary file formats alone for long-term archiving leaves you at the mercy of that one manufacturer. Adobe has been steadily working on their DNG (digital negative) file format. There's no doubt you should keep your RAW files—but consider exporting them to TIFF or DNG formats as backups.
- A great thing about shooting RAW files is that you can make non-destructive edits to them and not touch the original file. RAW file converters, such as Adobe Camera RAW, Phase One Capture One, Aperture, and Lightroom, all store your image edits separately from the original RAW file, so you can return to your digital original and edit as needed.
- In this sense, digital originals are superior to film, as long as you make backups. A film original suffers a little every time it is handled—but a digital file should not. And if you've made duplicates correctly, they will be every bit as good as the original file.
- One reason for trying to keep as broad a color gamut as possible in your image files, even after processing and editing, is that digital printing is improving all the time. Inkjet printers are getting better and better at managing and rendering color—and so is the software driving them.
- It's also true that image-processing software is improving. Not only is the variety of available programs increasing, but the capabilities of those programs to squeeze more quality out of your original file are improving, too. As I pointed out at the beginning of this book, it's wise to keep your options open, so you can take advantage of opportunities as they arise.

  Continuing this last point, a very clear advantage of storing RAW image files is that these files represent the unprocessed information from the camera sensor. If you assume that you will be able to read these file formats for the foreseeable future, there has to be some untapped potential in those images. In my own experience, I've found that I can successfully go back to my archives and successfully reprocess images to improve quality.

Storing and Archiving Film

I know many photographers who still shoot on film and many who have extensive libraries of negative and transparency film. First, if you can, use professional-quality film that has a valid date stamp. This helps assure you that the film was manufactured to higher standards and that it was stored in controlled conditions.

Once you bring the film back to the studio, keep it in the refrigerator until you need it. Let it warm to room temp for a couple of hours before use it, as using film that is chilled below environmental temperature can cause condensation on the film and in the camera. For long-term storage, freezing extends the life of the film almost indefinitely. Use plastic bags to protect the film while in cold storage.

Once you have completed a shoot, if possible, get the film developed right away. If you are using slide film, and you are having the developing work done by a vendor, be sure they use what's called a "dip-and-dunk" machine. Dip-and-dunk processing is kinder and gentler to your film.

And before you commit a large batch of film to any one vendor, have the vendor develop a few test rolls, on different days, and evaluate the quality and consistency of their work—this helps protect the color values in the film you've shot.

Next, once the film has been developed, you have the option of scanning it for archiving. Given the relatively reasonable cost of dedicated, high-quality film scanners, the real issue is finding the time to do this. An alternative is to ask a vendor to scan your film for you; this is of course more expensive.

For more information on this topic, see www.lightimpressionsdirect.com, www.kodak.com, and www.fujifilmusa.com.

Summary

Color management should involve protecting color and image integrity, not just manipulating images or managing devices. I learned this lesson when I realized that our family photo albums had protected and preserved images taken when my father was one year old.

I think that digital asset management is something of a misnomer. To me, it is photographic asset management, or art conservation. Film has its place in art and photography for the foreseeable future. Digital images may or may not turn out to be as durable and archival as the best films; time will tell.

In the last week I reviewed wildlife images I had taken in Florida several years ago. Using updated RAW conversion software, I was able to re-process the RAW files that I had previously thought were unacceptable and improve them enough that they are now marketable. I was also able to rescan some transparencies and get a much better result. These images are on their way to my stock agency as this is written.

A last thought: We can't know the importance or value of every image we create. What we now think of as an everyday, assignment photograph may, over time, become incredibly important as a documentary image or in other ways. You've worked hard to create images that speak to you; make sure they last.

A

Helpful Tips and Tricks

This appendix includes a hodgepodge of tips and tricks to help you on your way. Included in this appendix are the following topics:

- Tips for handling RAW files
- Tips for non-destructive image editing
- Tips for the best Photoshop setup and preferences
- Preventive maintenance tips for equipment
- Example software and equipment lists
- Example forms for the reproduction of prints
- Website resources

Tips for Processing RAW Camera Files

You have several choices when processing RAW files. Assuming you have Nikon Capture or equivalent software for your DSLR or your medium-format camera, you can make non-destructive adjustments (adjustments that leave the "original" pixels untouched) to the RAW file, save it as a RAW, and open and re-edit it at a later date. The file can then be re-opened in Nikon Capture/equivalent or in Adobe Camera RAW.

You can also open the file using Adobe Camera RAW (ACR). ACR now accommodates almost every RAW file format. You can make non-destructive adjustments in ACR. To keep this as an adjustable RAW-file format, you would click on Done, and the file will close, saving your adjustments. You can also click on Save and then designate Digital Negative format. This allows you to re-open the image as a RAW file, although only through ACR.

Last, you can use either RAW converter software package, make your adjustments to the file, and then choose to open it—it will come up in Photoshop as the type of file you specify—but you must choose the file specs. I suggest a 16-bit file in Adobe RGB (1998) or ProPhoto RGB, at the largest size possible in terms of pixels (X×Y). I suggest using TIFF file format, as it is one of the few that can be read by nearly every imaging application.

Tip

One quick tip: When processing in RAW, it is wise to experiment with color noise reduction and luminance noise reduction settings. These work quite well, but at the expense (sometimes) of image detail.

Figure A.1 shows the basic RAW file conversion process.

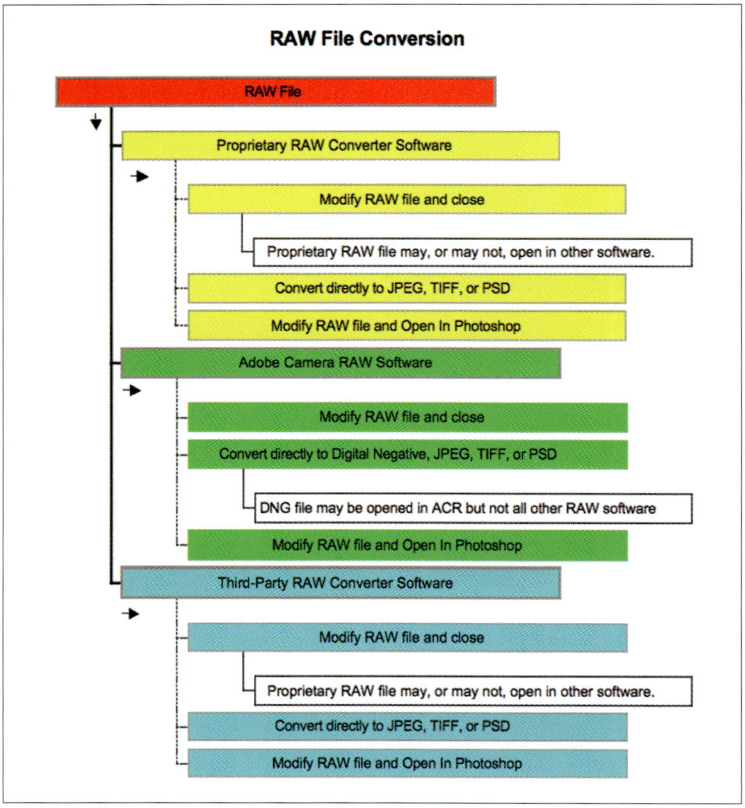

Figure A.1

This flowchart can help you choose among your options in RAW file conversion.

It's best to make basic color contrast adjustments in RAW but save your really heavy lifting and significant edits for a layered approach in Photoshop.

Tips for Non-Destructive Image Editing

The term "non-destructive" editing can be interpreted in a number of ways. First, it implies that whatever changes you make in your image, they leave the "original" pixels untouched. Another way to look at it is that if you have to change the pixels, do it in a way that lets you change them back.

File storage and archiving tips:

- Digital files are perishable. Make sure that you use reliable media, such as a high-quality hard drive or archival quality CDs. Make multiple backups and store your critical files in a separate physical location. You can't manage your color if there aren't any images to edit!
- It's common sense, but still: Store your film in a cool, dry, dark place (not under the bed, or in the attic, or the trunk of the car). Use storage materials that are made for proper film storage. Heat, light, and moisture are the enemies of your film.

Film scanning tips:

- Scan your film at maximum practical resolution. In 35mm, this may be as high as 4000 dpi, in medium format 3200.
- Make your scans in high-bit resolution, and use a color space like Adobe RGB (1998) or ProPhoto RGB.
- Be conservative in your scan adjustments. Avoid *clipping*, or over adjusting and distorting the details in highlight and shadow areas. See Figure A.2.
- Similarly, make conservative color corrections and adjustments. Leave the heavy lifting for Photoshop, where you can use layers.
- If you believe that you may need to try more than one group of settings when scanning, make multiple scans while the film is still mounted in the scanner. Remember, each time you handle a piece of film, it is damaged in some way.

Photoshop tips:

- If you open an image for editing, make sure that you have an untouched original stored in a different folder, on a different drive or disc.
- Check your color preferences in Photoshop. Make sure that the software will ask you if it is okay to change from the image's color space to your preferred color space.

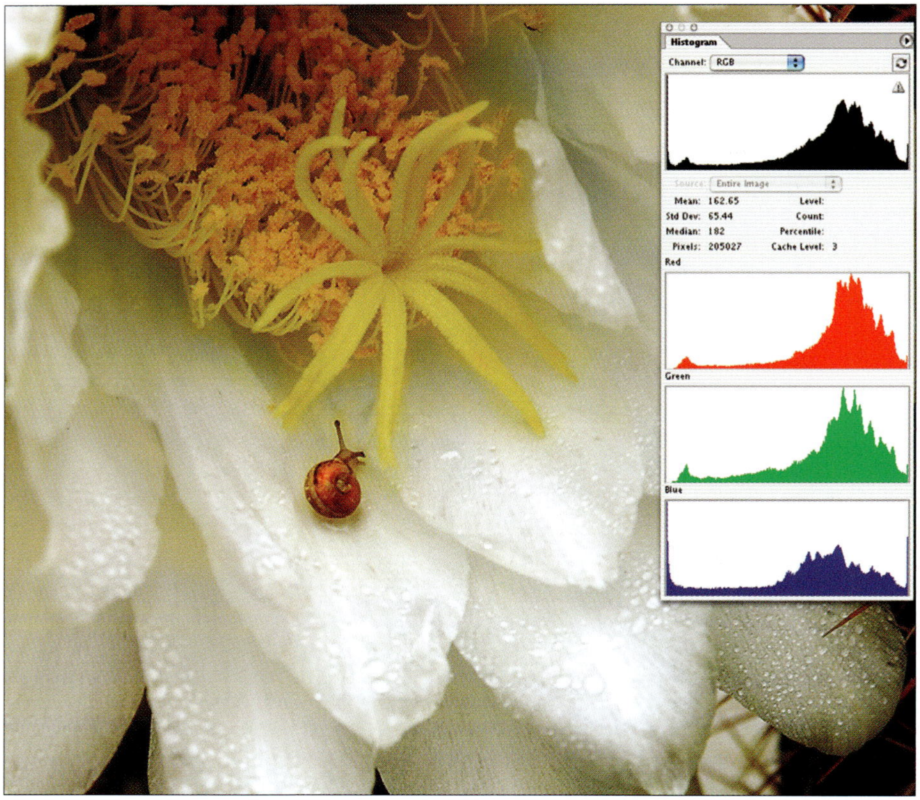

Figure A.2

The histogram for this image shows clipping, or loss of image information, in the shadow areas of the image. Note the spike at the far left in the histogram at the top and in the blue channel histogram.

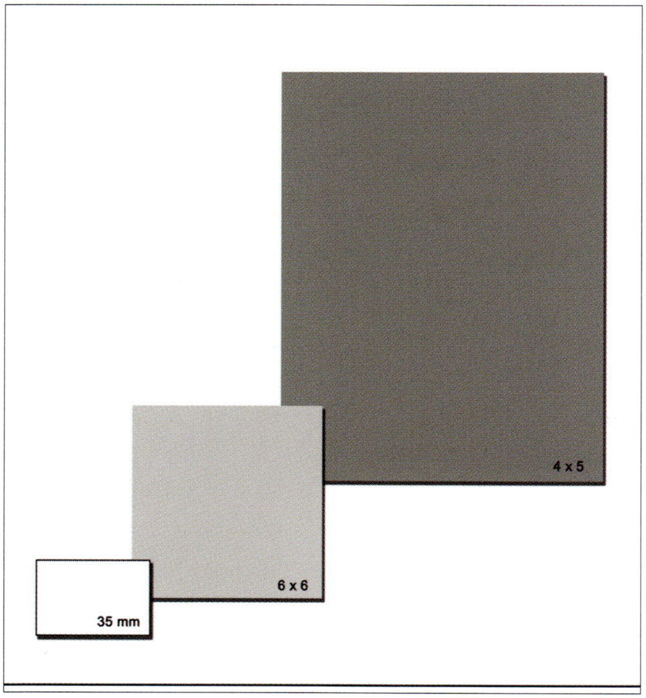

Figure A.3

Different film sizes, as compared to 35mm film.

- Use layers in Photoshop to make your adjustments and edits.
- Make your adjustments to Levels, Curves, Color on separate layers or better yet, use adjustment layers. Remember: one change, one layer.
- Add a last layer to perform retouching details such as smoothing skin or to remove spots from your skies and beer cans from your landscapes, as you prefer.
- Save the image as a layered TIFF or Photoshop file. Once flattened, saved, and closed, an image file cannot be re-inflated. There is no need to flatten the image for printing or storage. If you must give someone a copy, save a duplicate of the image under a modified file name.

You'll find more Photoshop tips in the next section in this appendix, called "Tips for Photoshop Setup and Preferences."

Tip

A super-tip for those who can't resist editing images during late night sessions, and who have accidentally flattened and saved an image: *Don't close the file.* Instead, go to the History palette and retrace your steps in your History palette to a stage where the image was not flattened. Voila! The layers reappear, and you can re-save the file under a different name.

Tips for Photoshop Setup and Preferences

Photoshop Machine Requirements:

For the most part, I use a Mac in the studio and in the field. In the end, you really want nearly as much speed and power as you'd want for top-end gaming or video editing, whether you are using a Mac or PC.

The short version of this is to use, at minimum, a Mac G5 dual or equivalent, running 2Ghz, with 4-8GB of RAM. A high-end graphics card with at least 256k on-board memory will help quite a bit. The new quad-processor machines are noticeably faster (according to www.systemshootouts.org, the PC equivalent to the Mac G5 quad is a Quad-Core 2.8 GHZ Xeon). The new Intel Macs are potentially faster, but not all software has caught up to take advantage of the hardware improvements.

A bit of essential gear is a second hard drive. Photoshop is much happier if you can provide a second drive, which is used by Photoshop for scratch or temporary files.

Color Settings

The basic principle underlying color settings is control. Photoshop default settings are not appropriate for photography or art editing. Here's some basic settings that will make your life a little easier:

1. Go to Edit>Color Settings.
2. In this dialog box, set your Working Space RGB to Adobe RGB (1998) or another, larger color space. Larger color space gives you, ultimately, easier image editing and better quality.
3. The default settings for CMYK, Grey, and Spot you can leave as-is.
4. Under Color Management Policies, choose Preserve Embedded Profiles under RGB, CMYK, and Gray.
5. There are three check boxes immediately underneath your color management policies drop-down menus: Profile Mismatches, Ask when Pasting, and Ask when Opening. These should all be enabled. Now, whenever you open an image file, Photoshop will *ask* you if you want to use the embedded color space or convert it. This gives you much more control over your color workflow.
6. Under Conversion Options, specify Adobe ACE and Intent: Perceptual. Use Black Point Compensation and Use Dither should be enabled. (Perceptual intent renders an image that's "most pleasing" to the eye; it also tries to map or transform colors from one color space to another, rather than discarding colors that don't fit.)

Photoshop Preferences

Under Photoshop>Preferences, you'll find a number of drop-down menus, including a range of dialog boxes. The range of choices may seem to be overdone, but there are a few to select that will make your work easier:

- Under the General tab, set History states to 20-30, which is a good compromise —this gives you reasonable "un-do" without hogging memory.
- Unless you really need it, turn off the Export Clipboard feature.
- Under the next tab, File Management, enable at least 10 recent file names used. I also disable Version Cue management.
- Under Plug-Ins and Scratch Disks, specify that Photoshop use your second hard drive, by name, as its main scratch disk.
- Under Memory and Image Cache, set the Cache levels to 4-6 and Memory Usage to between 50-70%. You'll have to experiment a bit with these settings, as the best levels depend on the combination of capabilities of individual machines.

Example Software and Equipment Lists

The following two tables show example software and equipment lists that you can use as a basis for your own needs. Please keep in mind that I think of this as a toolbox—I use the pliers, hammers, and screwdrivers as needed. A good way to evaluate equipment, other than reading technical reviews, is to borrow or rent it. Renting is much cheaper than buying, and you don't have to live with it if you don't think it's right for you.

Table A.1 Example Equipment List: Professional-Level Photography

Category	Examples/Manufacturers
Camera	8-10 MP digital SLR or better; 22MP medium format digital back
Lenses	Nikon, Canon, Zeiss, Fuji, Hasselblad, Contax, Leica
Image settings	High-bit (12 -16 bit) RAW
Color space	Adobe RGB (1998) or better
Exposure meter	Sekonic, Minolta, Gossen Digital or equivalent
Color meter	Minolta, Gossen, Broncolor
On-camera flash	Digital TTL-capable, with guide number of 100 or better
Studio strobes	Elinchrome, Hensel, Broncolor, Profoto, or equivalent Recycle time 2 sec or better. Color temperature consistent @ 5500-5600K
Film scanner	35mm: Nikon 5000 or equivalent Medium format: Nikon 9000 or equivalent Large format: Imacon Flextight 948 or equivalent
Color checker card	Macbeth color checker card or equivalent

Examples from my own equipment and software list: Nikon D2X, Nikon F100, Hasselblad H1, Phase One 22 MP digital back, Hasselblad H1 film back, Sekonic 358 digital exposure meter, Profoto, Hensel, and Calumet Elite strobes, Adobe Photoshop CS2, Phase One Capture One software, Minolta Multi Scan Pro, Epson V750 Pro Scanner, X-Rite Pulse Spectrophotometer, iOne Display calibration, Mac G5, Apple 30" Cinema Display, ImagePrint RIP, Onyx Postershop RIP, HP Designjet 130nr, HP Photosmart Pro 9180, Epson 9600, and the GTI GraphicLite viewing station.

Table A.2 Examples, Equipment and Software List: Professional-Level Image Editing and Color Management

Category	Examples/Manufacturers
Displays	Eizo ColorEdge, Apple Cinema Display, Lacie
Display calibration hardware	X-Rite, GretagMacbeth, ColorVision
Display calibration software	X-Rite Pulse Color Elite, iOne Match GretagMacbeth, ColorEyes
Printer profile calibration	X-Rite Pulse, GretagMacbeth
Image editing software	Adobe Photoshop CS2
Photo management software	Apple Aperture, Adobe Lightroom, Extensis
Stand-alone RAW file processing software	Adobe Camera RAW, Phase One Capture One, Bibble, Silverfast DC Pro
Print viewing box or booth	GTI GraphicLite or GretagMacbeth Spectralight or equivalent
Computer	Mac G5 Dual 2 Gz or Equivalent, 4GB RAM
Software RIP for printing	Imageprint, Colorburst, Onyx

Short-form Analysis: ROI on Large Format Inkjet Printer Using Color Managed Workflow

Initial Cost Of Printer and Display Calib. w/ Tax		$ 5,000.00
Initial Cost of RIP Software		$ 1,500.00
Subtotal		**$ 6,500.00**
Amortization/Month, Two Years		$ 270.83
Ink and Paper Cost Print/Square Foot, Satin, Lustre, Glossy		$ 2.00
Ink and Paper Cost Print/Square Foot, Fine Art		$ 4.00
# Prints/Month	**Satin, Lustre, Glossy**	**Fine Art**
13x19	20	5
18x24	10	20
24x36	5	10
Ink and Paper Cost/Each/Print		
13x19	$ 3.43	$ 6.86
18x24	$ 6.00	$ 12.00
24x36	$ 12.00	$ 24.00
Ink and Paper Cost for Printing by Size		
13x19	$ 68.61	$ 34.31
18x24	$ 60.00	$ 240.00
24x36	$ 60.00	$ 240.00
Number of Square Feet Printed		
13x19	34	12
18x24	30	36
24x36	30	144
Total Printing, Square Feet		286
Average Ink and Paper Cost/Square Foot		$ 2.46
Monthly Amortization, Hardware/software per sq foot		$ 0.95
Ink and Paper Costs, All Prints		$ 702.92
Total Cost/Square Foot		$ 3.40
Total Printing Cost/Month		$ 973.75
Printing Costs/Month If Printed by Outside Lab - Asssume $7/Sq Ft		$ 2,002.52
Printing Costs/Month If Printed by Outside Lab - Asssume $10/Sq Ft		$ 2,860.74
Approximate Cash Savings/Month		Approx $1,000 - $1,800
Approximate Cash Savings/Year		Approx $12,000 - $21,600

Figure A.4

These figures are based on my personal experience and feedback from other photographers and artists. Please feel free to massage the numbers to fit your situation.

Tip

One last tip—for all of us who have invested in Adobe Photoshop—the Help utilities provided with Photoshop, as well as the tutorials and information available through the Adobe website, are top-notch. And—they're free!

Preventive Maintenance Tips for Equipment

Tips for digital and film cameras:

- Keep the camera clean and dry. In fact, think of your camera as being about a durable as an uncooked chicken egg, and treat it accordingly. Prevent hard shocks and drops, vigorous shaking, and so on.
- One classic way to destroy your camera is to leave it on the car seat next to you while driving. A sudden stop, the camera flies to the floor or dash, and—it's dead. (Been there, done that.)
- Another favorite trick of photographers is to mount the camera on a tripod that is not well balanced, or is not on solid footing. A little nudge—and, again, it's dead.
- If you are using a camera strap, check the strap for fraying, loose buckles, and so on. Same thing for a camera bag; make it a habit to have a mental checklist about things like this.
- Do not leave the camera in a location where it can be exposed to high heat. This includes inside a car, but can also include simply leaving the camera sitting on a picnic table for an hour while you have lunch.
- If you are out in cold weather, remember that when you go back inside a heated area that moisture may condense on the lens, on the outside of the camera, or inside the camera. It is best to keep the camera in its bag or case until temperatures equalize.
- Keep the batteries well charged; do not leave the camera in storage for long periods with batteries installed. Use the correct charger for your batteries—don't improvise.
- Use recommended cleaners—household agents can ruin a camera or lens in an instant.
- Clean your lenses with materials specifically made for the purpose. PEC makes excellent products, as do many other companies. Wiping a lens with a Kleenex, or even worse, a paper towel, will scratch the lens.

- Change lenses in an enclosed environment, such as a room indoors, or in a car. Changing lenses out in the open can allow dust to enter the camera body. Blowing sand can "sandblast" your equipment.
- Lenses should mount and dismount from the camera with little or no effort. If you feel resistance, or there is significant grit in the mount, take the camera and lens to a qualified repair shop. Similarly, if a filter binds of the front of a lens, get qualified help.
- Similarly, use lenses that are made for your camera. Do not try to force a different lens onto the camera mount.
- If you need to remove dust from the camera, acquire a rubber squeeze bulb intended for the purpose. Do *not* blow into the camera with your mouth, and avoid using so-called "canned air."
- Use a lens cap. I know they are an inconvenience, but a $2 cap can save a $2,000 lens. Simple.
- If the camera is exposed to large quantities of water or becomes immersed, first take it out of the water. Remove the lens, the batteries, and the memory card immediately and gently wipe water from the outside of the camera. Take the camera to a qualified repair shop.
- A final note—your camera equipment and related items are a big investment. If you can afford it, purchase a lockbox or small safe for your most important camera gear. Don't leave it in the car, in view—lock it in the trunk if circumstances require.

Tips for inkjet printers:

- Use inks and papers that are provided by major manufacturers. Generic inks and papers from your local office supply store have no place in serious photography and art. Third-party inks and papers from reputable manufacturers should be okay.
- Check the instructions for the size paper and the weight of the paper your printer can handle.
- Inspect new packets of paper for dust. Remove dust if necessary; it can clog the printer and damage it.
- Locate the printer in an area that is protected from dust, water, and shocks. A sturdy table, at least a couple of feet off the floor, is best.
- Generally, inkjet printers do best in environments at around 70-75, and moderate humidity.
- Use a surge protector between the wall outlet and the inkjet printer.

- You can wipe the outside of a printer off with a soft, clean cloth. Do not try to clean the inside of the printer yourself.
- Insert and remove ink cartridges as per the manufacturer's instructions; the same is true with paper. Using force will usually break the device.
- Any indication of an ink leak is a signal to take the printer to a qualified repair shop.
- If you see streaks or bands of color on your printer, use the manufacturer's software utilities, supplied with the printer, to run cleaning and maintenance cycles.
- Do not leave the printer with an empty ink cartridge or an empty ink cartridge bay. In my studio, this means even 15 minutes. A clogged inkjet print head can mean a ruined printer.
- If a printer is running a job, it is best to let it finish the current page without intervention. Pulling a piece of paper from the machine while it is running can cause damage in a number of ways.
- Some printer manufacturer's recommend that you leave the printer turned on all the time; others will direct you to turn it off when not in use. Follow these directions to prevent ink clogs and similar problems.
- See the manufacturers instructions for information on moving the device from one location to another.
- I don't agree with those who indicate that you can clean dust and other foreign objects from the inside of a dedicated film scanner. Keep the scanner covered with a dust cover when not in use; when necessary, have a qualified technician clean it.

There isn't much to do in caring for scanners that is radically different than inkjet printers. Tips for scanners:

- If you are using a flatbed scanner, you'll find information in the instruction manual telling you how to keep the scanning glass clean. Don't improvise!
- Film holders are notoriously finicky. Their job is to keep the film flat for a sharp scan. Don't bend, twist, spindle, or mutilate them!
- You can use "canned air" to clean dust from film holders. Do not use canned air to clean film or the inside of the scanner.
- If you are using a dedicated film scanner, be careful when loading the film holder into the scanner. The scanner should "grab" the end of the film holder and slowly pull it in. Forcing the film holder, or even encouraging it with your finger, can damage the scanner's transport mechanisms.

- Use only approved brushes, cloth, and liquids to clean film or slides. If you improvise with a household cleaner, you'll probably permanently damage the film.
- See the manufacturer's instructions for information on moving the device from one location to another.
- When scanning is completed, remove film from the holder immediately and store it appropriately. Film that is badly warped or curled may not be suitable for scanning in some machines.
- Try to keep USB or Firewire cables connecting the scanner to the computer short. Longer cables seem, sometimes, to cause data errors.
- It is also a good idea to locate the scanner on a strong, sturdy table that will move very little during scanning. Some scanners will not function properly if the table is moved during scanning.

Website Resources

Here are just a few websites that I have had good experiences with—and remember, your mileage may vary!

- Adobe.com
- Alienskin.com: Plug-in and other software
- Artscans.com: David Coon's site—Color management and scanning—a real genius in this field
- Behladesign.com: Andrew Behla's site—Color management, printing, and digital imaging consulting (he is the tech editor for this book)
- Bhphotovideo.com: Equipment and software
- Calumetphoto.com: Equipment and software
- DavidSaffir.com: Digital imaging, tutorials, and photography
- Canon.com: Cameras and lenses
- Chromix.com: Color management software—one of the leaders
- Colorbytesoftware.com: ImagePrint software RIP
- Duganne.com: A leading fine art printmaker and consultant
- Epson.com: Printers and scanners
- Fredmiranda.com: Photoshop actions
- Greatoutput.com: Industry and technical news and information

- Gretagmacbeth.com: Color management—another leader
- Gtilite.com: Color-corrected viewing workstations
- Hasselblad.com: You guessed it…
- HP.com: Variety of imaging, scanning, and printing solutions
- Imagingbuffet.com: Andrew Darlow's site
- Inkjetart.com: Inkjet printing supplies
- Lexjet.com: Inkjet printing supplies
- Lightimpressionsdirect.com: Archiving materials
- Luminous-landscape.com: Reviews and digital info
- Lynda.com: Software training
- Lyson.com: Specialty inks
- Niksoftware.com: Software and plug-ins for digital imaging
- Nikon.com: Cameras, lenses, and scanners
- Pdnonline.com: Industry and technical info
- Phaseone.com: Digital camera backs and software
- Mamiya.com: Cameras and lenses
- Photoshopnews.com: You guessed it…
- Photoshopuser.com: The NAPP official website—incredible content on Photoshop, art, design, and so on
- PPA.com: Professional Photographers of America
- Reallyrightstuff.com: One of the better suppliers of specialty camera mounting hardware and tripods
- Wilhelm-research.com: The go-to site on technical issues related to film and print longevity
- WPPI.com: Wedding and Portrait Photographers International
- Dpandi.com: Harald Johnson's site (series reviewer for this book)
- Robgalbraith.com: Top-notch technical and equipment review site
- Smartshooter.com: A wide range of useful info and workshops for photographers
- Russselbrown.com: Amazing Photoshop tips and techniques
- xrite.com: A leader in color management

Permissions and Rights

I normally use the form on the facing page when artists leave their work with me. In some ways, the language is similar to that used by photo labs in regard to film and print developing. I ensure the artists that I will take every reasonable precaution to protect their work, and I also inform them that there is a small possibility that an event beyond my control will occur.

For safety's sake, I usually take a quick snapshot of the artwork, front and back, with a small digital camera before the artist leaves my studio.

Summary

Much of the information in this appendix is based on my own experience and research. It's important that you feel free to experiment and try things for yourself. Ask your colleagues for help, look on the Internet, compare information, and decide what's best for you. In the digital world, people are "often wrong, but rarely uncertain."

Some of my mentors and teachers are listed in the introduction to this book. Please take a look at their publications and websites—these are sources of incredibly useful information.

Right to Photograph Artwork and Produce Reproduction Prints

I, ____________ (ARTIST) by my signature below give my permission to ___________ (PRINTMAKER) to reproduce my paintings (ARTWORK) subject to the following terms and conditions:

ARTIST warrants to PRINTMAKER that ARTIST holds unrestricted ownership and copyright to ARTWORK.

ARTIST grants permission to PRINTMAKER to photograph, scan, and reproduce ARTWORK. ARTIST retains all copyright to artwork.

ARTIST releases and agrees to indemnify PRINTMAKER from liability for any injuries or damage to persons or property, and any loss suffered, including but not limited to any loss or damage to ARTWORK, equipment or film failure, loss of film, negatives or prints or any loss. ARTIST also releases PRINTMAKER from any liability or claims in connection with the use of the ARTWORK, including but not limited to claims for copyright infringement, libel, or invasion of privacy.

This authorization and release shall inure to the benefit of the legal representatives, successors and assigns of PRINTMAKER.

I have read the foregoing and agree to it by my signature below.

Date: ____________________________________

Print ARTIST Name: ____________________________________

ARTIST Signature: ____________________________________

PRINTMAKER Name: _________________________

PRINTMAKER Signature: _______________________________

B

Art Gallery

 The images shown here are arranged in groups, loosely by theme.

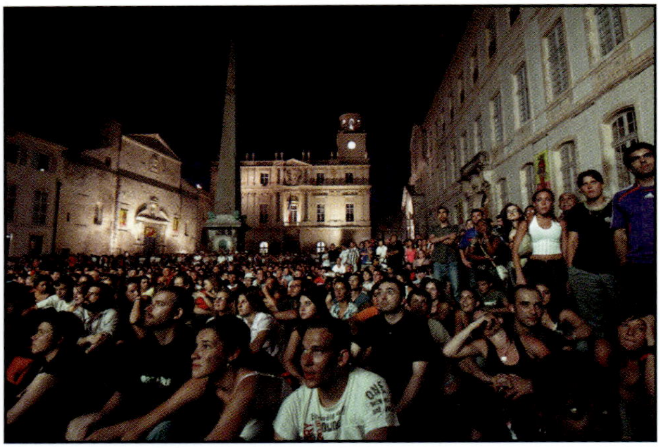

1. "Waiting" This image was taken in one of the central plazas in Arles, France, during the semi-finals of the world cup of soccer in 2006. The crowd are watching the game on a very large outdoor television screen. Nikon D2X, 12-24mm lens, ISO 1600.

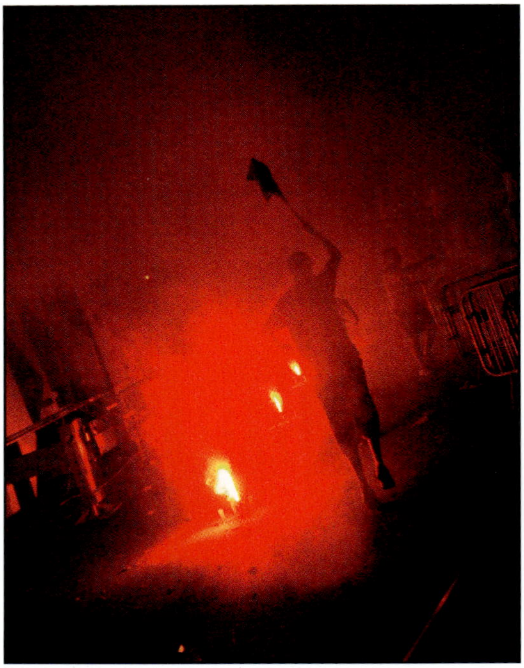

2. "France Wins!" Semi-final match. Nikon D2X, 12-24 lens, ISO 3200.

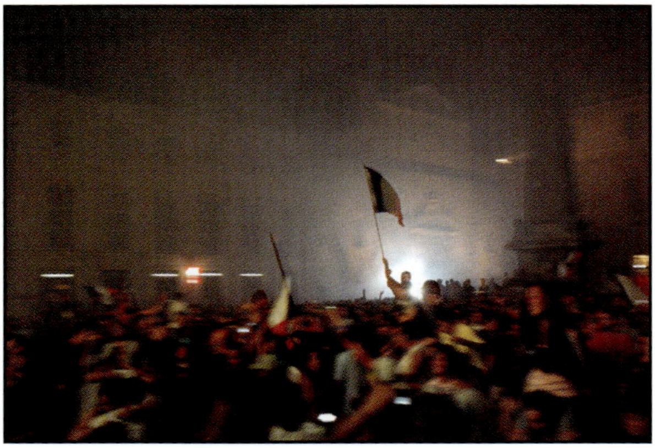

3. Same as image 1, holding camera high over my head for the coverage of the crowd.

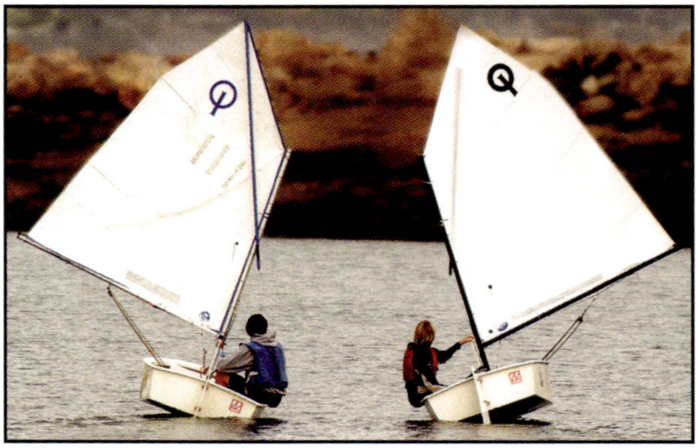

4. "Buddies" Santa Barbara Harbor, California, Nikon digital, exposure unrecorded, 200mm lens.

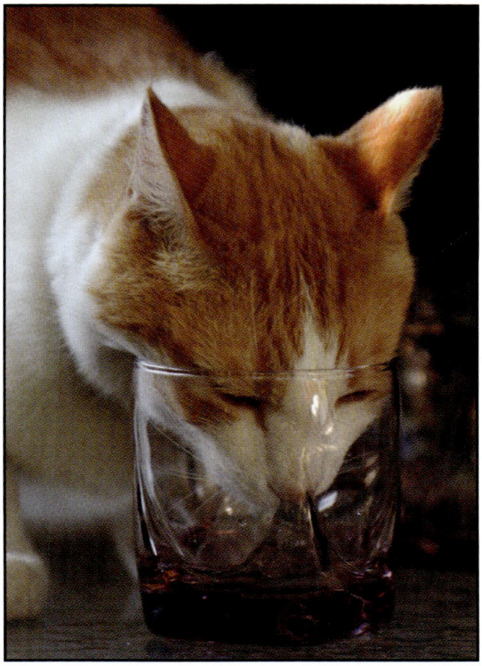

5. "Charlie's Margarita" Nikon D100, 70-200 lens, f/2.8, ISO 400. Charlie couldn't resist my client's unfinished drink.

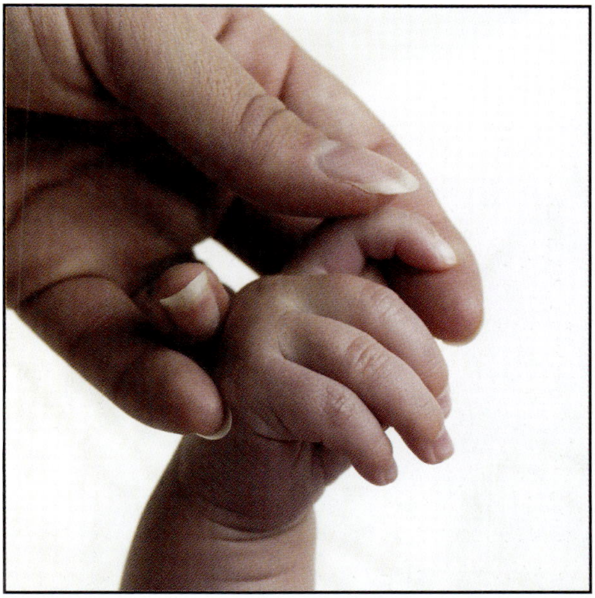

6. "Mommy and Me" Hasselblad H1 100mm f/2.2, ISO 50, studio lighting, for a campaign.

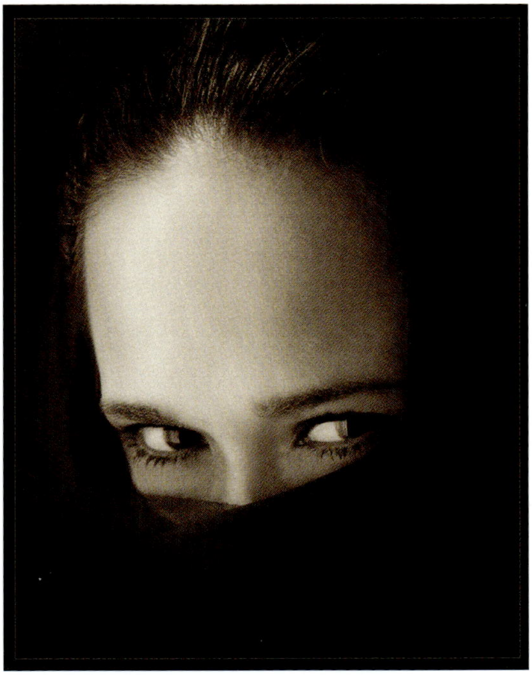

7. "The Mystery" Candid taken during a model shoot, by window light, Nikon D100, exposure unrecorded. Image shot in color, converted to black and white/sepia tone via Photoshop.

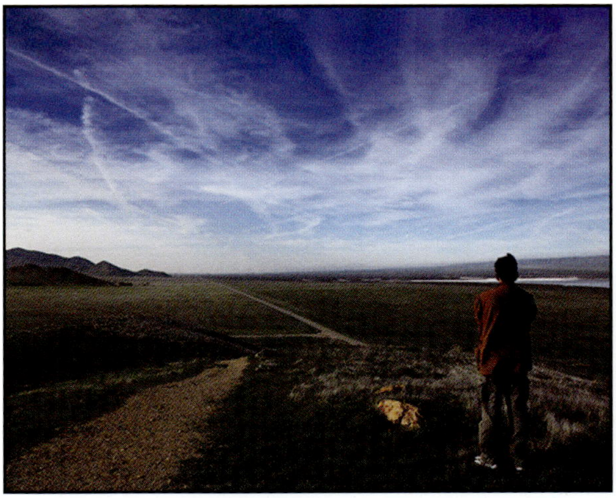

8. "Road to the Future" Hasselblad H1, 35mm lens, f11, Phase One Digital Back. Note that on this day the wind was blowing in very strong gusts, so even though temperatures were moderate, jackets were needed. Location: Carizzo Plain, California.

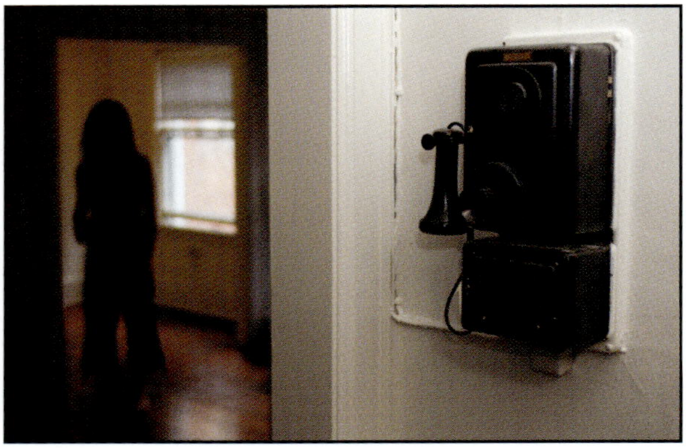

9. "Waiting by the Phone" Nikon D2X with bounce flash from ceiling, rear synch flash to bring up background illumination and silhouette, approx f/8 @ 1/200. (This is a working phone!)

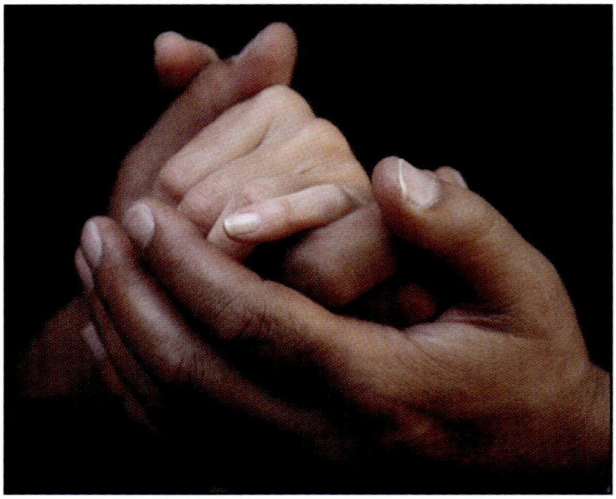

10. "I'll take care of you" A shot taken for an engagement portfolio, shot on Fuji Astia and scanned. Exposure unrecorded. Background burned in via Photoshop.

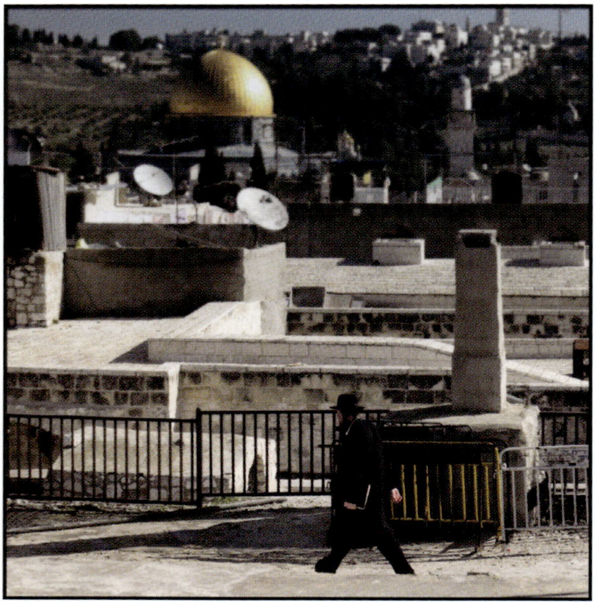

11. "Walking in Jerusalem" Note the Orthodox Jewish man walking on the rooftops in front of the Dome of the Rock, satellite dishes, chimneys, and power lines. Hasselblad H1, 60mm focal length, Phase One digital back. A lucky snap shot.

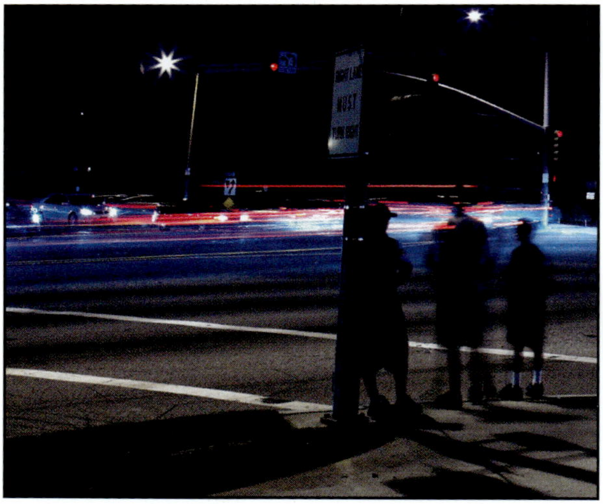

12. "Watching the World Go By" Teenagers hanging out on a corner near my home in Santa Clarita—a town famous for its lack of nighttime excitement. Hasselblad H1, Phase One Digital Back, exposure was five seconds at f/8 (on tripod), ISO 100. Note the absence of noise and color shifting one might see from reciprocity failure in film.

D

E

F

S

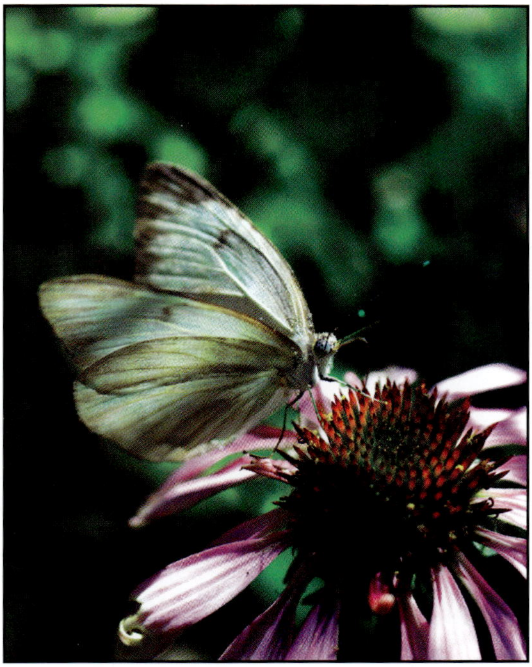

13. This butterfly was captive and part of an exhibit at the Los Angeles Museum of Natural History. I couldn't resist the green color coming through the insect's nearly transparent wings. Kind of a ghostly effect. Shot with H1, Phase One, 120mm macro lens, on a monopod, f/6.8, 1/160 sec.

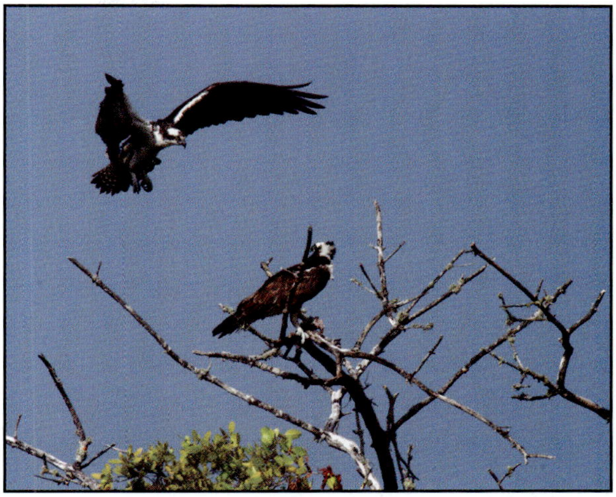

14. "The Landing Zone" This mated pair of ospreys were sharing a large fish they had caught. I used a Nikon 600mm lens with teleadaptor, shot with a Nikon D100, ISO 200, f/9 1/1000 of a second. Gitzo carbon fiber tripod, stabilized with sandbags. I also shot this using Fuji Velvia 50, pushed one stop, using the Nikon F100. No discernible difference between quality of the shots. This image is cropped about 50%.

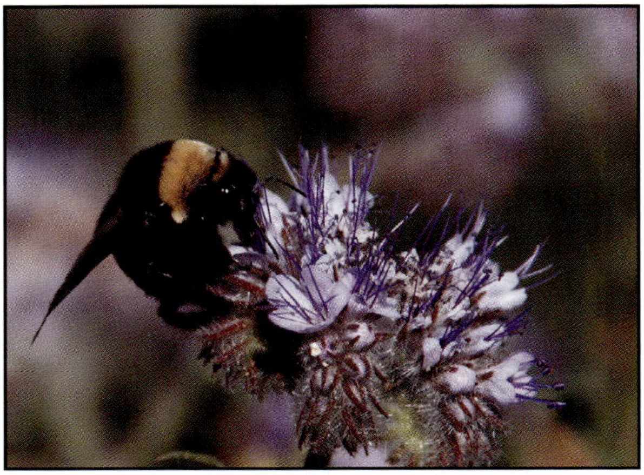

15. "BeeZilla" One of the biggest bees I have ever seen. Since I was a bit intimidated, I used Nikon 400mm lens, mounted on F100 and Velvia 50. It was a hot, sunny day, and the bees were behaving so erratically I was convinced they were drunk from fermented nectar. Exposure unrecorded. Image taken alongside the road near Carizzo Plain, California.

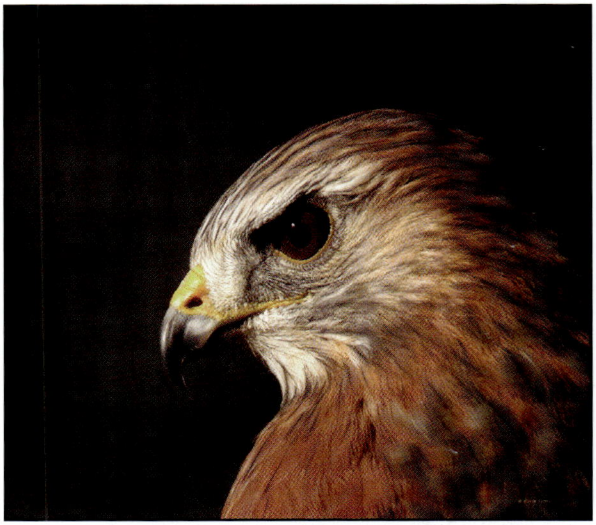

16. "Hawk" A captive bird, photographed at the Santa Barbara Botanical Garden. This bird was part of a recovery program for injured animals.

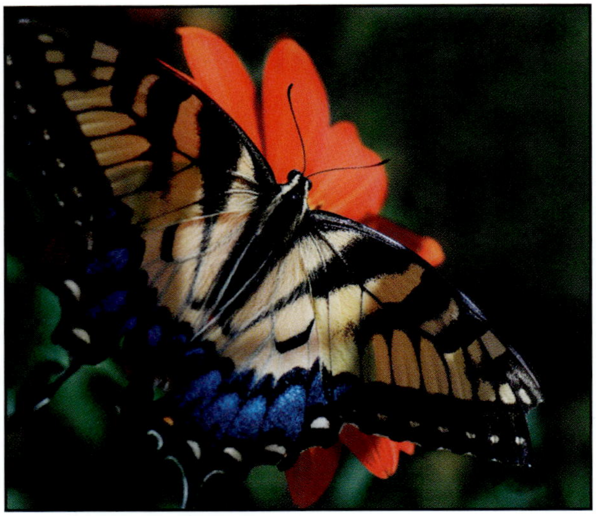

17. "All the Colors" Another butterfly at the Museum, captured with H1 and Phase One, hand-held.

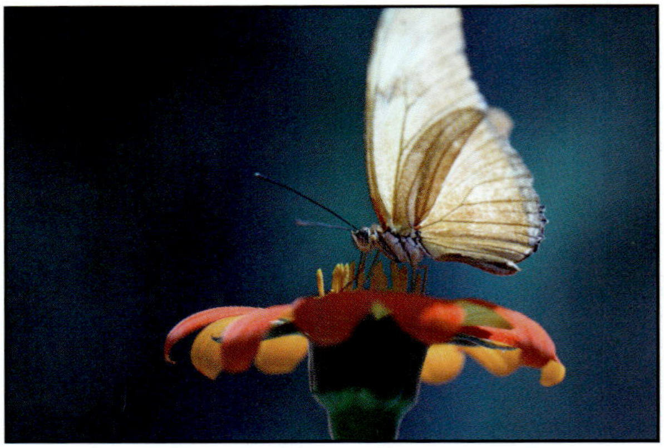

18. Same as 17; I'm pretty sure I used a monopod for this one; shutter speed is 1/160. Both 17 and 18 show the results of using ProPhoto RGB, in my opinion, as the color palette is just amazing, even after image editing.

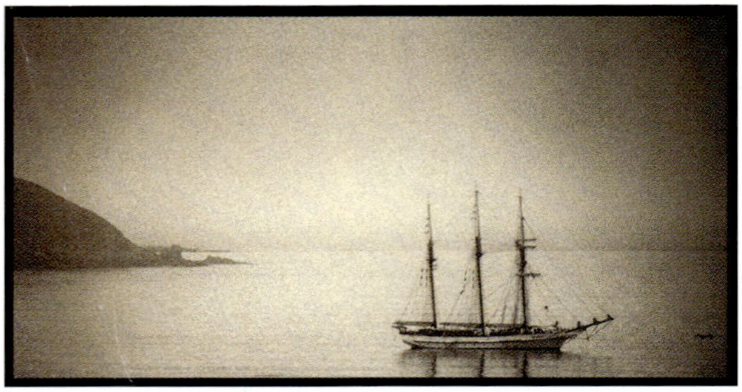

19. "The Ghost of Becher's Bay" Shot on an island in the Santa Barbara Channel. This was taken at the end of the day, using Fuji 800 film, and scanned into Photoshop. There is no color in the original; it is all shades of gray, so I converted to grayscale and added sepia toning later. Hand-held.

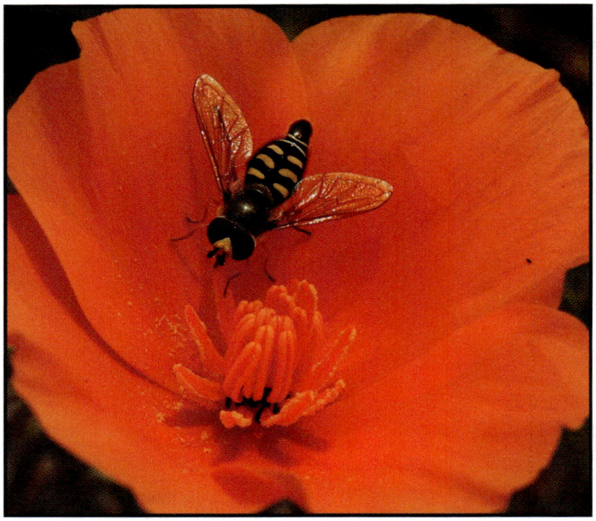

20. "The Visitor" Taken on a cloudy, windy day in California's Antelope Valley. Macro lens, hand-held. This image really requires great care in printing to hold detail in the orange flower.

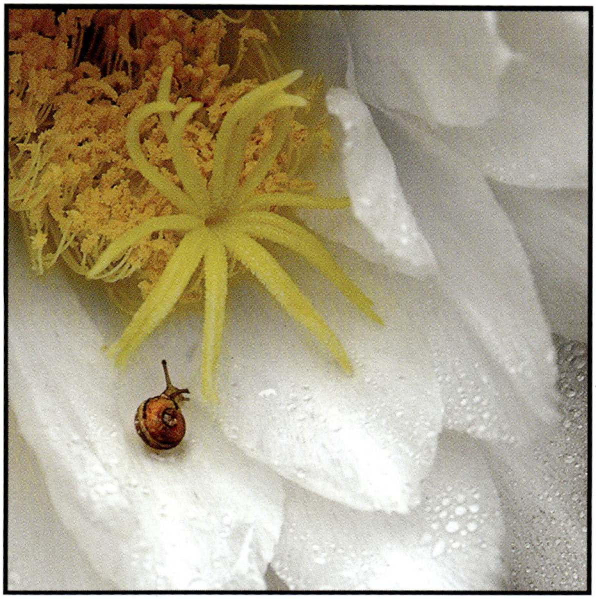

21. "The Race" Taken shortly after dawn in my father's cactus garden in San Diego. A hand-held shot, pure luck I think that it has decent sharpness. This particular cactus blooms very infrequently. Exposure not recorded.

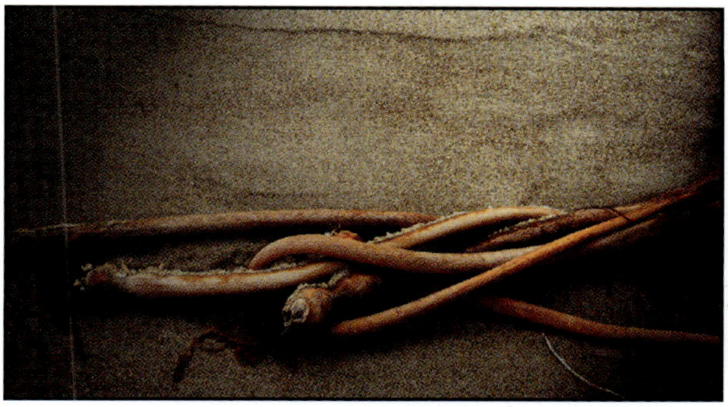

22. "Texture" Kelp washed up on the beach in Guadalupe Dunes, Calif. Taken w/ Nikon F100 on Fuji Velvia 50 and a 17mm focal length lens. Scanned to Photoshop. Note the subtleties of color (even though this seems like a duotone) and the sharpness of detail.

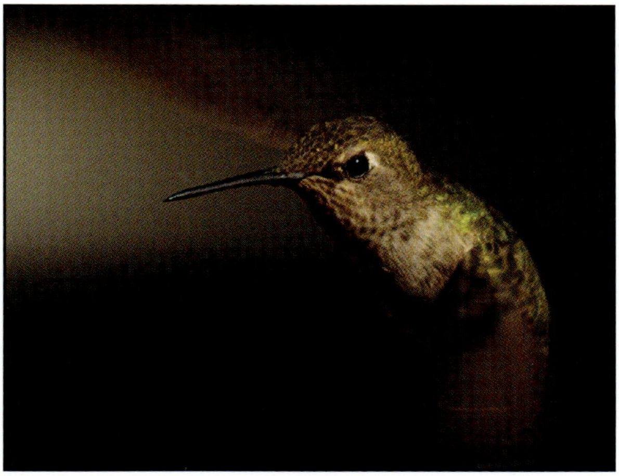

23. "The Green Flash" This Anna's Hummingbird was photographed using a Nikon D2x, 200mm focal length, 200 ISO, f 5.6 1/1000 exposure. Available light only, late in the day – note the warm colors and the background shadows.

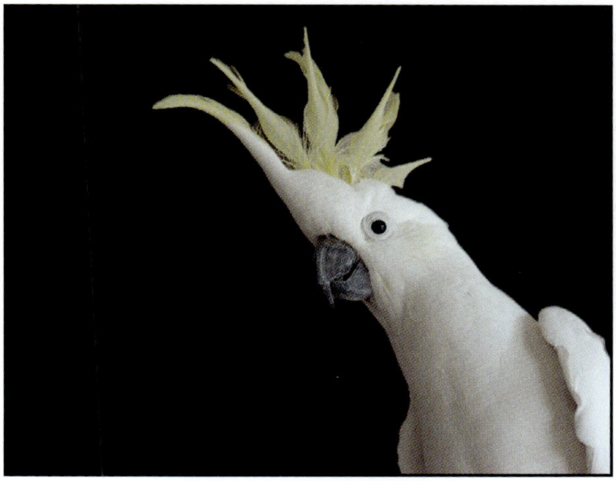

24. "What's Up Doc" Photographed with D100, aperture nearly wide open, by window light. Note the highlight detail and the color in the feather crown – I think this is partly the result of using daylight-balanced lighting and minimal editing in Photoshop.

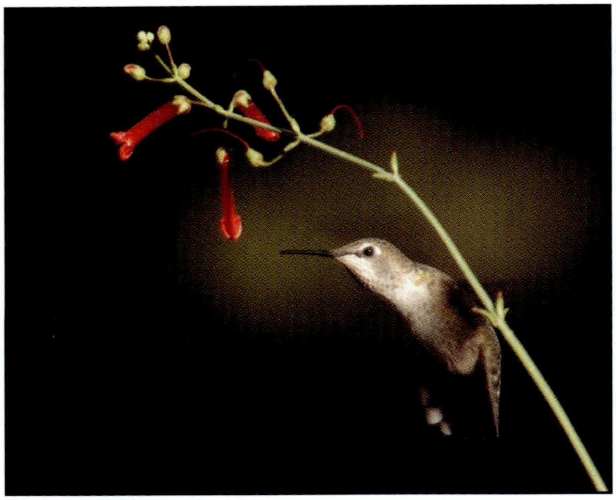

25. This hummingbird stopped for just a split-second in the sunbeam—amazingly, I was using a 400mm lens hand-held—just a lucky shot.

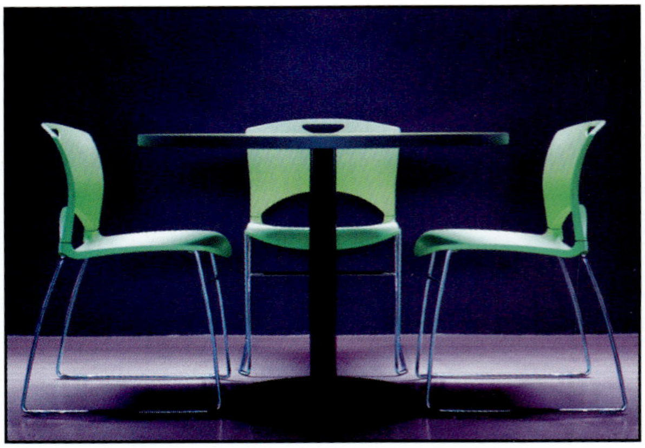

26. This tableau (no pun) was photographed as a commercial shot, in a hallway in an office building. I noticed a skylight immediately overhead, and came back an hour later for the shot. The reflected colors are amazing. Nikon D2x with 28-70 lens, ISO 400, hand-held.

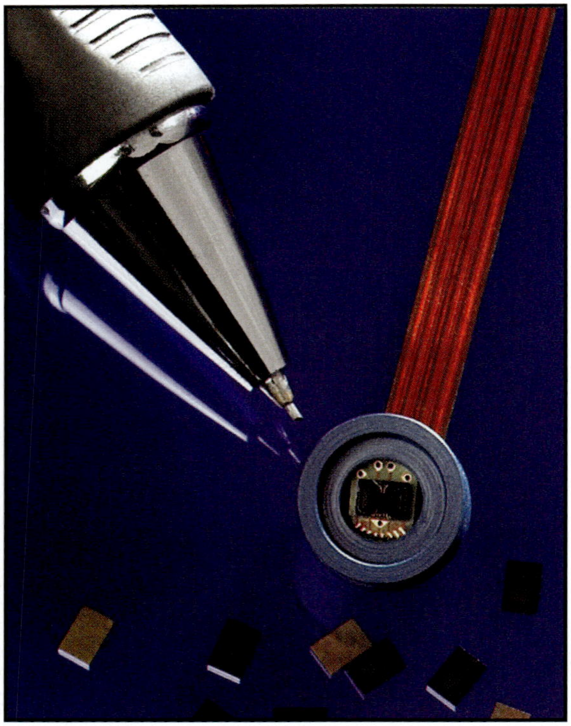

27. This commercial shot shows a miniaturized electronic sensor. Note the pencil point upper left for scale. The set was constructed using a lightbox underneath, with two dark blue CT gels covering it. Several strobes used for main light (soft box), and smaller strobes used for kickers and highlights. Hasselblad H1, 120mm macro lens, f/11.

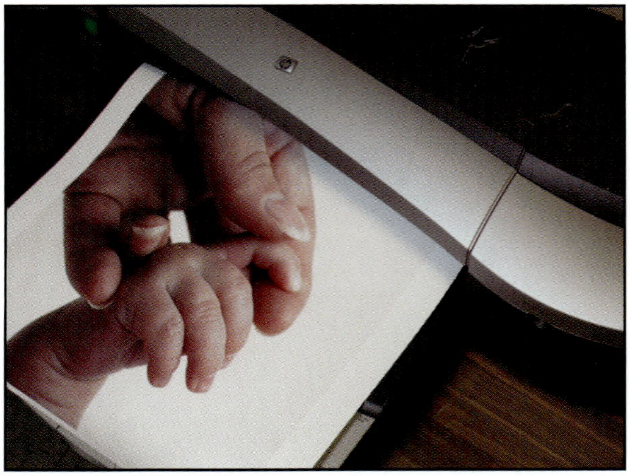

28. This commercial shot was set up with continuous lighting, not strobes, gelled to color temperature of about 4500K. We wanted a softer look, particularly since this was a real print coming from the printer, not "pasted" in later in Photoshop. Hasselblad H1 and Phase One, 70mm focal length.

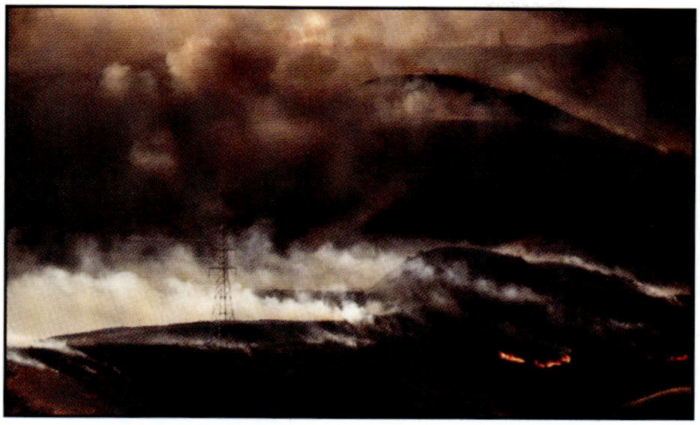

29. "Aftermath" An image taken after the disastrous fires in California in 2003. The color you see in the image is what we saw on-site—smoky, end-of-the-world dark.

30. Taken shortly after image 29, shows a water tanker climbing away from the fire at sunset.

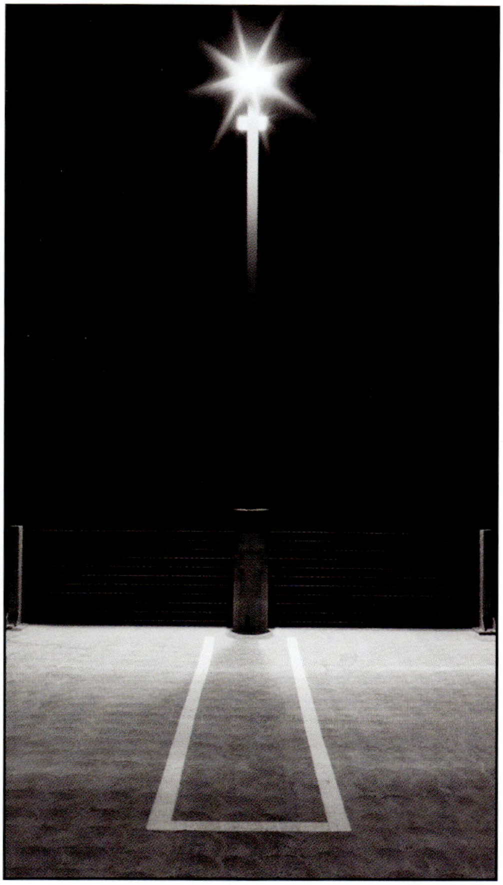

31. "Evening Star" Shot at 3 am, using Kodak TMAX 100, Hasselblad H1, several seconds exposure. Scanned via Minolta Multi Scan Pro.

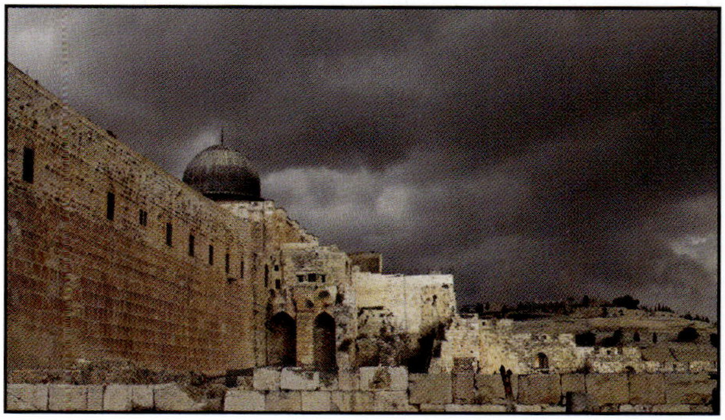

32. The Al Aqsa mosque in Jerusalem. Hasselblad H1, 35mm wide angle lens, Phase One, f/10 @ 1/1/25.

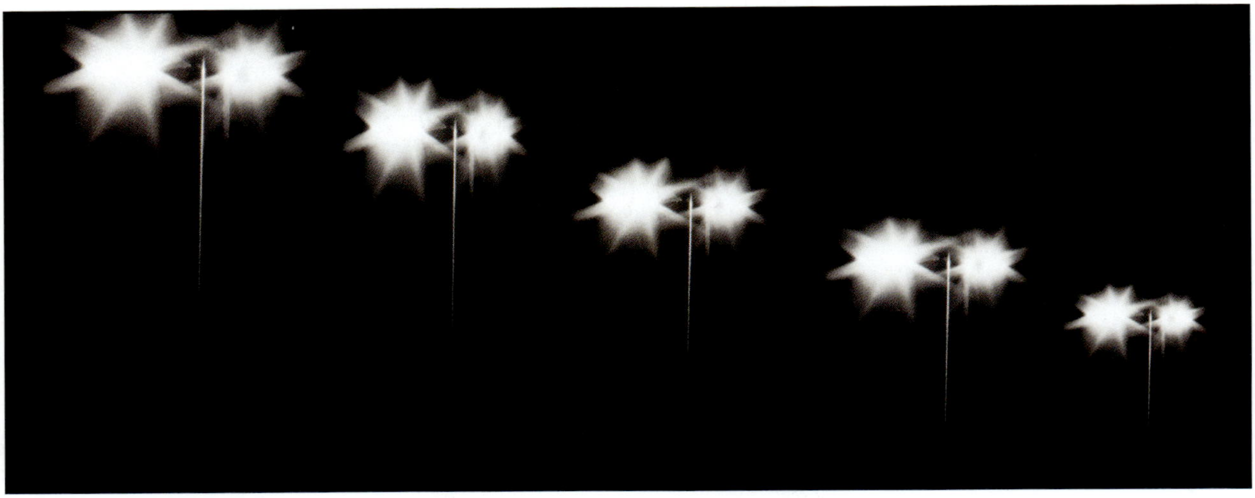

33. "Street Lights" Much the same as 34; some lights duplicated or manipulated in Photoshop.

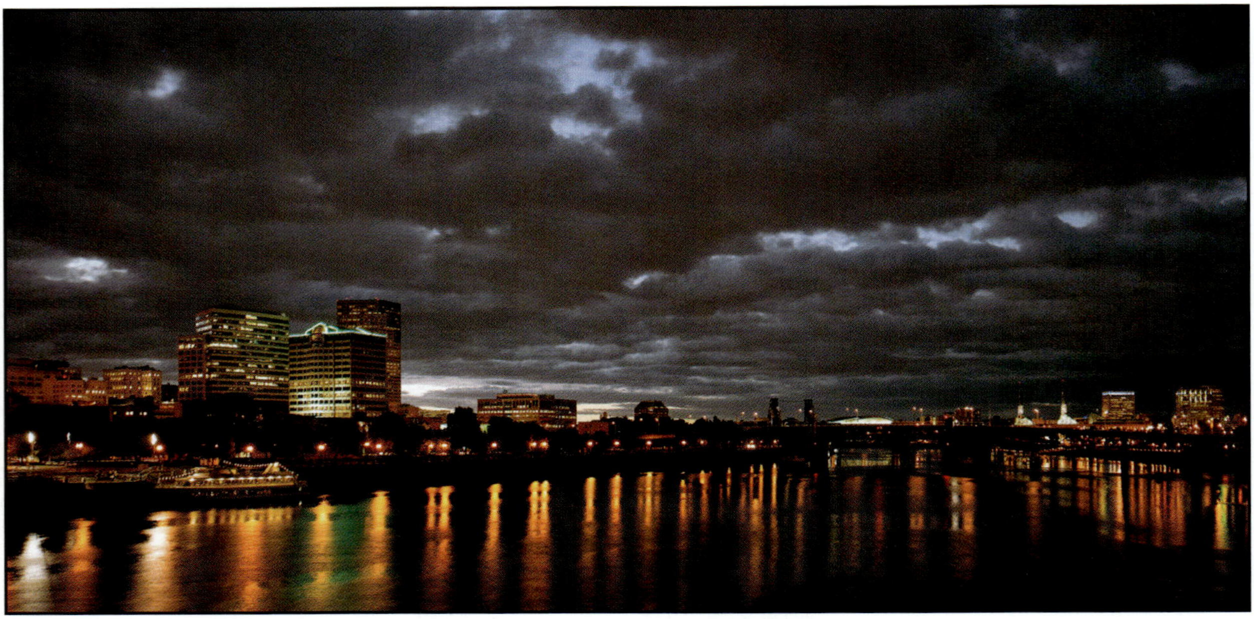

34. "View from the Hawthorne Bridge" Portland Oregon, four seconds at f/3.5, Hasselblad H1 and Phase One. A difficult shot due to wind and vibration.

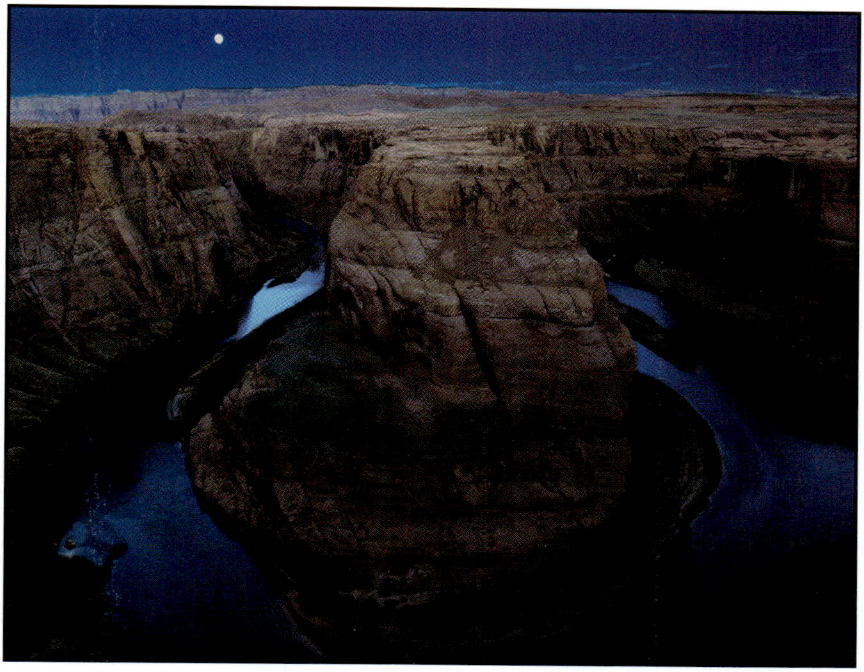

35. Moonset, Horseshoe Bend" Taken at approximately 5 am as the moon was setting. A six-second exposure at f/12, this image shows the strength of the Hasselblad 35mm wide angle, and the Phase One digital back. I can now see colors in this print that I never imagined were there when I took the shot. For a sense of scale, at the lower left (about 7 o'clock), the small white dot is a four-seater boat.

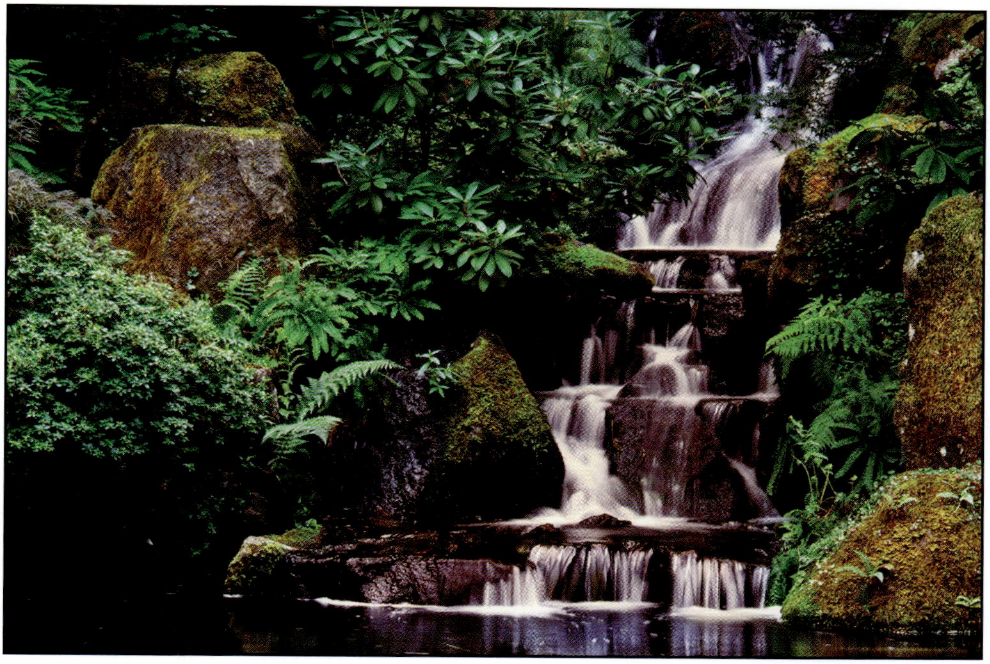

36. Waterfall, Japanese Garden, Portland Oregon. Shot on Fuji Velvia 50, scanned to digital. Hasselblad H1, exposure about three seconds.

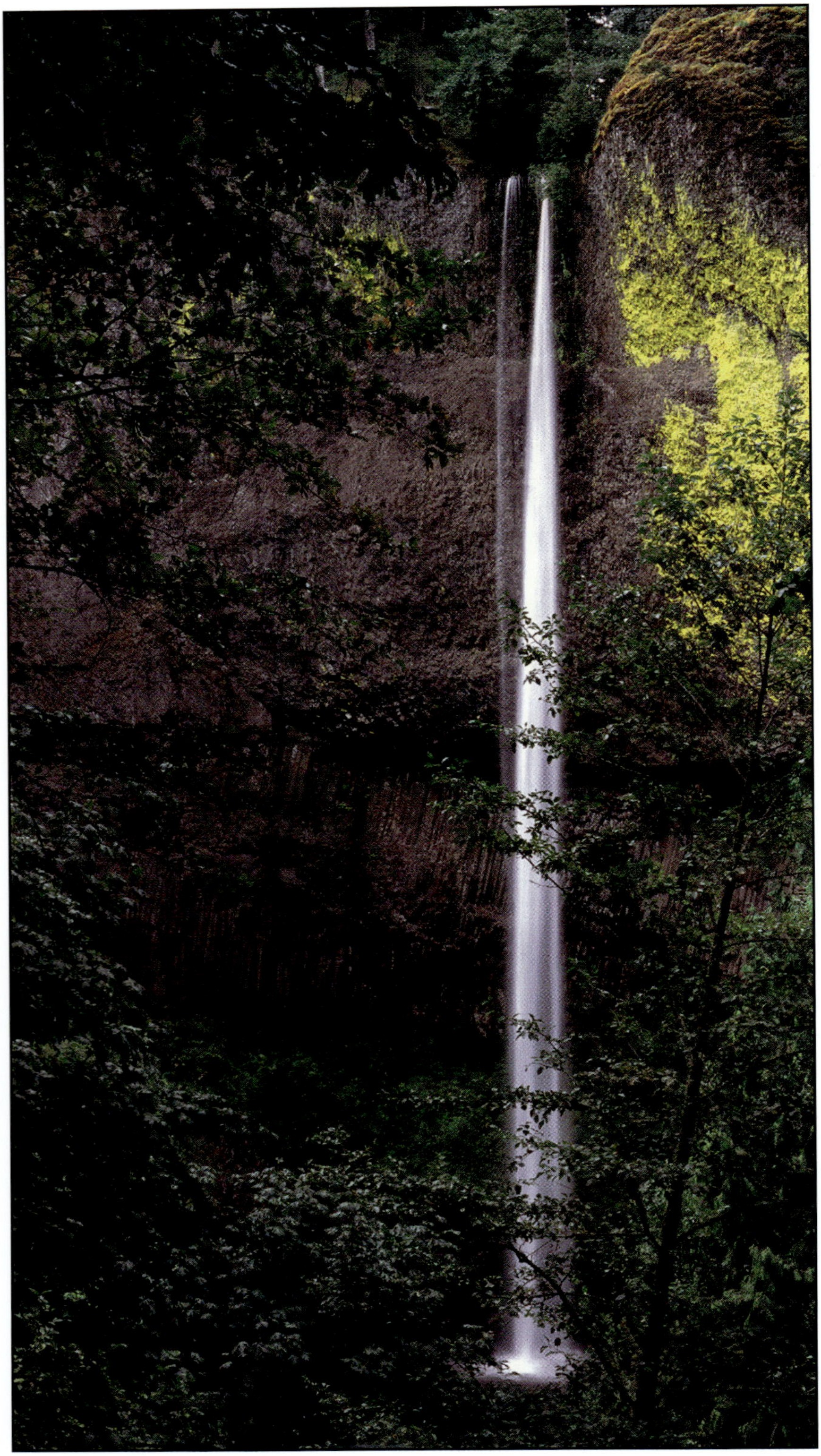

37. A waterfall in the Columbia River Gorge in Oregon. Hasselblad H1, Fuji Velvia 50, exposure about two seconds, scanned to digital. Luckily, there was no wind that morning.

Index

E

F

Q

R

S